OXFORD
G N V Q

Advanced
LEISURE & TOURISM

CAMBRIDGE
TRAINING AND
CTAD
DEVELOPMENT
LTD

Oxford University Press

Oxford University Press, Great Clarendon Street, Oxford OX2 6DP

Oxford New York

Athens Auckland Bangkok Bogota Buenos Aires Calcutta Cape Town Chennai Dar es Salaam
Delhi Florence Hong Kong Istanbul Karachi Kuala Lumpur Madrid Melbourne
Mexico City Mumbai Nairobi Paris São Paulo Singapore Taipei Tokyo Toronto Warsaw

and associated companies in
Berlin Ibadan

Oxford is a trade mark of Oxford University Press

© Cambridge Training and Development Ltd 1996

First published 1996
Reprinted 1997, 1998 (twice), 1999

A CIP catalogue record for this book is available from the British Library.

ISBN 0 19 832799 4

Typeset and designed by Design Study, Bury St Edmunds and Chris Lord Information Design, Brighton, East Sussex

Printed and bound in Great Britain by Butler & Tanner Ltd, Frome and London

Contributors include:
Marcus Colquhoun, Weald College
Abigail Concannon
Lisa Davis
Hugh Hillyard-Parker
Debra Howard
Caroline May
Suzanne Pattinson
Carol Schassens
Sheila White

Thanks go to:
Caroline Horrigan, The Travel Training Company Ltd

Thanks for permission to reproduce photos/extracts go to: Sports Council (logo, p.5, p.10, Sport For All logo, p.57); The Ramblers' Association (logo, p.5, Ramblers group, p.26, logo, p.321); The National Trust (logo, p.5, p.16, Beatrix Potter portrait, p.31, Acorn Camp, p.56, newsletter, p.173, logo, p.321); First Choice (tour operator brochure, p.6, extract, p.49); English Heritage (heritage leaflets, p.7); Social Trends 24, Office for National Statistics. Crown Copyright 119x. Reproduced by the permission of the Controller of HMSO and the Office for National Statistics (Graph 13.1, p.7, Table, p.22, Table 10.2, p.26); Department of National Heritage (leisure services department structure, p.11); British Tourist Authority (logo, p.11); Financial Times (FTSE index, p.15); Ipswich Youth Hostel Association Group (list of events, p.17); Bromley Leisure and Community Services (golf course, p.18); The Victoria and Albert Museum (the museum, p.19); The Royal Photographic Society (Victorian prints, p.22, 'satanic mills', p.27, early car, p.44); Social Trends 25, Office for National Statistics. Crown Copyright 119x. Reproduced by the permission of the Controller of HMSO and the Office for National Statistics (Household Survey, p.24/25); York Theatre Royal (Mystery plays, p.27); Bury St Edmunds Records Office (map, p.30); English Tourist Board (Crowns grading, p.36, disabled criteria, p.362, top tips, p.363); The Thomas Cook Group Ltd (logo, p.45, poster, p.269); Oxford Stage Company (leaflets, p.32); Social Trends 22, Office for National Statistics. Crown Copyright 119x. Reproduced by the permission of the controller of HMSO and the Office for National Statistics (table 10.20, p.34); Mayfair Cards of London (postcards, p.44); Lunn Poly Ltd (travel agent, p.49, travel agency, p.255);
Forte plc (facilities photos, p.50, gym instructors, p.187, receptionist, p.287, office staff, p.287, employee talking to one person, p.295, employee talking to a group, p.295, staff on phone, p.297, fitness instructor, p.325, receptionist, p.326, bartender, p.327); Stansted Airport Ltd (concourse photo, p.50); Tourism Concern (Tourism

Concern leaflet, p.54); Photobank (Clovelly, p.55); Country Holidays Ltd (brochure, p.68); Jonathan Markson Tennis (brochure, p.68); Forte Plc (staff computers, p.70, team, p.83, meeting, p.84, interview, p.97, interview, p.110, appraisal, p.119, bartender, p.462); Monthly Digest of Statistics, May 1994, Office for National Statistics. Crown Copyright, 1994. Reproduced by permission of the controller of HMSO and the Office for National Statistics (demographic statistics, P.70); Whitbread Hotel Company (recruitment information, p.72); Caterer and Hotelkeeper (front cover p.95) Crown Copyright is reproduced with the permission of the Controller of HMSO (leaflet, p.96); Cambridge Hi-Tech Recruitment (staff agency advert, p.96); Moswin Tours Ltd (brochure, p.130); KD River Cruise Holidays (brochure, p.130); Artro Garden Furniture (leaflets, p.133); McDonald's Restaurants Ltd (logo, p.143, counter staff, p.296, point of sales, p.317); Adidas (logo, p.143); Le Shuttle (logo, p.143); Pizza Hut (logo, p.143); Saga Holidays Ltd (logo, p.143); Crystal Holidays (promotional material, p.151); Office for National Statistics publications. Available through the Office Sales Desk, Room 131/4, Office for National Statistics, Government Buildings, Great George Street, London, SW1P 3AQ and/or HMSO book shops (Government publications, p.154); Haymarket Publishing, The Countryside Commission, The Leisure Media Company Ltd (trade journals: Campaign, Countryside, Leisure Management, p.155); ATMays (travel agency, p.157, travel agency, p.178, travel agent, p.327); Hayfield Farm Products (advert, p.167); Bury St Edmunds Leisure Services (advert, p.167, leaflet, p.403, meeting, p.412, fîte, p.429); SGR FM/Amber Radio (media costs, p.169); EMAP Anglia Newspapers Ltd (media costs, p.169); TSMS Ltd (media costs, p.169); Thorpe Park, Leisure Sport Ltd (brochure, p.170, direct response card, p.177); Advertising Standards Authority (logo, p.170); Independent Television Commission (logo, p.170); Radio Authority (logo, p.170); Linton Zoo (coupon, p.174); Reed Exhibition Companies (UK) (trade exhibition, p.175);

Jetset (catalogues, p.176); Outward Bound Trust (direct mail, p.176); British Airways plc (advert, p.167, spread of materials, p.180); The Rank Organisation (report and accounts 1995 extract, p.221); Commission of the European Union (and the Tidy Britain Group) (Blue Flag criteria extract, p.251); National Extension College (two women, p.257); Performance Sailcraft Europe Ltd (communications system, p.264); Philips Consumer Electronics (IMS) (interactive display, p.268); ASK Language Services (planner, p.256); Saga Holidays Ltd (brochure, p.303); Club 18-30, Flying Colours Leisure Group Ltd (brochure, p.303); World of Property (holiday sales presentation, p.315); Ipswich Tourist Information (booking form, p.320); Bury St Edmunds Golf Club (logo, p.321); Warwick Arts Centre (arts centre, p.330); Travel Trade Gazette, 6/3/1996 (top shop report, p.335); Post Office Counters Ltd (customer charter, p.339); Great Western Trains Company Ltd (customer charter, p.339); Stena Line Limited (direct mail, p.349); Dorset Evening Echo 23/3/1993 (health and safety disaster, p.359); Loss Prevention Council and Independent Television News (fire prevention campaign, p.359); Brighton Borough Council Arts and Leisure Services (deserted beach, p.363, crowded beach, p.363); Health and Safety Executive (advice booklet, p.369, logo, p.371, accident report, p.374, logo, p.368); Health and Safety Commission (logo, p.370, logo, p.365); Royal Society for the Prevention of Accidents (logo, p.368); St John's Ambulance (logo, p.368); Commission of the European Communities (logo, p.364); Fen Fever promotional material reproduced by permission of ADeC (Arts Development in East Cambs), designed by Sugar Free (leaflet, p.403); Hull Truck Theatre Company (leaflet, p.403); Theatre Royal (Norwich) Trust Ltd (pantomime, p.404); Allsport UK Ltd (tournament, p.405, athletics tournament, p.435, tennis tournament, p.438); British Telecom (swimathon, p.412); Silverblades Ice Arena, Streatham (ice rink, p.449); Cambridge Newspapers Ltd (folk festival, p.450); Suffolk Fire Service (fire, p.453).

Contents

ABOUT THE BOOK

This book contains the information you need to complete the eight mandatory units of your Advanced Leisure and Tourism GNVQ.

How it's organised

This book is organised in units and elements, like the GNVQ, so it's easy to find the information you need at any point in your course. Each element has several sections. They cover all the topics in the element, using the same headings as the GNVQ specifications. At the end of each element there are some key questions, so you can check your knowledge and prepare for the unit tests. There are also suggestions for an assignment, which will help you produce the evidence you need for your portfolio.

What's in it

The book presents information in several different ways so it's interesting to read and easy to understand. Some information is given in the words of people who actually work in leisure or tourism jobs – for example, a manager of a city centre entertainments venue, a travel consultant in a travel agency or a sales assistant in a museum shop. There are definitions of terms like 'disposable income' or 'products and services'. Graphs show you things like the amount of free time people have, occupancy rates in a hotel or the annual sales figures of a sportswear manufacturer. There are illustrations and diagrams, extracts from people's diaries, examples of brochures and leaflets. Case studies go into the details of leisure and tourism organisations like Virgin, major attractions like theme parks and events run by commercial and community organisations. And there are around 300 photographs showing all sorts of attractions, facilities and people working in them.

How to use the book

Decide which part you want to read. For example, you can go straight to any element and read through the relevant sections. You can find the information about any topic by looking at the list of contents at the front of the book and seeing which section looks most useful. Or you can use the index at the back to find a specific topic or organisation.

As well as information, the book has suggestions for things you can do to help you learn about leisure and tourism in a practical way. Discussion points suggest topics that you can think about and discuss with other people – other students on your course, your tutor or teacher, friends, family, people who work in leisure and tourism. Activity boxes ask you to do things like talk to a manager of a facility about the roles of people who work there, list the measures you would take to avoid health and safety risks at a venue, work out the profit a café makes in a year, and so on. They will help you to get a real life picture of leisure and tourism organisations and what it's like to work in them.

When you've finished an element, try answering the key questions at the end. You may want to make notes of your answers and use them when you're preparing for the unit tests. The assignment at the end of each element suggests what you can do to produce evidence for your portfolio. Some of the activities will also help you to build up the portfolio. You might want to make an action plan for each element to help you plan and carry out the work in the activities and assignment.

Other resources

By itself this book is an important and valuable source of information for your GNVQ studies. It should also help you use other resources effectively. For example, it suggests that you should find out more information about some topics, such as the 'life-cycle' of leisure products in the music industry or what forms of electronic technology a facility uses for communication.. You might be able to get this extra information in a local library or tourist office, or from other books about leisure and tourism. It also asks you to investigate facilities yourself, by visiting them, reading about them in magazines or watching relevant programmes on television.

Over to you

It's your GNVQ and your job to make the best of the opportunity to learn about leisure and tourism. Use this book in whatever way helps you most. For example, you could:

■ look at the contents page to give you the whole picture
■ use the index to find out specific bits of information
■ read a section at a time to help you understand a topic
■ look at the activities and assignment before starting an element so you know what you have to do
■ turn things on their head and start with the key questions to see how much you already know about an element.

It's over to you now. Good luck.

UNIT 1

Element 1.1

The structure and scale of the industries

Element 1.2

The development of the leisure and recreation industry

Element 1.3

The development of the travel and tourism industry

Element 1.4

The impact of the leisure and tourism industries

The leisure and tourism industries

ELEMENT **1.1**

The structure and scale of the industries

What exactly is leisure and tourism? Your aim in this element should be to answer this question by getting your own overview. You'll be looking at the main categories in travel and tourism and in leisure and recreation; you'll be finding out how many people work in them and how much money they generate. You'll also be investigating the contribution of the three sectors – private, public and voluntary – and how they work together. Use your own experience and the information in this book as a starting point, but carry out your own investigations yourself too.

Leisure and tourism is a mixed economy. There are many different types of business, from small guest-houses to multinational leisure groups, from local minibus operators to international airlines. The differences in scale are enormous. But all these businesses are linked together to form a national network of services. Guest-houses may make a living because they are close to airports, airlines provide booking services for hotel groups and car-rental chains, tourist information centres have leaflets on local attractions and sell products based on or produced by these attractions. No one in this industry is an island. We're all working for each other as well as ourselves.

marketing manager in a national tourist organisation

To work in leisure and tourism you sometimes need to be a jack of all trades. I work for a national heritage organisation. My job involves overseeing the day-to-day running of the property, opening it to the public, ensuring security and maintaining the property and the contents of the house. A marketing background is helpful, as is some knowledge of art history. And I need managerial skills for dealing with staff. What I most enjoy about my work is the variety.

administrator of a National Trust property

The structure of the UK leisure and recreation industry

Leisure is the opportunity and time outside working hours to choose and take part in activities or experiences which are expected to be personally satisfying.

Recreation is what people do in their leisure time. It may be active, like taking part in a sport. Or it may be passive, like watching the TV or reading.

Leisure and recreation is one of the biggest and fastest-growing service industries in the UK.

- More than 375,000 people are directly employed providing leisure and recreation services.
- Almost 30 million people take part in sport or exercise at least once a month.
- The average person in full-time employment has over four hours of leisure time each day.
- Walking is the most popular form of physical recreation.
- There are over 1,200 publicly owned leisure centres in the UK.

The purpose of all these organisations is to provide facilities, products and services that help people to make best use of their leisure time, alone or in groups.

Examples of facilities

Many organisations providing leisure and recreation facilities are privately owned. Others may be publicly owned, like sports halls and leisure centres run by local authorities. Some may be owned and run by voluntary groups such as the areas of land owned by local Wildlife Trusts.

Facilities are the buildings, equipment, structures or natural features which provide opportunities for people to take part in leisure or recreational activities.

Structure of the leisure and recreation industry means the different components or sectors in which organisations provide facilities enabling people to take part in and enjoy activities.

Leisure and recreation activities

- arts and entertainment – theatres, concert halls, galleries, art centres, museums, bingo halls, race tracks, theme parks, home-based entertainment
- sports and physical activities – sports centres, leisure centres, running tracks, sports stadiums, gyms, fitness centres, swimming pools
- play – playing fields, parks, adventure playgrounds, playschemes
- outdoor activities – natural spaces for walking and climbing, camp sites, open-air swimming pools, botanical gardens, nature trails, garden centres, activity centres
- heritage – historic sites, industrial attractions, working museums
- catering and accommodation – food and drink services in hotels, hostels, campsites etc., facilities such as meeting rooms

DISCUSSION POINT

The range of leisure and recreation products and services available might vary a lot from one area of the country to another. Why do you think this is?

ACTIVITY

Make a table with two columns using a wordprocessor. In the first column, list the six categories of organisation providing leisure and recreation facilities. In the second column, list three or four organisations in each category. Try to think of national organisations. For example, you could list the Canon cinema group under the 'arts and entertainment' category.

Save the file and add to your list as you learn more about the leisure and recreation industry in the UK.

The structure of the UK travel and tourism industry

A famous traveller once said that the reason for travelling is not to arrive, but to travel. But most people travel for a purpose, and the main purpose of travel apart from business is tourism. The industry today provides services that enable people to travel and tourist facilities when they get to their destinations. Today the word 'tourism' often includes travel.

A tourist officer in one of the regional Tourist Board offices explains that 'tourism' is going on everywhere, all the time:

> 66 *Tourism isn't just going on holiday or taking a day trip out somewhere. Whenever you take part in any leisure or recreational activity away from your own local area, you become a tourist. Our job in the industry is to try and make sure your needs as a tourist are being met. That applies whether you stay in our area half a day or half a year. As far as we're concerned, you can be a tourist if you're on business, visiting friends or family, travelling to watch a football match or on a religious pilgrimage. There will often be things you do at those times which turn you into a tourist.* 99

> **Tourism** is the temporary movement of people to places outside where they live and work, the activities they do when they get there and the facilities created to cater for their needs.

Travel services

The main travel services taking people to their destinations are:

- travel agencies – for tourists and business travellers
- tour operators – from the big holiday firms like Thomsons to smaller operators providing specialist services like trekking expeditions in the Hindu Kush
- transport providers – airlines, shipping companies, rail networks, car hire operators (these are all sometimes known as 'principals').

ACTIVITY

Take a trip to the nearest shopping centre or high street. Do a quick survey of the travel agencies. Make a few notes about each one to record:

- what services they offer – for example, currency exchange or specialist services for students
- what main holiday products they are displaying in their windows.

Tourism

The main tourist facilities once people get to their destinations are:

- tourist boards – national, regional and local
- tourist information centres

- At the start of the 1990s nearly 1.5 million people were employed in the UK tourism industry.
- More than 600,000 of them were employed in hotels and restaurants.
- In 1993, total UK spending on tourism was around £12 billion.
- In the same year, revenue from tourism was around £7.5 billion.
- There are nearly 2,000 historic properties in the UK open to the public.
- There are 83 historic houses in England which attract more than 50,000 visitors every year.
- The Tower of London attracts almost 2.5 million visitors each year.
- Three attractions owned by the same company – Madame Tussauds, Alton Towers and Chessington World of Adventures – account for more than 40% of visitors to theme parks.
- Center Parcs in Sherwood Forest opened in 1987 at a cost of £60 million.

- tourist attractions – everything from the prehistoric sites at Stonehenge or Avebury to the most up-to-date theme park or activity centre
- guiding services – such as two-hour tours round National Trust properties or week-long guided cycle rides in Wales
- currency exchange
- accommodation and catering
- transport – including bus and coach tours, and special transport to and from attractions.

Holidays taken by Great Britain residents: by destination

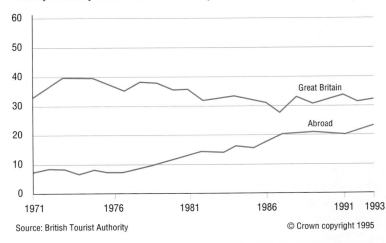

Source: British Tourist Authority   © Crown copyright 1995

ACTIVITY

Find out what are the top 20 tourist attractions in the UK. Using appropriate computer software, draw a graph showing:

- the number of visitors to them last year
- the amount of money they generated.

DISCUSSION POINT

Look at the graph of holidays taken by people living in this country from 1971 to 1993.

What does the shape of the graph tell you?

What do you think will happen in the next few years?

What sort of things does the government do to encourage more tourism in this country? Think of two or three recent examples.

How do the actions of government affect outgoing tourism (people living in the UK going on holiday to other countries)?

Section 1.1.3

The scale of leisure and tourism in the UK

You can measure the scale of leisure and tourism in the UK by looking at:
- how many people work in the industry (close to 3 million in 1995)
- how much money it makes for the economy.

Number of people in the industry

There are several sources of information for these figures. For example:
- government statistics – such as Social Trends, the General Household Survey and the Employment Gazette, compiled and published by Her Majesty's Stationery Office (HMSO)
- industry organisations such as the Association of British Travel Agents
- organisations such as Training and Enterprise Councils or the economic development departments of local authorities, which keep track of labour market information in their areas.

When you use these sources, remember that the figures may be approximate rather than exact.

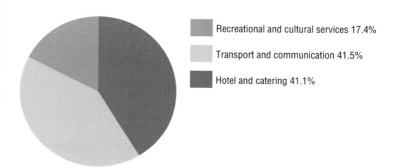

Recreational and cultural services 17.4%

Transport and communication 41.5%

Hotel and catering 41.1%

Contribution to the economy

Weekly expenditure on leisure items

	retired adult	retired couple	one adult with children	two adults with children	all households
holidays	1.66	4.09	4.92	11.36	10.75
alcohol away from home	0.73	2.44	2.37	8.20	8.19
meals out	1.25	2.76	2.42	7.46	6.83
TV, video, home computers	2.12	2.43	3.77	5.3	4.42
books, papers, magazines, hobbies	1.74	3.16	2.13	4.78	4.29
DIY materials	0.31	3.57	0.99	5.68	4.03
sports equipment, subscriptions	0.11	0.27	0.90	3.88	2.77
cinema, theatre and entertainment	0.16	0.38	1.02	2.43	1.82
total weekly expenditure	8.08	19.09	18.52	49.09	43.09
% of total household expenditure	10.90	13.60	10.90	13.40	15.60

Most of the money tourists spend when they visit an area is on leisure, recreation, transport and hospitality. So shops, facilities, transport companies and caterers all benefit from tourism. They pay wages to people who work in them, and those workers spend part of their wages buying goods and services from other businesses in the area. So the whole local economy benefits from the money tourists bring in.

Contribution to the balance of payments

The balance of payments compares the amount of money people spend on goods and services produced in their own country with the amount they spend on goods and services produced in other countries. When tourists from abroad visit the UK, they spend money here and make a positive contribution to the UK's balance of payments. When people from the UK go abroad, they take money out of the country and spend it somewhere else. So they make a negative contribution to the balance of payments. During the 1980s, people from the UK visiting other countries spent more than visitors from other countries spent in the UK.

year	value of incoming tourism £M	value of overseas tourism £M	balance £M
1977	2352	1186	1166
1978	2507	1549	958
1979	2797	2109	688
1980	2961	2738	223
1981	2970	3272	-302
1982	3188	3640	-452
1983	4003	4090	-87
1984	4614	4663	-49
1985	5451	4877	574
1986	5405	5927	-522
1987	6260	7280	-1020
1988	6184	8216	-2032
1989	6945	9357	-2412
1990	7475	9905	-2430

Tourists spend money in the local community

Increased demand for leisure, recreation, transport and hospitality facilities

Provides more local job opportunities, and workers' wages

Workers' wages are spent in the community

Local employment is created in the community

Local wealth is created

DISCUSSION POINT

The table above shows how the balance of payments in tourism changed from 1977 to 1990.

■ Why do you think there was such a big a change during the 1980s?

■ Do you think the balance will change back again during the 1990s?

The role of the public sector

Public-sector organisations are normally funded by national government or local authorities. Examples are tourist boards, arts centres and tourist information offices.

National provision

In the UK the government doesn't often get directly involved in providing leisure and tourism facilities. Instead it provides financial assistance through government agencies which make grants available to local authorities and voluntary organisations.

The government department that controls these agencies is the Department of National Heritage. The Department gets an annual budget from the Treasury. Since 1994, much of the money available to the agencies which support leisure and tourism comes from the National Lottery.

Other government departments providing funds for recreational activities are:
- the Department of the Environment – supports the Countryside Commission and English Nature
- the Department of Agriculture – supports the Forestry Commission
- the Department for Education and Employment – supports some recreational activities through education budgets
- the Welsh Office – funds the Wales Tourist Board and CADW (Welsh Heritage).

THE SPORTS COUNCILS

There are four Sports Councils in the UK – one each for England, Wales, Scotland and Northern Ireland.

Sources of funding:
- national government
- commercial activities
- sponsorship from the private sector for specific activities.

Aims:
- to increase participation in sport and physical recreation
- to increase the quantity and quality of sports facilities

- to raise standards of performance
- to provide information for and about sport.

Activities:
- make grants and loans to local authorities to fund community facilities and projects
- provide funds to national sports governing bodies for improving administration, participation, coaching and training standards
- run national publicity campaigns
- run the National Sports Centres
- administer and distribute sports and recreation grants from National Lottery funds.

THE NATIONAL TOURIST BOARDS

There are four National Tourist Boards: one each for England, Wales, Scotland and Northern Ireland.

Sources of funding:

■ national government.

Aims:

■ to promote tourism within Britain
■ to enhance the image of their parts of the country
■ to maximise the contribution of tourism to national and local economies.

Activities:

■ run promotional campaigns
■ advise the government and public bodies on tourism matters in their parts of the UK.

National Sports Centres

Bisham Abbey:

tennis, football, hockey, squash, weight training, golf

Crystal Palace:

athletics, swimming, boxing, martial arts, judo, basketball

Lilleshall:

football, table tennis, cricket, gymnastics, archery, hockey, golf

Holme Pierrepoint:

water-based activities

Plas y Brenin:

mountain activities

THE BRITISH TOURIST AUTHORITY

BTA 🇬🇧
British Tourist Authority

Sources of funding:

■ government grants from the Department of National Heritage.

Aims

■ to encourage people from abroad to visit Britain
■ to stimulate the quality of services offered to visitors to Britain, using the best available technology
■ to help areas of Britain develop their tourism potential, especially where there is high unemployment.

Activities

■ runs promotional campaigns
■ advises the government on tourism and opportunities to promote Britain abroad.

Local provision

Most local authority leisure and recreation services are financed by local taxes from:

■ businesses – they pay a tax known as the Uniform Business Rate
■ residents – they pay a Council Tax related to the value of their homes.

These taxes pay for a wide range of services, like education, housing and social services. So there isn't usually a lot left over for leisure. Local authorities have a legal duty to provide some amenities, such as public libraries. But in general the provision of leisure, recreation and tourism services is discretionary. These services are usually provided through leisure and recreation departments.

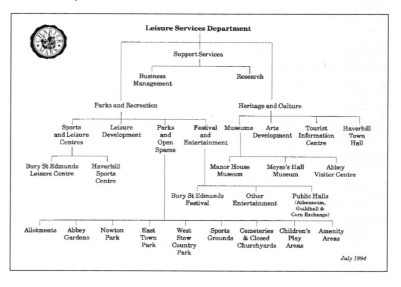

11

Local authorities often see their role as to provide facilities for people who live in the area, rather than people who come from outside. The chairperson of the Leisure and Recreation Committee on a town council explains why:

66 *We are elected by the people of this town to provide a service to them. That means our priorities on this Committee are to provide the services people living here want. For example, we subsidise the sports centre and swimming pool very heavily. Recently we sold some land in the centre to a developer on the condition that the firm built a new swimming pool. Over the last five or six years there's been a rolling programme to improve the parks and public spaces. New children's play areas have been put up and we've built a pavilion on the main green by the river to provide refreshments. Last month I asked officers to do a survey of residents to find out what they would most like us to do next – it will probably be a long list!* 99

Policy

Like other public-sector organisations, leisure and tourism facilities follow strategies and policies decided by their governing bodies. Policies are set at two levels:
■ by the government at national level
■ by local authorities at local level.

Local authorities are responsible for implementing as well as setting policies. They have to make sure their provision of leisure and tourism funds and facilities conforms to government policies and regulations. They also have to take into account the needs and expectations of the local people and the policies of the political parties elected to local council seats.

Contract management

The Local Government Act 1988 (Competition in Sport and Leisure Facilities Order) requires local authorities to put the running of its sports and leisure facilities out to tender. (This process is known as compulsory competitive tendering, or CCT.) This means that local authority departments have to compete with other businesses for contracts to run these facilities. Sometimes they win the contracts, but not always. So some of the facilities once run by the authority are now run by private-sector companies. Local authorities still control important aspects such as pricing, programmes and opening hours.

Funding

Money for spending on public-sector leisure and tourism activities and facilities comes from the public – people like you.

The government raises its money from taxation:
■ direct taxation like income tax
■ indirect taxation like VAT which is included in the price of many goods and services you buy.

DISCUSSION POINT

How might the leisure and recreational policies of an inner city area differ from those of a rural area?

ACTIVITY

When you visit local leisure and tourism organisations and facilities, look out for signs of public funding. Examples are:

■ exhibitions sponsored by the local authority

■ printed acknowledgements of funds received in programmes for theatres or sporting events

■ National Tourist Board or Sports Council logos on posters.

Make a note of them – collect examples of programmes etc. and take photographs of notices in facilities.

The Treasury allocates amounts of money to its departments responsible for the various aspects of public spending. The government departments responsible for leisure and tourism allocate money in the form of grants to national and regional organisations like the Tourist Boards and Sports Councils. They in turn make grants to leisure and tourism organisations and facilities at a local level.

Local government raises its money through the Uniform Business Rate and the Council Tax (described on page 11).

The diagram below shows the flow of money to and from central and local government.

WHERE THE MONEY COMES FROM

Joint provision

Sometimes, public- and private-sector organisations get together to provide facilities. This sort of partnership is getting more common. A local councillor who sits on the Leisure and Amenities Committee explains:

66 *We can't afford to incur big capital costs ourselves. So we work with others – for example, we put in applications to the National Lottery for grants where the matching amount of money is put up by private business. We are represented on the Board of the local theatre trust as well and recently helped them get a substantial grant from the Lottery for renovating their buildings. Quite often we have partnerships with much smaller organisations. For example, the café on one of our public parks is franchised out to a young couple who run it very successfully throughout the year, winter and summer. We wouldn't be able to do that ourselves.* 99

The Arts Council of England receives National Lottery funds and distributes them to deserving applicants. It uses guidelines to help it ensure that grants go to suitable causes.

THE ARTS COUNCIL OF ENGLAND

How will we assess the applications?

When we assess the applications we consider:

- the benefit to the public (including maximum access for disabled people);

- the long-term effect on the organisation's financial stability;

- the amount of partnership funding;

- the quality of design and construction;

- the quality of the artistic activities planned;

- the relevance of the project to local, regional and national plans for developing the arts;

- the contribution of artists, craftspeople and film and video makers;

- the quality of the organisations plans for education and marketing.

All these criteria are equally important but we will apply them flexibly to suit your own circumstances and the nature of your project.

The role of the private sector

Private-sector organisations are owned and funded by private individuals and normally aim to make a profit from the businesses they run.

Organisations in the private sector range from small businesses owned by one person to big multinationals with thousands of shareholders worldwide.

Because they aim to make a profit and because their investors want to see a good return on their investment, private-sector organisations usually operate in areas of the leisure and tourism industry where there are large numbers of potential customers.

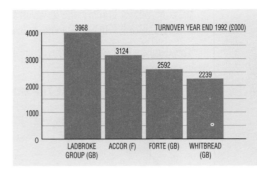

In the early 1990s, three of the top four hotel, catering and tourist groups in Europe were UK-based. In 1993, their combined turnover was just under £9 billion.

Providing facilities

Some examples of facilities provided by the private sector are:

- sports and recreation – sports clubs, water sports, snooker halls, bowling alleys, ice skating, fitness clubs, golf courses, tennis courts
- travel and tourism – travel agents, tour operators, transport services, tourist sites and attractions
- arts and entertainment – galleries, concert halls, arts centres, race tracks, home-based video and computer entertainment, theme parks, cinemas, theatres, bingo halls, amusement arcades
- catering and accommodation – hotels, hostels, pubs, boarding houses, bed and breakfast accommodation, self-catering accommodation, restaurants.

Managing facilities

Private-sector organisations also manage facilities or parts of facilities on behalf of public-sector organisations.

The Local Government Act (Competition in Sports and Leisure Facilities) 1988 states that local authorities must put the running of their sports and leisure facilities out to tender. This has given the private sector opportunities to bid for contracts from local authorities for facility management and service provision previously carried out by the public sector alone.

Finance and investment

Private-sector organisations can get the money they need to invest in their businesses from several different sources. Examples are:

- personal savings – owners of organisations provide money themselves
- loans – banks, building societies, insurance companies and pension companies all lend money to the private sector

DISCUSSION POINT

Do you think that using private-sector companies to manage facilities owned by the public sector is a good thing?

What benefits are there to people using the facilities?

What disadvantages are there?

- private shares – a private limited company can sell shares in the business to private individuals such as staff, friends and family who are connected to the business in some way
- public shares – a public limited company can sell shares to the public anywhere in the world through the Stock Exchange
- venture capital – venture capitalists are banks and companies who specialise in financing new business ventures
- government grants – the government may award grants if it thinks that the organisation will make a significant contribution to the local economy.

All investors in the private sector expect to earn money from their investment. Lenders earn money from the interest they charge on loans. Shareholders earn shares in the profits, known as dividends, and also from selling their shares when the share price increases.

Shares listing from the Financial Times

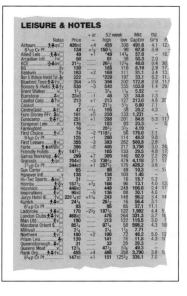

ACTIVITY

Look at the shares listings in the financial pages of a national newspaper. Pick one organisation from the leisure and recreation sector and one from the travel and tourism sector. Keep a note of the changes in their share prices over a period of six months. If you do this on a spreadsheet you will be able to calculate things like the percentage variance and the cumulative impact of movements in share prices.

Keep a lookout in the financial press for stories about your chosen organisations.

Risk ventures

Sometimes private companies can raise money for schemes that would not be suitable for public-sector organisations, which have to be more cautious because they are spending public funds. Private individuals and lenders may be prepared to risk their capital on a venture that may give them a good return – or it may not.

Examples of successful risk ventures in the leisure and tourism business are:
- Richard Branson's 'Virgin' label – a brand covering airlines, the music recording business and soft drinks
- pub groups like the Firkin and Tap & Spile chains
- theme parks like Alton Towers.

DISCUSSION POINT

Think of two or three more examples of risk ventures yourself.

- How successful are they?
- How is their success measured?

Joint provision

In the 1990s, the public and private sectors have become more interdependent and there has been an increase in facilities and services provided jointly by both sectors working together. The marketing officer for an inner-city music venue explains the benefits:

66 *We would never have got off the ground without the council. They helped us put together our grant application to the regional arts board and they provide funding for some of our educational work. We discuss our programmes with them and often do joint marketing – when people come here they also find out what's going on in other city venues.* 99

The role of the voluntary sector

THE NATIONAL TRUST

The National Trust, founded in 1895, is the largest voluntary organisation in the UK. It is the third largest landowner in the UK, after the Crown and the Forestry Commission. Its aim is to protect the countryside and properties of national and historical interest. Coastline, countryside, ancient monuments, nature reserves, waterways, buildings – the Trust protects and maintains a great variety of places of historic interest and natural beauty.

The Trust is a registered charity depending on the voluntary support of the public and its members. Its income is from membership fees, admission fees and trading activities like gift shops and tea-shops, as well as donations, grants and legacies. It uses its income to preserve the land and properties it owns and to buy land and property which would otherwise be destroyed by commercial redevelopment or decline.

As well as headquarters in London, the Trust has regional offices throughout the UK. Members can join voluntary associations, formed and run by Trust members themselves. The associations enable them to share common interests – activities include lectures, visits to properties and involvement as volunteers in the work of the Trust.

> **The voluntary sector** consists of not-for-profit organisations like charitable trusts and registered charities.

Organisations in this sector get their income from donations, legacies, grants, membership fees, admission fees and trading activities. The National Lottery also provides funds. The revenue raised by voluntary-sector organisations is always invested back into their facilities and services.

The voluntary sector is an important part of the UK leisure and tourism industry. Many smaller facilities are completely or partly run by volunteers – small, local concerns like local sports clubs, social clubs, conservation groups and youth clubs as well as large nationwide organisations like the National Trust. Volunteers often carry out the managerial, administrative and operational work, sometimes with paid staff and sometimes on their own.

Influencing national policy

Many organisations in the voluntary sector exist to promote special causes, issues and interests. They lobby government at national and local levels to support, protect and encourage the sector's aims, activities and interests. Two well-known examples in the leisure sector are Wildlife Trusts and the Ramblers Association.

ACTIVITY

Visit your local library or tourist information office and pick up some leaflets on leisure and tourism services and facilities provided by local and national voluntary-sector organisations. Choose one in leisure and recreation and another in travel and tourism. Find out:

■ what their main aim is

■ how they influence policy, nationally or locally

■ what facilities they manage.

Organising national interest

Many large voluntary organisations attract national interest in their activities by raising people's awareness of concerns and issues through campaigns and promotions. They put a lot of money into promotions, sponsorship, educational projects, radio and television features and interviews, newspaper and magazine adverts, articles and features, brochures and flyers, and direct mailing. Many of them have magazines and information services for their members. They may also offer advice to national government and their members may take part in government committees.

Developing facilities

The voluntary sector may provide facilities that the public sector can't afford or that won't raise a high enough or quick enough return for private-sector interest. All these facilities still have to be run on a commercial basis. To attract customers, facilities need to offer what the customers want by offering ease of access, value for money, services like food and drink, information and customer care.

The voluntary sector also develops facilities in parts of the industry that are too small or too specialised to attract funding from the public or private sector. For example, many local and amateur sports facilities are set up, managed and maintained by volunteers.

Managing facilities

The voluntary sector manages facilities using paid and unpaid staff. Many organisations are run by committees or boards of trustees. Large-scale operations like the national galleries and museums, city theatres, sporting bodies and heritage buildings have a core of full-time paid staff members. But they may also rely on volunteers. Small-scale, local operations often rely entirely on volunteers.

Organising local interest

Much of the voluntary sector operates at a local, 'grass roots' level. People join local groups, take part in activities in the area and campaign for better local facilities.

Providing for a common interest

Many organisations in the voluntary sector started because people with a common interest organised themselves into groups which could provide the facilities and services they wanted. Saga Holidays, which is now one of the largest holiday companies in the UK and specialises in holidays for older people, started as a voluntary organisation. Thomas Cook, who ended up with a travel agency of worldwide coverage which still flourishes today, started his career by organising a day trip for members of the local Temperance Society.

Some organisations started as a result of concerns like conservation and preservation – for example, the National Trust or the Royal Society for the Protection of Birds (RSPB). Others are a result of shared interests in sporting or leisure activities like the Wildfowl Trust and the Ramblers Association.

Raising funds

Being able to finance what they want to do is as much an issue for the voluntary sector as it is for the public and private sectors. Funding comes from trusts, donations, legacies, grants, membership fees, admission fees and any trading activities like gift shops. Organisations have staff responsible for fundraising activities like gaining sponsorships and grants and increasing membership. Fundraising is often part of marketing.

Ipswich YHA
Local Group Programme
October 1995

Mon 2 Tower St. Meeting 8pm Treasure Hunt.

Thur 5 Speedway at Foxhall Stadium. Ipswich v Reading. Meet 7pm at main gate. Admission £7. Contact Russell Mason for details 690950.

Fri 6 Chinese Meal in Ipswich. Meet 7pm at the Spread Eagle. Contact Gerry for futher details 745016.

Sun 8 Cycle ride led by Bob 01394 383074. Meet 10 am at Bob's. Bring a packed lunch.

Sat 14 AGM 7.30pm start at Cathy and Trevor's 747731.

Wed 18 RAFA club meeting 8pm.

Fri 20 Ten Pin Bowling. Contact Russell Mason for details 690950.

Sat 21- Sun 29 Lake District Walking Holiday led by Bob 01394 383074.

Section 1.1.7

Relationships between the sectors

All three sectors – public, private and voluntary – have a role in providing leisure and tourism services. The case studies on these two pages show that the three sectors can provide similar facilities in recreation and tourism.

THE GOLF BUSINESS

There are around 2,000 golf courses in the UK and 5 million players. The industry is worth around £3 billion a year and is still growing. In 1989 a report estimated that 700 new courses would be needed by the year 2000. Recently, many of the prime site courses in the UK have been bought by Japanese investors. Golf courses are run in three main ways – as private courses, municipal courses and as voluntary-sector clubs (sometimes known as private membership clubs).

Private clubs

are run as businesses and aim to make a profit for the owners. They are managed by employees of the company. Income is mainly from membership fees, green fees (payments made by non-members who play the course), tuition and retail sales of golf equipment, clothes and accessories. Many private clubs also provide other leisure and recreation facilities such as bars, restaurants, conference facilities, fitness suites and squash courts. Some diversify more widely into hotels and timeshare or second home developments.

Municipal courses

aim to provide a service to the local community. They are publicly owned and managed by employees of the local authority. Income is mainly from 'pay as you play' fees, although some municipal courses have members as well. Extra income comes from tuition, catering and retail sales. Less than 20% of golf courses in the UK are currently publicly owned.

Voluntary-sector clubs

are owned by their members. They aim to satisfy the needs and wants of members, and to break even (in other words, they don't have to make profits for owners). They are run by a committee of members and usually employ a steward to manage the facility. Their main sources of income are membership and green fees. Non-members pay a temporary membership fee allowing them to play the course for a limited time, such as a day.

DISCUSSION POINT

Why should all three sectors – private, public and voluntary – provide leisure and recreation facilities like golf courses, and tourist facilities like museums? Wouldn't it be better if they were all provided by just one sector?

THE MUSEUMS BUSINESS

The English Tourist Board lists over 900 museums in the UK. To qualify for their listing, the museum has to attract more than 5,000 visitors a year. Over a quarter of the museums listed attract more than 50,000 visitors a year. In the last 25 years, over 500 new museums have opened. Who owns them?

The government

owns at least 32 major museums. Twenty-one of them are classified as national museums. They include the British Museum, the Victoria and Albert Museum, the Science Museum and the Natural History Museum. These museums are grant funded through the Department of National Heritage and also rely on sponsorship to fund major exhibitions. In recent years the government has introduced admission charges to most of its museums.

Local authorities

own and run around 100 of the larger museums. Although mainly staffed by local authority employees, they have on average 20% of volunteer staff as well. Some, though not all, local authority museums charge admission. But they are not often profitable, so they still rely on grants from the authority.

Independent companies or voluntary organisations

own and run the rest. Over 70% of the new museums are run by the private sector. Fifty per cent of all staff are volunteers. Like other museums, the independents charge admission fees. They also rely on the provision of other facilities like shops and cafés to reach a level of income at which they can survive.

Although the number of museums has increased in the last twenty years, the number of visits is declining. Museums are facing growing competition from heritage attractions like the Jorvik Centre in York. Except for museums in big cities, attendance is seasonal. Bad weather is good news for museums!

ACTIVITY

Choose one type of service, in either leisure and recreation or travel and tourism. Find out how the three sectors work together to provide the service. Look out for examples of:

- dual use of facilities – e.g. the local authority hiring a privately owned swimming pool for school classes
- joint provision of facilities and cooperative ventures
- contracting by one sector to another.

Key questions

1 What do these terms mean?
  leisure, recreation, travel, tourism, facilities, structure, scale, balance of
  payments, return on investment, risk venture, joint provision, incoming
  tourism, outgoing tourism, public sector, private sector, voluntary sector,
  compulsory competitive tendering.
2 What are the six components of the leisure and recreation industry?
3 What are the four main types of travel services?
4 What are the nine components of the tourism industry?
5 In what two ways can you measure the scale of the leisure and tourism
  industry in the UK?
6 How does the government provide support for leisure and tourism?
7 What sort of leisure and tourism facilities do local authorities provide?
8 How do organisations in the private sector attract funds to provide leisure
  and tourism products and services?
9 What role do voluntary-sector organisations play in the UK leisure and
  tourism industry?
10 What are the five ways in which the three sectors – public, private and
  voluntary – can relate to each other? Give one example of each.

Assignment

Produce a report about the scale and structure of the UK leisure and tourism
industries. Your report could be in the form of:
■ a 'feature' article for a magazine
■ a radio-type programme, recorded on cassette
■ the script and storyboard for a TV programme – a storyboard is a sequence
  of images which show the main story.

The report should:
■ describe the structure of both industries (leisure and recreation, and travel
  and tourism)
■ give examples of facilities covering all the categories listed under 'Structure'
  in the range
■ show the scale of the two industries nationally, in terms of the number of
  people they employ and their contribution to the economy
■ explain the role of the public, private and voluntary sectors
■ give examples of organisations from each sector
■ describe how organisations in the three sectors can work together, with
  examples.

If you're writing a feature article, use illustrations such as photographs, graphs
and charts. If you're recording a radio-type feature, get two or three different
people to record the examples to give some variety. If you're doing a TV
programme, write a script for the presenter and keep the storyboard short –
twelve images in all should be enough. You might like to get help from
students on media and communication courses.

> ❝ The leisure industry has taken off in the last 20 years. It's a massive business now. Lots of our shows are doing well because people have more money to spend on entertainments. It's the same for other venues. There's a great deal of activity going on all over the country – probably more than there has ever been in the past. ❞
>
> *press and publicity officer at an entertainments venue*

> ❝ Riding is relatively cheap and accessible to the people at the top of the market – which is who I am aiming at. Now more people are becoming professionals and can afford to go riding – and we are able to do what they want to do. ❞
>
> *owner of a riding school which also provides holidays*

> ❝ We're seeing quite a lot of changes at the moment. It's possible that in future our service may be put out to tender to private companies. Some tourist information centres are already being run by private companies – in some cases by bus companies, as they have the financial backing to support the office. However, local authorities have been loath to make tourist information into a commercial venture – they see it as a service and they think a profit-making business might neglect the service side if it doesn't make money. ❞
>
> *manager of a tourist information centre*

ELEMENT **1.2**

The development of the leisure and recreation industry

In this element you will find out about leisure and recreation in the UK. You'll explore the reasons why industries like arts, entertainment, sports and heritage have developed over the years, by looking at major historical steps like the Industrial Revolution and the way people's leisure time has increased in the last hundred years. Where is the industry today? You'll answer that question by finding out about the products and services available across the country as a whole and in one area. As in element 1.1, use this book and your own experience as a starting point for your investigation.

Factors influencing development

The leisure and recreation industry includes:
- arts and entertainment – theatres, concerts, galleries, films, TV and video
- sports and physical activities – circuit training, swimming, athletics
- outdoor activities – walking, canoeing, climbing
- heritage – ancient sites, country houses, working museums
- play facilities – adventure playgrounds, summer play schemes
- catering and accommodation – food and drink, bed and breakfast, hotels.

The way people use their leisure and recreation time has changed enormously during this century. Most people now:
- have more time available for leisure activities because of social and economic developments
- have more personal disposable income – money which does not have to be spent on necessities such as housing, food and clothing
- are more mobile – more people own cars and the public transport system allows people to travel to areas outside their locality
- have different needs and expectations – for example, they are more aware of the importance of health and fitness
- have more access to the countryside.

Increase in leisure time

In the last century it was possible to talk about a 'leisured class'. It included landowners, politicians and wealthy industrialists – people who didn't have to spend all their time working for a living and who could afford to pay for their leisure activities. Most other people, including children, had to work long hours and did not have the time or the money to enjoy any leisure.

In the 1990s most people have time for leisure and are involved in some leisure or recreational activities.

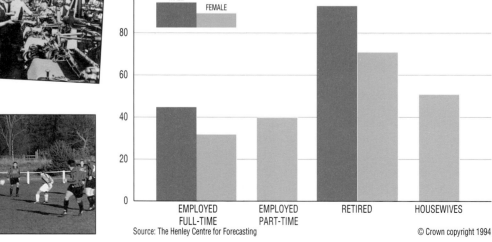

Free time in a typical week: by sex and employment status in Great Britain, 1992-93

Source: The Henley Centre for Forecasting

© Crown copyright 1994

Reasons for increased leisure time

■ the hours people work each week – since the end of the Second World War in 1945 the working week has become much shorter

■ the way people work – there's more job sharing and flexitime, part-time and short-term contracts, self employment

■ levels of employment – unemployment figures have been rising since the 1970s

■ changes in trading laws – Sunday is no longer thought of as a day of rest and more events like football matches, horse racing and theatre are now held on Sundays.

Changes in working hours and methods are not the only reason for the increase in leisure time. Many more activities are now possible because of technological advances like the invention of electricity and changes in transport. Most households now have washing machines, refrigerators and deep-freezes and many are centrally heated. In the past a lot of time would have been spent washing clothes, shopping for fresh food and making fires to keep the home warm.

Growth in personal disposable incomes

Some groups of people have higher levels of disposable income than others:

■ university students living on a grant and earnings from holiday jobs tend to have a very low level

■ single people or couples with jobs and no children tend to have quite a high level.

People can choose how to spend their disposable income. They can save, give to charity and invest in leisure activities – a trip to the theatre, or a season ticket to the football ground.

23

Household expenditure

United Kingdom

	1971	1981	1986	1990	1991	1992	1993
Indices at constant 1990 prices							
Food	87	91	95	100	100	102	103
Alcoholic drink	74	95	100	100	97	94	94
Tobacco	136	121	101	100	98	94	91
Clothing and footwear	52	67	92	100	100	103	108
Housing	68	81	93	100	100	101	103
Fuel and power	86	94	103	100	108	106	109
Household goods and services							
Household durables	53	69	86	100	97	98	107
Other	66	68	84	100	99	102	106
Transport and communication							
Purchase of vehicles	51	59	82	100	81	77	86
Running of vehicles	47	65	84	100	99	98	101
Other travel	56	70	84	100	97	101	101
Post and telecommunications	33	63	80	100	100	101	107
Recreation, entertainment and education							
TV, video, etc.	19	47	77	100	100	105	111
Books, newspapers, etc.	101	97	92	100	95	96	99
Other	36	62	76	100	99	100	104
Other goods and services							
Catering (meals etc.)	55	58	72	100	93	91	93
Other goods	44	60	75	100	100	98	100
Other services	30	43	68	100	97	94	96
Less expenditure by foreign tourists etc.	48	72	94	100	86	89	97
Household expenditure abroad	34	66	78	100	97	106	104
All household expenditure	59	72	85	100	98	98	101

Percentage of total household expenditure at current prices

	1971	1981	1986	1990	1991	1992	1993
Food	20.1	16.4	13.8	12.3	12.3	12.1	11.6
Alcoholic drink	7.3	7.3	6.9	6.4	6.6	6.3	6.1
Tobacco	4.8	3.6	3.1	2.5	2.7	2.7	2.7
Clothing and footwear	8.5	6.7	7.0	6.1	5.9	5.9	5.9
Housing	12.4	14.9	15.3	14.2	14.6	15.4	15.7
Fuel and power	4.5	5.1	4.6	3.6	4.0	3.8	3.7
Household goods and services	7.8	6.9	6.7	6.5	6.5	6.6	6.6
Transport and communication	14.3	17.2	17.5	18.3	17.3	17.3	17.5
Recreation, entertainment and education	8.8	9.4	9.4	10.0	10.0	10.1	10.2
Other goods, services and adjustments	11.4	12.5	15.6	20.0	20.0	19.9	20.0
All household expenditure	100	100	100	100	100	100	100

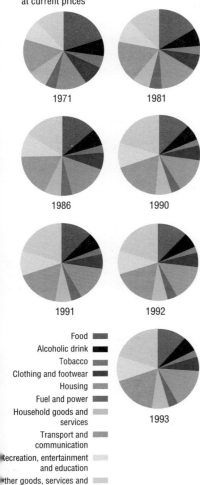

Percentage of total household expenditure at current prices

1971   1981

1986   1990

1991   1992

Food

Alcoholic drink

Tobacco

Clothing and footwear

Housing

Fuel and power

Household goods and services

Transport and communication

Recreation, entertainment and education

Other goods, services and adjustments

1993

© Crown copyright

An economist working in a local authority interprets the information in the table and charts:

66 *Figures like these give an idea of spending habits and how they have changed. As with most surveys of this kind, the picture is very broad. You can see that, in general, the amount of money spent on leisure has increased slightly in the recent past. But there are still many members of society today who cannot enjoy leisure facilities because they are short of money – the unemployed, single parents, the elderly, people on low incomes or short-term contracts. They all have very little disposable income. There are very few leisure activities which are free and yet many people who cannot afford to pay for recreation have more leisure time available.* 99

DISCUSSION POINT

Can you think of ways in which leisure could be made more accessible to people on low incomes?

DISCUSSION POINT

How would your leisure and recreation activities be restricted if you did not have access to a car or public transport?

Availability of transport

The various transport options now available – car, train, coach, bus – allow people to travel quite long distances to take part in their favourite leisure activity. People can:

■ drive to remote countryside for a day of climbing or walking
■ take a train to London to visit major exhibitions like the Boat Show or the Motor Show at Earls Court
■ organise coach trips to the seaside for the elderly or the young.

Personal needs and expectations

Leisure and recreation products and services develop as a direct response to people's needs and expectations. As these change, products and services have to change to match them. Organisations in the leisure and recreation industry use market research to keep up to date with changing demands.

Needs and expectations often reflect circumstances, social trends and fashions. For example, people have more information about health and fitness now than they used to. As a result the demand for sports and fitness facilities has increased. People also expect facilities to offer a wider range of products and services.

ACTIVITY

Make three lists and put down four or five activities in your area that:

■ are easier by car – for example, visiting an open day at a country house garden
■ can be attended by anyone with access to public transport – for example, a tennis tournament at a sports centre in town
■ require some form of transport – for example, a day trip to France organised by the local coach company.

Then list leisure and recreation activities which don't need any form of transport.

Social changes can also lead to changes in personal needs and expectations. A journalist on a leisure magazine explains how the change in the role of women in society has affected the leisure and recreation industry:

66 *The majority of women in the past were dependent on marriage to provide a home and financial security. Many more women are now able to live independent lives with an amount of choice that would have been unimaginable to someone living at the turn of the century. They can have careers, choose not to marry, vote, own their own homes – none of which was possible in the past. Importantly for the leisure and recreation industry, women now have more choice in how they spend their money and time.* 99

© Crown copyright

Weekly time use by employment status and sex, 1992–93

Great Britain

| | Full-time employees | | Part-time female | | Retired | |
Weekly hours spent on:	Males	Females	employees	Housewives	Males	Females
Employment and travel	47.1	42.2	20.8	0.4	0.5	0.6
Essential cooking, shopping and housework	13.0	25.5	32.5	38.1	17.0	33.0
Essential childcare, personal hygiene and other shopping	13.2	20.0	25.2	29.4	10.0	14.0
Sleep	49.0	49.0	49.0	49.0	49.0	49.0
Free time	45.7	31.4	40.6	51.1	91.5	71.4
Free time per week day	5.0	3.0	4.7	6.6	12.8	9.7
Free time per weekend day	10.3	8.2	8.5	9.0	13.8	11.5

Increased access to the countryside

The countryside has long been seen as a place where you can 'get away from it all'. As people's working lives have become centred in towns and cities, they look increasingly to the countryside for leisure and recreational activities. Developments in rail and road transport, especially the big increase in car ownership, have made getting to rural areas easier.

As well as providing places for simple pursuits like walking, animal and birdwatching and riding, the natural resources of the countryside also allow more active pursuits:

■ lakes and waterways are used for watersports and activities
■ cliffs and rocks are used for climbing
■ wilder areas like fells and moors are used for more adventurous pursuits like trekking, orienteering and survival games.

In response to people's increased demand for access to the countryside, governments have passed laws aimed at making rural areas accessible to the public and protecting the areas from damaging developments. For example:

■ ten National Parks and 33 Areas of Outstanding Natural Beauty have been established as a result of the National Parks and Countryside Act (1949)
■ the Countryside Act (1968) gave local authorities power to establish local parks and protect local areas of rural interest.

Major steps in development

Leisure activities have always been a part of society:
- competitive sports date back to the ancient Greeks and their Olympic Games held in honour of the god Zeus
- the Romans set aside as many as 200 days for celebrations and large-scale entertainment
- religion used theatre to express beliefs – an example is the York Mystery Plays, which are sometimes re-enacted today.

The Industrial Revolution

The Industrial Revolution describes the period of change from the early eighteenth century to the late nineteenth century. During this period the basis of the British economy – and the way of life of the people – moved from agriculture to industry.

The changes came about largely because of technological developments, particularly the discovery of steam power. Steam power could be used to drive large-scale machinery which made large-scale production possible. For example, the textile industry which had previously been organised around skilled craftspeople like spinners and weavers working at home was reorganised into a factory-based industry with large mechanised spinning and weaving equipment.

Mechanisation and periods of economic depression in agricultural areas meant that people began to move out of the countryside and into fast-growing industrial towns to find work in the factories and their service industries.

*I*t was a town of red brick, or of brick that would have been red if the smoke and ashes had allowed it; but, as matters stood it was a town of unnatural red and black like the painted face of a savage. It was a town of machinery and tall chimneys, out of which interminable serpents of smoke trailed themselves for ever and ever, and never got uncoiled. It had a black canal in it, and a river that ran purple with ill-smelling dye . . . It contained several large streets all very like one another, and many small streets still more like one another, inhabited by people equally like one another, who all went in and out at the same hours, with the same sound upon the same pavements, to do the same work, and to whom every day was the same as yesterday and tomorrow, and every year the counterpart of the last and the next.

Charles Dickens, *Hard Times*. London, 1854 (Chapter 5)

Working conditions in the towns were hard. Hours were long and the working environment was often unhealthy and dangerous. Housing put up for the increasing populations was often poorly built, cramped and insanitary.

From the 1830s onwards, social reform began to get a foothold. Poor working conditions and bad practices were brought to public attention by social, political and industrial reformers like Edwin Chadwick, John Stuart Mill, Charles

Dickens and Lord Shaftesbury. In response to growing social and political pressure, the government began to legislate to improve working conditions.

> *M*alformations of the spine are very frequent among mill hands; some of them consequent upon mere overwork, others the effect of long work upon constitutions originally feeble, or weakened by bad food. Deformities seem even more frequent than these diseases; the knees were bent inward, the ligaments very often relaxed and enfeebled, and the long bones of the legs bent. The thick ends of these long bones were especially apt to be bent and disproportionately developed, and these patients came from the factories in which long work-hours were of frequent occurrence.
>
> Testimony of Dr Ray, a doctor in Leeds, quoted in: Frederick Engels, *The Condition of the Working Class in England* (first published in 1845)

DISCUSSION POINT

How do you think traditional rural leisure and recreation activities were affected by the mass movement of people to cities during the Industrial Revolution?

ACTIVITY

Using your local library as a source of information, write a short account of family life during the Industrial Revolution. Include information about the kinds of leisure activities available to the whole family.

What use can be made of information like this in today's leisure and tourism industry?

The first improvements took place in the textile industry and were quickly expanded to other industries and areas of work. To ensure that the reforms stuck, the government established legal regulations and systems for factory and workplace inspections.

Reform concentrated on:
- reducing working hours
- improving pay and conditions
- developing systems of social welfare and local government
- increasing opportunities for education.

There was also increasing support for and development of the Trade Union movement. By the end of the nineteenth century, industrial workers had their average working day reduced to ten and a half hours a day, with Saturday afternoons and Sundays as holidays.

As conditions changed, people's expectations changed. A reduction in working hours meant more time for leisure and recreation. Improvements in pay meant an increase in people's disposable incomes.

The origins of football

Early forms of football were played as a running battle between villages. The game was played on a patch of open ground rather than a pitch. There were no limits to the numbers of players on each side and no written rules for the game. In the towns this kind of game was not possible – there were no rival communities, recreational land was in short supply and the work-force was restricted by a timekeeper's clock.

Some football firsts

1841 – First football match at Eton School

1852 – First inter-school football match

1857 – First football club with open membership: Sheffield FC

1861 – First public football match with an admission charge – Sheffield vs Hallam

1863 – Football Association formed

1868 – Sheffield Wednesday win the first football tournament

1871 – Cup Final – 2000 spectators

1872 – First football international

1885 – Professional football legalised

1888 – Football league matches played. Blackburn Olympics become first works team to win the FA Cup

1891 – Penalty kick introduced

1895 – Women's football played (at Crouch End FC)

1900 – The Cup Final at Crystal Palace attracted a crowd of more than 100,000

The game developed in various ways. In the public schools, when students were not studying, it was used as a way of channelling excess energy. Their game had rules, penalties for foul play, was played on a relatively small patch of ground and had a time limit.

Sabbatarians – a pressure group working to keep Sunday as a holy day – promoted the idea of introducing free time for leisure. Clergymen formed football clubs to try and stop drunkenness in their congregations. Clubs were also founded by local churches, chapels, publicans and companies.

The new form of football appealed to the factory owners and workers. Owners liked the idea that leisure activities could have rules and time limits. It meant they could allocate specific time for leisure – Saturday afternoons became the time when the factory workers were allowed to play. It was popular with the workers who were both spectators and players. With a common leisure time it became possible to form competitive leagues and the game became a spectator sport. The success of football teams became a matter of pride and the factory owners were happy to use the works football team for publicity purposes.

ACTIVITY

Describe how and why leisure activities grew during the Industrial Revolution.

- What were the effects of industrialisation?
- What were the factors which led to changes in the provision of recreation facilities for the working classes?

Bank holidays and paid holidays

Gradually during the nineteenth century, social reformers like Chadwick, Lord Shaftesbury and Charles Dickens helped improve the quality of life for the working classes by drawing public attention to poor working conditions.

Holidays came rather late in the process of improvement. The traditional holidays were Good Friday and Christmas Day. Sundays were also holidays and Saturday working hours were gradually reduced to a half-day. In 1871 the Bank Holidays Act made Easter Monday, Whit Sunday, the first Monday in August and Boxing Day into holidays.

Some employers recognised the benefits of fixed holidays and extended the Christmas, Easter, Whitsun and August holidays to longer shutdowns. In the 1920s and 30s, some enlightened employers allowed their staff paid holidays. But it wasn't until 1939 that the Holiday with Pay Act gave workers the right to paid holidays.

1925 – around 1.5 million workers had paid holidays

1939 – around 11 million workers had paid holidays

1961 – the basic holiday entitlement for full-time manual workers was two weeks

1971 – two-thirds of manual workers had a basic holiday entitlement of three weeks or more

1981 – the basic holiday entitlement was between four and five weeks

1991 – nine out of ten manual workers were entitled to more than four
weeks, with three out of ten getting five weeks or more

1993 – the average amount of paid holiday was 23 days for men and 25 days for women

Development of transport

The development of rail and road transport was possibly the most influential factor in the development of both sectors of the leisure and tourism industry. The rail networks which developed rapidly from the 1830s onwards meant that large numbers of people could travel around the country relatively easily and cheaply.

> In the first half of the nineteenth century 7.3 million people used the new railways. By the second half there were 1,142 million users.

The developments of cars, buses and the tarmac road surface meant even more mobility for even more people.

Increased mobility and holiday time meant people could go further afield for their leisure and recreation activities. Daytrips and stays of a week or two at the nearest seaside became favourite activities.

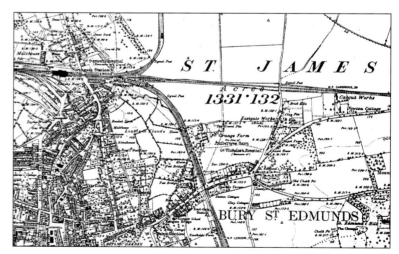

DISCUSSION POINT

What effect do you think developments of transport had on leisure and recreational facilities:

■ in seaside towns in Britain?

■ elsewhere in Britain?

Developments in sea and air travel had two main impacts on the UK leisure and tourism industry:

■ more people from the UK could take their holidays abroad

■ more people from abroad visited the UK.

Beatrix Potter, the author of Peter Rabbit, gave her Lake District farm to the National Trust after her death

Public-sector facilities

A major step in the development of local leisure facilities came when local authorities started to provide swimming pools, parks, recreation spaces and other facilities for people in the area. These were expensive to provide and many local authorities had to rely upon the generosity of local benefactors who gave money to finance them.

Local government reorganisation

In the past, local authorities managed their own leisure facilities or employed another company to manage all or part of it on their behalf. For example in a sports centre, the local authority might take responsibility for everything except the catering which would be managed by an independent company.

Nowadays local authorities have very little legal responsibility for provision of leisure facilities. In 1994 the structure of some local authorities changed. The idea is that these changes will lead to:

- more efficient and accountable local government
- an increased ability to identify the needs of the community
- less bureaucracy
- better coordination of services
- improved quality and reduced costs.

Compulsory competitive tendering

This method is now used by local government to provide cost-effective leisure and recreation services. Local authorities have to put out the management of their facilities to tender. This means that several companies bid for contracts such as:

- running a facility such as a leisure centre
- providing maintenance services for a parks department.

The contract is awarded to the company which submits the most effective management package, taking the objectives of the department into consideration. The winning contractor could be:

- the local authority – they will often have years of experience of running a particular department or facility
- a private company specialising in the management of particular facilities.

The performance of the contractor is regularly reviewed to make sure that the terms and conditions of the competitive tender are being met.

> ### DISCUSSION POINT
>
> How do you think the use of competitive compulsory tendering by local authorities affects users of local recreation and leisure facilities?

> ### ACTIVITY
>
> Make a chart outlining the major steps in the development of the UK leisure and recreation industry during the nineteenth and twentieth centuries.

Section 1.2.3

Leisure and recreation products and services

Products are what leisure and recreation organisations provide – for example, a hotel sells a special weekend break.

Services are what the product consists of – for example, the weekend break may contain several services such as meals, accommodation, entertainment and maybe travel.

The leisure and recreation industry offers many different products and services. The range provided by any one organisation depends on:
■ the needs and expectations of the customers and how much they are prepared to pay
■ the aims of the organisation
■ its size, resources and financial state.

A local authority, with limited financial resources, is likely to emphasise community leisure and recreation services for disadvantaged members of the community. A private-sector organisation will generally concentrate on products and services which are profitable.

Arts and entertainment

This sector of the industry is a major leisure and recreation provider with products and services provided by private, public and voluntary organisations.

Except for some specialist products the distribution of these products is widespread:
■ home-based entertainment is available to anyone who can pay for it
■ community entertainment may not be common in rural areas, but there are cinemas in most towns
■ bingo can be played in any village hall although private-sector companies will only open bingo halls where they think there is a big enough population to make a profit.

Products

■ home-based entertainment – TV, radio, video, computer games
■ community arts and entertainment – cinema, theatre, bingo, clubs, discos
■ specialist arts and entertainment – opera, ballet, contemporary dance, art films

Services

■ theatre booking agencies
■ arts clubs, children's party entertainment
■ mobile discos
■ home-based entertainment – cable TV, teletext, video rental

During the 1980s the percentage of people visiting the cinema grew from 38% to 64%. Seating capacity grew to over 400,000 – a result of the rapid growth of mutli-screen cinemas which by the mid 1990s accounted for almost half of all screens in the UK.

Opera, dance and other products may need special facilities or venues. This means that people living in small towns may only have the opportunity to see productions if they can travel to a nearby town or city. Large towns or cities will usually have at least one theatre or concert hall big enough to stage an opera or ballet production.

DISCUSSION POINT

Ballet and opera companies and orchestras are based in large cities, London in particular. What do you think can be done to ensure that other parts of Britain have access to these national companies?

26 Oct–4 Nov	Huddersfield	Lawrence Batley Theatre
6–11 November	Winchester	Theatre Royal
13–18 November	Bracknell	Wilde Theatre, South Hill Park
28 Nov–2 Dec	Barnstaple	Queen's Theatre
23–27 January	Watford	Palace Theatre
31 Jan–3 Feb	Crawley	The Hawth
5–17 February	Oxford	The Playhouse
20–24 February	Bury St Edmunds	Theatre Royal
27 Feb–2 March	Stirling	MacRobert Arts Centre
5–9 March	Canterbury	Marlowe Theatre
12–16 March	Cheltenham	Everyman Theatre

Sports, games and physical activities: average frequency of participation per adult per year.	
Persons aged 16 and over	Great Britain 1993
Walking	40.8
Any swimming	8.8
Swimming: indoor	5.9
Swimming: outdoor	3.0
Snooker/pool/billiards	7.4
Keep fit/yoga	12.8
Cycling	12.7
Darts	3.0
Weight lifting/training	5.5
Golf	2.7
Running (jogging etc.)	3.9
Any soccer	2.8
Soccer: outdoor	2.0
Soccer: indoor	0.9
Tenpin bowls/skittles	1.0
Badminton	1.2
Tennis	1.0
Fishing	0.8
Any bowls	1.6
Carpet bowls	0.9
Lawn bowls	0.7
Squash	0.9
Table tennis	0.7
Horse riding	0.9
Cricket	0.4
Basketball	0.4
Self defence	0.6
Ice skating	0.1
Field sports	0.3
Climbing	0.2
Water sports (excluding sailing, canoeing, windsurfing)	0.3
Motor sports	0.3
Sailing	0.2
Rugby	0.3
Athletics – track and field	0.3
Hockey	0.2
Netball	0.2
Skiing	0.2
Canoeing	[0.1]
Windsurfing/boardsailing	[0.1]
Boxing/wrestling	[0.1]

Sports participation

Many people participate in sporting activities.

- Two thirds of adults in the UK take part in some sport or physical activity.
- People are taking part in more sports now compared to five years ago.
- Walking is still the most popular activity – around half of adults go walking.
- Swimming, keep fit, yoga and cycling are all becoming more popular.
- Almost a third of adults visited a sports centre during a three-month period in 1993-94.
- Team sports are most popular among adults aged 16 to 24.

Levels of participation vary across the country, but even the smallest of villages will have an open space which is used for competitive football, rugby or cricket. Many have a tennis court and a village hall suitable for playing badminton. This provision exists because these kind of sports are products which attract mass participation.

Larger facilities like leisure centres and swimming pools which provide a service to the community are usually located in areas serving a population big enough to justify their provision. This is also true for private sports facilities such as:

- private heath clubs
- squash clubs
- golf clubs.

These often have high membership fees and there may be a waiting list to join. Their location will be dependent not just on population numbers but on the affluence or financial wealth of the area.

Sports spectating

Spectator sports attract large numbers of visitors and you can usually find a sports stadium in large towns and cities. Some facilities are built for specific spectators – for example, Chelsea football fans go to Stamford Bridge ground to watch home games. Sports fans often follow a particular club which may offer season tickets for games and other events. Some people travel all over the country and abroad to watch their favourite sport.

Spectator attendance at selected sporting events

	1971/72	1981/82	1990/91
			thousands
Football League (England and Wales)	28,700	20,006	18,828
Greyhound racing	8,800	6,100	5,121
Horse racing	4,200	3,700	4,698
Scottish Football League	4,521	2,961	3,377
Rugby Football Union	700	750	1,250
Motor sports		1,300	2,275
Rugby Football League	1,170	1,226	1,539
Test and County Cricket	984	994	
English basketball	2	85	140
Motorcycle sports	250	250	250
Scottish basketball	9	14	9

© Crown copyright

Outdoor facilities

Most local authorities have outdoor recreational and leisure facilities run by their parks and recreation department. Facilities might include:

- community playgrounds
- bowling greens
- outdoor lido or swimming pools
- public parks and gardens.

In rural areas these kinds of outdoor facilities may not be provided because the natural resources of the area are sufficient – for example, there is easy access to public footpaths and open spaces.

Recently, there has been an increase in facilities such as 'pick your own' farms and children's farms. These are normally easily accessible for people who live in towns and cities, providing an experience of the countryside.

Heritage sites

UK heritage sites are primarily tourist attractions. But they often have recreational and leisure services attached to them. Most stately homes provide catering facilities and sell souvenirs. Some larger stately homes provide added value to a visit, such as:

- adventure playgrounds for younger visitors
- live entertainers
- picnic sites
- exhibition spaces
- information centres
- wildlife parks.

Many of the sites which form part of the national heritage are located in the countryside. But there are important buildings, such as cathedrals and churches, in urban areas.

Some heritage sites offer services such as:

- special educational visits and information packs for visiting schoolchildren
- guided tours
- visitor centres.

ACTIVITY

Choose a local heritage site which is large enough to provide facilities for visits by local school parties. Find out the kind of educational resources provided by the site, such as:

- worksheets for school children to complete as they go around the site

- video shows which visitors watch before going round the site and which put the site into a historical context

- audio cassettes which visitors take round with them to explain what they are looking at.

Make a list of the resources provided. Then add two or three more you think the facility could provide.

Examples of play schemes

Some parks and recreation departments run their own play schemes for the under-fives.

Local authorities often provide financial assistance in the running of 'latchkey' projects – after-school schemes for children whose parents are at work.

Local authorities may run play schemes sponsored by large companies during school holidays.

Voluntary organisations often run schemes during the school holidays for children whose parents work full time.

For those who can afford it, there are many nurseries and holiday play schemes run by the private sector.

DISCUSSION POINT

What kind of products and services could a hotel provide in order to increase its use by business people and local companies?

Play schemes

These are provided by public, private and voluntary organisations.

Catering facilities

The catering industry is highly competitive. Most towns now support several fast food outlets with burger bars and pizza houses competing for business where once there were only fish and chip shops. Many of these offer free delivery services. The range of food is wide, reflecting the range of ethnic groups in the community.

Facilities in rural areas are more limited but many pubs now provide excellent catering and other services. As the landlord of a successful country pub says, they have had to adapt in order to survive:

66 *When I first came to take over this pub it was barely making a profit, with very few regular customers. Then my wife decided to provide Thai food and turn one of the rooms into a family room. As trade grew we put a bouncy castle in the garden and some swings. Now we're packed because people know they can come out with the whole family and eat cheaply and well.* **99**

Local authorities provide catering facilities in many venues – vending machines selling hot and cold drinks in swimming pools, large restaurants in concert halls.

Like other local authority services they are normally subject to compulsory competitive tendering.

Accommodation facilities

The range of products and services includes:
- self-catering products like caravan and camp sites, rented holiday apartments and holiday homes
- hostels
- bed and breakfast establishments
- guest houses
- hotels.

The range of services available depends on the price people are prepared to pay. Youth hostels provide basic accommodation at a very economical rate. Luxury hotels cost a lot more and may have shops, restaurants, hairdressing facilities, swimming pool, sauna and fitness centres to tempt the traveller.

Many self-catering facilities and smaller businesses operate on a seasonal basis. Accommodation providers with a wide range of services aim to achieve high levels of occupancy all year round by offering products and services for both business and leisure customers.

Reasons for distribution

The type and number of leisure and recreation facilities, products and services varies from one area to another. What is available depends on several things, for example:
- the location – urban, rural
- ease of access
- size of the population
- what local people want
- types of visitor attracted to the area
- types of investment the area attracts

■ type of population – age, culture, wealth, employment levels and so on
■ the amount of funding available from government and local authorities.

Natural resources

Some leisure and recreation facilities exist because of natural resources in the locality – examples are coastal areas, moorland areas like the Peak District or the North Yorkshire Moors and the Scottish and Welsh mountains. Some areas have artificial resources such as reservoirs and waterways. Rural areas can provide leisure and recreation opportunities not available in urban areas like fishing and rambling. Popular holiday areas are good places for establishing recreational and leisure pursuits that suit the holidaymakers' need to be entertained – facilities like golf courses, theatres and amusement arcades often grow up around holiday resorts.

Built facilities

Many old cities like Bath and York are full of sites and buildings of historical interest. Cathedral cities like Durham, Salisbury, Canterbury and Ely are well-established destinations which encourage a local economy to support visitors. More recently, areas with important industrial histories have begun to recognise their leisure and recreation potential. Because all these areas attract visitors, they provide opportunities for additional recreation and leisure facilities to develop alongside or as part of them.

City locations offer a wide range of opportunities for the leisure and recreation industry. Because their populations are big enough, cities can demand and support large-scale facilities like multi-screen cinemas, sports complexes, theatres and entertainment venues. They also have the related hospitality and catering facilities like restaurants, bars, hotels and so on close at hand.

National standards of provision

Professional associations representing different facilities give guidance to their members on national standards of provision. For example:
■ the Sports Council in its advisory capacity makes recommendations to local authorities about the minimum standard for provision of sports facilities in rural and urban areas
■ the English Tourist Board sets standards of provision which hotels and guest houses must achieve for grading.

Most leisure and recreation providers can get information on national or professional standards from trade or professional organisations.

DISCUSSION POINT

Think about the leisure and recreation facilities in your area.

How well do you think you are served by the leisure and recreation industry?

Are you satisfied with what's on offer?

Trade and professional organisations

■ Association of District Councils
■ The Arts Council of Great Britain
■ English Heritage
■ Institute of Leisure and Amenity Management
■ Playboard
■ The Countryside Commission
■ The English Tourist Board
■ The Museum Association
■ The Sports Council

The grading criteria used by the English Tourist Board

Listed Clean and comfortable accommodation; cooked or continental breakfast; adequate heating at no extra charge; bedding clean and in sound condition; hot water with no extra charge for baths or showers.

👑 Facilities and services as for Listed, plus: your own bedroom key; shared lounge area; washbasins in bedrooms or in private bathrooms.

👑👑 Facilities and services as for One Crown, plus: colour TV; early morning tea; minimum of 20% of bedrooms with ensuite/private facilities.

👑👑👑 Facilities and services as for Two Crowns, plus: evening meal; hairdryer; shoe cleaning equipment; ironing facilities; tea and coffee making facilities.

👑👑👑👑 Facilities and services as for Three Crowns, plus: evening meal with choice of dishes and selection of wine; colour TV, radio and telephone in bedrooms; laundry services, toiletries; quiet seating area.

👑👑👑👑👑 Facilities and services as for Four Crowns, plus: all bedrooms with full ensuite facilities; restaurant serving breakfast, lunch and dinner; night porter and room service; 24 hour lounge service.

Investigating local products and services

What is available – and why

You can get a good idea of local distribution patterns by looking at what leisure and recreation products and services are available in your own area. Some of the products and services may be common to all areas of the UK, although their size, ownership and management may differ. Examples are social clubs and sports facilities. Others may be more specialised because of their location – for example, an urban area may have different facilities from a rural area, a coastal area will differ from an inland area and so on. Factors like local government, the population and the structure of the local economy also affect the products and services available.

DISCUSSION POINT

Think about whether there are any unusual leisure products or services available in your area and why they are provided. For example, a local riding school may provide riding lessons for disabled children because there is a residential school nearby for disabled children.

Then think about the things which are more usual.

Are there are any products or services normally available nationally which are not available in your locality?

Can you explain why this is?

Part 2 of the assignment for this element asks you to carry out your own in-depth investigation of products or services in a locality.

Key questions

1 What do these terms mean?
the working week
flexitime
personal disposable income
social changes
customer demand
household expenditure
leisure time
transport system
compulsory competitive tendering
minority entertainment
mass participation
high levels of occupancy
minimum standard provision
trade or professional organisations

2 How did the development of road and rail systems in the nineteenth century benefit the leisure and recreation industry?

3 What facilities did local authorities start to provide as a result of the lobbying by social reformers in the nineteenth century?

4 What main pieces of legislation improved the work and leisure of factory workers in the nineteenth century?

5 How might competitive tendering improve the provision of leisure and recreation services provided by local authorities?

6 What are the differences between a product and a service in the leisure and tourism industry?

7 What kinds of facilities are most likely to be provided by:
■ a local authority?
■ a private-sector organisation?

8 How has the geography of the UK affected the provision of leisure and recreation facilities in different parts of the country? (Give three examples.)

9 Why do so-called 'inner-city' areas in Britain often lack leisure and recreation facilities? What historical and geographical factors do you think may have caused this?

10 Why do you think leisure and recreation facilities decide to offer certain products and services?

Assignment

Part 1

Produce a written report on the UK leisure and recreation industry.

Do the report in two sections. The first section should give the historical background – the main factors affecting the development of the industry and the major steps in its development. The second section should describe the main products and services provided by the industry nationally and explain why some of them can only be found in certain areas.

Include one example from each of the eight categories listed at the start of the element. You could do them as short case studies. Include illustrations such as photographs, graphs and charts.

Part 2

If you are working on your own, select a small geographical area in your locality. You could choose a larger area if you work together with others and share your findings.

Research and produce a comprehensive information leaflet which could be distributed by your local tourist centre or library. The leaflet should:
■ list all the products and services available in your area for each of the eight categories of facility listed at the start of the element
■ explain why these services are available in your particular area
■ identify which services are provided by the local authority and which are provided by private- or voluntary-sector organisations.

Design the leaflet as attractively as you can, using illustrations such as a map showing the position of each facility.

> 66 We're finding that more people are travelling now compared to ten years ago and they are going further afield than before. India used to be considered a far-off destination but now it's very popular. The sort of holidays people want are also changing – they have done the package holiday and now want something tailor-made. 99
>
> *travel consultant in a travel agency*

> 66 There has been a growth in car hire recently. Businesses are hanging on to their vehicles for longer than they used to (often until they have done 80,000 miles – it used to be about 40,000) and this means that their cars are more likely to break down. Then they need to hire cars. 99
>
> *car rental manager*

ELEMENT 1.3

The development of the travel and tourism industry

In this element you will find out about travel and tourism in the UK. You'll explore the reasons why tourist attractions have grown up all over the country and why there's a tourist information office in almost every town. You'll look at major historical steps like the start of the railways and the rapid changes in transport over the last hundred years. Where is the industry today? You'll answer that question by finding out about the travel and tourism products and services available across the whole country and in two local facilities. As in element 1.2, use this book and your own experience as a starting point for your investigation.

Factors influencing development

The travel and tourism industry includes:

- travel services – retail travel agencies, business travel agencies
- tour operators and principals – organisations which provide transport, accommodation and other facilities
- national and regional tourist boards
- tourist information centres
- tourist attractions
- guide services, such as guided bus tours
- currency exchange
- accommodation, catering and transport relating to travel and tourism.

Economic, social, political and environmental changes since the Industrial Revolution have had a major impact on the travel and tourism industry. Since the Second World War tourism has grown into one of the largest industries in the world. The UK – London in particular – has become a popular tourist location for visitors from abroad.

DISCUSSION POINT

In 1990, 43% of all holiday nights spent in the UK by foreign tourists were spent in London. In the same year, only 3% of holiday nights spent by UK residents were in London.

What do you think are the main attractions for foreign visitors to London?

Why do so few UK residents choose to spend the night in London?

- About nine million people are employed in tourism in the European Union – around six per cent of the workforce.
- In the UK, over 1.5 million people are employed in tourism-related industries.
- Holidays abroad now make up more than 40% of all holidays taken.
- In 1993, 23.5 million holidays were taken by British residents, more than three times as many as in 1971.
- Until 1986 tourists visiting the UK spent more money than UK tourists in other countries – there was a surplus on the tourism balance of payments.
- In the early 1990s nearly half the money spent on tourism by people living in the UK was spent on day trips (including visits to friends and relatives) – over 630 million day visits per year, at a total cost of £5.2 billion.
- More than half the foreign visitors to the UK base their holiday in London.

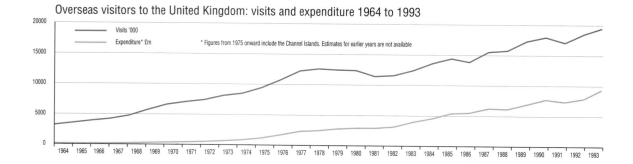

Overseas visitors to the United Kingdom: visits and expenditure 1964 to 1993

Visits '000
Expenditure* £m   * Figures from 1975 onward include the Channel Islands. Estimates for earlier years are not available

The main factors which have affected the growth of travel and tourism during the last two hundred years are:

- an increase in individual leisure time – people at work have an average of 24 days paid holiday per year
- a rise in personal disposable income
- a change in needs and expectations about travel and tourism – international business travel, increased interest in foreign travel
- a rise in the number of people coming to the UK from abroad – encouraging more tourist developments and investment.

Increased leisure time

Industrial and social change from the time of the Industrial Revolution to the present day has meant that people have more time when they can choose what they want to do. Regulations and reforms from the mid-nineteenth century onwards have reduced the number of working hours to an average of around 40 hours a week.

Advances in transport have made travelling quicker, easier, cheaper and more accessible so more people are able to use their leisure time for travel for pleasure.

See pages 22–23 for more information on how leisure time has increased.

Increased personal disposable income

Disposable income is money which does not have to be spent on necessities such as housing, food and clothing.

Over the last 50 years, people in Western Europe have gained progressively more disposable income. Once they've covered essential expenses such as housing, food, clothing and household bills, they have more money left over to spend on things like holidays and outings.

Estimated expenditure incurred on holidays abroad and party size 1974–93

	Holidays abroad of one or more nights													
	1974	1976	1978	1980	1982	1984	1986	1987	1988	1989	1990	1991	1992	1993
Average cost of holiday per person(£)*	107	162	201	287	327	351	376	419	443	480	507	550	547	555
Average size of expenditure party	1.9	2.0	2.1	2.0	2.0	2.0	2.0	2.1	2.1	2.2	2.1	2.1	2.1	2.1

Source: British National Travel Survey

Note: The expenditure party is paid for as one unit (including children)

* includes cost of accommodation

See pages 23–24 for more information in how personal disposable income has increased.

Percentage of holidays taken abroad (for four nights or
more) in the eight most popular countries*, 1974 – 1993

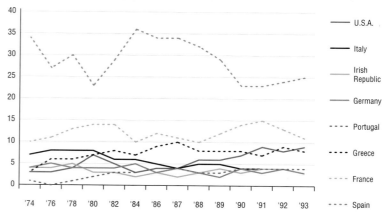

Personal needs and expectations

What people expect from travel and tourism has changed dramatically over
the last fifty years or so. Advances in sea and air transport have made holidays
abroad a normal expectation of most people. Journeys from one side of the
world to the other are now possible in hours rather than weeks. Advances in
communications and media systems have also made people more interested in
travelling abroad. Closer international business links and the spread of multinational companies have meant an expansion in business travel.

Growth of incoming tourism

In 1991, visitors to the UK spent almost $10 billion – around ten per cent of the
total amount spent on international travel by people in 25 countries across the
world. The table below shows how much money was spent by visitors to the
UK from other countries in the decade from 1983 to 1993.

Overseas visitors to the UK: Expenditure (by market countries/areas) 1983–93

	1983 £m	1984 £m	1985 £m	1986 £m	1987 £m	1988 £m	1989 £m	1990 £m	1991 £m	1992 £m	1993 £m	% change 1983/93	% share 1993
Country of permanent residence													
North America	992	1,271	1,709	1,464	1,710	1,579	1,700	1,907	1,542	1,743	2,057	+107	22
Western Europe** †	1,083	1,194	1,383	1,717	1,934	2,018	2,272	2,551	2,743	2,870	3,362	+210	36
Western Europe non-EU	317	369	440	491	617	613	699	822	828	804	895	+182	10
Rest of world	1,612	1,780	1,911	1,881	1,999	1,975	2,274	2,468	2,272	2,473	3,061	+90	33
All countries	4,003	4,614	5,442	5,553	6,260	6,184	6.945	7,748	7,386	7,891	9,376	+134	100

* less than 0.5%

** Spending by residents of the former East Germany are included with spending by residents of Eastern Europe up to 1990

† Expenditure by foreign visitors departing directly from the Channel Islands is included in the total expenditure but excluded from the
  figures for individual countries of residence.

Major steps in development

Tourism, like leisure, has existed for thousands of years:
- the ruling class of ancient Rome went to villas by the coast when summer temperatures became unbearable in the city
- religious pilgrims to holy sites needed accommodation when they reached their destination and on the way there, travelling the famous pilgrims' routes across Europe.

The major steps in the development of modern tourism happened partly as a result of massive economic and social change brought about by the Industrial Revolution:
- new technology powered an increase in trade and the need to import raw materials such as cotton for the new cloth mills – steamships were developed to carry such cargo, and soon these were used for cross-channel and transatlantic services for people wanting to travel abroad
- the invention of tarmacadam improved road surfaces and made travelling by stagecoach more comfortable
- the development of railways meant that people could move about the country more quickly and easily.

Paid and bank holidays

The introduction of paid and bank holidays was a result of the nineteenth century reforms of working conditions. But it was a gradual development, brought about partly by legislation and partly by more enlightened employers. Up until 1871, workers were allowed the traditional holidays of Christmas Day and Good Friday. Sundays were also traditional days of rest. A reduction in working hours over the second half of the nineteenth century brought the working hours down to ten and a half per day and Saturdays became half-days.

In 1871 Parliament passed the Bank Holidays Act. This created four bank holidays: Easter Monday, Whit Sunday, the first Monday in August and Boxing Day. Some industrial employers recognised the benefits of having fixed shut-down periods during the year and the Bank Holidays were the starting point for shut-down weeks.

Some employers in the 1920s and 30s allowed their staff paid holidays but a right to paid holidays didn't become law until the 1939 Holidays with Pay Act. For more information on the development of paid holidays, see pages 29–30.

Development of seaside towns

The seaside had long been considered good for the health but you had to be rich to afford the time and the expense of travel. Rapid development of the railways from the 1830s onwards led to a boom time for seaside resorts. As train fares became cheaper, more and more people made day trips to the seaside. And as holidays became longer the annual week or fortnight by the sea became increasingly popular.

Miles of railway in the UK

1848	4,646
1886	16,700

Resorts popularised by rail travel:
- Blackpool
- Fleetwood
- Southport
- Skegness
- Clacton
- Southend
- Folkestone
- Hastings
- Eastbourne
- Bournemouth

Morecambe Bay

O'tis a lovely country! The grey solemn-looking Carboniferous Limestone is the prevailing feature, soft-toned and exquisitely varied by sweetest natural woodland fringing the shores of the famous Bay . . . we had each day, also, four regular passenger trains, and charming it was to be playing in such trains a game of bo-peep with old father Ocean – a minute or two sweeping along his gently rippling shore – then a grand headland in view against which he wages eternal war of foam and fury. We several times visited this ground of enchantment . . .

From a letter written by Adam Sedgwick to his neice, 26 August 1870

Resorts developed to suit the needs and tastes of their visitors. Blackpool attracted holidaying textile and heavy industry workers from the nearby industrial regions. Southend, Hastings and Margate attracted the city workers from London. Other resorts, like Southport and Eastbourne, aimed to attract wealthier visitors. Popular attractions included piers, promenades, music halls and pleasure gardens as well as beaches.

The influx of holidaymakers meant a rapid increase in the service side of the travel and tourism industry. Hotels, boarding houses, lodgings, eating houses, entertainment and amusement facilities and transport systems sprang up to meet the needs of the visitors.

The introduction of motor vehicles like cars, buses and coaches increased people's mobility further. For some resorts like Blackpool, well served by the road system, this was an added boon. But for those without good road access, like nearby Southport, it meant a loss of business.

From the 1950s onwards, advances in air and sea transport and the increased availability of cheap holidays abroad led to a decline in the popularity of UK seaside resorts. They now rely far less on the annual holidaymakers' one- or two-week stays and more on weekend and Bank Holiday day-trippers.

Development of transport

Tourism owes much of its growth to improvements in transport by road, rail, sea and air during and after the Industrial Revolution.

Road transport

Until the nineteenth century the only form of road transport – other than by private carriage – was by goods wagon. Journeys like this were slow: a

ACTIVITY

Do a survey of holiday and day trip destinations of twelve to fifteen people, including friends and family. Make a chart to show the results.

DISCUSSION POINT

How do you think increased access to road transport affected society during the 1920s and 30s?

THOMAS COOK

Thomas Cook

Thomas Cook was the first person to organise a day trip on the railway. In 1840 he chartered a train to take the local temperance organisation – a group which promoted abstinence from alcohol – on a day excursion from Leicester to Loughborough. The trip was so successful that within five years he and other entrepreneurs were running excursions as fully commercial enterprises. It was the beginning of the Thomas Cook Travel Agency which is still in existence today.

On his first excursion between Leicester and Loughborough – a round trip of 24 miles – Cook attracted 575 customers who each paid one shilling (5p) for their day out. He took a great deal of care with the planning of his excursions and soon developed a programme of escorted tours around the world. Through his contacts with other tourism providers such as hotels and shipping companies he was able to negotiate reasonable prices for the services which he sold.

journey from London to Brighton would take two days. They were also unsafe and uncomfortable because of the uneven roads or tracks. Improvements came with the development of the stagecoach and, after 1815, the surfacing of roads with tarmac.

They were little more than a stage out of Grantham, or about half way between it and Newark, when Nicholas, who had been asleep for a short time, was suddenly roused by a short jerk which nearly threw him from his seat. Grasping the rail, he found that the coach had sunk greatly on one side, though it was still dragged forward by the horses; and while – confused by their plunging and the loud screams of the lady inside – he hesitated for an instant whether to jump off or not, the vehicle turned easily over, and relieved him of all further uncertainty by flinging him into the road.

Charles Dickens, *Nicholas Nickleby*, London, 1838, Chapter 5

Steam coaches – the forerunners of cars – went out of use once the railway network started to expand. The first petrol engines, developed by Daimler and Benz in Germany, were made in the 1880s – the first car to be sold was made by Benz and could travel at ten miles an hour. By the start of the 20th century, cars were more common. The first production-line techniques were used in Henry Ford's factories in the USA in the 1900s; European companies like Wolseley, Rolls Royce, Peugeot and Renault also began making small cars in factories.

In the 1920s, lorries developed during the First World War were converted into public transport vehicles, replacing horse-drawn buses. The private motor car increased in popularity and availability. People started to have more choice about how, when and where they travelled by road and were no longer reliant on the railway system.

Rail transport

The first passenger rail link was built between Liverpool and Manchester in 1830. In its first three months, it carried over 70,000 passengers and 4,000 tons of freight. In a very short time a network of railway lines between the major cities had developed. By 1846 there were over 4,500 miles of track in England. At first, travelling by train was expensive and working class people could not afford to take advantage of the network. The railways were used mainly by businessmen or wealthy travellers. They were also used for transporting goods around the country.

DISCUSSION POINT

Many people regularly travel for business purposes.

Do you think this could be described as tourism?

When do you think a trip to another part of the country can be described as tourism?

What are the essential characteristics of tourism as opposed to travel?

Not everybody approved of the new system of transport:

'The terrifying speeds (around 30mph) cannot but affect delicate lungs'

'To pass through cuttings and tunnels will occasion catarrhs and multiply agues'

'The movement of the trains will produce apoplexy in those of a sanguinous disposition'

Sea transport

Britain has always been a seafaring nation. Until the nineteenth century, ships were built mainly for defence and trade. If people did travel by sea, the journey was uncomfortable, long and dangerous. Sea travel was improved by the introduction of passenger steamship services. When the Suez Canal was built in 1869 these ships could operate on a round-the-world basis.

... Whatever you do, whatever folly you commit, never, never be tempted to take a sea voyage. It is quite the nastiest thing you can take – I have had three days of it now, so I know...

I know you are never sea-sick, unlovable creature that you are, so you won't sympathise with us as we lay limp and wretched in our deck-chairs on the damp and draughty deck... At last it became too miserable to be borne... we zigzagged to our bunks where we have remained ever since... Our steward tries to cheer us by tales of the people he has known who have died of sea-sickness, 'Strained their 'earts, Miss, that's wot they done!' It isn't very cheerful lying here...'

Anna Buchan, writing home about her journey to India on the steamship *Scotia*, 1913.

As well as transatlantic services, domestic services became popular in nineteenth century Britain. These were introduced from London to Gravesend and other resorts on the Thames estuary and the South Coast. The pleasure boats needed landing stages and so piers were built, followed by hotels and guest houses as visitor numbers grew.

In recent years, sea transport has lost out to air travel. In 1983, the number of journeys to European destinations by sea and air was almost the same. By 1993, for every traveller getting to Europe by sea, two chose to travel by air instead.

Air travel – some key dates

1903 Wright brothers became the world's first aviators

1914 first passenger flight – 22 miles took 23 minutes

1919 Alcock and Brown made the first trans-Atlantic flight

1947 an American pilot broke the sound barrier

1949 the first jet airliner came into service

1969 first flight of a Boeing 747 jumbo jet

Major tourism development in Britain

1830 First passenger train service between Manchester and Liverpool

1840 First leisure steamship built for Cunard

1869 Suez Canal opened

1871 Bank Holiday Act

1879 Thomas Cook organises his first overseas package tours

1895 Foundation of the National Trust

1903 The first Trust House opens

1936 Billy Butlin opens his first holiday camp at Skegness

1938 Holidays with Pay Act

1949 National Parks Act

1955 First packaged air holiday organised by Horizon

1969 Development of Tourism Act

1974 Concorde goes into service

1995 Eurotunnel carries its first passengers

Air transport

The need to move troops during the Second World War prompted the development of passenger-carrying aircraft. After the war, surplus aircraft were used for fare-paying passengers. The invention of the jet engine meant that air travel was fast, comfortable and relatively inexpensive. As air travel became more popular, twentieth-century entrepreneurs realised the potential for package holidays in the same way that Thomas Cook had done a century before.

DISCUSSION POINT

What effects do you think the development of air travel had on other forms of transport?

How does increased competition among airlines affect the travel business?

Overseas package tours

The most popular holiday destinations overseas for people living in the UK are France and Spain. The popularity of European destinations and the United States is shown in the table on page 42. Overall, eight out of ten UK tourists travel to other European countries, rather than go further afield. Most of them stayed in hotels, rented villas or flats – many of them sold as part of a package tour.

The great majority of package tours are to the popular European resorts and the big operators compete ruthlessly on price. But there is still a good market for different packages, such as:
■ upmarket holidays in exotic locations
■ activity holidays – watersports, cycling, walking, hobbies
■ special interest tours to remote places.

Development of Tourism Act

Until 1969 the organisation of tourism in the UK was very irregular. In that year the Development of Tourism Act created the statutory tourist boards and the British Tourist Authority. Tourist boards have two main functions:
■ to provide marketing support to tourist facilities within their region
■ to provide general tourist information about their region.

The legislation also authorised grants to be made available for the development of hotels and a hotel grading system.

ACTIVITY

Work in a small group with three other people. Choose one form of transport each and research its development during the nineteenth century. Use reference works about social and economic development in nineteenth and twentieth century Britain.

When you have done your research, share your findings with the group.Using your own notes and those of others in the group, produce a short description of the major steps in the development of the travel and tourism industry in the nineteenth and twentieth centuries. Include brief profiles on the four forms of transport.

Travel and tourism products and services

Travel and tourism services

- holidays
- tours
- activities at the destination – diving, water skiing, trips to historic sites
- accommodation, catering and transport
- information services
- guiding services
- currency exchange

DISCUSSION POINT

Think about your last holiday. What products and services did you make use of?

Who provides the products and services?

ACTIVITY

Find out the names of ten companies which provide principal services and products. For example, airports are principal providers – Heathrow is the largest airport in the UK – who owns it?

ACTIVITY

Collect some brochures from tour operators – either from your local travel agent or companies advertising in the Saturday or Sunday newspapers. Make a list of:

- the different types of tour operators
- the kinds of products and services they provide.

Products and services in the travel and tourism industry can be:

- domestic – UK residents travelling in and around the UK
- outgoing – UK residents travelling abroad
- incoming – foreign visitors travelling to the UK.

Each of these categories might include:

- leisure travel – annual holidays, day trips, weekend breaks
- business travel – to conferences or regional offices, corporate entertainment
- visiting friends and relatives.

There are three main suppliers of products and services in the travel and tourism industry:

- principals, e.g. airlines, rail, car hire companies, shipping
- tour operators
- travel agents.

Principals

They provide the basic travel products – transport and accommodation – and facilities such as:

- airports
- ferry terminals
- railway stations
- coach stations
- hotels and similar accommodation facilities
- travellers cheques
- holiday insurance.

Passenger travel products provided by principals include:

- rail transport – schedule and charter rail services
- road transport – coach companies, public bus services, car rental, chauffeur-driven hire cars, taxi and mini-cab services
- sea transport – cruise lines and ferry services
- air transport – scheduled and chartered airlines and helicopter services.

Principals also supply accommodation products such as:

- hotels and guest houses
- time-share resorts
- serviced accommodation
- self-catering accommodation.

Tour operators

Planning a holiday can involve a great deal of time and effort – as the couple below explain.

❝ Last year we decided we'd spend a few days away in the Lake District. Our idea was to tour around and keep the accommodation costs down as much as possible. We didn't have a car then so we had to make other travel arrangements. Hilary organised the travel, I arranged what we would do when we got there. We thought it would be a fairly easy task but it wasn't. First Hilary had to compare coach and train prices and timetables, and book seats for the cheapest option – the coach. Then she rang several car hire companies, compared prices and arranged to collect a car. I contacted the English Tourist Board to find out about bed and breakfast accommodation and bought a copy of The Good Pub Guide to find out where we should eat. One Saturday morning I

went to the library, looked through guide books and made a list of places to visit. Next year we've decided to go on a package holiday abroad! **99**

Why do you think principals and tour operators use travel agents when they might make more money selling direct to the customer?

Tour operators take a lot of the hard work out of going on holiday. They plan, organise, finance and sell holiday packages – including transport, accommodation, food and other services such as sightseeing tours, babysitting and local information. They buy each component of the holiday from the principals and create their own product which they then sell either directly to the public or through a travel agent.

Some people like to plan their own holidays. But for many, the tour operator means they can book the holiday well in advance and then relax until the day of departure arrives. Many tour operators specialise in holidays for specific groups of people – students, the elderly, wildlife enthusiasts – to make choices even easier.

First Choice... Price Pledge

No 'ifs', no 'buts', no 'extras.' With First Choice the price of your holiday is fully guaranteed and will not be subject to any surcharges. We reserve the right to change our prices at any point up until the time you book, but once you've made a booking and paid your deposit, the price of your holiday will not go up. (see our Booking Conditions on pages 130 - 131)

First Choice... Price Guarantee

We're confident that our prices are unbeatable. So much so, in fact, we offer you this price challenge: If, within 14 days of booking with First Choice, you find an identical holiday offered in another British tour operator's brochure available from a travel agent, and that identical price is cheaper - then tell us about it and, if it turns out to be exactly identical, we'll cut our price to match it! You may have already compared prices, in which case you'll know this is no mean task. Remember though, the following elements of the holiday must be identical, since even the slightest variation can greatly affect the price:
Do be careful to match • Date and time of departure Morning (6am-12noon) Afternoon (12.01pm-6pm) Night (6.01pm-5.59am) • Departure Airport • Holiday

Services provided by travel agents

Information:

- on means of travel – schedules, prices and availability
- location, price and availability of accommodation
- travel requirements – baggage allowances, passport, health and visas
- suitability of destinations – climate, topography, access

Reservations:

- find out where the customer wants to go – for example, Paris by plane or Portsmouth by coach
- check availability and cost of flights
- confirm the customer is happy with the time and cost
- buy the ticket from the airline or coach company
- sell the ticket direct immediately to the customer

Extra services:

- foreign exchange
- holiday insurance
- passport and visas.

Travel agents

The number of holidays available is huge and can be confusing. Travel agents provide easy access to information and help about the choice and suitability of a particular holiday. They supply prospective travellers with details of travel and related services, bridging the gap between the consumer and the principals or tour operators. Income is from commission paid by the principals or tour operators for every product, service or package the travel agent sells.

WELCOME TO LUNN POLY

Types of travel products

- leisure travel – services to the general public wishing to buy leisure holidays
- business travel – services for the business community
- visiting friends and relatives – seat-only sales where customers do not require accommodation
- conference and incentive travel – conference facilities and special promotions, associated with business travel.

From the information you have collected so far, produce a 'fact file' describing six types of tourism products or services – holidays, tours, activities at destination, accommodation, catering, transport, agency and information services, guiding services and currency exchange. Give examples which cover domestic, outgoing and incoming travel and tourism.

Other providers

As well as principals, travel agents and tour operators there are many smaller organisations which provide specialist services like tour management, guiding, courier services and resort representation.

There are also the tourist information centres. These are usually funded by local authorities and situated in towns to provide local tourist information. Most tourist information centres offer an accommodation booking service and sell travel-related products such as guide-books, souvenirs and maps.

Section 1.3.4	Investigating selected facilities

Most people employed in leisure and tourism probably work in one very specific area.

So why is it useful to have an overview of the complete range of travel and tourism products and services?

What do you think all the products and services listed in this element have in common?

If you spent time investigating travel and tourism facilities, you could come up with a list of products and services they offer. You could also describe what they are and who buys them. Part 2 of the assignment for this element asks you to do just that.

Key questions

1 What do these terms mean?

   European Union   tourism facility

   business travel   leisure travel

   retail travel agencies   principals

   excursions   tourist information centres

   tour operators   regional tourist boards

   guiding services   tourist attraction

2 What were the major effects of the Industrial Revolution on travel and tourism?

3 What legislation in the past 150 years has contributed to the growth of travel and tourism in the UK?

4 What did the Development of Tourism Act 1969 introduce?

5 What are the three types of organisation that provide travel and tourism services?

6 What facilities are principals responsible for?

7 How do tour operators create the product which they are selling to the public?

8 What role do travel agents play in the industry?

9 How has the structure of the travel and tourism industry changed in the last 150 years?

10 Do you think there is any way in which the industry could become more efficient – for example, by changing the relationship between tour operators, travel agents and principals?

Assignment

Part 1

Produce a written report on the UK travel and tourism industry. Do the report in two sections. The first section should give the historical background – the main factors affecting the development of the industry and the major steps in its development. The second section should describe the main products and services provided by the industry.

Include three examples of travel products or services and six examples of tourism products or services. You could do them as short case studies. Use illustrations such as photographs, graphs and charts.

Part 2

Select two facilities – one from the travel sector and one from the tourism sector. Find out what you can about the products and services available through these facilities. Produce a description of your chosen facilities.

ELEMENT **1.4**

The impact of the leisure and tourism industries

What impact does leisure and tourism have on people's lives, on their jobs and on the environment? In this element you'll be asking yourself what is good and bad about the industry. You'll look at how it affects people who live in a tourist area, the kind of jobs they get, the benefits of conservation – and the disadvantages like noise, overcrowding and pollution that can come along with successful tourism and transport systems. Start by looking at the situation across the whole country, then see what the benefits and the problems are in one area.

❝ *We're good for business! Leisure and tourism organisations tend to employ local people – we prefer them because they know the area. Part of our economic effect on the area is to boost trade. In one city, shopkeepers are up in arms because the tourist information centre might have to close. These traders know how much benefit the centre is to them.* **❞**

manager of a tourist information centre

❝ *We are in a well-known tourist area, so we get visitors from all over the world. As far as involvement with the local community goes, I employ local people and we provide lessons for locals as well as running riding holidays. My guests stay in nearby hotels, bed and breakfasts and pubs. I make recommendations according to what people say they want.* **❞**

owner of a riding school which also provides holidays

❝ *We provide employment for both paid and voluntary staff here. Along with other similar properties we help the area appeal a lot more to tourists. Our own research shows that one of the reasons why tourists come to this part of the country is that there is such a lot they can see and do within a 50-mile radius.* **❞**

administrator of a National Trust property

❝ *We contribute to the local community because our guests go to the local teashops, shops, restaurants and pubs. Eight people wanting dinner in a pub is good business here, and the network of guesthouses is important to the economic livelihood of the town. It does get a bit overcrowded sometimes, and I've heard quite a few local people complain about the seasonal nature of the work. But I suppose you're bound to get that variation in the tourist business.* **❞**

owner of a guest-house

The economic impact

Impact means the effects of the UK leisure and tourism industry on the country in economic, social and environmental terms. It refers to both positive and negative effects.

The leisure and tourism industry has grown rapidly in the past century. Growth is positive and negative – it presents opportunities and also problems.

Positive impact

- job creation – during construction and for local people in the longer term
- increased income to an area – visitors spend money in local shops, on locally made goods
- increase in local trade – visitors use other local facilities such as restaurants
- increase in wealth – people provide specific services to visitors

Negative impact

- a destabilised local economy – sudden changes in the population numbers, seasonal work
- loss of local industry
- loss of amenities – local shops close in favour of shops for tourists
- environmental damage

Positive economic impact

The leisure and tourism industry is one of the UK's largest and most profitable industries, and it's continuing to expand. Every sector of the industry provides employment, and large leisure and tourism organisations such as British Airways or Granada employ thousands of people in the UK and world-wide.

In June 1994:

- 330,000 people in the UK worked in hotels and other tourist accommodation
- 307,000 people worked in restaurants, cafés, etc.
- 323,000 people worked in pubs and bars
- 133,000 people worked in night clubs and licensed clubs.

An economist writing for the financial pages of a newspaper explains how important the industry is to wealth creation:

66 *There is an argument that recession affects leisure less than tourism – people in full-time jobs use leisure centres in their spare time whereas the unemployed use leisure centres and recreation areas to fill their time. The reality is that facilities will only be used if people can afford to use them.*

Leisure and tourism generally make a positive contribution to an area because facilities attract income and the people who earn that income spend a large part of it elsewhere in the local community. It all creates wealth in the area. Many schemes have been sold to communities on the basis that they will create jobs or wealth. By and large it's true. But the question they have to ask is, how many jobs, how much wealth? 99

So these three questions are important for a community to assess the economic impact of the leisure and tourism industry in their area:

- How much money is spent directly on leisure and tourism goods and services?
- How much money do the providers of leisure and tourism facilities spend on goods and services to run their business?

DISCUSSION POINT

Think of an example of a local leisure and tourism facility which has created wealth for your local community. List the ways in which you think it has done this.

53

■ How much of the profits earned from leisure and tourism is spent within the local community?

Negative economic impact

Growth in leisure and tourism does not necessarily mean that the community really benefits. Some negative economic impacts of tourism can be surprising: visitors to Windsor Castle arrive mainly by coach, which causes very bad traffic congestion and as a result local traders lose business. There could also be hidden negative economic effects, as the economist explains:

66 *I'll give you an example. A small factory closes in a rural town with a loss of 200 jobs. A leisure facility is opened at the old factory site creating 120 jobs. The facility is reliant on holiday visitors and so 40 of the jobs created are seasonal – staff only work there from May to October. Another 50 are casual, unskilled labour offering poor pay and no training. So there's a high level of staff turnover. The local community undoubtedly suffered with the loss of the original factory jobs. At first it seemed that the new leisure facility would help but in fact only 30 jobs are permanent, full-time positions and many local people are either unemployed or insecure in their jobs. Better than nothing, maybe, but still the overall impact is negative.* 99

Many people are worried that the development of tourism causes serious damage to some communities. For example, the British charity Tourism Concern has campaigned about many of the problems associated with modern tourism. Its magazine, In Focus, features examples of tourism's impacts and promotes the idea of sustainable tourism – tourism that will benefit everyone in the long term.

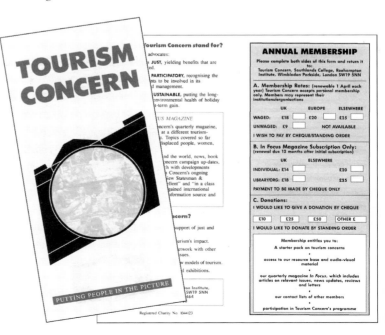

The social impact

Positive impact

- creating jobs and wealth
- meeting the local community's needs
- providing extra facilities and amenities

Negative impact

- inconvenience to the local community
- disruption to the structure of the local community
- increase in crime related to tourism

Positive social impact

Nationally, the beneficial social effects of the leisure and tourism industry are:

- the country is provided with a variety of resources to entertain its population
- people's lives are enriched by access to culture, entertainment and the opportunity to enjoy different parts of the country
- people can use their leisure time productively and enjoyably.

Locally, the effects of the leisure and tourism industry include:

- people having a choice in how to spend their leisure time
- work in facilities which make a positive contribution to the community
- continuation of local customs and cultures.

Negative social impact

Leisure and tourism can cause great inconvenience to both communities and individuals. People living in popular tourist areas can have their day-to-day lives severely disrupted as a result of the intrusive or anti-social behaviour of tourists:

- the village of Lacock near Chippenham is owned by the National Trust – each year up to 500,000 visitors come to admire the village. Two hundred people live in the village, many of whose families have lived there for several generations. The visitors intrude on their lives by allowing them very little privacy.
- Clovelly is a picturesque village in North Devon, with a very steep, car-free, cobbled main street lined by cottages and leading down to a small harbour – at the height of the season the main street is thronged by visitors peering through windows and even wandering into homes.

Another negative social effect of the leisure and tourism industry can be the disruption to the structure of the local community. Crime levels can also go up – things like theft of cameras or holiday money and traveller's cheques.

DISCUSSION POINT

Think about the different kinds of leisure and tourism facilities in your area.

- Do people have enough choice in how to spend their leisure time?
- What sort of facilities would more travel and tourism provide?

ACTIVITY

The activity on page 54 asked you to identify a leisure or tourism development which has caused debate. Using the same sources of information, find out the positive and negative impact of the development on the community.

DISCUSSION POINT

Do you think that, in the future, tourism in the UK will have to be restricted by legislation in order to protect local communities? What would such legislation try to do?

The environmental impact

Positive impact
- increased environmental awareness
- conservation – areas of outstanding natural beauty
- preservation – buildings and sites important to our national heritage

Negative impact
- destruction of natural resources
- wear and tear on resources
- visual pollution – developments out of keeping with the surroundings
- noise pollution – traffic

Positive environmental impact

Increased access to the countryside means that many people now have the opportunity to see wildlife and plants in their natural environments. The increase in money available for schemes to protect the environment is a direct result of people becoming more aware of its importance. Once they have seen flora and fauna in their natural surroundings people are more likely to understand the importance of protecting the environment.

Some organisations run holidays for young people which give them the chance to help on conservation projects. By learning how to build a stone wall or tidy hedging, participants can learn to appreciate traditional rural skills and practices.

Negative environmental impact

It is easy to see how the industry, and tourism in particular, has a negative impact on the environment:
- in National Parks, overcrowding has led to the erosion of footpaths and damage to the ecological balance
- in historic buildings and heritage attractions, the wear and tear created by visitors destroys what they are coming to see
- many tourist attractions become very crowded at peak times of the year – traffic congestion disrupts the day-to-day life of local people, car parks overflow and pollution is made far worse.

DISCUSSION POINT

Why do you think it is important for the leisure and tourism industry that the environment is preserved?

DISCUSSION POINT

Think about the environmental impact of tourism.
- Does it pose a major threat to the environment?
- Do you think the positive economic impact of tourism outweighs the negative environmental impact?

DOES TOURISM SPOIL OUR NATURAL HERITAGE?

Dovedale in the Peak district used to receive a million visitors a year – so many people caused damage to footpaths. Most of the visitors used a privately owned car park which had space for 900 cars. There was considerable traffic congestion, and therefore air pollution, on Bank Holidays and at other peak times.

The Norfolk Broads have been a tourist attraction for hundreds of years. Part of the problem is that nitrate run-off from agricultural land has damaged the reed beds which act as a natural filtration system. Continual boat wash exposes them to further erosion. The increased phosphate levels in the water encourage algae which threaten the balance between fish and plant life and some areas of the broads are gradually silting up. The conversion of marshland to arable land and the reduction in planned management of the marshes and woodlands have destroyed a characteristic landscape.

Kynance Cove is a famous beauty spot near Land's End. It is owned by the National Trust and attracts 200,000 visitors a year. A privately owned car-park, shop, café and house are highly visible and out of keeping with the remote and unspoiled character of the cove.

Westminster Abbey attracts 2.5 million visitors a year. There is often serious noise and disruption. A greater problem is the damage caused by wear, theft and vandalism. The ledgers in the Nave and places where queues form have become worn, and a thirteenth-century pavement in front of the altar is starting to disintegrate. Over the years there have been many thefts from the abbey's monuments.

The English Tourist Board encourages visitors to respect the area they are visiting and minimise the environmental damage they cause.

ACTIVITY

The two activities on pages 54 and 55 asked you to identify a leisure or tourism development which has caused debate. Using the same sources of information, find out the positive and negative impact of the development on the environment.

Section 1.4.4 — The impact on a locality

A good way of understanding the economic, social and environmental impact of the leisure and tourism industry is to study the impact of a development on a local area.

THE FAST-FOOD RESTAURANT

For many years young people living in a small town wanted a burger bar to open in the high street. Supporters of the project argued that:

- a busy fast-food restaurant would provide employment for young people
- it would become a meeting place for teenagers in the evening – much as the youth clubs and coffee bars had been in the 1950s and 60s.

A burger chain bought a shop in the high street which had previously been occupied by a family-run grocery business established for over 50 years. The owner had decided to sell his business and retire because of the increased competition from the supermarket. The shop was a listed building originally designed and built by a local builder on a traditional design out of local materials. Many local residents objected to the proposal to open the burger bar. After much debate the local council gave planning permission for the change of use on the basis that the outside of the building was not changed in any way. The members of the council agreed with supporters of the project that the burger bar would create jobs and bring in extra trade to the high street.

What actually happened:

- The developers used their own labour – there were few building jobs for local people.
- Both the manager and assistant manager were existing employees of the burger company and lived out of town – there were no other full-time jobs available, but several part-time jobs were created.
- The bar was popular in the evenings but there was a lot of rivalry between local groups of teenagers which led to arguments and fighting in the street.
- Litter from the take-away service caused a problem with scavenging cats and dogs.
- Rubbish from the restaurant was only collected by the council twice a week and rats had been round the bins in the access yard behind the building.
- Delivery lorries caused congestion in the high street three mornings a week.

DISCUSSION POINT

Do you think the local councillors could or should have predicted some of the problems caused by the burger bar? What do you think could have been done to reduce the negative impact of the development?

ACTIVITY

The burger bar site featured in the case study is now empty. Think about what other leisure or tourism business could use the facility. Draw up an outline proposal for your chosen leisure or tourism business. Identify the positive and negative impacts – economic, social and environmental.

Describe the impact your development might have on the local community.

DISCUSSION POINT

The management team focused on the positive impact their policies would have on the community. What problems do you think might arise from their promises?

SPORT FOR ALL?

The management of a small leisure centre on the outskirts of town was put out to compulsory competitive tender. The contract was awarded to a management team who gave a commitment to the council that they would

promote the 'Sport for All' campaign run by the Regional Sports Council. This meant that they had to develop, promote and put on activities which encouraged as many members of the community as possible to take a greater interest in sports participation.

The management promised to:

■ identify and develop leisure activities which would meet the needs of all the community

■ only employ people who lived locally.

They believed their campaign would result in:

■ a fitter and healthier community

■ increased social interaction.

They were committed to 'green' issues, promising to:

■ introduce a regular shuttle service from the leisure centre to the town centre

■ ban the use of CFCs in their cleaning materials

■ recycle all their waste material.

The leisure and tourism industry can have both positive and negative impacts on local economies, communities and the environment. The impact varies from one area to another:

■ In an urban area the impact of leisure may be far greater than the impact of tourism.

■ In the countryside the environmental impact may be of greater importance than the economic impact.

■ The social impact of tourism may be far greater than that of leisure in areas where the tourism industry is not well-established.

Key questions

1   What do these terms mean?

job creation	local wealth
recreation areas	destabilising of the local economy
casual labour	high turnover of staff
listed building	seasonal jobs
traditional culture	visual pollution
erosion	national parks

2   Can you list three positive and three negative effects of the economic impact of the leisure and tourism industry?

3   Can you summarise what the social impact of the leisure and tourism industry might be on a small rural community?

4   can you give three examples of how the leisure and tourism industry can positively affect the environment?

5   What factors need to be taken into consideration when planning to introduce a leisure facility into a local community?

6   How should tourists behave responsibly when visiting the countryside and historic sites?

Assignment

Produce a report about the impact of the leisure and tourism industries in the UK. If you have done the assignment for element 1.1, this report could be a follow-up to that one. It could be in the form of:

- a 'feature' article for a magazine
- a radio-type programme, recorded on cassette
- the script and storyboard for a TV programme – a storyboard is a sequence of images which show the main story.

The report should:

- describe their social impact – positive and negative
- describe their impact on the environment – positive and negative
- describe the economic impact of the industries – positive and negative
- give examples of all three types of impact on a selected locality.

If you're writing a feature article, use illustrations such as photographs, graphs and charts. If you're recording a radio-type feature, get two or three different people to record the examples to give some variety. If you're doing a TV programme, write a script for the presenter and keep the storyboard short – twelve images in all should be enough. You might like to get help from students on media and communication courses.

UNIT **2**

Element 2.1
Organisational structures

Element 2.2
Leisure and tourism teams

Element 2.3
Recruitment and selection

Element 2.4
Workplace standards and performance

Human resources in the leisure and tourism industries

ELEMENT **2.1**

Organisational structures

What are leisure and tourism organisations like from the inside? In this element you'll be finding out how organisations are structured. Big companies like airlines or hotel chains are likely to have several different departments and many layers of management. Smaller local organisations may have a simpler structure – for example, a leisure centre might have one general manager and just two or three department managers. You'll be looking at how these structures affect the way employees in organisations work. You'll also have a chance to see what the people at the top of the organisations do in their jobs.

❝ *The organisation is run by the chairman and managing director with various managers reporting to them – the sales manager, the parts manager, the service manager and me, the car-rental manager. We have monthly management meetings together.* **❞**

car-rental manager

❝ *The key roles at our property are those of head gardener, restaurant manager, shop manager, plant centre manager, house steward, secretary and myself as administrator. We communicate through meetings which we hold as and when we need them.* **❞**

administrator of a heritage site

❝ *The two of us tend to divide our responsibilities so that we are responsible for slightly different things but most decisions are taken together. We employ four part-time staff: two for cleaning rooms, two who come and house-sit and someone who does the bookkeeping. They've all got to be trustworthy and the important thing is that we get on with them as people. They've got to appreciate what we are trying to do – and they have to be non-smokers!* **❞**

guest-house owner

❝ *We normally make important decisions at regular management meetings. People bring up ideas and we then decide whether or not to act on them. We tend to have a collective decision-making process rather than one dominated by one person.* **❞**

sports centre development manager

Types of organisational structures

DISCUSSION POINT

Think of reasons why organisations need a formal structure. What do you think might happen to an organisation without a clearly defined organisational structure?

All organisations have a structure to help them function smoothly and efficiently. Organisational structures are based on:

- how the organisation is divided into areas of operation
- the way authority, responsibility and control are allocated amongst staff in the organisation
- the relationships and communication channels between different levels of staff – for example, sales staff report to a sales manager, who in turn reports to the sales director.

Types of organisational structures

simple	a small scale organisation where the manager is in direct contact with all staff
functional	an organisation where people are grouped together according to the similarity of jobs they do
divisional	an organisation divided into separate areas of business activity
centralised	an organisation where overall authority and control is held by a single person or group of people
decentralised	an organisation where authority, responsibility and control are allocated to people at a local, functional, or divisional level
hierarchical	an organisation structured into tiers where levels of authority, responsibility and control increase at each successive tier

Simple structures

In a simple structure, all staff report to one person, who will probably also be the owner of the organisation.

Organisations with simple structures have enough staff to manage the day-to-day running of the business. But they often need to buy in help from specialists, such as:

- accountants – to prepare annual accounts and VAT returns
- graphic designers – to produce promotional brochures and company stationery
- solicitors – for legal advice.

Functional structures

Bigger organisations are often divided into functions. Each function will be run by a manager. The managing director of a travel agent explains:

Functions are specialised areas of business activity carried out in an organisation – for example personnel, finance and marketing.

66 *When I first set up this business, it was a small-scale thing – me and two staff. As the business grew and I took on more staff, it became impossible for me to manage everything. So I separated the business activities into departments based on functions and appointed a manager for each one. The most logical structure was to have three departments: finance, marketing and sales. The managers report to me but have responsibility for the activities and staff within their departments. We've grown again in the past year and we're now thinking of dividing the sales department into two separate departments – sales and customer service.* 99

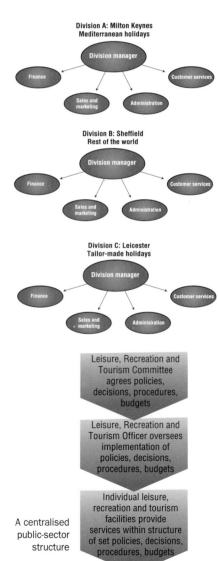

A centralised public-sector structure

Divisional structures

Large organisations often structure themselves into divisions. The divisions may be:

- geographical – operating in different areas of the UK or in other countries
- product- or service-based – concentrating on specific products or services from the organisation's range
- operational – where services like retail, production or transport operate as separate divisions
- commercial – where divisions operate in different areas of a single industry or in several different industries
- subsidiary – where smaller companies are owned by a large parent company.

Each division may be divided into functional departments with department managers reporting to division managers. In big organisations, each division may be organised like a separate company, with directors who belong to or report to the board of the parent company or a company headquarters. Examples in the leisure and tourism industry are:

- Granada – a very large organisation with a number of business divisions in the UK and abroad including rental and retail, television production and broadcasting, leisure and business services. In January 1995 they bought the Forte group, with its extensive hotel and catering business
- Rank – owns companies in a number of different leisure and tourism sectors, including cinemas.

Centralised structures

In a centralised structure, a few senior managers have overall responsibility and authority. They set policies, establish procedures and make decisions for the rest of the organisation to follow.

Centralised structures can be:

- small organisations run by the owner-manager
- large organisations where control rests with a head office
- public-sector organisations where policies and budgets are set by local or central government.

DISCUSSION POINT

Think about facilities in the leisure and tourism industry that are part of a large chain – for example, fast food restaurants, big travel agents, cinemas. Can you see any evidence of centralised control over the way individual facilities and outlets operate?

A centralised private-sector structure

Decentralised structures

In a decentralised structure, complete responsibility and authority are given to managers. In large organisations, divisional managers make decisions, set policies and establish procedures based on their own judgement of how the division should operate. In smaller organisations, department heads are free to choose how to run their departments rather than have the managing director tell them how to do it.

Hierarchical structures

> **Hierarchical structures** have different levels of status or authority ranked one above the other.

A hierarchical structure

Organisations with **tall** structures have many layers of management.

Organisations with **flat** structures have as few layers of management as possible.

A hierarchical structure exists as soon as one person or group of people has authority, control and responsibility over another person or group of people. So most organisations will have some form of hierarchy.

There are two types of hierarchical structure:

- tall
- flat.

65

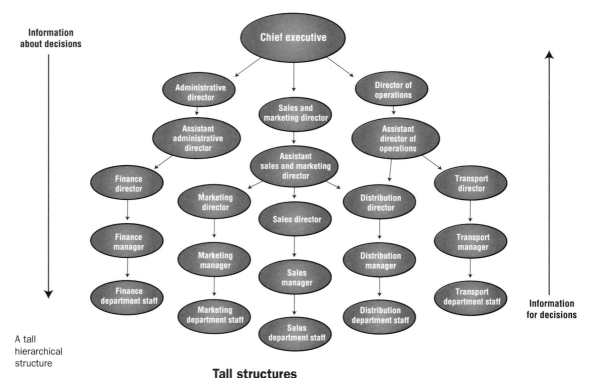

Information about decisions

Information for decisions

A tall hierarchical structure

Tall structures

In an organisation with a tall hierarchy, the limits of authority, responsibility and control are strictly defined. The manager or director responsible for each layer:

■ reports directly to a manager or director in the layer above

■ instructs the director or manager in the layer below.

The higher up the hierarchy you are, the wider span of authority, responsibility and control you have.

Characteristics of a tall hierarchy

■ Decisions are made at the top of the hierarchy by senior management and passed down through the hierarchy for implementation.

■ Information is passed up the hierarchy to the top to provide the basis for decision-making.

■ Communication lines are long because information has to be passed up and down through a number of people.

Characteristics of a flat hierarchy

■ Fewer decisions are made at a highest level.

■ Few layers of management.

■ Information flows up, down and across the organisation.

■ Fewer layers of management means shorter communication lines.

Flat structures

In organisations with flat structures, staff who carry out the operational aspects of the organisation's business have more authority to make decisions about the way they carry out their roles and responsibilities. Staff speak directly to the relevant people rather than pass information through one layer of management to another until it reaches the relevant person.

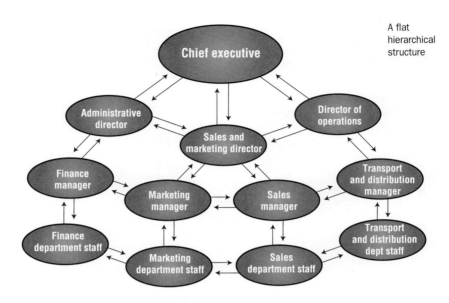

A flat hierarchical structure

Flat structures are becoming more and more popular. A manager in a medium-sized entertainment complex explains how it works for them:

66 *People here take their own decisions. That's the rule we go by – if you can take a decision, take it. If you can't, ask your manager or supervisor. But don't go on asking, once you've learned how to do it. I think a lot of organisations are going this way. You don't need as many staff and people have more interesting jobs if they can decide for themselves what to do in a situation.* 99

A management consultant explains the choices an organisation has to make in deciding on its structure:

66 *You can't say that any one structure is better than any other. You have to consider which is most appropriate. An organisation should choose the structure that best supports what it does and helps it to operate in the most effective and efficient way. This means taking into account the size of the organisation, its culture, the type of market it is in, how its competitors are structured and so on. Also, many organisations – particularly the larger ones – will be made up of a combination of types of structure. For example, a large organisation may have a mixture of centralisation and decentralisation. Some decisions will be made centrally and the whole organisation will follow them. Some decisions will be decentralised and made at divisional or departmental level by the managers or staff members using their own judgement.* 99

ACTIVITY

Choose three leisure and tourism organisations you know something about or can find out about. Find out what type of organisational structure each one has and draw a chart to show each one. Make brief notes on why the organisations have structured themselves in these ways.

Section 2.1.2

Factors which influence organisational structures

Internal factors

- the size of the organisation
- the organisation's location
- the type of product or service it offers
- the organisation's management style

External factors

- ownership of the organisation (whether it is public or private)
- competition
- changes in:
  - markets
  - technology
  - demographics
  - government, or government policy

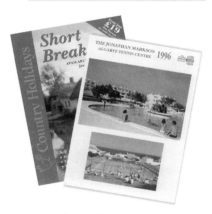

Internal factors

Size

Organisations with a large number of staff may need more than one layer of management to:

- support and monitor staff
- manage the operation so that it provides products and services efficiently
- manage in different locations.

A small organisation working from a single office can usually use a simple organisational structure, without different layers of management.

Location

When an organisation is small and based on just one site, it can have a fairly simple structure. If it expands to more than one location, it may need to change its structure and become more divisional and decentralised.

Nature of product or service

Some products and services provided by leisure and tourism organisations are exclusive or specialised – for example, guided walking holidays in Nepal, or special-occasion candlelit dinners for two. These types of service are usually provided by small organisations with a simple organisational structure, which can offer a more personal approach than large, hierarchical organisations.

Large organisations often offer products and services to mass markets regionally, nationally or internationally. These types of organisation will be more complex. They may also be more centralised to ensure a consistency of quality, standard and promotional methods across their wide-ranging activities.

Management style

The way in which managers work with staff can have a major influence on an organisation's structure. For example:

- if senior managers have an autocratic management style and like absolute power over decision-making, the organisation will probably have a centralised structure with a tall hierarchy
- if managers have a more democratic management style and prefer to delegate decision-making and authority to others, the organisation will probably have a decentralised organisational structure with a flat hierarchy.

External factors

Ownership

Who owns an organisation can have a powerful influence on its organisational structure. For example:

- Public-sector organisations are controlled by national or local government officers or by specially appointed boards. They are often run on fairly complex hierarchical lines, with decisions taken by committees.

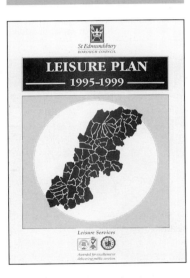

- Private-sector organisations choose the structure which is most in keeping with their management style and which is likely to produce the most profit for owners and shareholders.

Competition

An organisation keeps a close eye on the competition from other organisations offering similar products and services to make sure they are not gaining a competitive advantage. Competing organisations often have similar organisational structures. For example, major fast-food chains all need the same type of organisational structure because they are doing very similar things – providing large amounts of fast food quickly and to strict cost controls.

Change

The organisational structure of a company can be influenced by changes in:

- markets
- technology
- demographics
- government, or government policy.

Changes in markets

If there is an increase in demand for an organisation's product or service, it may need to expand. As a result, the organisational structure might change to accommodate the increase in staff and offices.

Changes in technology

New technology affects people's jobs which in turn can affect the organisational structure. For example, an organisation launching a new computer network may need to centralise or streamline its administration department.

Changes in demographics

Changes in demographics can have two main effects on an organisation:
- a change in the nature and availability of customers
- a change in the nature and availability of people to employ.

Changes in demographics can occur locally as well as nationally.

Changes in government or government policy

All political parties have policies which affect leisure and tourism businesses. A change in government, or in government policy, can affect finance, legislation, regulatory policies and trading, forcing both public- and private-sector organisations to change their organisational structures.

AGE DISTRIBUTION OF ESTIMATED RESIDENT POPULATION AT 30 JUNE 1992										
Resident population										
	England and Wales		Wales		Scotland		Northern Ireland[2]		United Kingdom[2]		
	Males	Females	Males	Females	Males	Females	Males	Females	Males	Females	Persons
0–4	1771.5	1683.1	98.3	93.6	167.3	159.1	66.4	62.9	2005.1	1905.1	3910.2
5–9	1674.0	1584.9	97.2	92.2	164.2	156.9	67.4	63.8	1905.5	1805.6	3711.1
10–14	1607.6	1518.9	93.8	88.6	163.6	155.9	66.0	63.7	1837.2	1738.5	3575.7
15–19	1598.6	1508.0	91.9	86.6	165.9	157.3	65.2	60.9	1829.6	1726.2	3555.8
20–24	1984.4	1894.5	106.0	100.4	205.5	198.4	68.7	64.1	2258.6	2157.1	4415.7
25-29	2168.8	2086.8	107.4	104.8	212.0	207.6	62.9	62.9	2443.7	2357.2	4800.9
30–34	1967.8	1913.8	100.7	100.4	199.5	197.9	57.6	59.6	2224.9	2171.4	4396.3
35–39	1711.8	1695.6	92.2	92.8	174.2	175.5	51.7	51.7	1937.7	1922.8	3860.5
40–44	1760.5	1756.1	99.2	98.9	169.9	172.1	48.2	48.7	1978.6	1976.8	3955.4
45–49	1700.0	1694.9	94.8	95.2	159.5	162.1	46.3	47.6	1905.8	1904.7	3810.5
50–54	1360.9	1362.0	79.9	79.6	136.4	143.9	38.4	39.9	1535.7	1545.7	3081.4
55–59	1281.8	1295.2	75.2	76.8	130.0	140.7	34.9	37.4	1446.7	1473.4	2920.1
60–64	1228.1	1305.5	73.6	78.7	123.6	140.6	31.9	37.3	1383.6	1483.4	2867.0
65–69	1129.3	1293.2	71.5	81.5	109.7	132.9	29.4	35.8	1268.3	1461.8	2730.1
70–74	919.9	1195.2	57.6	75.3	84.5	118.0	23.3	31.5	1027.8	1344.8	2372.6
75–79	638.1	987.3	38.1	59.6	56.8	94.5	15.5	24.8	710.5	1106.5	1817.0
80–84	389.8	761.6	22.1	45.1	33.6	70.6	8.8	17.7	432.2	849.9	1282.0
85 and over	205.9	641.6	11.5	37.2	16.5	54.5	4.3	13.3	226.7	709.3	936.0
0–14	5053.0	4787.0	289.3	274.4	495.0	471.9	199.8	190.4	5747.9	5449.2	1197.1
15–64	16762.7	16512.4	920.8	914.4	1676.6	1696.1	505.7	510.1	18945.0	18718.6	37663.5
65 and over	3282.9	4878.9	200.9	298.8	301.2	470.4	81.3	123.0	3665.4	5472.3	9137.7
All ages	25098.6	26178.2	1411.0	1487.6	2472.8	2638.4	786.8	823.4	28358.3	29640.1	57998.4

1 Figures may not add due to rounding.
2 Provisional

From: Monthly Digest of Statistics, May 1994, Table 2.2
Crown copyright 1994

DISCUSSION POINT

What would be the effects on a sports centre of the following demographic changes:

■ longer life expectancy leading to an increase in the proportion of the population aged 60 and over

■ a past drop in birth rates leading to a reduction in the proportion of 16- to 18-year-olds in today's population

■ an increase in the number of students nationwide taking courses in leisure and tourism?

ACTIVITY

Imagine you work in the marketing department of a small bus company that specialises in tours of historic cities, such as Bath, Edinburgh and Oxford. To keep a competitive edge the company decides to start running tours to visit other areas of interest and scenic beauty, such as the Cotswolds and Rutland. It is estimated this will increase the company's activities and profitability by about 25%. The company restructures with the intention that this increased workload can be dealt with by existing employees. How could the company handle the change to help employees cope with the effects of the change? Write a memo to the managing director outlining your views.

How organisational structures affect operations

The way organisations are structured can have a big effect on the way the business works. The general manager of a health studio explains:

66 *We used to be a very small organisation, owned by just one person. I was brought in as general manager, responsible for just two staff. I dealt with everything to do with the business, from paying the wages to buying new equipment. We offered a personal service, we changed things whenever we felt they needed to be changed, and we just shared out the jobs, doing whatever needed to be done. Because we were a small business we knew everyone personally and there was a sort of family atmosphere here. A year ago the owner of the studio sold out to an American organisation and everything changed. Things are really different now because we are answerable to our main branch down south, and they are answerable to head office in Boston in the States. Now the type of fitness facilities we offer is decided at head office, we have more staff, there is a clear division between jobs – instructors deal with the members, the office staff deal with the paperwork – and I'm much more involved in managerial tasks.* 99

In this case, changing the organisation's structure had all sorts of repercussions for the day-to-day running of the business.

Internal effects

Internal effects

- on work relations
- on job opportunities
- on communication
- on decision-making
- on response to internal change (in staff and management)
- on productivity
- on profitability

External effects

- on the way an organisation responds to external changes in technology, competition, government and markets

DISCUSSION POINT

If the structure of an organisation changes, how do you think this might affect people who use the products or services which it provides?

Work relations

Effective work relationships rely on people knowing:
- what is expected of them
- what they can expect from their colleagues.

The organisation's structure should help to support working relationships. People need to know how much authority they have and who they have to report to.

DISCUSSION POINT

What do you think would be the effect on work relationships if the organisational structure is inappropriate – too many or too few managers, complicated or inadequate reporting structures or too much responsibility and too little support?

Job opportunities

The structure of an organisation can shape job opportunities. In a tall hierarchical structure, people can move up the hierarchy, gaining more responsibility and authority. They have the benefit of a clear, step-by-step career progression. On the down side, waiting until someone in the job above moves on can hold good people back. In a flatter structure, job opportunities can be more flexible. Progression through the organisation tends to be sideways rather than just upwards. People can extend the scope of their jobs by taking on new areas of responsibility or acquiring new skills. On the down side, it can mean that people's roles become muddled or overstretched and the opportunities for progression are not so clear.

Whitbread Group Leisure Organisation Chart

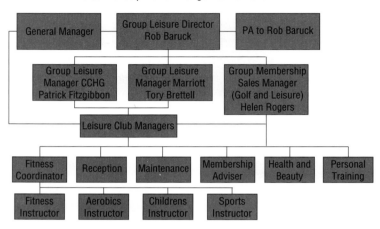

Creating job opportunities also depends on managers who believe in the importance of developing everyone's potential. They use the organisation's structure to make it happen.

Communication

The structure of an organisation defines how people at different levels report to their managers or supervisors. If the structure is right it should support good working lines of communication. Fast, effective and responsible communication is vital to any organisation. So communication lines should be as direct as possible. But they also need to be efficient in terms of time.

Here's the experience of the managing director of a tour operator:

❝ *Before I started up this organisation, I had several jobs in the travel and tourism business. One organisation had a long and rigid communications route. Staff talked to supervisors who in turn talked to managers who talked to directors who talked to the managing director who made all the decisions. There were only 25 people in the organisation! It took so long to get information and you never felt you had a say in any decisions. When I started my own organisation, I thought 'I'll be different. It'll be open door and open ears to all whenever they need me.' I spent my days talking to various members of staff – and my evenings and weekends catching up on the work I didn't get done because I'd been talking to people. So I asked all the staff to define what information they needed and who they needed to get it from. We then got together and worked out the best way to get information around the organisation.* ❞

Investing in People

- in 1993, 90 per cent of employers in Center Parcs took part in a 'job rotation' day where people tried out other people's jobs

- IDV UK, a drinks marketing company, spends an amount equivalent to two per cent of the organisation's staff costs on training

- when it opened three new hotels, the De Vere group filled all key appointments internally – i.e. from people already employed by the organisation

- at Bettys and Taylor's of Harrogate, which won the 'Tea Place of the Year' award in 1993, the best idea put forward each month by staff gets a prize.

All these organisations have received the Investors in People award, which means that they have achieved the national standard for developing their employees to meet business objectives.

INVESTOR IN PEOPLE

DISCUSSION POINT

Think of a time when you've had difficulty getting hold of the right person to talk to.

■ What problems did it cause you?

■ Why was the right person so hard to find?

DISCUSSION POINT

■ How do you feel when decisions are made for you?

■ When does it annoy you, and why?

■ When do you prefer it, and why?

Decision-making

In hierarchical structures decisions are made at the top of the organisation then passed down as instructions for lower levels to follow. In flat structures as many decisions as possible are made by the people who do the work.

Response to internal change

Most organisations want to minimise the disruption caused by changes in staff and management. It's particularly important when changes happen at strategic and policy-making level. For example, an organisation which has a centralised structure, with decisions made by one person, will find it hard to operate if this person leaves. In contrast, an organisation with a decentralised structure has a range of managers who can keep things running smoothly if a key member of staff leaves.

Productivity

Productivity is the measure of the efficiency of a business's output – the products it makes and the services it provides. An increase in productivity is achieved when more products are made, or services provided, with fewer or the same resources.

An organisation's structure should help everyone to do their job efficiently and effectively. If people are bogged down with long reporting lines, lengthy decision-making processes or masses of paperwork which don't actually contribute to the main part of their job, it will reduce their productivity levels. Productivity levels are also affected if people are overstretched by too much responsibility or underused by having too little responsibility.

Here's how a sales representative of a tour operator feels about the negative effects of the department's structure.

66 *My main role is to make sales but because we haven't got any administrative staff in the department, a lot of my time is spent filling in, photocopying and filing sales forms. I spend the official working day concentrating on my sales role, but an hour or two after office hours doing all the paperwork and filing.* 99

DISCUSSION POINT

What links do you think there are between levels of staff morale and productivity?

73

Profitability is the amount of surplus money an organisation can generate from the income it has left over from sales once it has paid the costs of producing and selling its products and services.

Profitability

An organisation can use its structure to make sure it isn't wasting money. For example, it can keep costs down by ensuring that it is employing the right number of staff with the right levels of skill.

ACTIVITY

Look at the quote from the sales representative for a tour operator. Suppose there are four sales representatives in the department, each putting in an average of eight hours' overtime each week at a rate of £9.00 per hour. Taking into account holidays, they work 46 weeks a year.

■ How much will that cost the organisation over a year?

■ How could it reduce the negative effects of this overtime on its profits?

External effects

An organisation's structure can affect the way it responds to external changes in:

■ technology
■ markets and competition
■ government.

ACTIVITY

Keeping staff informed of changes, their reasons and their effects can be a difficult task – particularly for large organisations where management decision-makers can seem remote from staff at operational levels. But being informed helps staff to feel valued and raises their morale.

Make a list of ways an organisation can keep its staff informed. Contact a large leisure and tourism organisation and find out what they do to keep staff informed. Add to your list any methods they use that you hadn't thought of.

Changes in technology

Organisations have to make quick, well-informed decisions about whether to introduce new technology in order to remain competitive.

Changes in markets and competition

These can have an immediate effect on profitability – good or bad. To make the most of change, organisations have to respond quickly, effectively and aggressively to the situation. A leisure and tourism organisation without a clear marketing function in its structure will not be able to compete well. A rigid, hierarchical structure may slow down the decision-making process and make an organisation unable to respond quickly to changes in the leisure and tourism markets.

Change in government

An organisation's structure will affect its ability to respond effectively to changes in government policy on finance, legislation, regulatory policies and trading. For example, the opening up of the single market in Europe will continue to present many opportunities to go-ahead businesses in the leisure and tourism sector – but only if the organisation is structured to take advantage of them.

Key job roles

If you look at the organisational structure of a number of leisure and tourism organisations, you'll find a number of common job roles. Job titles may differ in the private, public and voluntary sectors but the activities of the job-holders are often similar.

Key job roles fall into three main categories:

- strategic planners – they decide on long-term objectives and strategies for the organisation as a whole: what the organisation is going to do and why
- tactical planners – they decide on the how the different sections of the organisation can contribute to the long-term objectives and follow the strategies: how the organisation is going to do it
- operational planners – they decide on the short-term activities which get the work done.

The three boxes below show the key roles in private-, public- and voluntary-sector organisations.

PRIVATE SECTOR

Board of directors	elected by the company owners (private individuals and shareholders) to take overall strategic charge of the business. Also responsible for ensuring that the company operates according to legal regulations.
Chair of the board	also chair of the company. Elected by the board of directors to have overall responsibility for the actions of the board
Executive directors	managing director and other directors who have responsibility for the tactical planning and day-to-day running of the company. May also be board members.
Non-executive directors	an independent, advisory role. They have no involvement in running the company but may be investors or represent an investing body such as a bank.
Managers	responsible for the operational planning needed for the day-to-day running of departments and sections within a company. Report to the executive directors.

PUBLIC SECTOR

Elected members	councillors elected to parish, city, county and district councils. They hold council and committee meetings to make the decisions, allocate budgets and set policies.
Officers	paid staff employed by the councils to manage the budgets and run the facilities and services provided by local government. Usually have responsibility for specific areas – for example, Recreation Officer, Heritage Officer.

VOLUNTARY SECTOR

Board of trustees	the governing body elected to oversee the use of trust funds
Directors	responsible for the overall management of an organisation. Report to the board of trustees
Treasurer	responsible for managing the organisation's finances
Officers/Managers	responsible for the day-to-day running of sections or departments

Comparing organisational structures

Public-sector leisure and tourism facilities

- arts centres and theatres
- libraries
- museums
- parks and playgrounds
- public halls
- sports centres and swimming pools
- tourist information centres

Most leisure and tourism facilities are in the private sector – they are privately owned and aim to make a profit. Private-sector facilities range from tiny coffee shops run by one person to international travel and hotel chains.

Private limited companies:

- have two or more shareholders (usually the owners of the company). Shares cannot be bought by the general public
- have the word Ltd or Limited in their name.

Public limited companies:

- are owned by shareholders, who can be private individuals, banks, trade unions, insurance companies, pension funds, etc.
- have the letters plc in their name.

Voluntary-sector leisure and tourism organisations

- clubs
- community centres
- play schemes
- societies
- sports grounds

Some facilities are funded and organised by government and the voluntary sector to provide services for the local community.

Two sets of factors influence organisational structures in all three sectors:
- internal factors – for example, size, location, nature of product, nature of service, management style
- external factors – for example, ownership (private, public, voluntary), competition, changes in markets, technology, demographics, government, government policy.

DISCUSSION POINT

Think about the factors listed above.

Do you think they affect organisations in the private, public and voluntary sectors in the same way? For example, would the private sector be influenced more or less than the public sector by a change in technology?

Private sector

If you look at a number of private-sector organisations, you'll find quite a variety of structures. Because private-sector organisations exist to make a profit, they choose the structure most likely to help them do that. In general, they have more freedom in their choice of structure than organisations in the public sector.

The most common types of private-sector companies are:
- sole traders – owned and run by one person
- partnerships – jointly owned and run by two or more people
- private limited companies – owned by two or more private shareholders (people with a direct personal interest in the company like executive and non-executive directors, company staff, friends and family)
- public limited companies – owned by public shareholders (members of the public, banks, trade unions, insurance companies, pension funds).

The Feelgood Factory is a fitness centre. It is a private limited company owned by three share-holding directors, the managing director, the marketing director and the financial director, who are all executive directors working for the company. The centre was set up by the directors six years ago.

The business is located in a market town with a population of about 11,000. It is situated behind the market square and close to a small shopping mall. It provides gym facilities, aerobics classes and four squash courts. It also has a small cafeteria serving hot and cold drinks and light snacks.

The organisation employs 23 staff. The organisation chart below shows how the organisation is structured and what the reporting lines are.

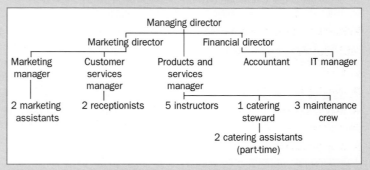

The centre is open from 7.00 a.m. to 10.00 p.m. The customer service staff, instructors, catering and maintenance staff work a shift system.

There is a hierarchy, but because the organisation is small its structure is simple and flat. The managing director favours a democratic management style. Directors concentrate on making strategic plans to grow and develop the business and keep ahead of the competition. They discuss these plans with managers and staff to agree on ways to achieve targets. Managers and staff themselves make most of the day-to-day decisions about how to organise and carry out their work.

Communications are mostly face to face. Issues affecting parts of the organisation, like customer complaints or equipment repairs and replacements, are discussed by the staff with the relevant responsibility. The organisation also has a monthly meeting of all staff members to discuss company policies and share information on performance and achievements.

Public sector

The aim of public-sector organisations is to use public funds to provide facilities and services. Because they are funded by public money – from national and local taxation – their structures tend to be more rigid than private-sector organisations. People who pay taxes naturally expect value for money. To ensure a clear chain of accountability, public-sector organisations usually have a hierarchical structure. The decision-making process is often a long one – investigation by working parties, discussion by committees, consultation with interested parties and approval by planning and financial bodies.

Public-sector organisations have three types of management:

- elected members – people elected to seats on councils who decide on policies and budgets
- officers – people employed by the council to manage facilities and services and control budgets of organisations and the council funds
- managers – people employed by the council to carry out the day-to-day, on-site management of a facility.

The Brent Row Centre is a sports and fitness centre funded by a local district council. It is open from 10.00 a.m. to 10.00 p.m. seven days a week and offers a range of fitness and exercise classes, indoor facilities for squash, badminton, volleyball and five-a-side football. These activities are seen as part of the council's

BRENT ROW CENTRE

commitment to providing local recreation facilities. It also has a small cafeteria which is run by a private catering company under contract. Maintenance work is also carried out by an outside contractor.

Funding for the centre comes from the council's leisure and recreation budget. The centre employs 25 staff, eight of whom work on a part-time basis. A cut in the centre's budget at the beginning of the financial year meant that two instructors were put onto part-time hours. Three of the instructors rent exercise studios for their classes.

The centre's director reports to the council officials. The organisation chart below shows how the centre is structured and what the reporting lines are.

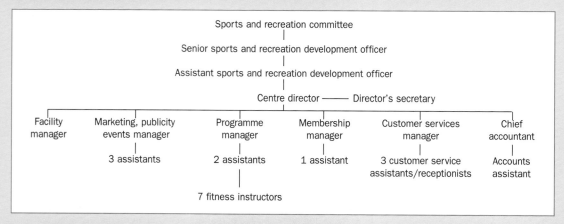

The centre's budget is set by the council and reviewed annually.

Strategic and policy decisions are made by council officials, who also set targets for financial performance. Day-to-day running of the centre is the responsibility of the management team headed by the director. They have to make sure the centre operates within its budget.

Communications between the centre and the council and its officials are formal, usually in writing. The council have set procedures for issuing information – decision-making can be lengthy as many decisions go through several committee stages. Communications inside the centre about day-to-day issues are a lot less formal – mostly face-to-face meetings and written memos.

Voluntary sector

Voluntary-sector organisations provide facilities and services for the benefit of particular groups. They are similar to public-sector organisations in that they are largely funded by other people's money. Like the public sector, they have to demonstrate value for money, so their structure ensures a clear chain of accountability. Organisations in the voluntary sector can concentrate on specific or minority areas of interest.

Voluntary-sector organisations are usually charities or charitable trusts. Their main income comes from grants, donations, legacies and membership fees. They are governed by laws and regulations which define what counts as a charitable or voluntary organisation. They are not-for-profit organisations and any profit they make from their activities must be invested back into the organisation.

SportsKids is a gym club for children aged between five and eleven in a small village a few miles from town. It was set up two years ago by two local PE teachers and is run entirely by volunteers. The club's aim is to provide a recreational activity for children in the village. The club was set up to replace the

after-school activities lost when the village school closed down. It holds two three-hour sessions a week in the village hall – the first hour is for the under-sevens, the second for the seven-to-nine-year-olds and the third for the ten-and-eleven-year-olds. The two teachers attend every session and they're helped by a rota of parents of the children who go to the club.

The club is run by a committee of five:

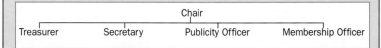

		Chair		
Treasurer	Secretary	Publicity Officer		Membership Officer

They hold general meetings every two months at the Chair's house. These meetings are attended by the committee and volunteer helpers. The Treasurer reports on the financial affairs of the club and they all discuss any issues, problems and fundraising ideas. The Secretary organises the meetings, sends out the agendas, takes notes during the meeting and writes them up as minutes to be sent out later to all the club's volunteers. Apart from this formal meeting, they hold occasional meetings to organise specific fundraising events. Any other necessary communication goes on informally either face to face or by phone.

The club is funded from a small membership fee of £5 per child per term which covers the rental of the hall. It also received a donation from a local trust fund to buy basic gym equipment and gets a small grant towards running costs from the local parish council. The club also runs fundraising events like jumble sales and sponsored activities.

DISCUSSION POINT

The organisations in the three case studies above are all small organisations.

- Do you think the issues that affect them would also affect larger organisations?
- What issues and factors would be different?

Organisational diagrams

The diagrams on pages 77–79 show the job titles and reporting lines in three different organisations. Diagrams like these show functions and lines of responsibility. You may come across them in:

- annual reports
- staff handbooks
- newspaper and magazine articles describing businesses.

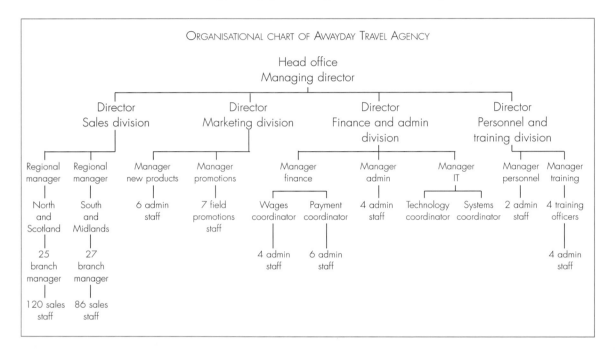

ORGANISATIONAL CHART OF AWAYDAY TRAVEL AGENCY

Head office
Managing director

| Director Sales division | Director Marketing division | Director Finance and admin division | Director Personnel and training division |

Regional manager — North and Scotland — 25 branch manager — 120 sales staff

Regional manager — South and Midlands — 27 branch manager — 86 sales staff

Manager new products — 6 admin staff

Manager promotions — 7 field promotions staff

Manager finance — Wages coordinator — 4 admin staff / Payment coordinator — 6 admin staff

Manager admin — 4 admin staff

Manager IT — Technology coordinator / Systems coordinator

Manager personnel — 2 admin staff

Manager training — 4 training officers — 4 admin staff

Key questions

1 What are the differences between:
   – a centralised and a decentralised organisational structure?
   – a flat hierarchical structure and a tall hierarchical structure?
2 Why do organisations have structures divided into different functions or divisions?
3 What are the main internal and external factors which influence an organisation's choice of structure?
4 Give three reasons why an organisation might change its structure.
5 Can you explain each of these key job roles?
   – chair of board
   – executive director
   – non-executive director
   – manager
   – elected members
   – government or local authority officers.
6 Why do organisations in the public, private and voluntary sectors have different organisational structures?

Assignment

Part 1

Pick two leisure and tourism organisations from different sectors (public, private and voluntary). Find out:

■ how they are structured – include an organisational diagram of each one
■ what factors have influenced their structures – look at internal and external factors
■ how their structures affect the way the organisations work.

Produce a summary of your findings, including illustrations.

Part 2

Produce a report about the structure of leisure and tourism organisations. Your report should be a general one, outlining:

■ different types of structure
■ factors influencing the structures
■ how these factors affect the way the organisations work
■ the key job roles.

If you have done the activities in this element, you may already have a lot of the information you need to complete the assignment.

ELEMENT **2.2**

Leisure and tourism teams

Anyone who works in leisure and tourism has to like being part of a team. A lot of the day-to-day work is done by people working together – the front-of-house team in a theatre, a coaching group at a sports centre, the reception team at a big hotel. Teams are also set up for one-off events or projects such as a summer festival or the launch of a new arts centre. People in teams have different roles; it helps the team work together well if everyone knows what role they have to play. In this element you'll be examining what teams are for, how they work and the relationships within them.

66 *Because the pool is run by a large leisure group on behalf of the council we have to adhere to specifications the council lays down. So in a sense we work as a team with the council officers. There are advantages to this arrangement. For example, the council provides extra funding which enables us to put on coaching courses. And it works both ways – we've even contributed to their video on tourism.* 99

swimming pool manager

66 *I work in two sets of teams. The national organisation we belong to is a bit hierarchical and has a managing agent based at each regional office. I'm a member of the regional team. Decision-making at our property is collective, so we work together as quite a close team. But we also use advice from relevant experts from the national team in areas such as painting, ceramics, sculpture and gardens.* 99

administrator of a heritage site

66 *The key roles in the organisation are the marketing manager, publicity officer and bookings manager – they're the management team. The marketing manager is answerable to the director of the venue, who is in turn answerable to the head of leisure services at the council.* 99

press and publicity officer at an entertainments venue

Section 2.2.1

The structure and purpose of teams

Team structure and purpose

A team always has:

- an objective
- a team leader
- team members
- team roles and responsibilities
- the right balance of skills and knowledge to achieve the objective.

Teamwork helps people to work in an organised and effective way.

Examples of teams in the leisure and tourism industry

- a marketing team which works together to promote products and services
- an airline in-flight team which works together to get passengers to their destination safely, in comfort and on time
- a customer services team which works together to make sure customers get what they want
- an orchestra which works together to play a piece of music
- a maintenance team which works together to make sure premises and equipment are clean and safe
- a finance team which works together to make sure the organisation's finances are allocated and used effectively
- an entertainments team which works together to provide entertainments

Organised teams

Organised teams work together long-term. They are:

- part of the organisation's permanent structure
- involved in a particular area of its activities
- have a continuing role.

For example:

- a customer services team
- a reservations team
- a tour-guide team
- a sales team.

All the members of an organised team have knowledge and skills relating to the functional area they work in.

Ad hoc teams

Ad hoc teams are put together to work on short-term projects, one-off projects and special events. For example:

- to identify ways of cutting costs
- to devise an induction programme for new staff
- to organise a fundraising event for charity.

83

ACTIVITY

Make a list of all the teams you belong to – at school or college, at work and in your leisure time. Decide whether each team is:

■ organised

■ ad hoc.

Explain why in each case.

Unlike organised teams, they aren't part of the organisation's permanent structure. They come together to work on a particular project and disband once the project is complete. The project will have set deadlines and the work the team members do will be fitted in around their more usual workload. The team members often come from different areas of an organisation and are chosen because the project needs the combination of their particular skills.

TEAMS IN ACTION

The customer services manager in a branch of a chain of travel agents describes some of the teams they use:

66 *The customer services function includes customer information services, reservations and promotions. Each of these activities is handled by an organised, long-term team and supervised by a team leader. From time to time, we need to set up short-term, ad hoc teams to handle particular projects or temporary changes in workloads. In February, we had a special promotion for Easter breaks to European capitals for senior citizens. The demand was huge and we put together a team of three – two from the customer information team and one from the reservations team – to concentrate solely on handling the Easter break enquiries and bookings. In the autumn, we're launching a new range of winter activity holidays. We've got a special projects team handling that. They've been working on it since last December and everything has to be ready for the launch date. The team is made up of staff with specialist skills – a couple from the promotions team, one from the customer information team, one from the finance team, myself and a couple of support staff. As the project develops, each of the team will lead smaller teams who will take on different chunks of the project like getting promotional literature printed and preparing information briefings for staff.* 99

ACTIVITY

Contact a couple of local leisure and tourism organisations and find out what sort of teams they use.

Factors which influence the effectiveness of teams

An effective team is one which works together well to achieve a common goal.

In a happy and effective team:

- the team's objectives and purpose are clearly understood and agreed
- people listen to each other and express their views and opinions
- meetings are lively, enjoyable and productive
- the team leader is respected and is treated as a valued member of the team
- people are willing to look at new ideas and ways to improve
- people will do whatever it takes to get the job done.

In an unhappy and ineffective team:

- people don't understand the team's objectives, or work to their own objectives
- people don't listen, and keep their good ideas to themselves
- meetings are seen as unnecessary and a waste of time
- the team leader is either feared or ignored by other team members
- people are unwilling to change: 'We've always done it like this, so why change?'
- people are prepared to do what is expected of them, and no more.

Resources

Without the right resources, a team won't be able to meet its targets and objectives.

It is the team leader's responsibility to make sure a team has all the resources it needs in order to achieve its aims.

Resources needed by teams

- time
- people
- equipment
- space
- finance

DISCUSSION POINT

Can you think of occasions when you have been in a team which failed to meet its objectives because it didn't have the right resources? How can teams plan to ensure this doesn't happen?

Team structure

Whether a team is organised or ad-hoc, short-term or long-term, it needs a structure to make sure everyone knows what they are supposed to do to help the team achieve its goals.

A training officer working in local government explains why a team needs a structure:

Processes are the established and agreed ways in which things are done.

66 *An effective team has to have a clear structure. Every team member must have a role, and every role must have its own clearly defined responsibilities. If there's no structure, it's not a team – it's just a group of people.* 99

Processes

Establishing processes is an important part of teamworking because it means that everyone takes a similar approach to the work. For example:

- the communication process: regular meetings, memos, reports
- the decision-making process: jointly, individually, the team leader decides
- the monitoring and review process: targets, review dates, who's involved.

DISCUSSION POINT

How do you think a team should go about establishing its processes?

Group dynamics means the way team members react and relate to each other. Reactions and relationships within a team will evolve over time.

FORMING
- Individuals selected
- Roles and responsibilities are discussed
- Members are weighed up

STORMING
- The team is established
- Processes and procedures are considered
- Conflict may arise
- Personalities start to show

NORMING
- Individuals settle down
- Roles and responsibilities are clarified
- Processes and procedures are agreed
- Trust is established

PERFORMING
- Team is working together
- Roles and responsibilities are carried out
- The team is united
- Efforts are recognised and appreciated

Group dynamics

Experts who have studied how teams work together have identified four stages a new team will go through from when they're brought together to when they are working effectively as a team.

Forming
- A set of individuals are selected for the team.
- They discuss the roles and responsibilities they will have and how they will operate.
- They weigh each other up.

Storming
- Individuals start to establish themselves in the team.
- Different processes and procedures are considered and argued about.
- Some conflict may arise as strengths and limits are tested.
- Different personalities start to show.

Norming
- The individuals begin to settle down into a team.
- Roles and responsibilities are clarified and accepted.
- Processes and procedures are established and agreed.
- Trust is established amongst team members.

Performing
- The team is working as a team.
- Everyone is carrying out their roles and responsibilities.
- The team is united in their approach and support each other.
- Team members recognise and appreciate their own and each other's efforts.

DISCUSSION POINT

Think of teams you've belonged to. Did they go through any of the forming-storming-norming-performing stages of team development? What happened and what effects did it have on the team as a whole?

The effectiveness of a team depends on all team members working together well. If everyone on the team gets on and is prepared to work hard and contribute, then the team is likely to succeed.

An effective team member is willing to:

- cooperate with others
- take responsibility
- share in the decision making
- listen to and accept other people's suggestions
- give their views and opinions
- adapt their own ideas to meet the needs of the team
- accept praise and recognition for the team's achievements, not just their own contribution
- recognise the importance and value of everyone on the team
- support and encourage other team members
- accept responsibility when things go wrong.

DISCUSSION POINT

What effects will there be on the team if there is a lack of balance? What effects will there be if any team member doesn't pull their weight?

A good team will be a balanced team. There will be a balance of:

- personalities
- roles
- skills
- responsibilities.

Management styles

The effectiveness of a team often depends on the effectiveness of its leader.

A good team leader:

- knows what the team is supposed to achieve and communicates these goals to other team members
- supports, encourages and motivates people on the team
- encourages open communication within the team
- takes a pride in the team
- sets a good example.

ACTIVITY

Draw a four-column table. Head the columns Forming, Storming, Norming and Performing. In each column, note down:

- qualities and characteristics a team leader must have to manage that stage of team development
- actions a team leader could take to help the team through that stage.

How a team operates often depends on the management style of the team leader. There are four main styles:

- autocratic
- democratic
- easy-going
- charismatic.

This is how a management consultant described the four main categories:

❝ Autocratic leaders make decisions without consulting the team and don't expect the team members to challenge them. They expect to be listened to but don't spend much time listening to others. They give instructions and expect them to be carried out.

Democratic leaders encourage every team member to contribute. They consult team members before making a decision, let people express their opinions, and listen to what they say. They still have authority and can insist on their own plans if they feel it is necessary.

Easy-going leaders leave the other team members to get on with the task. They give limited and very general directions or instructions.

Charismatic leaders have strong personalities. They trigger feelings of liking and admiration in their team members. They set their teams an example to follow and aspire to. ❞

DISCUSSION POINT

Discuss the pros and cons of each of the management styles described. Are any better than the others for all situations? Or are there times when one style would be more appropriate than others because of the circumstances of the situation?

ACTIVITY

Think about the teams you are part of. What is the management style of each of the team leaders? Note down each management style, with a list of the ways you think it affects the team's effectiveness. Comment on whether or not the style suited the circumstances.

The working environment

The working environment has a strong effect on how the team operates. It should suit the type of work the team is carrying out. If it doesn't, the team can't work effectively and will quickly become demoralised.

DISCUSSION POINT

Think of a time when you've had a task to do but didn't have the right surroundings to do it – for example, an essay to write, but nowhere quiet to work. What effect did it have on you and your ability to do the task?

Team roles and responsibilities

A **role** is what someone does in an organisation or team. For example, a team organising an event might appoint a publicity officer.

Responsibilities depend on role. For example, the publicity officer would be responsible for making sure that as many people knew about the event as possible.

People's roles in leisure and tourism teams can be:

- managerial – deciding what needs to be done and delegating the work to others
- supervisory – making sure the work gets done but not actually doing it
- operational – doing the work
- technical – helping people carry out their work by providing technical support and advice.

Responsibilities in leisure and tourism teams include:

- product delivery – making sure the product is ready, is right for the customers and is in the right place at the right time
- service delivery – making sure the service is provided in the right place, at the right time and to the right people
- customer care – dealing with customers, finding out what they need and helping them to get it
- health and safety – identifying health and safety needs and making sure products, services and premises meet health and safety regulations
- security – identifying security needs and making sure products, services and premises meet security regulations.

Within leisure and tourism teams, people are usually given roles and responsibilities which match their skills, knowledge and experience.

TEAM ROLES, RESPONSIBILITIES AND RELATIONSHIPS

An outdoor activity centre is holding an open day as a promotional event. The team of organisers are:

Member	Role title	Responsibilities	Role type
Suki	Team leader	Managing the team, making sure they have the right resources, organising and running team meetings, monitoring the budget, monitoring the schedule	Managerial
Alan	Finance	Managing the budget, planning and recording spending	Technical
Liam	Publicity	Organising publicity materials, selecting target customers, monitoring publicity budget	Supervisory
Chris	Publicity	Writing promotional literature, briefing designers and printers	Operative
Vim	Sales	Taking bookings, monitoring booking levels	Operative
Cindy	Catering	Organising catering facilities, staff and services, monitoring catering budget	Supervisory
Val	Event management (staff)	Organising staff for the day, organising venues and activities	Supervisory
Jo	Event management (premises)	Identifying and providing for health, safety and security needs	Supervisory/ technical

In this team, they all share responsibility for product and service delivery. Vim, Cindy, Val and Jo share responsibility for customer care. Jo's responsibilities make her role a combination of supervisory and technical because health, safety and security procedures will affect other areas like catering, venues and activities.

ACTIVITY

Choose a local leisure and tourism organisation, such as a travel agent, hotel or sports club. Talk to the manager or a senior member of staff, and find out how many teams they have within the organisation. Draw up a chart showing the teams and the roles and responsibilities of each team member.

Team objectives

An **objective** is something that you want to achieve; for example, getting a job as a receptionist in a hotel, or completing GNVQ Leisure and Tourism before next summer!

All leisure and tourism teams have objectives which they want to achieve, and every member of the team works towards achieving these objectives.

DISCUSSION POINT

How does making an objective SMART help you to:

■ understand the objective

■ feel that you can achieve the objective

■ know when you've achieved the objective?

Team objectives should be SMART:

■ Specific – clear, straightforward and easy to understand

■ Measurable – state quantities

■ Achievable – within the team's abilities and resources

■ Realistic – based on circumstances which exist or can be brought about

■ Time-bound – state a timescale.

ACTIVITY

Look at the objectives below, each set for a team of five people. Say whether or nor they meet the SMART formula and why.

■ To organise and run the staff Christmas party within a budget of £250.

■ To beat last June's sales total of 1000 holidays to Italy by making a sales total of 5000 holidays to Italy this June.

■ Each sales-team member to make a minimum of ten extra sales calls every day.

■ To write a 16-page report in one week's time on a replacement visual display unit for the sales reception desk computer.

Now think of an objective you would like to achieve. Write it down using the SMART formula.

Team roles and responsibilities

To achieve a team objective, team members are given different roles depending on their skills, knowledge and experience. Their roles give them specific responsibilities for particular aspects of the team's work towards its objective. They may also have individual targets that contribute to the overall target.

The type of roles and responsibilities which team members have depends on the objectives they are trying to achieve. Members of a team which is organising a children's party will have very different roles and responsibilities to people who are involved in a sales campaign.

Because a team is a group of people working together, they need to use their interpersonal skills in a beneficial way. So as well as specific areas of individual responsibilities based on practical skills, knowledge and experience, team members will also have responsibility for contributing to the overall team objectives of:

- supporting the team
- encouraging individuals.

The team leader of a tour operator's sales team explains how team roles and responsibilities were allocated in response to the objective of selling £500,000 of holidays in two months:

66 *Each team member took responsibility for one aspect of working towards this objective. The 20 salespeople were each given individual sales objectives of selling £12,500 of holidays for each month of the period. The five sales support staff each looked after the administrative and computer support needs of four salespeople. As team leader, I made sure the team had all the resources they needed like telephones, computer terminals, adequate desk space and so on. I also arranged team meetings when team members could talk about their progress and highlight any problems they'd had with resources. I also held individual progress meetings with each team member throughout the period. If any team member had a particularly good day, I took the opportunity to congratulate them. If they'd had a bad day, I spent time helping them to put it into perspective.* **99**

The relationship between objectives, roles and responsibilities

There is a clear relationship between objectives, roles and responsibilities:

- the objectives define what is to be done
- the roles define who will do it
- the responsibilities define how they will do it.

ACTIVITY

Think about a team you belong to now or belonged to in the past. Write down its main objectives. Then write a list of the different roles and responsibilities of each team member. How do these roles and responsibilities relate to the team's objectives?

Lines of authority

Lines of authority define who is responsible for different aspects of a team's work, and who reports to whom.

DISCUSSION POINT

What do you think would be the effects of:

■ too many lines of authority
■ too few lines of authority?

ACTIVITY

In the activity on page 89, you chose a leisure and tourism organisation and found out what sort of teams it used. Find out what the lines of authority are for the teams and how they relate to the lines of authority within the facility or organisation as a whole.

The purpose of lines of authority

Lines of authority create clear paths for:

■ control
■ accountability
■ communication
■ responsibility
■ reporting.

They show:

■ who is in charge of different aspects of team activity
■ who to report to
■ who to go to for advice, information and instructions.

Control

Lines of authority help to control how information gets around, how authority, accountability and responsibility are allocated and how decisions are made.

Accountability

Lines of authority show who is answerable to whom – where the buck stops. Each person along the line must account for their actions to the person in the line above. For example, team members are accountable to their team leaders. Team leaders are accountable to their managers for their own action and for the actions of their team members.

Communication

Lines of authority help to make communication more efficient. When people know the reporting and decision-making structure they know who to go to when they need to give or get information. For example, to get information to a whole department, you just need to give it to the department head who will then pass it on.

Responsibility

Lines of authority establish who is responsible for what. This is important because it means that there is someone in charge of each aspect of activity who will make sure that the right things happen at the right time.

Reporting

Lines of authority help to make sure that progress and problems are reported efficiently. This ensures that:

■ everyone is up to date with progress
■ people are only given the information they need.

Lines of authority within a facility or organisation

Lines of authority exist at every level within a facility or organisation. The diagram on the left shows the way they can extend from team members to the board of directors.

Key questions

1 Can you describe three different purposes of teams?
2 What is the main difference between an organised team and an ad-hoc team?
3 What are the main qualities which an effective team member should bring to a team?
4 How can a team leader's management style affect the overall success of a team?
5 Can you explain the relationship between team members' roles and responsibilities?
6 Why is it important for teams to have objectives?
7 Why do teams need clear lines of authority?

Assignment

Part 1

The senior management of a leisure and tourism organisation are reviewing their working practices. They want to include more teamworking. Prepare a report for them which:

■ describes the structure of teams
■ explains the purpose of teams
■ explains the factors which affect team effectiveness.

Part 2

Carry out an in-depth investigation of two work teams in two different leisure and tourism organisations. Find out:

■ how they are structured
■ how they operate
■ what roles and responsibilities team members have and how they relate to each other
■ what lines of authority there are and what their purpose is.

Use the results of your investigations to create a display of information about the teams in your selected leisure and tourism organisations. Use charts to show the similarities and differences between team structures.

ELEMENT **2.3**

Recruitment and selection

How do people get jobs in leisure and tourism? And what do employers do when they need new staff? This element gives you the chance to find out about recruitment and selection from both sides. You'll be looking at the process employers go through when they recruit and select staff, from putting in advertisements to the final interviews with candidates. This will help you see what employers are looking for in new staff – what they can do, their personal qualities, qualifications and other achievements. You'll also be taking part in the process yourself.

❝ *If you were starting out you could get an assistant teaching qualification to begin with, but as that isn't valid for very long you would need to get a full teaching qualification. You could then go on to train up to club coach level. There are also various specific areas you can train and specialise in: working with the disabled, running Aquafit or working with parents and toddlers.* ❞

swimming pool manager

❝ *When recruiting staff, companies normally advertise in local papers. If the job is for someone who already has experience in the industry, they may also advertise in the trade journals such as TTG and Travel Weekly which go to all travel organisations. Not all jobs are advertised so it can be a good idea to write in to an agency about jobs.* ❞

travel consultant in a travel agency

❝ *There are 60 people in our company and what we look for in recruits are good communication skills – an ability to give a good first impression on the telephone, to be smartly dressed, to be able to work alongside other people. They should also be able to work independently, on their own initiative. We want them to have common sense and be prepared to work hard to achieve targets. Being good at selling is probably more important in this job than having academic qualifications. We mostly advertise for people in the local press.* ❞

car-rental manager

❝ *Posts in our organisation are usually advertised in the creative and media sections in national papers, and we also advertise in the local paper. Another way for people to get into the field is as students gaining work experience. In my particular job you need press or public relations experience – working on a newspaper gives you a sense of what makes news and what would be good photocalls. People often get involved in student papers – that's another good way to get experience. We have someone working in our box office who is doing a course in arts administration. She has also gained invaluable experience by working as a volunteer doing publicity for a theatre group at the Edinburgh Festival.* ❞

press and publicity officer at an entertainments venue

Recruitment and selection procedures

The recruitment and selection process

- Prepare a job description summarising the tasks, activities and responsibilities the job entails.
- Prepare a person specification describing the skills, qualifications, experience and personal qualities the job-holder should have.
- Advertise the job.
- Evaluate the applications.
- Short list the suitable applicants to interview.
- Interview the applicants.
- Decide which of the interviewees is the best candidate.
- Offer the job to the best candidate.

Organisations invest a great deal of time and money in recruiting and selecting staff. Leisure and tourism organisations rely on keeping their customers happy, and to do this they need staff who are:

- hard working
- cheerful, enthusiastic and motivated
- skilled and experienced or willing to learn.

Recruitment is the process of attracting possible candidates for a job.

Selection is the process for assessing and choosing the most suitable candidate.

Once an organisation is sure about the job they need someone to do, the type of person they are looking for and the conditions of service (hours, salary, leave entitlement, etc.) it can start the search for suitable candidates.

Advertising vacancies

Job vacancies can be advertised both within the organisation, to allow existing staff to apply, and externally.

Places to advertise

- in national or local press
- in trade publications and professional journals
- on radio and television
- through recruitment agencies

National press

All national newspapers sell advertising space on their recruitment pages. They often have certain days for jobs in particular skills areas. For example, media and marketing on Mondays, education on Tuesdays, computer technology on Wednesdays and so on. Local newspapers also have jobs pages.

Trade press

All commercial areas have their own specialised publications aimed at people working in those areas.

ACTIVITY

Find out what trade journals there are for the sector of the leisure and tourism industry you'd most like to work in.

EMPLOYMENT AGENCIES 371

CAMBRIDGE HI-TECH RECRUITMENT

RECRUITMENT CONSULTANTS

Technical Specialists for the Software I.T., Telecoms, Electronics, Computer and High Technology Industries

Tel (01223) 467724
Fax (01223) 321273

ACTIVITY

Use the *Yellow Pages* to find out how many recruitment agencies there are in your area. Contact a few and ask about the sort of jobs they deal with. Keep a note of any agencies you think might be useful to you when you're looking for work in the future.

DISCUSSION POINT

What are the pros and cons of each of the means of recruitment advertising given here?

A **job description** is a written document describing the role, responsibilities, activities and duties involved in a job.

A **person specification** is a written document describing the skills, qualifications, experience and personal qualities needed by the person who will do the job.

Radio and television services

Radio and television stations offer advertising services for job vacancies. Information services like Teletext are also used to advertise job vacancies.

Recruitment agencies

Recruitment agencies are private businesses which help organisations to fill vacancies. People looking for work give their details to the agencies and the agencies match them against details organisations give them of vacancies. Many agencies specialise in recruitment for particular skills, like secretarial skills, or particular industry areas, like the catering industry.

In the public sector, the Department for Education and Employment runs Jobcentres where local vacancies are advertised. Jobcentre staff are trained to give advice on careers and to put people in touch with employers advertising relevant vacancies. They also provide free leaflets which give advice on job-finding and interviewing skills.

JOB HUNTING

a guide for _____ Managers•

_____ Executives•

_____ Professionals•

ACTIVITY

Look through newspapers, magazines and journals and collect different examples of advertisements for jobs in leisure and tourism, keeping a record of where you found them. From your research, where do you think you are most likely to find advertisements for your first job in leisure and tourism?

Shortlisting applicants

An advertisement for a job vacancy will bring in many applications. Shortlisting is the process for picking out the ones which most closely match the type of skills and experience the vacancy demands. They will go on the shortlist as people to interview. The key tools in this process are the job description and the person specification. Any applicant who matches them is someone to interview. People with skills and experience outside the industry are also worth interviewing if their skills or experience would be useful to the job.

Dealing with references

References are comments and appraisals given by people (referees) who know or have worked with the applicant. They are used by the recruiting organisation to check on the information the applicant has given them and to find out more about what the applicant is like as a person and a worker. Most people choose the following to act as their referees:

■ their current employer or manager

■ a previous employer or manager

■ a teacher or tutor.

Dealing with records of achievement (ROAs)

A record of achievement is a good way of relating school achievements to possible career opportunities and is particularly useful for people looking for their first job who have no previous work experience to help demonstrate their abilities. Here's what the facilities manager of a local sports complex thinks about the ROAs:

❝ *The information they provide – the final school reports, examination certificates, the personal statements of achievement, career plans and so on – helps me to build up a picture of the applicants. They give a good, all-round view through their contributions from teachers who know the applicants and the statements by the applicants themselves. They're an excellent starting point for talking to applicants at an interview. They also give applicants a means to prove that they have something to offer an employer even though they're new to the job market.* ❞

Interviews

Interviews are the opportunity to meet the applicant and discuss in detail what the job involves. The key to an effective interview is careful preparation. The interviewer and interviewee must prepare all the information the other might need and questions that will help bring out the right sort of information.

Here's how the personnel officer for a cinema complex prepares for interviews:

❝ *I read the interviewees' CVs very thoroughly and make notes on any aspects I want to know more about. I also prepare a list of questions I want to ask all the interviewees to find out about their reasons for wanting the job, their background, experience and achievements and so on. I use the job description and person*  *specification to prepare questions that give the interviewees a chance to talk about their suitability for the job. An interview is a two-way process, so I think about the information the interviewees will need from me – information about the organisation, the job, the opportunities and so on. There's also a practical side – I prepare an interview room, tell all staff that interviews will be going on and make sure there won't be any interruptions during any interview.* ❞

Assessing applicants

Interviewers will assess applicants during the interview and also spend some time after the interview reviewing their assessment. They'll consider the answers the applicants gave and the questions they asked, what sort of personality traits they showed, how they came over and so on. The interviewers will use their observations to assess the applicants further against the job description and person specification.

Some organisations also use assessment techniques like job skill tests and aptitude tests.

The leader of a team of fitness instructors explains what she does to assess potential recruits to the team:

❝ We do a three-part assessment: an interview, a mock class and a written test. At the interview, the candidate is interviewed by me and a team colleague. We have a form we've prepared with questions to ask and space for notes on the candidate's responses. The form also includes boxes we tick on personal qualities we pick up on through asking questions and observing the candidate – things like personal appearance, confidence, communication skills, levels of knowledge demonstrated and so on. During the mock class, I and a colleague act as observers and other team members act as class participants. Again, we have a form to help us note down our observations and after the class we add notes on the feedback from the team members who took part in the class while the candidate does the written test. The written test is made up of questions on health and safety, good instruction practice, planning and running fitness classes and so on. We then go through all the information we've collected from the assessment and decide which of the candidates best matches the job we're offering. ❞

Confirming employment

Once the interviewers have made their choice, they will contact the person to offer them the job. Usually, job offers are made in writing.

Notifying rejections

Once the successful candidate has accepted the job, the next stage is to notify all the others that their applications have been unsuccessful. The personnel officer who works for a sports complex financed by a local authority explains how he approaches rejection letters:

❝ Being told you haven't got a job you wanted can be a painful experience, so it is important that letters bringing this news are as kind as possible. It's best to get the bad news over with first. It also helps to pay a compliment like 'you were a very strong candidate and we were impressed by your knowledge of our facilities' and to wish them success in future applications. ❞

LIFESTYLE
LEISURE LIMITED

14th May 1996

Janice O'Rourke
12 New Close
Bilbourne
Buckinghamshire
MK14 3PT

29 Market Hill
Bilbourne
Buckinghamshire
MK41 1WB
Tel: (01296) 346838
Fax: (01296) 346839

Dear Janice

Fitness Instructor

Following your interview last week, I'm pleased to offer you the post of Fitness Instructor.
I'm enclosing two of the copies of a draft contract which sets out the terms and conditions for the post.
If you wish to accept the offer you should sign one and return it to me as soon as possible.
Please feel free to call me if you have any further questions.
I look forward to hearing from you.
Yours sincerely

B. Lubienski

Bruno Lubienski (Programmes Manager)

LIFESTYLE
LEISURE LIMITED

14th May 1996

Martin Crewe
51 Meadowcroft
Bilbourne
Buckinghamshire
MK14 8AP

29 Market Hill
Bilbourne
Buckinghamshire
MK41 1WB
Tel: (01296) 346838
Fax: (01296) 346839

Dear Martin

Fitness Instructor

I'm sorry to tell you that your application for the post of Fitness Instructor has not been successful.
You were a strong candidate and we were impressed with your performance at the interview.
I will keep your details on file in case a suitable vacancy arises in the future and I wish you every success in your applications elsewhere.
Yours sincerely

B. Lubienski

Bruno Lubienski (Programmes Manager)

Legal and ethical obligations

All leisure and tourism employers have legal and ethical obligations they must comply with when recruiting and selecting new members of staff.

> **Legal obligations** are laws which aim to ensure employers promote equal opportunities and are fair when recruiting staff.
>
> **Ethical obligations** are morally correct ways in which employers should behave when recruiting staff. They are not laws.

Equal opportunities

In the United Kingdom, equal opportunities legislation covers three key areas:

- sex (including marital status)
- race
- disability (physical, mental and sensory).

Equal opportunities refer to people's rights to be recruited, employed and paid without discrimination on the grounds of sex, race or disability.

The following table shows the legislation employers must comply with when advertising for, selecting and employing staff.

Act	What it states
Equal Pay Act 1970 Equal Pay (Amendment) Regulations 1983	Men and women must be paid equally for the same or similar work or for work judged as being of equal value.
Sex Discrimination Act 1975 Sex Discrimination Act 1986	Employers are not allowed to discriminate on the basis of sex or marital status in recruitment advertising, selection or dismissal, or in the terms, conditions and benefits of employment offered.
Race Relations Act 1976	Employers are not allowed to discriminate on the basis of race, colour or ethnic origin in recruitment advertising, selection or dismissal or in the terms, conditions and benefits of employment offered.
Disabled Persons (Employment) Act 1958 (this Act will be replaced by the Disability Discrimination Act 1995 from 1996 onwards)	Any firm which employs more than 20 people must make every reasonable effort to ensure that at least 3% of its workforce is made up of people who are registered as disabled.
Disability Discrimination Act 1995 (to come into effect in various stages from 1996 onwards)	Employers are not allowed to discriminate on the basis of disability in recruitment advertising, selection or dismissal, or in the terms, conditions and benefits of employment offered.

A solicitor who specialises in employment law explains what equal opportunities legislation means in practice for recruitment and employment:

66 *Discrimination in employment covers recruitment advertising, selection procedures and terms and conditions of employment.*

There are two types of discrimination: direct and indirect. Direct discrimination is where one person or group of people has been treated less favourably than

acās

The 1996 annual report of the Advisory Conciliation and Arbitration Service (ACAS) showed that industrial tribunals dealt with 90,000 complaints in 1995 – a record number and an increase of 15% on the figures for 1994. The biggest rise was in complaints against unfair dismissal. Sexual discrimination cases were also up but racial discrimination cases were down.

another in similar circumstances. For example, a recruitment advert asking for a man where the job could be done equally well by a man or a woman. Indirect discrimination is where unnecessary qualifications or conditions are set which the job doesn't justify. For example, stating that a job-holder must have English as their first language would exclude people who were perfectly fluent in English but had another language as their first language.

All the terms and conditions of a job must also be non-discriminatory – that means pay, hours of work, training, promotion prospects, benefits like health insurance and pensions and so on. Again, direct and indirect discrimination rules apply. An organisation who only sent women on management training courses could be guilty of direct discrimination against its male staff. An organisation who always arranged training courses during the evenings or at weekends could be making it more difficult for staff with young families to attend.

The Disability Discrimination Act 1995 makes it unlawful for employers to discriminate against the disabled in their methods of recruitment and terms and conditions of employment. It also obliges organisations with more than 20 employees to take reasonable steps to ensure that its premises and facilities don't put disabled people at a disadvantage in comparison with people who aren't disabled. For example, where access to a building means getting up a flight of steps or where the layout of a building or its offices makes it difficult for a disabled person to move about safely. This is a new law and organisations will be expected to comply with it over a period of time, not overnight.

There are some exceptions to the discrimination laws – known as genuine occupational qualifications – but they have to be very well founded. For example, where the job involves close contact with people of one sex, it is lawful for the employer to choose a job-holder of the same sex – a male changing room attendant for a male changing room, a female instructor for a women's swimming class.

Any breach of the discrimination laws can land an employer in front of an industrial tribunal. They will decide if discrimination has taken place and impose a penalty on the offending employer. **99**

Contract of employment

The rights of employers and employees are mainly set out in the Employment Protection (Consolidation) Act 1978 and the amending Acts of 1980, 1982, 1988 and 1989.

The terms of employment are agreed by an employer and an employee – their agreement is defined in law as a contract. Once employees starts work, they and their employers are bound by the contract of employment. Strictly speaking, the contract of employment doesn't have to be in writing but all employees are entitled to a written statement of their employment terms within two months of starting work. So in practice, most organisations give employees a written contract which includes all the employment terms.

Employers can choose to state sick leave and sick pay entitlement, pension

What the written statement of employment should include:

- the employer's name
- the employee's name
- the date when employment began
- a job title or brief job description
- pay and when it will be paid (weekly, monthly, etc.)
- hours of work
- holidays and holiday pay
- sick leave and sick pay entitlements
- pensions and pension schemes
- length of notice which an employee or employer is required to give and is entitled to receive
- for temporary jobs, the length of time the job is expected to last
- for fixed-term contracts, the date when the employment will end
- the place or places of work
- disciplinary procedures and grievance procedures (for organisations employing more than 20 people)
- the name of the person an employee can go to with a grievance (for organisations employing fewer than 20 people)
- name, title and location of the organisation's grievance officer.

and pension schemes, disciplinary and grievance procedures in separate documents rather than in the written statement – for example, in a company handbook or manual. However, if they do this, they have to make sure that the employees have easy access to these documents and have the opportunity to read them.

(4) Holiday entitlement accrued but not t...

3   Date of commencement of employment

 **LIFESTYLE** LEISURE LIMITED   **Contract of Employment**

An agreement made on the 27th day of May 1996 between Lifestyle Leisure Ltd whose registered office is situated at 29 Market Hill, Bilbourne, Buckinghamshire MK41 1WB (hereafter called "the Company") of the first part and Janice O'Rourke of 12 New Close, Bilbourne, Buckinghamshire MK41 3PT(hereafter called "the Employee") of the second part.

Whereby it is agreed as follows:

1   Definitions

In this agreement

(a)   "the Act" means the Employment Protection (Consolidation) Act 1978 and subsequent additions and amendments

(b)   "the Board" shall mean the Board of Directors of the Company for the time being

(c)   All references to any statute shall include references to any statutory amendment or re-enactment thereof

(d)   The headings are for convenience only and shall not affect the construction of this agreement.

2   Appointment and job title

(1)   The Company hereby agrees to employ the Employee and the Employee hereby agrees to act as Fitness Instructor on the terms and conditions herein appearing. The Employee will be expected to perform all the duties necessary to such a post and customarily performed by a person holding such a post. The Employee may be asked to serve the Company in another capacity but any permanent change of post will be agreed with the Employee in advance by the Company.

'We are committed to an equal opportunities recruitment policy. Registered disabled people are currently under-represented within our workforce and their applications will be considered first.'

'We particularly welcome applications from Asian, African, Carribean and people from other ethnic minorities who are currently under-represented in our workforce. Suitably qualified/skilled/experienced applicants with a disability will be guaranteed an interview.'

'We are an equal opportunities employer and positively welcome applications from all sections of the community.'

ACTIVITY

Talk to the manager of a leisure and tourism organisation in your area. Find out how they make sure that their recruitment and selection procedures comply with the laws governing equal opportunities and contracts of employment.

Objectivity means viewing things factually and not allowing personal emotions, opinions or prejudices to affect the view.

DISCUSSION POINT

The owner of a small sports shop has a vacancy which he advertises in the local newspaper. Twenty people send in letters of application. Before he's had a chance to look at them, a friend tells him that his son is looking for a job. He's a school-leaver with a GNVQ in Leisure and Tourism. The shop owner knows the young man and feels that he will be a hard-working and trustworthy employee. So he gives him the job. He then writes to the 20 applicants and tells them that their applications have been unsuccessful and the vacancy has been filled. Has he complied with the law? Has he acted ethically?

Objectivity

Employers have an ethical obligation to make sure the recruitment and selection process is carried out in an objective way. If interviewers or members of the personnel department aren't objective when recruiting, they may allow personal opinions and preferences to interfere with fair selection.

To ensure objectivity, employers must:

■ look at and consider all the applications they receive
■ compare the applications with the job description and person specification, and decide who to interview on the basis of how well applicants meet the criteria listed
■ conduct interviews fairly and objectively, and not allow subjective decision-making.

Honesty

Employers have an ethical obligation to be honest throughout the recruitment and selection procedure. They should describe the job, the pay, the terms and conditions exactly. They should also be honest about the career prospects the job may or may not offer. They should also give honest reasons for accepting or rejecting an applicant.

ACTIVITY

Draw up a checklist of all the considerations a recruiter must bear in mind to ensure that they recruit legally, objectively, fairly and honestly.

Job descriptions and person specifications

Most leisure and tourism employers prepare job descriptions and person specifications for job vacancies in their organisations.

Job descriptions

When organisations produce a job description, it gives them a chance to really think about the tasks and responsibilities involved in the job they are advertising.

A **job description** summarises what a job involves – day-to-day tasks, responsibilities, location, and so on. It gives applicants a useful overview of a job and is often included in the successful applicant's contract of employment.

A **person specification** summarises what type of person the organisation is looking for to do the job – skills, experience and qualifications needed, personal qualities which would be helpful and so on.

Job Description

Organisation	Awayday Travel, Billington
Job title	Senior travel sales consultant
Reporting to	Assistant branch manager
Responsible for	Not applicable
Job description	- Sales of full range of package holidays, flight-only, ferry and rail tickets, foreign currency and other ancillary services
	- meet given sales targets
	- provide information and advice to customers on above range of products and ancillary services
	- control and monitor use of air ticket stocks and provide returns to supplier
	- operate booking administration and filing system and liaise on a day to day basis with principals
	- maintain and control stock of brochures
	- such other actions as reasonably requested by assistant branch manager

Contents of a job description:

■ job title – for example, senior sales advisor, promotions supervisor, bookings assistant

■ reporting structure – who reports to the job-holder and who the job-holder reports to, for example, 'responsible for a team of two people'; 'reporting to the section manager'

■ job responsibilities – for example, 'establishing and maintaining a client database'; 'writing copy for mailshot brochures', 'selling European holidays to customers'

The recruiting officer in a public-sector entertainments venue describes how job descriptions help him when he's looking for new staff:

66 *The job description makes it clear what is expected from the job-holder. It defines what tasks they have to do, how much authority they have and who is in charge of them. When I'm considering applicants, the job description tells me what sort of experience the job-holder should have and what sort of things they need to be able to do.* 99

Person specifications

A person specification gives a picture of the ideal applicant; they are often used by leisure and tourism organisations to show clearly the type of person most likely to fit into their team.

As the personnel manager for a large hotel chain explains, preparing both job descriptions and person specifications is a very important part of the recruitment process:

66 *Before I advertise a vacancy I always check the job description and person specification I used last time I recruited, just to make sure that there haven't been any changes. For instance, I need to make sure that the job itself hasn't*

How effective would the recruitment and selection procedure be without a job description for the vacant post?

A person specification usually includes the following information:

- personal attributes (e.g. must be outgoing, enthusiastic, capable of leading and motivating a team)

- personal qualities (e.g. must be a creative thinker)

- personal achievements (e.g. must have at least two years' experience running a similar department)

- vocational qualifications (e.g. GNVQ in Leisure and Tourism)

- academic qualifications (e.g. GCSEs, A levels)

- competence (e.g. experience of preparing successful fund-raising proposals).

changed, and I also need to make sure that we are still looking for the same type of person we looked for when we last advertised. For example, last time we recruited a conference manager we needed someone with considerable knowledge of the catering trade and with experience of managing staff. The job itself has now changed because the organisational structure of the organisation has changed. Now, a conference manager working for us needs to be multilingual and computer literate. This is because we are doing a lot of conferences for foreign trade fairs, so languages are important, and we've installed a complete new IT system. In the case of the conference manager I needed to change the job description and the person specification to make sure that they realistically described the job we were offering and the person we were looking for. 🍯

Person Specification

Job title	Senior retail travel consultant	
Qualifications	Academic	GCSE Maths and English
	Vocational	GNVQ Leisure and Tourism (Advanced) or NVQ Travel Services Level 3 or ABTAC (Association of British Travel Agents Certificate) Advanced
	A sales qualification would be desirable	
Experience	Minimum two years experience in retail travel agency	

Personal attributes and qualities
- good communication and administration skills
- selling skills
- be able to work on own initiative
- lively and friendly personality
- effective team skills

Evaluating job descriptions and person specifications

Effective job descriptions and person specifications are useful tools in the recruitment and selection process. If they've been properly thought out, they should help an organisation to:

- match applicants to vacancies
- minimise the possibility of inappropriate appointments
- match business objectives to jobs
- plan training and development needs of job-holders.

Matching applicants to vacancies

Clearly defining the types of tasks the job-holder will be doing and the aptitudes and qualifications the job-holder will need creates standards applicants must match. For example, if you know that the job requires a teamworker, you can look for evidence of teamwork or an aptitude for teamwork in the applicants' letters and CVs.

Minimising the possibility of inappropriate appointments

The job description and person specification should provide a good guide to what a job entails and the sorts of skills and aptitudes needed by the job-holder. Having a clear picture of the job helps to create a clear picture of the appropriate person for that job.

Matching business objectives to jobs

All jobs within an organisation should relate to its business objectives. The job description and person specification should make clear how the job contributes to the business objectives.

A team leader at an outdoor activity centre explains how the jobs of the instructors in his team relate to the centre's business objectives:

66 *The centre's key objectives are to provide outdoor activities for all age ranges, to comply with all health, safety and security rules – those set by law and our own guidelines – and to have happy customers.*

My team are all qualified instructors with experience of working with different age groups. The nature of the work demands a high level of physical fitness. They are all trained in first aid and we regularly update their skills and knowledge in health, safety and security practices and procedures.

All the team members are energetic, outgoing people who believe that life should be fun. In addition to the right qualifications, they also need strong interpersonal skills. These help them to be good team workers and to deal well with the customers. **99**

Training and developing job holders

Most people expect their jobs to develop in terms of skills and responsibilities. Job descriptions and person specifications can be useful for training and development in three ways:
- they identify existing skills and aptitudes which can be developed
- they identify skills and aptitudes people can acquire in order to move into the job
- they provide a measure of how far the job-holder has developed.

ACTIVITY

From the job descriptions and person specifications you collected for the activity on page 104, pick one from the leisure and recreation sector and one from the travel and tourism sector. Make notes on how well you think they each meet these criteria for effectiveness:

- help to match applicants to the vacancy
- minimise the possibility of selecting the wrong person for the job
- show how the job relates to the organisation's business objectives
- set a basis for future training and development needs.

Discuss your evaluation with a partner. What's their view of the job descriptions and person specifications you've looked at? What's your view of the job descriptions and person specifications your partner has looked at?

Letters of application and CVs

The two most common ways to apply for jobs in leisure and tourism are:

- through application forms
- with a CV and letter of application.

Employers usually specify on job advertisements how they want people to apply, and it is important that applicants follow their instructions. If they want people to fill in an application form, they won't be impressed by a CV and covering letter.

Content of CVs

> **CV** is short for 'curriculum vitae', which is Latin for 'course of life'. The aim of a CV is to give employers enough information about your qualifications, skills and experience to enable them to decide whether to interview you for a job.

A CV should include enough information about experience and qualifications to show the person's suitability for a job. Too much information can be as bad as too little. A CV should be no more than two pages long – any longer, and the employer may not bother reading it.

Quality of presentation of CVs

The layout and presentation of a CV is very important. It should be typed or word processed, printed out clearly, and checked carefully for mistakes in spelling and grammar. Photocopied, creased, misspelled and otherwise untidy documents often go straight in the bin.

The example below shows one standard approach to laying out a CV.

Information to include in a CV:

- name, address and telephone number
- date of birth
- education and training – giving details of schools and colleges attended
- vocational qualifications (e.g. GNVQs, NVQs)
- academic qualifications (e.g. GCSEs, A levels)
- employment record (details of jobs done to date)
- skills (e.g. driving licence, foreign languages spoken)
- other achievements
- interests and hobbies.

Name:	Trevor Marshall
Address:	29 Lindwell Court Walthamstow London E17 3JH
Telephone:	(0181) 576 3481
Date of birth:	18/9/73
Marital status:	Single

Employment to date

1994 to present Exotic Holidays
I joined the organisation in March 1992 in the capacity of Customer Care Liaison Officer. I am currently responsible for liaising with hotels throughout Europe and dealing with all the verbal and written complaints which the organisation receives. In 1995 I began working towards my NVQ in Customer Care and so far have achieved Units 2 and 3.

1990 to 1994 Hindmarsh Travel
I joined Hindmarsh Travel in the capacity of telephone booking clerk, taking bookings from customers for foreign holidays. In 1991 I was promoted to section leader and was given responsibility for two junior members of staff. My duties included dealing with customer queries and complaints and handling all the associated paperwork.

Personal qualities
I am a good communicator and enjoy working with customers and helping to solve problems. I enjoy working alone and am able to use my initiative and take decisions on my own. I also enjoy teamwork and like to be part of an effective and energetic team.

Qualifications
Units 3 and 4 of the NVQ in Customer Care
GCSE passes in English, French, German, Maths, Geography, Art, Religious Studies

Interests and hobbies
I enjoy walking, travelling and listening to music. I am the drummer in a local band and I am an active member of the local amateur dramatic society and the local rugby club.

Content of letters of application

Unless the organisation states otherwise in the advert, it is usual to send a letter of application with a CV. You can use the letter to explain why you are interested in the job and why you feel you should be considered for the job.

Quality of presentation of letters of application

Letters of application should follow a standard letter format.

They should be on good quality paper and preferably typewritten or wordprocessed. The content should be concise and to the point. Spelling and grammar should be accurate and the tone of the letter should be polite yet friendly.

Mrs Lynne Wentworth   Andrew Forster
Personnel Manager   82 Breacon Drive
Devon Hotel   Crawley Park
Parkway   Ampthill
York YO2 7UY   MK20 2BE

                                       17th January 1996

Dear Mrs Wentworth

Hotel Receptionist — 'York News' 15th January, 1996

Following your recent advertisement in the 'York News', I am enclosing my Curriculum Vitae for your consideration.

As you will see I have an Advanced GNVQ in Leisure & Tourism and have worked part-time, during my school holidays, as a receptionist at the Hunter's House Hotel in Stafford.

I am very keen to work in York and am available to come for interview at any time which is convenient for you.

I hope that this application is of interest to you, and look forward to hearing from you.

Yours sincerely

A. Forster

Andrew Forster

Interview techniques

Job interviews have two aims: to assess whether an applicant is suitable for the job; to give the applicant a chance to get more information about the job.

In the leisure and tourism industry, depending on the organisation's procedures, interviews may be conducted by:

- the owner
- a director
- a manager
- a team leader or supervisor
- a personnel manager.

Sometimes there may be an interview panel made up of two or more people.

Techniques for interviewees

An interview is your opportunity to show prospective employers what you're like as a person. Your CV and letter of application will have convinced them of your possible suitability. The interview gives:

- them a chance to find out more about you
- you a chance to find out more about them.

Because an interview is a face-to-face meeting, your appearance and your communication skills play an important part.

Preparation

Careful preparation for an interview is crucial.

A personnel manager explains how she looks for evidence of preparation by the interviewee:

66 *There are certain things I always look for in an applicant – I expect them to arrive on time and to look neat and tidy. I am impressed if they bring a portfolio of work or a Record of Achievement as evidence of what they've put about their skills and aptitudes in their CV. I like candidates to know something about our company – it shows they've taken the time and the trouble to find out about us. And I expect someone who is serious about working here to ask relevant questions. Not 'How much holiday will I get?', but sensible questions about opportunities for training and promotion, and the people they are likely to be working with. I always give serious consideration to anyone who shows that they have prepared carefully for the interview and thought about what they want to say.* 99

Personal presentation

People can't help making judgements based on their first impression. Once an impression is made, it's difficult to shift. So it is important that the first impression you make on an interviewer is a positive one.

Before an interview:

- find out as much as possible about the organisation
- ring up and confirm the address and directions for getting there, and the name and job title of the interviewer
- reread the advertisement, job description and person specification, and try to 'match' your skills and experience with what is required
- prepare and practise answers to the questions most likely to be asked
- prepare question you want to ask
- decide what you're going to wear.

DISCUSSION POINT

What is your immediate impression of the people shown in the three illustrations above? What is it about each illustration that triggers your response?

ACTIVITY

Make a checklist of things to consider about personal appearance that will help you when you're preparing for an interview.

Body language means the non-verbal messages you give out through your posture, facial expressions, gestures and eye-contact.

Interview questions to be ready for

- Why do you want this job?
- What personal qualities do you have to offer?
- What ambitions do you have?
- Why did you leave your previous job? Why do you want to leave your present job?
- What can you offer this organisation?
- What do you do in your spare time? What are your hobbies and interests?
- What is your greatest achievement?
- Do you have any questions?

Presenting a confident image

- Calm your nerves with a few deep breaths.
- Stand up or sit up straight.
- Look at the interviewer while you are talking and listening.
- Smile.
- Speak clearly and positively.
- Remember that the interviewer wants you to be there because you're a good candidate for the job.

Body language

Body language works in two ways:

- it can support your verbal messages
- it can undermine your verbal messages.

ACTIVITY

Get together with a partner. Sit facing each other as if you were the interviewee and your partner the interviewer. Fold your arms, cross your legs and look at the floor, then stay in that posture while you tell your partner about something that interests you – for example, a hobby, a sport or the sort of music you like. Then tell them again, but this time sit up straight, with your hands clasped loosely and resting on your lap and your shoulders relaxed.

Change roles and repeat the exercise.

Discuss with your partner the effects body language had in each case.

Make notes on what you've learned from the exercise and how you can use it to help your performance at interviews.

Asking and answering questions

An interview is an opportunity to give and get information. Your performance at an interview will be improved if you think beforehand about the sort of questions you might be asked and the sort questions you want to ask the interviewer. Listen carefully to questions you are asked and answers you are given. Don't be afraid to give yourself time to think before you answer or to say if you don't understand the question.

Confidence

Interviews can be nerve-racking. But you can help yourself feel more confident by careful preparation. On the day, you can use your body language to present a confident appearance.

The facilities manager for a heritage site made this point on confidence:

66 *Being asked to come for an interview should give you confidence in itself. It means that your letter and CV were amongst the few that stood out from all the others. You've been picked out as someone interesting, someone with potential.* **99**

Techniques for interviewers

Interviewers want to assess whether an applicant is suitable for the job and also to give the applicant a chance to get more information about the job. Interviews range from being very structured and formal to very loose and informal.

Planning and preparing for an interview

■ What should the interview cover?

■ How should it be structured?

■ What questions will help me get the information I need from the interviewee?

■ What questions might the interviewee have?

■ Which areas of the interviewee's CV do I want to discuss?

■ How will I measure the interviewee's performance?

■ Where will I hold the interview?

■ How long should it last?

DISCUSSION POINT

How can interviewers use their body language to positive effect during an interview? What sort of body language should they avoid?

Preparing for an interview

Whichever type of interview an organisation uses, the interviewers have to plan and prepare carefully.

DISCUSSION POINT

What extra considerations would a panel of interviewers have to make in planning, preparing for and carrying out an interview?

Here's what the programmes manager for a city centre entertainments venue does:

❝ *I put together a series of questions that I will ask all the candidates. Then I look through each CV very carefully and list some questions I want to ask individual candidates. I make sure I have all the information I need about the job we're offering. On the day, I give the reception staff a list of the people coming to interviews and the interview times. When the interviewees arrive, I go to reception to greet them and to introduce myself and then I show them to the interview room. I try to put them at their ease as much as I can. I offer them refreshments, ask them to make themselves comfortable and ask them about their journey – it all helps to break the ice and gives them a chance to settle down. I then start off the interview with some simple questions such as 'What was it that interested you in the job?'. The interviewee will usually be prepared for this sort of question so it gives them a chance to start off on a positive and confident note. I listen very carefully all the time and I nod and smile to show that I'm listening and to encourage the interviewee.* **❞**

ACTIVITY

Visit a local leisure and tourism organisation in your area and talk to someone involved in recruiting and selecting staff. Find out how he or she:

■ prepares to interview applicants

■ encourages applicants to perform well during an interview.

Use your findings to draw up a checklist to help interviewers prepare for and carry out an interview.

Asking and answering questions

Good interviewers use different types of question depending on the type of information they want.

Question types to use

Type	Use	Example
Closed	To get specific information or simple yes or no answers.	How long did your holiday job last?
Open	To encourage the interviewee to open up on a topic, give broader answers or express their opinions.	What did you like about your holiday job?
Probing	To find out more on a particular point.	What did your holiday job teach you about dealing with customers?
Clarifying	To check understanding.	By 'children', do you mean the under-18s or something more specific like five-to-eight-year-olds?
Hypothetical	To test an interviewee's ability to apply their knowledge or experience to other areas.	What similarities might there be between the way you handled a difficult customer in your holiday job and the way you might handle a difficult customer in this job?

Good interviewers will also avoid certain question types because they:

- cause confusion
- undermine objectivity.

Question types to avoid

Type	Example	Reason
Rambling	When you've been at work – or not at work – how have you tried to develop your skills at dealing with customers – or people – that you think might help you in this job or at work in general?	It's confusing, unspecific and tries to cover too much.
Multiple	What do you see yourself doing in three years' time, what do you hope to achieve and how do you plan to achieve it?	It's trying to ask three questions in one which makes the interviewee's task of answering an unnecessarily difficult one.
Leading	Don't you think that swimming is healthier than walking?	The expected answer is disguised in the question and the interviewer is imposing their subjective opinion rather than gaining the interviewee's opinion.

The programmes manager for the city centre entertainments venue explains how he uses questions:

66 *Mostly I use open questions because they encourage the interviewee to give fuller answers, bring in their own ideas and show me what they know. I use clarifying questions when I'm not sure I've understood what the interviewee has said or to bring an interviewee back on track when nerves have made them lose their thread. I use probing questions to test out the interviewee's knowledge or to focus on something they've said that needs exploring further. I use closed questions sparingly to get basic information or as a starting point for a new topic which can then be broadened out with open and probing questions.* 99

Demonstrating and evaluating interview techniques

To perform well in an interview means having confidence in your communication skills. As with all skills, they can be improved with practice and feedback. Recruitment experts recommend that people get the help of friends they can rely on to give them honest, constructive criticism and helpful advice.

ACTIVITY

Get together with a couple of friends. Go through the recruitment pages of the local, national or trade press and pick a job in the leisure and tourism industry you would like to apply for. You can all choose the same job or you can each choose a different one. Contact the organisation and ask for the job description and person specification for the job you've picked. Prepare a CV and a letter of application for the job. Prepare to be interviewed and prepare to interview your friends for the jobs they've chosen. Carry out the interviews and give each other feedback on your performance as interviewee and interviewer. You might find it useful to make a video recording of each interview so you can see for yourselves how well you did. Make a list of any skills you want to improve and arrange with your friends to help you practice them further.

DISCUSSION POINT

In this unit, you've looked at the recruitment and selection process from both the employer's and the potential employee's viewpoint. How has this helped you to understand the skills and attitude you need to have when you come to look for a job in the leisure and tourism industry?

Key questions

1 What is the difference between a legal obligation and an ethical obligation?
2 What information should be given in a contract of employment?
3 What is the difference between a job description and a person specification?
4 Why do organisations ask for a letter of application?
5 What information should be included in a CV?
6 How should an interviewee prepare for a job interview?
7 How should an interviewer prepare to interview candidates?
8 What sort of questions should an interviewer:
   ■ use
   ■ avoid?

Assignment

Part 1

Prepare a leaflet or short booklet for students hoping to work in personnel in the leisure and tourism industry. The leaflet or booklet should:
■ describe in general terms the recruitment and selection process
■ explain the legal and ethical obligations in recruitment and selection.

Part 2

Get together with two or three other students. Pick two jobs from the recruitment pages of the local, national or trade press. One job should be from the leisure and recreation sector and one from the travel and tourism sector. Get hold of job descriptions and person specifications for each of the jobs. Discuss them with the other students and make notes on your evaluation of them.

Prepare your CV and letters of application for each job and give them to the other students to evaluate. Evaluate their CVs and letters. Give each other feedback and note down your evaluations.

Part 3

Roleplay interviews for each job with one other student. Arrange to have the roleplays recorded on video and ask your tutor to act as an observer. Review your own and each other's performance and give each other feedback. Ask your tutor for an evaluation. Make notes on the comments you make and receive and evaluate your own performance as interviewer and interviewee.

Use all the notes you've made to write a brief account of what you did for the assignment and summarise the evaluations you made on each aspect.

ELEMENT **2.4**

Workplace standards and performance

High standards are important in leisure and tourism in many different ways. Facilities have to come up to health and safety standards, employees have to follow the standards of the organisation in things like dress and timekeeping and employers have to maintain good personnel records. Some of these standards are required by law, others are laid down by the organisations themselves. The point about all of them is that they help to create a working environment that is fair for everyone and protects their rights.

66 *National legislation which affects us includes the health and safety regulations, which have an enormous effect on us, and building regulations. There are strict rules about what we can and can't do to the buildings, although these can also be affected by the provisions under which the property was donated. If we wanted to build we would obviously have to seek planning permission.* **99**

administrator of a heritage site

66 *We are affected by fire and health regulations. When we wanted to extend the building last year we had to get permission from the planning authorities. It took time but it shows that our standards of accommodation are high.* **99**

guest-house owner

66 *All staff have annual appraisals where they can look at how things have gone in the previous year with their manager. This is a chance to discuss every aspect of their jobs. Staff are told about what they are doing well and about areas where they might be able to improve. It is also an opportunity for them to talk about areas in which they would like some more training.* **99**

press and publicity officer at an entertainments venue

66 *Targets can be a good thing as they give people a goal and sense of achievement when they are reached. They should not be impossible to reach – that can be demoralising and unproductive.* **99**

manager of a tourist information centre

The workplace and legislation

In the UK, a range of legislation is in place to make sure that the workplace is safe and secure and that people are employed under fair terms and conditions. Some of the most important laws cover:

- safety of premises and equipment
- fire precautions
- health, hygiene and sanitary measures
- the working environment
- anti-discrimination measures
- statutory obligations for employers and employees
- contracts of employment.

Customers – 'consumers' – are also protected by legislation.

The purpose of legislation is to:

- prevent injuries, accidents and unsafe practices
- promote fair employment practices
- protect employers, employees and consumers.

It gives employers, employees and consumers:

- clear regulations and standards to follow
- responsibilities for the effects of their failure to follow regulations and standards
- a right to seek compensation for loss, damage or injury caused by the failure of others to follow regulations and standards.

Health and safety legislation

Health and safety legislation aims to make the workplace a safe one for everyone who uses it – employees, employers, visitors and customers. The major Acts and regulations are covered in unit 7.

The main legislation which sets standards for health and safety in the workplace is the Health and Safety at Work Act 1974 and the Workplace (Health, Safety and Welfare) Regulations 1992.

Although the law places responsibility for providing safe and healthy premises on employers, it also says that employees have a duty to take reasonable care for their own health and safety and that of anyone who may be affected by what they do at work (for example, work colleagues and customers).

Legislation also ensures that consumers visiting the working environment are safe. The Health and Safety at Work Act specifically states that employers must 'make sure that customers and other people visiting the workplace are not exposed to any health and safety risk'. Like employees, customers and visitors are expected to take reasonable care of themselves and to make sure others aren't put at risk by their actions or behaviour.

DISCUSSION POINT

Why does legislation give responsibilities for health, safety and welfare to employees and consumers as well as to employers?

The Health and Safety at Work Act (HASAWA) 1974 states that employers must:

- provide and maintain equipment, appliances and systems of work which are safe and without risk to health
- arrange for the safe handling, use, storage and transport of articles and substances
- provide information, instruction, training and supervision to ensure the health and safety of employees
- maintain the premises in a safe condition
- provide safe entrances and exits on working premises
- provide and maintain a working environment that is safe and without risk to health
- provide facilities such as rest areas and dining areas for the welfare of employees at work
- provide all employees with a written statement of the current policy with respect to health and safety at work.

The Workplace (Health, Safety and Welfare) Regulations 1992 sets minimum workplace standards governing:

- cleanliness
- workspace allocated to each employee
- temperature
- ventilation
- lighting
- sanitation and water
- floors, passages and stairs
- dangerous machinery.

Rules, standards, policies and procedures

- responsibilities for health and safety
- fire precautions
- emergency procedures
- training
- waste disposal
- maintenance of buildings and equipment
- safe use and storage of hazardous substances
- safe use of equipment
- working practices

ACTIVITY

The box above lists some of the areas covered by an organisation's health and safety rules, standards, policies and procedures. Contact a leisure and tourism organisation and find out what standards they set for health and safety. Find out:

- how they make sure all staff are aware of the standards
- how staff are encouraged to keep to the standards
- what action is taken if standards are not met.

ACTIVITY

Write an information sheet for an employer – either a leisure centre or a travel agency – summarising the main health, safety and employment legislation they have to comply with in order to:

- protect themselves
- protect employees
- protect consumers.

Organisations use health and safety legislation to:

- draw up rules for employees to follow
- set maintenance standards for premises and equipment
- establish policies and procedures.

Employment

The aim of employment legislation is to ensure that employees are:

- given reasonable terms and conditions of employment
- treated fairly and without discrimination.

The table on the next page lists some of the major laws which govern employment. Legislation deals with minimum and general requirements such as:

- workplace conditions
- health, safety and welfare
- fair treatment
- written terms and conditions of employment
- terminating employment
- maternity leave
- sick leave
- equal opportunities.

In some cases, an employee has to have worked continuously for the same employer for two years to qualify for rights under employment legislation – for example, the right to redundancy payments.

An employment adviser gave this overview of employment legislation and practices:

❝ *Many of the things employees take for granted such as paid holidays, set hours of work, sick pay and so on are not actually legal rights. They are terms and conditions to be agreed between the employer and the employee. In law, agreements between two parties are called contracts. Under the Employment Protection (Consolidation) Act of 1978, employees have a right to a written statement of the terms and conditions of their employment contract. This is the document which sets out the hours of work they have agreed to do, the number of days' holiday they can take, what sick pay they can have and so on. These are known as 'contractual rights' – in other words, entitlements an employee and employer have agreed to and therefore must abide by.*

There are some exceptions where the law decides on minimum requirements. For some types of work, hours have to be restricted on health and safety grounds – coach-driving, for example.

Pregnant women have certain statutory employment rights. These include the right to paid time off to attend antenatal clinics and classes, the right not to be dismissed for being pregnant and the right to at least 14 weeks' maternity leave. They are in most cases entitled to return to work after their maternity leave. Women who have worked for the same employer for at least six months at the 15th week before their baby is due are entitled to up to 18 weeks' Statutory Maternity Pay (SMP) from their employer. Women who've worked for the same employer for two years are entitled to an additional period of maternity leave of up to 28 weeks after their baby is born.

Employees can claim Statutory Sick Pay from the employer from the fourth day of sickness so long as they comply with the contract's instructions for notifying the employer of their absence. **99**

ACTIVITY

Find out what employees can do if they think their employer has broken employment legislation or the contract of employment. Your local library, Citizens' Advice Bureau and Jobcentre should all have leaflets and other information which should help you. Make notes on what you find out.

Employment Protection Act 1975, and Consolidation Act 1978	Employees have the right to a fair contract of employment and written terms stating: the rate of pay; notice of termination rights of both employer and employee; sick-pay rights; holiday entitlement; protection of employees from unfair dismissal; grievance procedures.
Employment Acts of 1980 and 1982	Employees have the right to choose whether or not to join a trade union. Employees also have the right to have reasonable time off work for community duties, such as being a magistrate or councillor, or for trade union representative training. An employer has to have fair grounds for dismissing an employee (e.g. redundancy, gross misconduct, incompetence).
Equal Pay Act 1970 Equal Pay (Amendment) Regulations 1983	Men and women must be paid equally for the same or similar work or for work judged as being of equal importance.
Wages Act 1986	Employers may only make lawful deductions from employees' pay, such as income tax and National Insurance contributions, payments towards a company pension scheme and agreed trade union subscriptions.
Sex Discrimination Act 1975 Sex Discrimination Act 1986	Employers must not discriminate against or victimise employees on the basis of sex or marital status in the terms, conditions and benefits of employment offered or allow employees to discriminate or victimise each other.
Race Relations Act 1976	Employers must not discriminate against or victimise employees on the basis of race, colour or ethnic origin in the terms, conditions and benefits of employment offered or allow employees to discriminate against or victimise each other.
Disabled Persons (Employment) Act 1958 (this Act will be replaced by the Disability Discrimination Act 1995 from 1996 onwards)	Any firm which employs more than 20 people must make every reasonable effort to ensure that at least 3% of its workforce is made up of people who are registered as disabled.
Disability Discrimination Act 1995 (to come into effect in various stages from 1996 onwards)	Employers must not discriminate against or victimise employees on the basis of disability in the terms, conditions and benefits of employment offered or allow employees to discriminate or victimise each other.

Procedures for maintaining standards of performance and behaviour

All leisure and tourism organisations expect certain standards of performance and behaviour from their employees. Only if everyone cooperates – with a positive attitude to each other, customers and the work environment – will an organisation succeed.

In order to maintain these standards, most organisations establish their own set of rules and procedures.

Workplace rules

Every organisation has rules about standards of behaviour. In many cases, organisations issue staff with a set of written rules covering things like:

- eating, drinking and smoking at work
- health, safety and hygiene standards
- dress and appearance (dress codes are particularly important for people who have regular contact with customers and for staff in the catering industry)
- timekeeping and attendance
- attitude towards customers, colleagues, company property and work premises.

If an employee regularly fails to follow these rules, then most organisations begin a disciplinary procedure (see below).

Workplace standards

Workplace standards cover the health, safety and welfare of all people who work in or visit the workplace. They are largely established by legal regulations like the Health and Safety at Work Act 1974 and the Workplace (Health, Safety and Welfare) Regulations. Employers and employees share responsibility for maintaining workplace standards. Employers are responsible for setting standards, devising procedures in line with legislation and for training their employees so they can keep to standards. Employees are responsible for taking part in training, keeping to standards and following procedures.

Attendance records

Attendance at work for the right number of days and hours is a contracted obligation for an employee. It is also a performance standard. Attendance records are kept by either line managers or the personnel department and they show how often a person is absent from work and for what reasons – for example, sickness, injury, holiday, unauthorised absences. If someone is frequently off work, the attendance record can be used to draw their attention to their failure to meet the expected performance standard.

Performance records

Performance records show expected standards of performance in measurable terms and how far people are meeting or exceeding the standards. Performance standards are usually agreed between each person and their line manager. Performance records are useful ways of keeping track of people's achievement and identifying any performance problems they may have.

ACTIVITY

Ask the manager of a local leisure and tourism facility if you can have a copy of their staff rules.

Examples of performance standards

- processing 35 customer bookings per day
- implementing twelve promotional campaigns within six months
- increasing sales of off-peak breaks by 20% per annum.

Supervisory feedback

Most employees are given feedback informally, day-to-day by their supervisors. In addition, many employers use an annual review or appraisal to:

- let employees know whether they are meeting the standards
- give employees a chance to discuss their jobs
- identify training and development needs.

In preparation for an appraisal or review, the supervisor or manager will look at written records which have been kept on the employee's work, including:

- attendance records
- performance records
- notes and reports made by supervisors and other managers
- details of compliments about performance
- details of criticisms about performance
- records of what took place at any previous appraisals.

These are then discussed with the employee, giving both the supervisor and member of staff an opportunity to talk about all aspects of the work and review the progress the staff member has made over the year. The supervisor and staff member then:

- plan standards for performance for the coming year
- agree targets for achievements.

The supervisor of a team of customer care assistants at a travel agency explains how they use the appraisal system:

66 *We like to make sure that an appraisal is a constructive and positive process – a time to:*

- *review job responsibilities and tasks*
- *look at recent achievements*
- *assess current levels of performance*
- *praise where performance meets or exceeds the standards*
- *reflect where performance is not up to the standards*
- *discuss possible future career development*
- *assess training needs.* 99

Disciplinary and grievance procedures

All organisations have their own disciplinary procedure, which is either included in employees' contract of employment or issued as a separate document. When a disciplinary procedure is underway employees have the right to involve a work colleague or trade union representative if they think their employer is treating them unfairly.

A disciplinary procedure usually involves giving the employee:

- a formal verbal warning; if things don't improve, this is followed by
- a written warning; if there is still no improvement, this is followed by

- a final written warning or suspension; if conduct or performance is still unsatisfactory, then
- the employee is dismissed.

A grievance procedure is the formal means of complaining about treatment or conditions at work. Grievances can range from simple, easily resolved complaints like lack of blinds in an over-sunny room to serious breaches of terms and conditions of employment. The grievance procedure must be outlined in the written contract of employment. The procedure should state:

- who to complain to initially and how
- who to complain to if the initial complaint is not dealt with satisfactorily
- who will make the final and binding decision on how to resolve the grievance.

The personnel officer at a theme park describes how they deal with grievances:

66 *Minor grievances are usually resolved informally through a chat between the staff member and a supervisor. More serious grievances may have to be dealt with more formally and involve more senior management. For serious grievances where a breach of contract or infringement of employment or other laws is involved, it might be necessary to seek the help of a trade union or professional association. If the matter can't be resolved, it may need to go to an external body like ACAS for their judgement.* 99

If you have a grievance about your treatment as an employee you should normally inform your head of department or, if you feel unable to do so, you should inform the executive director, either verbally or in writing. If, after a reasonable period of time you have not been able to resolve your problem with either your head of department or the executive director, you should approach the disciplinary committee of the board of trustees.

An example of an internal grievance procedure from a contract of employment

Employee charters

Many organisations now have an employee charter, which sets out clearly:

- employees' rights and responsibilities
- the way the organisation aims to treat its employees.
- the standards the organisation expects of its staff.

Customer charters

Some organisations also have a customer charter, which sets out:

- the standards of service and customer care which customers can expect from the organisation
- what action customers should take if they are dissatisfied with a product or service.

DISCUSSION POINT

What difference would it make to your view of an organisation if you knew it had an employee charter or a customer charter?

The benefits of occupational standards

Many leisure and tourism organisations now have occupational standards for job functions. Occupational standards describe standards of work performance. For example:

- an accounts assistant must be able to use a range of spreadsheet software
- an administrator must be able to establish and maintain a database of information
- a sales assistant must be able to communicate clearly and appropriately with customers
- a product manager must be able to control and monitor stock.

Employers in each industry determine occupational standards by deciding what someone working in a particular function should be able to do.

Defined by industry and incorporated in NVQs

Many industries have now put together sets of occupational standards, each of which makes up a National Vocational Qualification (NVQ). Each set of standards applies to a sector within the industry. For example, in the Leisure and Tourism industry there are different sets of occupational standards for Sports and Recreation and Travel Services (as well as for the many other areas of the industry). The way the NVQ in Travel Services was defined is shown on the left.

The benefits for individuals

Anyone can show they meet occupational standards by working towards NVQs – there are no time limits, age limits or entry requirements. People who achieve an NVQ prove they are able to do their job, resulting in a range of benefits.

Promotion

Occupational standards have been developed at five levels – level 1 covers basic work activities, while level 5 is designed for senior management. These five levels provide a useful framework to help people work towards promotion.

A personnel manager at a city arts centre explains the benefits she sees in occupational standards:

66 *By completing an NVQ, our staff show that they can do their job well, improving their promotion prospects. By then aiming higher and working towards the next level NVQ, they can also show their potential for the future.* 99

Qualifications and skills recognition

Occupational standards and NVQs are based on what people do in their day-to-day jobs, rather than on written exams and theoretical learning. Because of this, they give many people who wouldn't want to take traditional exams the chance to gain valuable qualifications.

A careers adviser made this point on occupational standards:

66 *Because occupational standards are national, and defined by industry, they are recognised and respected by employers all over the country. When individuals achieve occupational standards by working towards NVQs, it is proof*

that they have the skills needed for the job. So whether individuals want to get a new job, progress in their existing job, or go back to work after a career break, having an NVQ can help. 🙸

Job competence

Occupational standards define what individuals should be able to do in order to be competent in their jobs.

An employee in the leisure and tourism industry describes how occupational standards help her to feel confident in her skills:

🙶 *By looking at the written standards, I can identify skills and knowledge I need to develop, and the level of competence I want to achieve. Achieving the standards shows me that I'm good at my job and I get more satisfaction from my work because I can see my job leading somewhere.* 🙸

The benefits for organisations

Industry plays an important part in defining occupational standards, ensuring that NVQs really do have benefits for organisations.

Appraisals

Occupational standards and NVQs are an effective way for organisations to measure their employees' developing skills and recognise their achievements. Therefore, an individual's progress towards occupational standards can provide important evidence for use during an appraisal or review.

Skills audit

By looking at the occupational standards being achieved across its workforce, an organisation can identify areas where skills are strong and areas where skills need strengthening. They can then either provide extra training to existing staff or recruit new employees with the skills needed.

Assessing training needs

Having carried out a skills audit and established overall needs, an organisation can then identify training needs for individual employees.

Assessing development

Occupational standards and NVQs provide a way to measure employees' skills. By aiming at set standards, employees can monitor their progress towards new skills and have their achievement officially recognised.

Job descriptions

Because occupational standards define clearly and consistently what individuals should be able to achieve for particular jobs, they can be an excellent starting point for organisations wanting to write job descriptions and person specifications.

Sources of information and advice on legislation

You don't need to know all the laws relating to work and workplace legislation, but you do need to know where you can get information and advice if you need to.

National sources

The main national sources are listed below – many of them have local branches or offices which will be listed in your local telephone directories:

- the Department for Education and Employment
- the Department of Social Security
- the Health and Safety Executive
- the Arbitration, Conciliation and Advice Service (ACAS)
- the Equal Opportunities Commission
- the Commission for Racial Equality
- the National Council for Disability.

Trade associations and advisory bodies

Trade associations and advisory bodies provide information specific to the relevant industry. Here are the key ones for leisure and tourism:

- ABTA – Association of British Travel Agents
- English Tourist Board
- IBRM – Institute of Baths and Recreation Management
- ILAM – Institute of Leisure and Amenity Management
- ITT – Institute of Travel and Tourism
- the Sports Council
- the Tourism Society.

Trade Unions are also a useful source of advice and information.

Local sources

Useful information and advice on work and workplace legislation can be obtained from local sources such as:

- Training and Enterprise Councils
- Local Enterprise Councils (in Scotland)
- Chambers of Commerce
- Citizens' Advice Bureaux
- local authority environmental health officers
- the local fire service
- Jobcentres
- libraries
- the personnel departments of leisure and tourism organisations.

Published sources

Your college and local libraries should have reference books on work and workplace legislation. Leaflets and booklets are also available from many of the organisations listed under national and local sources above. The trade press also carry features from time to time on legislation and its implications for the industry.

ACTIVITY

The organisations listed below all help to ensure that work and workplace legislation is kept to. Carry out some research into the responsibilities and activities of each organisation and write a report on your findings:

- The Health and Safety Executive
- The Arbitration, Conciliation and Advice Service (ACAS)
- The Equal Opportunities Commission
- The Commission for Racial Equality
- The National Council for Disability.

ACTIVITY

Find out which trade unions represent the interests of employees in the leisure and tourism industry.

ACTIVITY

Write a letter to an employee, advising her:

- where to find information about her legal right to maternity leave
- what to do if she thinks her employer is in breach of health and safety regulations

Investigating workplace standards and performance

All leisure and tourism organisations have to comply with legislation on health, safety and employment rights. Meeting legal requirements establishes a good basis for workplace standards and rules for behaviour. But most organisations do more than just the basics.

In the case study below, the operations manager of a heritage site explains some of her responsibilities for making sure that health and safety standards are met and the personnel manager describes some of his responsibilities for ensuring that employment legislation is followed and performance standards are established.

The operations manager

66 *It's my responsibility to make sure that health and safety standards are met and that all staff know their responsibilities for maintaining a safe working environment. All staff attend a week-long induction course when they join the organisation and health and safety standards and procedures are a key part of the course. All staff are given a copy of the company handbook. This includes sections on the main health and safety laws we have to abide by and describes all the procedures that have to be followed. It also includes a statement of our organisation's health and safety policy, information on what to do in the case of an emergency, who to contact if there's been a breach of any health and safety procedure, and so on.*

I'm also responsible for arranging health and safety training. And I have to keep myself up to date with changes in legislation or new codes of practice. For example, under a new law, the Disability Discrimination Act 1995, we have to make sure that our premises are suitable for disabled employees and customers. So we're in the process of investigating the changes we may need to make to our buildings, grounds and facilities so that they are accessible and safe for disabled people and still comply with all the other health and safety legislation. 99

The personnel manager

66 *I'm responsible for ensuring that employment legislation is followed in our recruitment, selection and terms and conditions of employment. As with health and safety, details of what employees can expect from us and what we expect from them is given in the company handbook. My responsibilities also cover the setting of general performance standards like attendance, personal standards of dress, hygiene and behaviour and for making sure staff know about them and keep to them. I have a personnel file for each employee where I keep their personal details, performance and attendance records, copies of appraisal reports and so on. I also have a responsibility for the personal welfare of each employee. If they have any problems which affect their ability to perform well –*

problems at home or with colleagues or in their working conditions – that they don't want to discuss with their supervisor, they can discuss it with me and I'll do what I can to help them find a solution.

Job-related performance standards are worked out by me and the relevant managers and supervisors. We work together to produce job descriptions and person specifications and to identify the relevant occupational standards for each job. The managers and supervisors are responsible for making sure their team members are doing what's expected of them in their jobs and for discussing training and development needs. **99**

Brolling Castle Heritage Site: Company Handbook

ACTIVITY

Contact two leisure and tourism organisations and arrange to speak to staff with responsibility for ensuring that health, safety and employment legislation is kept to and performance standards are met. Find out:

■ the key health, safety and employment laws and regulations they have to observe

■ what procedures and systems they have in place to ensure that legal, occupational and organisational standards are met

■ how they make staff aware of their rights and responsibilities

■ how they make sure staff can meet all relevant standards.

Ask if you can have any copies of rules, handbooks or manuals issued to staff.

Write a brief report on what you find out.

Contents

Key questions

1 Can you name two acts that include legislation to protect employees in the workplace?
2 What is meant by equal opportunities?
3 What are the key laws governing equal opportunities at work?
4 What are the differences between standards of behaviour and occupational standards?
5 What is the purpose of an annual appraisal?
6 For employees, what are the main benefits of occupational standards?
7 For employers, what are the main benefits of occupational standards?
8 Can you name five main sources of information and advice on legislation in the workplace and explain what they offer?
9 How can an organisation make sure that all staff know what standards are expected of them?

Assignment

Part 1

Carry out an investigation into the workplace and performance standards of a selected leisure and tourism facility. Your investigation should cover:
■ the legislation the facility has to keep to and the purpose of the legislation
■ the facility's procedures for maintaining standards
■ the occupational standards the facility uses and the benefits they have for the facility and for individual staff members.

Use the results of your investigation to write an induction booklet for new employees at the facility that would help them understand:
■ the purpose of all the standards
■ the procedures for keeping to standards
■ the benefits of having standards.

Part 2

Make a set of handouts that could be used at a employers' conference on workplace and performance standards in the leisure and tourism industry. The handouts should cover:
■ the purpose of health, safety and employment legislation
■ procedures for maintaining standards of performance and behaviour
■ ways of ensuring that standards are understood by employees
■ relevant occupational standards and their benefits
■ sources of information and advice relating to work and workplace legislation.

UNIT **3**

Element 3.1

The principles, activities and objectives of marketing

Element 3.2

Marketing research in leisure and tourism

Element 3.3

Marketing communications

Element 3.4

A marketing plan

Marketing in leisure and tourism

ELEMENT **3.1**

The principles, activities and objectives of marketing

You can see the results of organisations' marketing activities all around you: advertisements on TV and in magazines. A lot of it is selling or promoting leisure and tourism activities. Organisations often spend large amounts of money to make sure their products or services are well known and easily available to people who want to buy them. Marketing does not happen by accident: it's the result of hard work and creativity. In this element you'll be looking at the way organisations set about marketing and how the results of all this marketing activity affect the way they change their products.

66 *Marketing is a process that starts with research and ends with new products. We collect statistics on how many visitors we've had in the area and and where they come from. We produce promotional literature and sell advertising to help pay for it. We also promote the area by placing adverts ourselves in national magazines.* **99**

manager of a tourist information centre

66 *Marketing is always a very difficult thing – you can spend a fortune and get little or no return. I have advertised my classes in newspapers in the past, but now I find it more effective to advertise every month in the specialist riding magazines.* **99**

owner of a riding school which also provides holidays

66 *We have tried a marketing campaign in the past, advertising in the broadsheet press at weekends. We tried about five different papers but it was a bit of a waste of time. For us, the response never seemed to justify the price of the advert, so on principle now we don't advertise in papers and magazines. We rely much more on word of mouth and on information passed on to potential customers through guidebooks and the local tourist centres. We want everyone to go away from here very happy with what they have had; I designed a questionnaire to find out from people what they liked best. But the British being what they are, it is quite difficult to get people to answer everything we ask – they are usually just very polite!* **99**

owner of a guest-house

66 *My job is to liaise with the press and other media, both nationally and locally. I write and send out press releases and arrange press interviews. I set up photo opportunities, try to encourage press interest in all the acts we have appearing and liaise with promoters. I'm also responsible for arranging for posters and photos to be available. Sometimes I arrange competitions to increase interest in our productions. When we were putting on an opera we got in touch with a local restaurant which had the same name as the opera and arranged for children to design a pizza. The winner's idea was then on the menu for the following week.* **99**

press and publicity officer at an entertainments venue

The principles of marketing

Marketing activities are based on five key principles:

- identifying customers' needs and wants
- satisfying customers' needs and wants
- finding new markets for the organisation's products or services
- influencing customers' buying attitudes
- getting the products and services into the right markets.

All marketing activities aim to provide customers with:

- the right product or service
- at the right price
- in the right place
- using the right method of promotion.

Customers' needs and wants

Leisure and tourism is a service industry – it is geared towards providing products and services which meet customers' needs and wants. An assistant in a travel agency explains the difference between a 'need' and a 'want':

66 *I'd say that a need is an essential requirement, whereas a want has more to do with providing a luxury or fulfilling hopes and dreams. The travel business aims to meet both needs and wants. For example, this morning a business client telephoned in a panic and said: 'I need to catch the first flight to Glasgow tomorrow morning. It's the last thing I want to do, but I have to sign an important contract.' Half an hour later, a customer came into the shop, looked at the brochure display and announced with a smile: 'I want a holiday.'* 99

> ### DISCUSSION POINT
>
> The Institute of Marketing defines marketing as 'the management process responsible for identifying, anticipating and satisfying customer requirements profitably.' Look at the two lists above which describe marketing principles and the aims of marketing activities and think about the Institute of Marketing's definition. Is marketing just the responsibility of the marketing department, or would other areas of the organisation be involved?

> ### DISCUSSION POINT
>
> Think of two or three organisations that provide different leisure and tourism products and services.
>
> For each organisation, think of a range of customer needs and wants it aims to satisfy.
>
> In general, do the organisations focus more on satisfying customers' wants or customers' needs?
>
> What implications does this have for the way the organisations market themselves?

A huge amount of marketing resources goes into identifying customers' needs and wants. The marketing director of a leisure complex explains why:

66 *Knowing what your customers want defines what the organisation should be providing. When you know what you should be providing, all the organisation's resources and activities can be geared towards providing it.* 99

Customer satisfaction

One of the main aims of marketing is to make sure customers are satisfied. The marketing manager of a fitness centre sums up the importance of satisfying customers:

❝ *Good customer care encourages repeat business – if customers are satisfied they are likely to buy the product or use the service again. That means you stay in business. They're also likely to recommend you to their friends. So that means you could increase your business. If customers aren't satisfied, they'll look around for an organisation that can satisfy them. That means you'll lose business – and your loss is your competitor's gain.* ❞

Analysing and targeting markets

To meet customers' needs and wants, organisations have to:

■ know who their customers are

■ target marketing activity towards them.

This means analysing the markets carefully.

Market analysis:

■ by segmentation – classifying potential customers according to what segment of the market they fall into. This is done by assessing factors such as age, social class, income and lifestyle. By classifying customers in this way products, services and marketing activity can be geared towards a particular market segment.

■ by looking at the competition – finding out what products and services competitors provide, which customers they aim for, what gaps there are in the markets.

■ by targeting – focusing marketing activity on particular clients or groups of clients. This helps ensure that promotional time and money is spent attracting the right customers.

■ by positioning – the part of the market the organisation aims to occupy in relation to the market position of its competitors.

Who is likely to buy these products?

Influencing buyers' decisions

People buy products or services for many different reasons. Marketing identifies:

■ why people want to buy products or services

■ who decides what to buy (for example, in families and organisations).

The behaviour of buyers changes as their lifestyles change. For example, as people get older their needs, wants, income, likes and dislikes change – all of which affect the decisions they make about what they buy. So a teenager and an elderly person are likely to want very different things from a holiday.

DISCUSSION POINT

How can marketing influence
buyers as they go through the
process of deciding what to buy?
Read through the different stages
in buying listed above and talk
about which offer opportunities
for marketing.

The **marketing mix** is the
combination of factors used to
achieve marketing goals.

Effective marketing makes use of what motivates people to buy products and services. Customers usually go through several stages when deciding whether to buy a product or service, or choosing which one to buy. They might:

■ compare different products and services
■ look for more informarion or advice about them
■ ask questions about them
■ talk to their family or friends
■ decide to buy the product or service they like best.

Their final decision will be based on which option best meets their needs.

ACTIVITY

Think of a purchase you've made recently. List the steps you went through in making your purchase and the factors that influenced you at each step.

Balancing the marketing mix

The components of the marketing mix are often called the four Ps.

The four Ps

■ Product – establishing a product range, quality, level, name
■ Price – selling the products at the right price
■ Place – selling products in the right places
■ Promotion – publicising the products in the right way and to the right people

Applying the four Ps to product strategy and marketing activities helps an organisation to:

■ concentrate its resources in the right areas
■ increase the likelihood of selling its products and services
■ achieve customer satisfaction.

The marketing officer of a local authority sports hall explains:

66 *We match the four Ps to what we know about our customers – who they are, where they are, what they like. The right products are defined by what our customers want. The right price is what we know our customers are willing to pay. The right place is where we know our customers are and where our customers can make use of our products. The right promotion is the best way to make contact with our customers to let them know about our products.* 99

Marketing activities

Marketing activities happen at every stage of the buying process in leisure and tourism – from encouraging people to buy a product or service to providing after-sales service and customer care.

Marketing research

This is where marketing starts. It tries to predict the future based on research and analysis of the present and the past. There are two types of marketing research:

- primary research (also known as field research). This involves direct contact with current and potential customers. It is usually based on questioning or direct observation of customers.
- secondary research (also known as desk research). This involves analysing data about customers from different sources. It is usually used to identify and predict market trends based on statistics.

Analysing the marketing environment

The products and services a leisure and tourism company offers – and the way it markets them – can be influenced by factors outside the industry. Organisations need to analyse the whole marketing environment in order to market their products and services well. To do this, they consider a range of different factors, or 'environments'.

Environment	Possible influences
Political	Changes in international, national and local governments, policies and legislation.
Economic	Effect of factors such as unemployment, rises or falls in taxation, the cost of living, interest rates and so on.
Social	Changes in local or national population (e.g. growing numbers of retired people), fashions, lifestyles and cultures.
Technological	Effect of new technology on how organisations operate and on people's buying habits

This type of marketing environment analysis is known as a PEST or STEP analysis – an acronym using the first letters of the four factors listed in the box.

Analysing the market

Companies must have a good understanding of the market in which they operate so that they can target their marketing activities well.

The most common method of analysing the market is called a SWOT analysis. Organisations use this to evaluate their current and potential performance under four headings:

- Strengths
- Weaknesses
- Opportunities
- Threats.

ACTIVITY

Think of any leisure and tourism organisation. Do a PEST analysis of the changes outside the organisation that might influence the products or services it offers. What benefits might come from these changes? What problems might they create?

Planning

Successful marketing depends on planning. The marketing director of a theme park in south-west England uses a seven-stage approach to planning.

Key stages in the marketing plan

1 Assess or evaluate the current position – internally (using SWOT analysis) and externally (using STEP analysis).
2 Define future marketing strategies or activities.
3 Consider different marketing options.
4 Cost the plan.
5 Prepare a time plan or schedule
6 Implement the new or revised marketing plan.
7 Review and evaluate the plan.

Marketing plans are always linked to the organisation's business objectives and look ahead over a number of months or years. Within this broad plan, there are also short- and medium-term objectives. Companies review plans regularly to see whether marketing activities have been successful.

Communicating

Marketing is all about understanding and communicating with customers – 'getting the message across' about the products and services on offer.

Organisations communicate with customers in many different ways:

■ advertising – in newspapers, magazines, on television, on radio, at point of sale or point of delivery

■ publicity material – brochures, leaflets, events guides, guides to services, posters

■ public relations – press releases, sponsorship, lobbying, community relations, corporate communication

■ sales promotion – to consumers and trade

■ direct marketing – mail order, catalogues, telemarketing, direct response, electronic shopping

■ personal selling – product-orientated, service-orientated, customer-orientated, face-to-face, telephone sales.

One of the challenges of marketing is choosing the right forms of communication for the target audience.

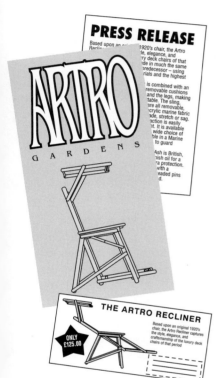

PRESS RELEASE

ARTRO

G A R D E N S

THE ARTRO RECLINER

ONLY
£125.00

DISCUSSION POINT

Publicity that works well stays in your mind for a long time. What publicity for a leisure and tourism facility or service can you remember best? Why has it stayed in your mind? See if other people remember the same things as you.

Sales and customer service

Organisations know marketing is right if their customers are satisfied. In the leisure and tourism industry, good customer care is essential at every stage of contact with customers:

- before they buy – communicating effectively, providing information, creating a positive image of the organisation
- while they are buying – giving information, checking that their needs are being met
- after they have bought – being available to deal with queries or problems, responding quickly and courteously to complaints.

Marketing activities in profit-making organisations

Profit-making organisations use their marketing activities to:

- keep hold of existing customers
- identify ways of expanding their range to bring in new customers
- gain an edge over their competitors
- identify new products and services to bring in new customers
- identify products and services no longer wanted by customers.

Because they are in business to make a profit, the marketing activities of profit-making organisations are linked to their plans for growth, so they aim to increase the profits they make. The success of marketing activities is judged by how much extra business they generate and how much profit they produce.

Marketing activities in not-for-profit organisations

Marketing activities are just as important in not-for-profit organisations. Being a not-for-profit organisation doesn't mean your aim is to break even or make a loss. It means that you aren't in business to make a profit for the private benefit of the organisation's owners. Any revenue left over from business and funding activities goes back into the organisation.

Organisations like charities and charitable trusts use marketing to:

- promote their causes
- increase income through increased membership
- promote products and services
- publicise fundraising activities
- encourage donations, grants and legacies.

Marketing activities in public-sector organisations

Marketing is an increasingly important activity in the public sector, particularly where organisations are competing with the private and voluntary sector or competing for public funds. They use marketing activities to:

- publicise their products and services to existing and new customers
- demonstrate to potential funding bodies like the government their viability and effectiveness as product and service providers.

Key marketing objectives

Good marketing plans have clear objectives which state exactly what an organisation hopes to achieve through its marketing activities. The organisation can then use these objectives to evaluate different activities by looking at:

- how far objectives have been achieved
- whether objectives need to be reviewed and amended
- what new objectives may have been created.

Adding 'how' and 'why' to an objective helps organisations decide what marketing activities to carry out, and then makes it easier to evaluate whether they have been successful.

Objective	How	Why
To analyse market needs	Identify customers' needs and wants through primary and secondary research	To change existing or develop new products or services to meet customers' needs
To satisfy customer requirements	Deliver the goods or services which customers need and want	To increase the likelihood of repeat business and maintain or improve current levels of business
To manage the effects of competition	Maintain market share by promoting products and services	To keep market position
To manage the effects of change	Through public relations	To minimise the bad effects change may have on the market
To coordinate marketing	Provide marketing information to staff involved in the delivery of products and services to customers	To ensure that staff are aware of developments in the market which may affect their ability to deliver a quality service and provide cost-effective marketing
To maximise income and generate profit	Develop and implement pricing and sales strategies	To ensure the continuing survival and profitability of the organisation
To generate community benefit	Provide or sponsor services which offer a direct social or cultural benefit to the community but which are not necessarily profitable	To create goodwill in a competitive and changing environment and to ensure that customers are not deprived of leisure and tourism products or services because of disadvantage, disability or discrimination
To help customers see the product in the best possible way	Run special promotions emphasising quality and value for money	To maintain or improve levels of sales in the long term

CASE STUDY

Melanie is head of marketing for a large entertainment venue which puts on events ranging from rock concerts to opera, Shakespeare plays to alternative comedians. She is responsible for:

- the box office – where tickets are sold, information is available and publicity material is displayed
- front-of-house staff – including stewards who check tickets and sell programmes at events
- promotion and publicity officers – who deal with the press, write promotional material and so on
- customer service staff – who deal with customers' queries, problems and complaints
- a team of distributors – who deliver leaflets, put up posters and so on.

Melanie tells all her staff that they contribute directly to marketing the venue. They help to promote events, have contact with customers, and provide direct customer care. She also says they are great sources of information about what customers want, think and feel – information which is fed back into the department's research into the market.

Melanie is convinced that she also needs to involve staff from other areas of the organisation in marketing activities. This includes the financial, catering and technical (backstage) staff, as she feels their work has an important effect on whether the venue meets customers' needs.

ACTIVITY

Look through the different objectives given at the start of this section. Choose three that you think would interest Melanie. Why would these interest her so much? How should she try to achieve them? Make notes on your ideas and discuss them with one or two other people.

Key marketing objectives of profit-making organisations

The key marketing objectives of a profit-making organisation will characteristically focus on growth and increasing profit.

Key marketing objectives of not-for-profit organisations

The key marketing objectives of not-for-profit organisations will characteristically focus on promotion, continuation and expansion of the public or charitable service it offers.

How organisations grow

One of the main aims of marketing is to help organisations succeed, become more profitable and grow. In order to grow, organisations need to maintain or improve their position in the market. This means finding good ways to survive and grow in the face of competition and declining markets.

Achieving growth

There are five basic ways of achieving growth:

■ existing markets
■ new markets
■ existing products and services
■ new products and services
■ market share.

Growth through existing markets

This means using marketing activities to:

■ sell more to existing customers in existing markets (also known as market penetration)
■ identify new customers in existing markets (also known as market development).

The marketing manager of a travel agency explains how they did this:

66 *We wanted to increase the take-up of special offers for business travel. So we researched into the types of customers we had and found that we weren't attracting much business from small firms. So we did a direct mailing specifically targeting small firms with business links abroad.* 99

Growth through new markets

This means using marketing activities to sell existing products and services in new or different markets.

The marketing director of an outdoor activity centre explains how they did this:

66 *Our customer database showed that most people who used the centre were over 16 but under 40. That meant there was a potential new market of the under-16s and the over-40s. So we put together a series of promotional activities to encourage new customers from those market areas.* 99

Growth through existing products and services

This means selling more existing products or service or making them more profitable.

The managing director of a family-owned coach business explains how they did this:

66 *We bought a couple of minibuses to run at off-peak times of the day. We offer the same service but it's cheaper for us to run. As a result, we're thinking of increasing the frequency of the minibus service and taking on another driver.* 99

Growth through new products and services

This is also known as product development. Offering new products and services can help an organisation:

■ keep existing customer

■ gain new customers.

The marketing officer of a theme park explains how they did this:

66 *Sales of some of our attractions were slumping so we used a questionnaire to find out why. The main reason was that people were becoming bored of them and wanted something new. So we invested in two new attractions that we added to our range. As a result, we kept our existing customers and attracted new ones which had the added benefit of a new source of interest in our existing attractions.* **99**

Growth through market share

Market share is the percentage of customers in a market who choose your products and services. There are two ways an organisation can increase its market share:

■ by attracting customers away from competing organisations

■ by picking up customers from organisations who have moved out of the market.

The marketing director of a council-funded sports centre explains how they increased their share of the local leisure and recreation market:

66 *With the increasing popularity of fitness as a recreational activity, our centre was in danger of losing its customers to two new private-sector fitness centres in the area. We identified that we had a market advantage because our public funding meant that we could offer low membership and concessionary fees. So we promoted that aspect heavily. As a result, our membership has gone up and our share of the local market has increased from 28% to 35%.* **99**

Ansoff's matrix

Ansoff's matrix was developed by Igor Ansoff. It is a tool for identifying ways an organisation can grow through increasing sales. The options are:

■ sell more existing products or services to existing customers (i.e. getting further into the market – market penetration)

■ sell existing products or services to new customers (ie expanding existing markets or getting into new ones – market development)

■ develop new products or services to sell to existing customers (product development)

■ develop new products or services to sell to new customers (developing new products for new markets – diversification)

Organisations can use Ansoff's matrix to ask:

■ Will existing customers continue to buy existing products?

■ Can the existing products attract new customers?

- Will new products appeal to existing customers?
- Will new products have to attract new customers?
- Can the existing and new products both be marketed to existing customers?
- Can the existing and new products both be market to new customers?
- Will any of the above strategies increase the market share?
- Can the existing products or services be sold by targeting a different group of customers?

Answers to these questions will help them to decide whether marketing activity should be customer-focused or product-orientated:

- If the market is saturated, i.e. no new business is being generated, they will need to consider new markets.
- If there is no scope for growth in new markets, they will need to focus on new products.

Product life-cycle

Most products and services have a limited life-span. There are many reasons for this, including changes in fashion and technology that can quickly make a product obsolete.

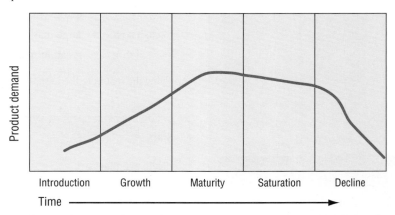

Products and services often go through a five-stage cycle, as shown in the graph.

Introduction	Low initial sales until product or service awareness develops
Growth	Steady, sometimes rapid, increase in sales as demand increases
Maturity	Sales continue to increase but at a slower rate, as the market for the product is fully targeted
Saturation	All customers needs and wants for the product are satisfied
Decline	Sales of product decline as the popularity of the product decreases.

The Boston matrix

The strategies adopted to promote them will vary according to which point in the life-cycle they have reached. A sportswear manufacturer comments:

> **❝** *We put a lot of promotion effort into a product as it is introduced, including things like special offers, promotional events and an advertising campaign.*
>
> *As the product matures, our aim is to maintain a high profile in the market and ensure that as many potential customers as possible are being reached through targeted direct mail or selective advertising, for example.*
>
> *As the product nears the end of its life-cycle, we cut down promotional activity and change focus, perhaps offering reduced prices or special terms to milk the last few sales out of the product.* **❞**

The Boston matrix

The Boston matrix is used to assess where products are within the product life-cycle.

Different types of products or services produce different levels of income for organisations. They are classified according to their position, in terms of relative market share and how quickly the market is growing:

star	=	high share in a growth market
problem child	=	a product in a growing market but with a low market share
cash cow	=	large market share in a mature market
dog	=	weak in market share or in a declining market.

Applying the matrix to the leisure and tourism industry might give you:

Stars	**Problem child**
Health and fitness	Virtual reality
Rollerblades	Holidays to Turkey
Theme parks	
Compact discs	
Cash cows	**Dogs**
Holidays to Benidorm	Vinyl discs
Traditional swimming pools	Roller skates
Cassette tapes	

◄─────── Market share ───────

Factors which influence pricing

Pricing products and services – deciding what price to sell them for – is an important part of marketing. If an organisation charges too much, people will buy competitors' cheaper products; if it charges too little, it won't make a profit.

So how do organisations decide what price to charge for their products and services?

Direct and indirect costs

When making pricing decisions, organisations have to consider the costs involved in making a product or delivering a service. This includes:

- direct costs – the costs of raw materials and labour
- indirect costs – overheads such as rent, rates, heating, light, and so on.

Some of these costs are fixed and others are variable:

- fixed costs do not vary, regardless of the number of items produced (e.g. rent and business rates)
- variable costs vary in direct proportion to the number of items produced. They may also be affected by other factors (e.g. changes in exchange rates may mean that the cost of holidays abroad rises or falls).

Organisations work out the overall cost of producing an item – the production cost – by adding up direct and indirect costs. They then decide on a selling price by adding a mark-up to the production cost.

Economies of scale

A large organisation would be able to produce goods and services at a lower price than a small business. This is because of economies of scale – the more items an organisation produces, the lower its costs for each unit become. And it's easier for a large organisation to produce large quantities.

Competition

Organisations may reduce the cost of products and services if they face direct competition from other companies. This is because they need to be competitive in order to keep their market share.

Multifit and Megafit are two leisure centres in the same town. Both offer similar facilities and are easy to get to on public transport.

Both used to charge £3 for an aerobics session. Then Megafit increased its charge by 50p a session with a major effect on sales. By the third week so many extra people were going to Multifit's classes that it was able to reduce its charge by 50p.

	Aerobics	Multifit	Megafit
Week 1	Cost per person	£3.00	£3.00
	Class size	20	20
	Number of classes	3	3
	Instructors	3	3
	Customers	45	45
	Income	£135	£135
Week 2	Cost per person	£3.00	£3.50
	Class size	20	20
	Number of classes	3	3
	Instructors	3	3
	Customers	50	40
	Income	£150	£140
Week 3	Cost per person	£2.50	£3.50
	Class size	20	20
	Number of classes	3	3
	Instructors	3	3
	Customers	60	30
	Income	£150	£105

Promotion

Promotion and pricing are very closely linked. If an organisation is going to promote a product or service through an expensive advertising campaign, it needs to consider this cost when setting the price.

Often pricing is actually part of promotion – an organisation promotes its product or service as the cheapest on the market or runs a special promotional campaign based on price-cutting. For example, many organisations run short-term campaigns aimed at increasing market share by temporarily reducing the price of a product or service. This may reduce profitability in the short term but increases it in the long term by attracting new customers who continue when the normal prices have been reestablished.

How do you perceive these products?

Customer perception and quality

It's essential to establish an image for a product or service. The aim is to strike a chord with customers – to make them think that a product or service is tailor-made for them.

The way organisations price and promote their products and services can affect customers' perceptions of quality, service, value for money, consistency and availability.

Some organisations create an up-market image for their product or service by charging high prices and using promotional terms which suggest quality:

Other organisations aim to sell at the cheapest price and imply that their product or service is of a more basic quality:

Public- and voluntary-sector support

When organisations depend on support from the public or voluntary sectors, the prices they charge for products or services may be influenced by several factors:

■ the amount of support received – some organisations may be fully funded, others only partially funded
■ whether the organisation must make a profit
■ conditions laid down by the supporting organisation.

> Westport City Council introduced a Leisure Card scheme for people living within the city boundaries who were students, disabled, senior citizens, low-waged or unemployed. It guaranteed to fund half-price tickets to certain facilities and venues for anybody with a card, regardless of the number of applicants. The aim was to increase access to local leisure services.

ACTIVITY

Collect a range of holiday brochures for destinations in different parts of the world:

- British coastal resorts
- Southern Spain
- Egypt
- Thailand.

For each destination, draw a graph showing how the price of the same holiday changes at different times of the year. When is 'high season' in each destination?

How do holiday firms try to attract people to destinations during the low season? What marketing strategies do they use?

DISCUSSION POINT

Look at the graph on page 139 showing a product life-cycle. Think of several different leisure and tourism products or services, including some that have now disappeared from the market. Discuss how prices changed during their life-cycles.

Legislation

All leisure and tourism organisations have to comply with different types of legislation; for example:

- health and safety
- food hygiene and safety
- public liability insurance
- consumer protection.

Complying with this legislation can be expensive and when new legislation is introduced organisations may have to increase prices to cover the cost of changes. For example, when strict, new regulations on spectator seating were introduced at football grounds, many clubs had to carry out major alterations to their grounds. To help cover the cost of this, they had to increase entrance fees.

Seasonality

Price and time of year are particularly closely linked in the leisure and tourism industry. A quick look at any holiday brochure shows that the same holiday varies enormously in price at different times of the year.

Position in the product life-cycle

Where a product is in its life-cycle can also affect its price. For example, a new product incorporating new technology or an unusual feature may be relatively expensive when it first appears – think of the price of CD players and Gameboys when they first appeared on the market. Alternatively, an organisation may deliberately reduce the price of a product or service early in its life-cycle to attract attention and establish its market position.

Pricing in profit-making organisations

Because profit is a key measure of business performance for profit-making organisations, their pricing strategies are often based on what will:

- recover costs in the shortest time
- generate the most profit over a reasonable timescale.

This doesn't mean they just go for big, fast profits. A modest profit over a longer period is usually better than a big, short-term profit. Profit-making organisations also need to take into consideration what their competitors are charging for similar products and services.

Pricing in not-for-profit organisations

Because not-for-profit organisations are subsidised by public money – either by the state or by voluntary donations – people expect to pay less or even nothing for the products and services they provide. Not-for-profit organisations tend to focus more on perceived benefits to customers and demonstrating that they are not wasting funds.

Private- and public-sector pricing influences

The managing director of a newly opened private-sector fitness centre explains their choice of pricing:

❝ *We looked at the competition in the surrounding area and decided that the lower cost end of the market was covered by facilities financed by the local council. So we decided to go for the 'exclusive' tag and target people with lots of money to spend. We promote ourselves as a select private-membership club. Membership fees are high but we do offer members up-market facilities like the members-only bar and restaurant, saunas, jacuzzis. People will pay more for what they perceive as a higher value of product or service* ❞

The marketing manager of a council-funded fitness centre explains their choice of pricing:

❝ *Our pricing structure is based on our aim to provide access to all. We do face competition from the private sector but we have the advantage of council funding which means we can keep our prices low. We also know exactly how much money we have to spend for the year and how much additional income we need to supplement the council funding. Our funding also allows us to offer discounts on subscription fees, concessionary rates and flexible payments like per class, per month or per quarter. We can't offer anything fancy but we have all the basics like showers and lockers.* ❞

ACTIVITY

Give examples of local marketing activities carried out by two leisure and tourism organisations in your area, one from the private sector and one from the public or voluntary sector. Make notes on the differences and similarities of their aims, approaches and target customers.

Investigating leisure and tourism organisations

Virgin is a group of companies owned by Richard Branson. He started as a sole trader and since then the business has grown into one of the world's leading leisure organisations with interests in entertainment, travel, catering, publishing and broadcasting.

Key features of Virgin's marketing activities.

- Most although not all Virgin products are branded.

- The product range of Virgin follows a reasonable logical sequence of diversification.

- The products are marketed both internally and externally (e.g. Virgin drinks are available on Virgin Airlines and in Virgin pubs).

- Virgin is a high-profile sponsor of national and community events and voluntary causes.

- The organisation has an effective public relations division which succeeds in placing Virgin or Richard Branson in the news.

- Virgin products are widely merchandised through special promotions at point-of-sale (T-shirts and baseball caps).

- The market segmentation of Virgin products is targeted primarily at teenagers and young professionals.

- Pricing is geared towards achieving mass-market penetration by undercutting the prices of Virgin's main competitors.

ACTIVITY

Using the case study above as a model, select two nationally known leisure and tourism organisations and write a short report on their marketing activities. Your report should identify their marketing activities, objectives and pricing policies and investigate how they achieved growth.

Key questions

1 What do you think is the most important element in marketing: the customer, the organisation or the product or service being offered?
2 Which elements make up the marketing mix? Why are they important?
3 In what ways does the status of an organisation (profit-making or not-for-profit) influence or determine the sort of marketing activities it undertakes? Give examples of each sort of organisation.
4 Why do organisations need to set marketing objectives?
5 What do you think would happen to an organisation which had several 'stars' but no 'cash cows'?
6 In what ways can an organisation grow through:
   – its products and services
   – its customers?
7 What do these factors mean and how do they each influence pricing decisions?
   – direct costs
   – indirect costs
   – economies of scale
   – competition
   – promotion
   – customer perception
   – quality (actual and perceived)
   – public- or voluntary-sector support
   – legislation
   – seasonality
   – stages in the product life-cycle.

Assignment

Write a brief report explaining:
■ the principles of marketing
■ what marketing activities are carried out in leisure and tourism organisations
■ their marketing objectives
■ the link between marketing and organisational growth
■ factors influencing pricing.

Pick one leisure and tourism organisation from the profit-making sector and one from the not-for-profit sector. Find out as much as you can about:
■ their marketing activities and objectives
■ how they have used the development of products and markets to help them grow
■ the factors they take into account in their pricing decisions.

Use your findings to create case studies to add to your report. The case studies should show how the theory of marketing is put into practice.

ELEMENT **3.2**

Marketing research in leisure and tourism

The starting point for most marketing is getting to know your customers. In a small business owners and staff can develop relationships with individual customers and get to know what they want. Some leisure and tourism organisations have customers coming from far afield, so it's not possible for staff to get to know them individually. But the organisations still have to find out what customers like and don't like. Marketing research helps organisations to get information like this and make use of it. Some information can only be got by interviewing a sample of customers or asking them to complete a questionnaire. Other information can be obtained from published sources like trade magazines.

66 *In the past we have carried out our own market research here for this property, and the organisation as a whole carries out market research across the country. We sometimes put together a questionnaire to see if there is a market for a particular event or to test customers' reactions to a new service or facility, such as extended opening hours for the restaurant at weekends.* 99

administrator of a heritage site

66 *We ask everyone who comes to us a set of questions: how they heard about us, whether the accommodation is as they expected from the description, whether there is anything we don't provide them with, what they'd expect for the sort of price they are paying, why they chose to stay at our property and what they particularly liked and disliked about their room. Then each year we analyse the information and use it to improve our service. We also use it to highlight certain features of the service in our publicity.* 99

owner of a guest-house

66 *Whenever a company hires a vehicle I try to get the name of the most suitable contact – for example, it could be the transport manager or the administrator. Then I arrange to go and see them so that I can sit down and spend time with them finding out their requirements.'*

car-rental manager

66 *Our target market is really everybody in the community. One of the ways we carry out marketing research is to develop a 'ticketing history' which alows us to see what has sold well and who likes coming to what. We have also distributed questionnaires to selected audiences to see what people thought ticket prices, whether they liked the shows we were offering and what they thought about the venue.* 99

press and publicity officer in an entertainments venue

66 *We carry out our market research in schools to find out what children like and want. Provision for children can actually be difficult to get right because what they want tends to change within the space of six months. It is clear that the media influences them – at the moment a lot of basketball is being shown on Sky TV and is very popular amongst the children.* 99

community play officer in a local authority

Objectives of marketing research

Organisations carry out marketing research to find out as much as they can about the customers they want to sell to. Through marketing research they identify:

- what markets exist
- the characteristics of potential markets
- market trends and changes
- opportunities for market and product development
- promotion opportunities and the effectiveness of promotions
- who their competitors are and what they are doing.

The information they gather helps them to make sure they're offering:

- the right product or service
- to the right people
- at the right price
- in the right place.

A marketing consultant made this comment on the importance of marketing research and the cost of not doing it:

66 *Some organisations think that market research is too costly. Their approach is to use their money to develop products or services they think are good ideas and then try to find customers who agree with them. If they can't find enough customers, they're not going to sell enough products or services to be profitable or even to cover their costs. And nothing is as expensive as making a product or providing a service that nobody wants to buy.* 99

Identifying markets

The marketing manager of a multipurpose venue explains why she sees identifying markets as one of the most important objectives of marketing research:

66 *It tells you who your customers are now and who may become customers in the future. We do a lot of research by asking people that use the venue what they do and don't like about it. We also try to find out why some groups of people don't come here often. It helps us to improve our existing services and think of ways of reaching new customers.*

By carrying out this sort of research we are able to remain competitive by making sure that our existing customers are getting what they want and by attracting new ones. 99

Identifying the characteristics of markets

Once an organisation has worked out who its customers are (its market), it needs to find out the characteristics of these customers.

The organisation can then use this information to make sure its products and services match what the customers want.

Characteristics of a market

- what customers want
- what customers need
- what customers prefer
- how, where and when they buy products and services

Recent trends in leisure and tourism

- Leisure complexes offering a range of recreational, leisure and sports activities
- Multiscreen cinema complexes
- Fun exercise activities like aerobics and dancercise
- Home-exercise equipment
- Themed amusement parks
- Working museums

DISCUSSION POINT

Think of some new activities, products or services in the leisure and tourism industry. How many of them would you describe as trends and how many as passing crazes?

The manager of a leisure centre explains why the centre decided to change its timetable:

66 *There's a large number of serious swimmers who want to do lane swimming before they start their day, so we have introduced a lane session from 7.00 a.m.–8.00 a.m. each weekday morning. There is also a growing number of retired people who regularly make use of the centre. We now hold special sessions just for them – in the pool, keep-fit classes, badminton, etc. – which they prefer to general public sessions.* 99

Identifying trends

A trend is a noticeable pattern in tastes or activities. They can modify or completely change demand and the nature of the market. Marketing research can pick up on trends and make use of them. Some trends work in a market's favour and some work against it. There are two tricky bits to trend-spotting for marketing research analysts:

- deciding whether they've picked up on a trend or just a passing fad
- deciding if the trend is one the organisation should follow or not.

Identifying changes in markets

Markets change constantly as a result of:

- new competition
- new ways of selling products
- changes in environmental factors
- changes in trends
- changes in customers' tastes.

Organisations need to find out why their business may change so that they can take action in time. For example, a television advertisement by one company can have a major short-term effect on other companies selling the same type of product. Or the closure of a large factory in the area may have a long-term effect on business, as people can afford to spend less – they have less spending power.

DISCUSSION POINT

In the two situations just described, what threats are there to the organisation? How could you turn these threats into opportunities? Think of different ways of responding positively to changes in the market.

Identifying opportunities for market and product development

Marketing research helps organisations:

- decide which existing markets to develop
- identify new markets it can reach

How could an organisation use marketing research to assess the effectiveness of these promotional activities?

- decide which existing products to change, repackage and relaunch
- identify new products to replace those which are falling in popularity.

The owner of a Mexican restaurant explains how marketing research helped ensure the successful relaunch of his restaurant:

66 *I asked all the staff to find out from our customers what they liked most and least. Everyone loved the food – I supervise the kitchen myself. But they told us the restaurant looked a bit scruffy, the walls needed repainting, the tiles on the floor were cracked and we weren't providing the right atmosphere. So we redecorated it completely, gave the place a new style with new decor and live music at the weekends, and now we are almost too busy!* 99

Assessing the effectiveness of promotion

Marketing research can help organisations work out how best to promote a product or service. Promotional activities can be very expensive (for example, television advertising) and organisations need to know that they are using their money wisely. Promotion is a waste of money if it doesn't bring in any more sales.

Assessing the competition

All leisure and tourism organisations face competition from other companies offering similar products and services. One of the objectives of marketing research is to keep a close eye on this competition. If an organisation knows what the competition is doing, it can plan what to do in order to prevent its own sales dropping.

Marketing research into competition looks at how other organisations:
- are set up (equipment, staff, facilities)
- perform
- plan ahead and market themselves
- offer something new to customers.

When a new leisure centre opened in Marston the existing centre, which had been open for a long time, was worried that it might lose some of its customers. It immediately carried out research to find out what would tempt customers over to the new centre, and made the following list:
- large, free carpark (compared to the old centre's small carpark)
- lower prices for some facilities (although prices were higher for others)
- a wider range of family membership and discount offers
- more up-to-date equipment.

Based on this research, the old centre planned a promotional campaign, updated its equipment and reviewed its prices. It hoped this would be enough to keep its regular customers.

Section 3.2.2

Sources of secondary market research

Sources of marketing research data can be:

- primary sources – customers and service users themselves
- secondary sources – published data and information.

There are two main types of marketing research data collected from secondary sources:

- internal data – information collected from inside the organisation, such as visitor records
- external data – information collected from other organisations, such as national statistics on the number of foreign visitors coming to the UK.

Internal sources of secondary data

Most organisations working in leisure and tourism collect information about their customers and service users from:

- sales records
- occupancy/usage figures
- financial information
- the customers themselves.

This information may be collected by one department in an organisation and used by another. For example, the marketing department may use financial data collected by the accounts department. Because of this, people involved in marketing often have to work closely with other departments to collect and interpret information.

To be useful, data must be:

- relevant – to the subject area, to the research objectives, to the time period
- accessible – easy to get hold of, easy to understand, easy to share.

Sales records

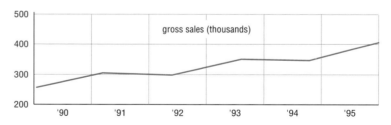

These are usually presented as a graph showing sales over a period of time. Leisure and tourism organisations use sales records as part of marketing research to spot trends and seasonal variations in sales.

Occupancy and usage figures

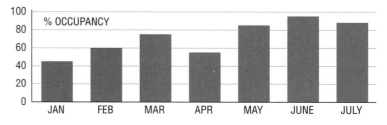

Hotels and leisure facilities such as sports centres use occupancy and usage figures as a source of secondary data. They use these figures to work out when they are likely to be busy and, more importantly, when they have space for more customers. Occupancy and usage figures are measured by 'time' and 'capacity'.

Financial information

Leisure and tourism organisations use financial data in secondary marketing research to find out:

- overall sales
- growth or fall in sales of particular products and services
- the profitability of different products and services.

Customer databases

Customer databases are made up of information collected in many different ways. For example, customers may fill in membership application forms or complete booking forms for events or holidays or they may supply information in surveys. This information is then stored in a database; organisations can use this database to find out marketing research data such as where customers live, their age, sex, income and preferred activities (what, when, where and how often).

ACTIVITY

All information stored on computerised databases is covered by the Data Protection Act 1984. Use your local reference library or college library to find out about this Act and make notes on its effects.

If you prefer to pay by cheque, please put your Booking Reference Number on the back to ensure it is correctly attributed to your holiday and ensure it is fully completed before posting.

Data Protection: 'Summerside Holidays' may forward your name and address to other reputable companies whose products and services may be of interest to you. Please tick here if you do not wish to receive information from these companies. ☐

I am over 18 years of age, I have read the Booking Conditions and agree to be bound by them.

Signed _____   Date _____

External sources of secondary data

To get a clear picture of what is happening in the marketplace as a whole, organisations use data from external sources, as well as internal data.

153

Government publications

The government publishes a wide range of data which can help leisure and tourism organisations decide how to meet their customers' needs and wants. This data is collected from many different sources including:

- population census returns
- household surveys
- industry surveys
- information provided by government departments.

Useful government publications include:

- *Annual Abstract of Statistics*
- The *British Household Survey*
- The *Employment Gazette*
- *Social Trends*.

Professional organisations, trade journals and periodicals

There are a range of leisure and tourism associations – professional organisations – which play an important role in the industry. They provide information, promote training, and speak on behalf of the industry.

Useful trade journals and periodicals include:

- *Annals of Tourism Research*
- *Campaign*
- *Coaching Journal and Bus Review*
- *Countryside Commission News*
- *Floodlight*
- *Holiday Which?*
- *Insights*
- *Journal of Leisure Research*
- *Leisure Management*
- *Leisure Studies*
- *Marketing Week*
- *The Caterer*
- *The Travel Trade Gazette*.

 ABTA (Association of British Travel Agents) is a trade organisation which regulates the industry and operates on behalf of the customer and its member organisations, for example, travel agents and tour operators.

 ITT (Institute of Travel and Tourism) is a professional body which is concerned with maintaining and improving professional standards as well as training and education within the travel and tourism sector.

 ILAM (Institute of Leisure and Amenity Management) is a professional body which encourages professionalism through the endorsement and development of career paths and qualifications within the sports, leisure and recreation industries. Its particular focus is at management level.

They also produce and contribute to publications – trade journals and periodicals – which are an important source of secondary data for leisure and tourism organisations. These give information about new products, services, competition, trends and general developments in the industry.

National organisations

Government-funded organisations – such as the Sports Council, tourist boards, English Heritage and other national heritage bodies – also publish useful data about leisure and tourism markets. For example, the English Tourist Board publication *Insights* regularly includes statistical data on tourism, examples of good marketing, descriptions of new tourism products and services, and summaries of articles from other publications. This type of external secondary data is particularly useful to the tourist industry.

Commercial data

Some companies specialise in collecting information and passing it on to organisations to use for marketing research. These include cuttings services which collect articles and reports on the industry from national, regional and local newspapers.

ACTIVITY

Produce a short report listing and briefly describing the most popular leisure activities in the United Kingdom. Compare your findings with a period in the past, for example, ten years ago.

To do this, you will need to carry out secondary marketing research using publications available in either your school or college library or your local reference library.

Other external sources

- national, regional and local newspapers
- on-line databases, which provide statistical information using computer technology
- annual and financial
- opinion polls
- reference libraries

Primary marketing research methods

Organisations usually carry out primary marketing research by talking to the people who buy their products or services – the consumers. Primary marketing research gives organisations a clearer picture of their customers' needs, preferences, attitudes and feelings.

Leisure and tourism organisations use a range of different methods to collect primary data.

Sampling

Sampling is the process of selecting a small part of any leisure and tourism market and taking their views as representative of the whole. For example, a leisure centre manager who wanted to find out what customers thought about a new reception area used sampling:

66 *We'd been having complaints about the amount of time it took to book in, and long queues were forming at busy times. So we reorganised the whole area, separating out the booking facilities from general services. Customers were certainly going through faster but I wanted to know if they had any other problems. It would have been very time-consuming talking to every customer! So we simply decided to interview every twentieth person and hoped that the sample would reflect people's views generally.* 99

Opinion polls are a good example of large-scale sampling. The two largest organisations in the country producing opinion polls are Gallup and MORI. Both carry out polls for private companies, and also run opinion polls on public events such as general elections. Gallup and MORI interview thousands of different people and ask them questions about particular products and services.

Qualitative and quantitative research

Primary marketing research is either qualitative or quantitative.

- Qualitative marketing research looks in depth at consumers' feelings, desires and views. Organisations usually carry out qualitative research by asking customers to fill in a questionnaire or by interviewing them. It provides useful information on customers' needs, wants and attitudes.
- Quantitative marketing research is more formal and structured than qualitative research and the results can be measured as statistics. Organisations usually carry out quantitative research by watching and counting the number of customers behaving in a particular way and then producing statistical data from these numbers. For example, a football club would use quantitative research to find out how many spectators are at a football match.

Interviews

Interviews – with individuals and groups – are one of the most common ways to collect primary data. Marketing research interviewers ask two main types of questions:

- closed questions – these can either be answered 'yes' or 'no', or the interviewee can choose an answer from a list of options. Interviewers use closed questions to collect quantitative data.
- open questions – these allow customers to talk freely and express an opinion in their own words. Interviewers use open questions to collect qualitative data.

ACTIVITY

Design a questionnaire to use in a survey of a local leisure and tourism organisation. The survey can be about any aspect of the organisation.

Look at the guidelines for writing questionnaires first.

Surveys

Surveys – often involving questionnaires – are another way that leisure and tourism organisations find out customers' views on their products and services. Surveys may be carried out face-to-face, over the telephone, or in writing.

A marketing researcher who was asked to sample 100 customers at a museum to find out their views on a new exhibition hall explains his approach:

66 *The first question I asked was : 'Do you like the new exhibition hall?' Of the 100 customers, 63 said 'yes' and 37 said 'no'. This gave me the quantitative evidence that most customers liked the hall, but a significant proportion didn't. I then asked two further questions: 'What is it that you particularly like about the exhibition area?' and 'What do you particularly dislike?'*

These questions enabled customers to give an qualitative opinion about the design and layout of the facility. I found out that those who disliked the hall thought the lighting was too bright, so we reduced the brightness of the lighting by 10%. A month later I repeated the survey and 90% of those interviewed said that they liked the exhibition hall. 99

Observation

Carrying out marketing research by watching and counting people – observation – is useful if organisations need to collect data quickly, but don't need to know what customers think. For example, a travel agent might decide the best place to put a brochure rack by watching the way customers walk around the agency.

Experiments

Experimental trials – sometimes called market testing – are used to work out how successful new products might be.

In experimental trials, organisations ask customers a range of questions about a product or service, its packaging, price, and how it should be promoted. They then use these findings to work out how to promote the product or service.

Contact methods

Marketing researchers make contact with consumers in three main ways:

- by mail
- on the telephone
- face to face (personal contact).

Mail

Leisure and tourism organisations often use mailshots to carry out primary marketing research. This usually involves sending questionnaires either to a large number of households or to people in a particular socioeconomic, geographic or age group. It's a good way to gather quantitative information.

A large sports and leisure shop publishes a magazine which it mails free to all customers on its database. The shop collects the names, addresses and telephone numbers of customers when they buy products under guarantee.

The magazine contains some articles of general leisure interest and others about new products and services. After it has been sent out to customers, researchers telephones a sample of customers and ask them questions about the magazine. They then look closely at the data they collect and develop future marketing plans.

RELAY
THE FREE SPORTS AND LEISURE MAGAZINE

The more carefully organisations choose their targets, the more likely they are to get a response and to get relevant information.

The disadvantages of using mail methods are:

- it's a one-way flow of information, so if the response isn't clear you can't ask the person what they meant
- there's a lot of it about and people often regard mailshots as junk mail and put them straight in the bin.

To encourage people to fill in and return a mailshot, organisations often offer incentives, such as entering the names of people who reply in a prize draw or giving them a reduction on products and services.

As well as generating primary research data, mailshots can give organisations useful information about their customers. They can then store this in a database and use it for future mailshots and promotional activities.

Telephone

Telephones are useful for gathering quantitative and qualitative information. They can be used in a number of ways, for example:

- as a first method of contact (also known as cold calling) when marketing researchers pick a number of people and interview them over the phone
- as a follow-up method of contact when marketing researchers ask people who've taken part in a written questionnaire or responded to a mailshot to say if they'd be willing to take part in further research over the telephone
- as a follow-up to a sale or loss of sale to find out why the person has chosen to buy or not buy the product or service.

The advantages of using the phone are:

- it's direct
- it's personal contact
- it can't be thrown in the bin unanswered like a mailshot can
- it allows an immediate two-way flow of communication.

The disadvantages are:

- finding the right people to talk to and the right time to call them can be time-consuming
- people are sometimes guarded because they suspect you might be trying to sell them something
- it uses time from the person's working day
- callers need training to ensure they get the relevant information from what people say and to keep the conversation on track.

Personal contact

Although marketing researchers can usually collect very useful information if they speak to customers face to face, this is not always possible. Samples are often too large for everyone to be interviewed individually, and one-to-one surveys are time-consuming and expensive. Many leisure and tourism companies are now replacing personal contact with telephone research, and are exploring electronic methods such as e-mail.

How does market research contribute to marketing decisions?

Organisations don't carry out marketing research for the sake of it. They use its findings to make decisions about products, prices, place and promotion – the 'four Ps' of the marketing mix.

A sporting goods manufacturer was planning to introduce a new range of clothing in purple, green and blue and decided to carry out marketing research to find out customers' views.

Summary of primary marketing research

The clothing was displayed at 30 leisure centres around the country. Customers at the centres were asked their opinions on the design, range of colours and logo on the clothing. They were also invited to enter a prize draw to win a family holiday in Florida. More than 30,000 people entered the competition.

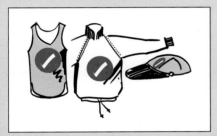

Key results

- 40% of competitors were from the C1/C2 socioeconomic grouping (office supervisors/skilled manual workers).
- Most competition entries came from leisure centres in the North.
- Most customers liked the design range but quite a lot of people disliked the purple colour.
- Ten per cent of people said that even though they were not regular sports players they would be prepared to wear the clothing as leisure-wear.

The range of children's wear was particularly popular.

Summary of secondary marketing research

- The most popular leisure wear carries a logo.
- The most popular leisure wear manufacturers spend a lot of money on sponsorship of professional sports players.
- Leisure wear stays fashionable for about eight months.
- Similar clothing produced by a competitor was selling in the shops for £60 per outfit (children's range £22).
- The busiest sales time for leisure clothing is in mid-July, just after the Wimbledon Tennis Championships.

As a result of the marketing research findings, the sporting goods company made the following decisions about the marketing mix for its new clothing.

Price

The adult's range of clothing should be priced at £58; the children's at £20.

Everything not sold in the January sales (if not sooner) should be sold off at a very reduced price.

Place

The range of clothes should go on sale in the men's and ladies' leisure wear departments of stores rather than in sports departments.

Product

As a result of its primary marketing research, the company decided to market the green and blue ranges only – the idea of a purple range was abandoned.

Promotion

The company decided to promote the children's range particularly strongly and to use children as much as possible in the advertising campaign. It targeted the Manchester area as a particularly good market and decided to run special promotions there.

DISCUSSION POINT

Why did the leisure wear manufacturer take these decisions? Based on the research findings, what else might you do to sell this range of leisure wear?

Undertaking market research

Carrying out marketing research needs careful thought and planning. Organisations work through five main steps to make sure all goes smoothly.

Steps in research

1 Decide what you hope to achieve and write it down clearly.

2 Decide the best ways to carry out your research, bearing in mind cost and time. Will you use primary or secondary research methods? Make sure that the methods you choose are likely to give you the information you need. Think in advance about problems you might face; for example, how long it will take, the money it will cost and the number of people you will need.

3 Carry out the research.

4 Collect information.

5 Work out what you have learnt from your research and use the information to decide your marketing mix.

Setting objectives

Organisations need to set both broad and specific marketing research objectives.

A company which manufactures rollerblades set the following broad and specific objectives.

Broad objective	Specific objective
To identify market trends (e.g. whether the market for rollerblades is growing)	To determine the growth in sales of rollerblades in Wales and north-west England in the last six months
To spot opportunities for products (e.g. rollerblades for the under-5s)	To find out what parents think about their young children wearing rollerblades. What are their top three worries?
To find out what the competition is doing (e.g. special offers on rollerblades in the run-up to Christmas)	To find out what were the top and lowest prices for rollerblades in all city stores in the six weeks before Christmas last year.
To evaluate how effective our promotion is	To find out how many more rollerblades we sold in the three months after a regional TV advertising campaign

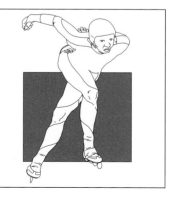

DISCUSSION POINT

Think of a project you carried out recently which involved research. What were the broad objectives of your research? What were your specific objectives? Do you think it would have helped you achieve your objectives if you had identified them clearly before starting your research?

Selecting suitable research methods

As you have already seen in this section, there are many different ways to carry out primary and secondary marketing research. Organisations need to ask themselves a range of questions in order to decide which research method to use in a particular situation.

Questions	Examples
How much will it cost to use this research method?	If a company is considering carrying out a detailed telephone survey, it needs to work out whether it will cost too much.
How much time will it take to use this research method?	If a company does decide to carry out a telephone survey, it needs to consider how much time it will need to carry out the interviews. Working with a short multiple-choice questionnaire would be quicker than working with a number of long answers.
How accessible is the method – how easy is it for people to understand?	If a company designs a questionnaire, it needs to assess how easy it is for respondents to fill in.
Will the results be valid (well-grounded and fair)?	If a company wants to carry out a survey of leisure facilities for young people in a town, it would be wrong to go to just one school. For results to be valid, it would need to go to several schools to see what a range of young people think.
Will the response, and the results, be reliable (consistent and accurate)?	If a company hands over a large number of questionnaires to respondents, how can it be sure that it will get any replies back? Or that the replies it gets will be honest?
Is the method fit for its purpose – is it suitable for the customers involved and will it produce the information needed?	If a company is dealing with people with learning difficulties, it can't give them a long written questionnaire. A short questionnaire with simple questions worded in plain English would be fit for the purpose.

Carrying out the research

Once an organisation has determined its marketing research objectives and the research methods to use, it can carry out the research.

Putting research into practice can be an expensive business – primary marketing research is usually more expensive than secondary research, because people have to be paid to collect the information. Secondary research is cheaper and quicker but may not produce the information an organisation needs. The owner of a small, local agency specialising in marketing research explains:

66 *There's no point advising clients to spend a lot of money on primary marketing research if the information they get isn't going to help them make at least twice as much money. We can give clients a lot of information from secondary sources – it's quicker if we do it because we know the sources and it's not an expensive service. If we do set up a survey for them, our policy is to do it quickly and in the most cost-effective way. For example, we recently sent a team of six researchers with a questionnaire into an airport mall for a day and got a mass of data which couldn't have been got in any other way.* 99

> **Collating information** means organising and presenting it in a form which makes it easier to understand.

Collating information

Once marketing researchers have got the information they need – from primary or secondary sources – it needs to be collated. Quantitative data is often collated in the form of charts, tables and graphs. Qualitative data is usually collated in written reports. It is a lot easier to collate information if it has been collected in a suitable form in the first place, as the owner of the marketing research agency explains:

❝ *People think that writing questionnaires is easy, but actually you have to think very carefully about the questions so you get the information in a form that's easy to analyse. If we're wanting mainly quantitative data, we try to ask closed questions with a 'yes' or 'no' answer or use a scoring system – for example, 'How good is the signposting in the airport on a scale of 1 to 5?'. Asking qualitative questions is harder, because you're trying to find out people's attitudes or feelings but you also want to collect as much precise data as you can. We are very experienced at collating this type of 'soft' data.* **❞**

Using the information

It's a waste of money collecting information that you can't use. For example, if you're selling rollerblades in Liverpool, information about the sale of rollerblades in Cornwall and Devon isn't much use. But if you know that sales in Manchester doubled in the last six months, you might use this information to double your order to the manufacturer.

A company manufacturing roller skates would be very interested to know about sales of rollerblades nationally. It might think seriously about launching its own rival product or running an advertising campaign encouraging people to buy skates rather than blades.

Using marketing research for product innovation

Before launching a new product or service, organisations need to be sure that there are customers to buy it. So they use marketing research techniques to test and analyse new product or service ideas and opportunities.

There are two main ways of creating a new product or service:
■ the organisation has an idea for a new product and service and uses marketing research to test people's response to the idea – this is product-led development
■ the organisation asks the customers what new products or services they would like and then creates a product or service to fit the customers' wants – this is market-led development

The aim of marketing research into possible product innovations is to find out if there's a sufficient number of potential customers to make it worth the development, production and launch costs of the new product or service.

Using marketing research for product modification

No organisation can afford to be complacent about its products and services. Markets change, people's tastes change, competitors move in. Keeping up to date with changes is an important and continuing aspect of marketing research. The information the research produces tells an organisation when it's time to update or modify their products and services so they keep up with what the market wants.

The sales director of a theme park explains how their marketing research activities contributed to product modification:

66 *Our figures showed a drop in interest in the log-ride – where people travel along a rapid water-course in hollowed-out logs. We conducted some on-the-spot interviews with customers who used the ride and customers who looked at it but moved on to other attractions. The general opinion was that you got too wet. So we did some tests and modified the logs to cut down the amount of spray thrown up as the logs went along.* 99

ACTIVITY

Choose a leisure and tourism organisation in your area which provides products or services aimed at your age group (for example, a cinema or a nightclub). Plan and carry out marketing research to identify opportunities for the organisation to develop new products to appeal to your age group. Make sure you cover the five steps described in this section:

■ set objectives

■ choose suitable research methods

■ carry out the research

■ collate the information

■ explain how the organisation could use the information.

Section 3.2.6   Presenting research findings

Organisations usually summarise and present marketing research findings in a report with figures and charts. The aim is to make data eye-catching, clear and interesting.

Presenting research findings

■ Decide on the best way to present the findings –usually in a report.

■ Think about who is going to read the report and what they want to do with the findings.

■ Think about the order in which the findings should be presented.

■ Write a summary of the research and how it was carried out.

■ Present any numerical data in graphs, charts or tables.

■ If there are a lot of figures, it may be a good idea to group them at the end of the report.

■ Summarise the research findings in a few sentences.

■ Suggest what the organisation should do next.

DISCUSSION POINT

How do you think the travel agency should present the information in its final report? Why?

A travel agency investigated the European destinations of business travellers and presented the results in a report.

They questioned 200 business travellers and found that 110 used Heathrow Airport, 47 used Gatwick Airport, 20 used Stansted, 15 used Luton and the rest used Eurotunnel.

They could present this information more clearly in a number of different ways:

As a table

Travelled from	Passengers
Heathrow	110
Gatwick	47
Stansted	20
Luton	15
Eurotunnel	8
Total	**200**

As a pie chart

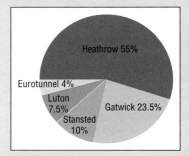

Bar chart

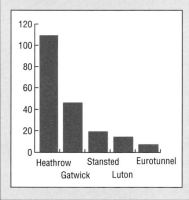

3D bar chart

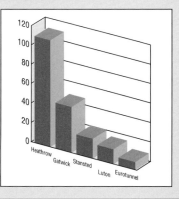

ACTIVITY

The organisation you focused on for the activity in section 3.2.5 (see page 163) has asked you to present your marketing research findings in a report. Decide the best way to present the information you have collected – consider using tables, pie charts, bar charts and 3D bar charts – and prepare a report. Include a brief explanation of why you have chosen to present your findings in this way.

Key questions

1   What does 'marketing research' mean?
2   What are the aims of the following marketing objectives and why they are important to an organisation?
    – identifying markets
    – identifying characteristics of markets
    – identifying trends
    – identifying changes in markets
    – assessing the effectiveness of promotions
    – assessing the competition.
3   What are the differences between primary and secondary sources of marketing research data? Give three examples of each type.
4   What information can you get from
    – quantitative research
    – qualitative research?
5   What do the following primary research methods involve? Give an advantage and a disadvantage for each:
    – sampling
    – interview
    – survey
    – observation
    – experiment.
6   If you were planning a market research project, which of the following contact methods would you use? What sort of information would you gather with each one?
    – by mail
    – by telephone
    – face to face
7   How important do you think marketing research is to marketing decisions? Explain your reasons.
8   What steps would you take if you were carrying out a marketing research project?
9   How would you use marketing research to decide whether or not to:
    – introduce a new product or service
    – introduce changes to an existing product or service?

Assignment

Part 1

Pick a leisure and tourism organisation you know or can find out about. Carry out a market research project to identify opportunities for product development the organisation could benefit from. Prepare a report on your findings to present to the organisation. As well as your findings, you'll need to include in your report details of how you conducted the research project.

Part 2

You work in the marketing department of a leisure and tourism organisation. Your manager is preparing a marketing handbook for the department staff and has asked you to help. She's asked you to prepare notes on:
■   the objectives of marketing research
■   sources for secondary marketing research (desk research)
■   primary marketing research methods (field research)
■   how information collected through marketing research is used to make decisions on marketing strategies and activities.

ELEMENT **3.3**

Marketing communications

Communication is at the heart of marketing leisure and tourism. Brochures, holiday catalogues, posters, TV adverts, travel programmes – they are all designed to get across a message about the value of travel and recreational activities. This element focuses on the different methods of communicating with potential customers, including advertising, public relations (PR) and special offers. You'll be looking at many examples of printed material and at the way people in leisure and tourism organisations communicate directly with their customers. You'll also assess how effective all these methods of communication are.

66 We do press and radio advertising. We also produce an A4, two-fold, colour leaflet which is used to promote the property and give visitors information about our events. We use a distribution company for some of our material and sometimes mail it out ourselves. We tend to target existing customers to try to ensure that they come back over and over again. We are also looking for new customers in the local area and tourists. 99

administrator of heritage site

66 In order to get admitted into one of the holiday brochures which features activity holidays you need to belong to some kind of association. I joined 'Ponies UK' because they are concerned with improving the standards on riding holidays. 99

owner of a riding school which also provides holidays

66 Our income is from two sources: competitors' entry fees and sponsorship. Sponsors provide the prizes and cover the fixed overheads that we have to pay. Our first sponsor was a family shoe shop. The race gave them a chance to advertise themselves to families and young people. 99

organiser of a regatta

66 It's essential to plan publicity so that we are communicating with customers when they are ready to book. For a May festival we aimed for the end of January. We did some research and found out that the longer the selling period for tickets the greater the box-office income. Once when we slipped with the publicity by a week and a half our income slipped too. There are definitely two distinct periods. You need to get the early birds and then those that like to make late decisions. So you need maximum exposure at these two times. 99

arts festival organiser

66 We have found that mailing lists are an excellent way of bringing people in to our concerts. So now we are building up our own database and we mail everyone on it every six months. This is definitely the most successful way of getting an audience. We have tried advertising but that isn't very successful. We've tried newspaper adverts and putting posters in music shops but it doesn't really work. The direct contact is much more effective. 99

leader of a band

Advertising

Advertising is the process of publicising a product or service. It is used to raise awareness, to inform, to attract inquiries, to generate or increase sales and to create an image.

DISCUSSION POINT

Which media do you think the following organisations are likely to use for advertising:

■ a new theme park expecting to attract people from all over the UK

■ a new children's play area for local people

■ a leisure wear company considering advertising a range of leisure wear which they realise is about to go out of fashion

■ a small public-sector organisation, such as a local sports centre

■ a large voluntary sector organisation, like the National Trust?

A successful advertisement must:

■ catch the attention of the public

■ keep the interest of the reader, viewer or listener

■ persuade the audience that they need or want the products or services advertised

■ make the audience take action.

Advertising is a powerful way to promote a product or service, but it can be expensive and most companies have to think carefully about what to advertise, when to do it and where to place advertisements.

The media used for advertising include newspapers, magazines, television, radio, posters, point-of-sale materials and brochures. Advertising in national newspapers, magazines and on television is much more expensive than advertising in the local media. If the market for a product or service is large, organisations will have more to spend on advertising. Some organisations use only one or two different media, either because that's all that their budget will stretch to or because they have analysed them as being the most effective way of advertising their products and services. Some organisations – usually the larger ones – will put together an advertising campaign which uses a range of media.

Newspaper advertising

There are three basic types of newspaper:

■ national press, which report national and international news and items of national interest

■ local press, which report mainly local news and items of local interest

■ specialised press, which report on particular areas of industry, commerce or special interest.

Every newspaper aims itself at a particular type of reader. Most people have a favourite national newspaper which they always buy because its news-reporting style, coverage and feature articles appeal to them. Local papers are designed to appeal to people in the areas they cover. Specialised papers are read by people with an interest in the special area the paper covers.

Advertising is a source of income for newspapers as advertisers have to pay for the space they want to use. To make it worth the money, advertisers have to decide carefully what type of person they want to appeal to and then advertise in the papers that type of person would read. Or they may advertise in a range of papers but change the style of the advert to fit in with the style of the paper and the type of reader.

Full time chef/cook required for our modern but busy kitchen, serving top quality bar meals. Must be enthusiastic and hard working.
Own transport essential.
Apply to Clare or Jo,
The White Horse, Eastford,
01842 331986

ACTIVITY

Make a collection of classified and display advertisements from national, regional and local newspapers that have been placed by leisure and tourism organisations to promote products or services.

- Do they do what is listed above – catch attention, keep interest, persuade and stimulate action?

- What links can you see between the types of products and services being advertised and the people likely to read the newspapers?

- Find out the cost of placing a classified advertisement and a display advertisement in your local newspaper.

ACTIVITY HOLIDAYS IN SNOWDONIA
Feel the trill of floating on the wind – drift through the valleys and get a view that will never be equalled. Our fully qualified training staff will take you through all the safety procedures and techniques to enable you to *FLY* solo after one week.
Call FREEPHONE Activity Now!

Classified advertisements

Classified ads are usually very short and don't cost much to buy. They are used to sell products or promote services, but give little information about quality.

Loot, Exchange and Mart and *Daltons Weekly* are papers which just have advertising – they contain no news items.

Display advertisements

Display ads give much more information about the product or service being offered. They make use of logos and headlines to catch the eye.

Magazine advertising

Like newspapers, magazines and journals all have different kinds of readers. Some cover quite specialised subjects, while others are more general. Many magazines cover a particular leisure activity, and these are important places for suppliers of products or services to advertise. For example, a magazine on angling would be a good place for a supplier of fishing products to advertise.

DISCUSSION POINT

Collect examples of five national magazines. Make sure they are very varied, e.g. a TV listings magazine, a women's issues magazine, plus one or two on leisure activities. What sorts of advertisements appear in these magazines? Why have the advertisers chosen these magazines?

Television advertising

Advertising on television is a very effective way of reaching large numbers of people. But it's very costly – particularly at peak viewing times between 6.00 p.m. and 11.00 p.m. – so only very large organisations can afford to do it.

Radio advertising

There is an increasing number of commercial national and local radio stations. Radio advertising is cheaper than television but audiences are smaller.

Posters

Posters are a particularly important way of advertising local events, activities, venues or services. Where they are positioned is important, and they need to include photographs or drawings that will stay in the public's mind for a long time.

The manager of a small concert hall talks about how he uses posters to promote a concert:

66 *Sharp, attractive posters are very important for our concerts. We have a number of regular sites for posters: inside and outside the hall itself, but also in the local libraries, in selected shops (often music shops and bookshops), certain cafés and restaurants, noticeboards in nearby villages and schools. We also have a number of display cases in sites around the town. When we print posters, we usually have smaller versions printed as handbills which can be left in places where we think people interested in coming to our concerts will see them.* 99

Most towns and cities also have a number of large poster or billboard sites. These are often very expensive and are used mainly by national organisations.

Point-of-sale material

Think of the number of times you go into a record store not intending to buy a tape or CD but come out having bought several. The atmosphere of the shop might have made you buy something, but there are also all the posters, special promotions and special offers. These are all materials which promote products at the point-of-sale.

Point-of-sale materials are aimed at the impulse buyer – the sort of person who sees something and buys it straight away, even though they hadn't thought of buying it before going into the shop. Some people take longer to make their minds up, but even they may be persuaded to buy something when there is a special discount, bright packaging or a leaflet packed with useful information.

Brochures

Brochures aren't designed for the impulse buyer, but for customers who have already decided they might buy something but need more information before

buying. Holiday brochures, for example, promote a particular country, region, resort or activity – and use words and pictures to persuade the customer to buy.

The brochure is particularly useful for promoting services: a holiday is not like a piece of leisure wear – it cannot be bought off the shelf, taken home, tried on and returned if unsuitable.

ACTIVITY

Visit a local tourist information centre, your local library and some local leisure and tourism facilities. Collect any handbills, leaflets and brochures they have on leisure and tourism products and services. Pick out the two you like best and the two you like least and make notes on what you like and dislike about them.

Regulatory standards for advertising

The Advertising Standards Authority is the regulatory body for these advertising media:

- advertisements in newpapers, magazines,brochures, leaflets, circulars, mailings, catalogues and other printed publications, facsimile transmissions, posters and aerial announcements
- cinema and video commercials
- advertisements in non-electronic media such as computer games
- viewdata services
- mailing lists except for business-to-business
- sales promotions
- advertisement promotions
- advertisements and promotions covered by the Cigarette Code.

All advertisers using these media have to abide by the rules set out in the British Codes of Advertising and Sales Promotion. The key principles of the advertisements should be:

- legal, honest, decent and truthful
- prepared with a sense of responsibility to consumers and to society
- within the generally accepted principles of fair competition in business.

Adverts appearing on television and cable are regulated by the Independent Television Commission (ITC). Its guidelines are called The Code of Advertising Standards and Practices. As well as placing a ban on using television to advertise certain products – such as cigarettes – the ITC also have strict rules about advertising aimed at children and adverts using child actors or models.

Advertising on radio is regulated by the Radio Authority.

Public relations

Examples of public relations activities

- sending out press releases
- building relationships with sponsors
- lobbying
- developing community relations
- promoting corporate communications

Press releases can cover a wide range of subjects, including the announcement of:

- a new person taken on to work for the organisation
- another company taking over the organisation
- the launch of a new product or service
- a large new contract being given to a company
- forthcoming events and activities.

ACTIVITY

Imagine you work for a local tourism or leisure organisation. Write a press release giving information about an important event or activity which you are organising. Use your imagination to think of an interesting event to publicise. Make your press release punchy, but include all the information people will need. Remember to add details such as a contact name and phone number.

Public relations (PR) is now an important part of the marketing of leisure and tourism organisations. It is a way of making sure that the public hears or reads about what an organisation is doing.

Larger organisations either employ their own PR officers or press officers, or bring in consultants to work on particular campaigns.

Press releases

Organisations use press releases to make sure their events and activities are covered in newspapers and magazines and on radio and TV. Press releases are a good way for organisations to promote themselves because, if successful, they result in free publicity.

A press release is usually sent out several days before an event or activity. This gives journalists time to plan how and when to cover the story. Ideally, a press release should contain enough information for a journalist to write an article without having to attend the event or activity.

The owner of a drama centre talks about the press releases he writes:

66 *We take great care over press releases for new shows because we know that extracts from them may appear in the papers exactly as we wrote them, especially if the reviewers are too busy to come. This amounts to us writing our own previews or reviews! Brilliant!* 99

PRESS RELEASE　　　**PRESS RELEASE**　　　**PRESS RELEASE**

from MEGATOURS

Date:　29 September 1995

Time: 12h00

<u>Embargo until 06 October 1995</u>

Megatours to take delivery of new cruise ship 'Caribbean Sunrise'

Directors of Megatours will take delivery of a new cruise ship on Thursday 6 October. The ship will be named 'Caribbean Sunrise'.

This is a luxury 300-cabin cruise ship which will sail between Miami and Kingston (Jamaica) and will make its first trip in March 1996.

As part of its expansion programme, the company has appointed the advertising agency Brown, Patel and O'Reilly to manage a £2 million advertising campaign.

For further information please contact Sajel Makwana, Press Officer.

Telephone:　(0159) 111111

Fax:　(0159) 111112

An **embargo** on a press release means that journalists cannot use the information until the date given.

Sponsorship

Organisations involved in sponsorship offer support – money, staff, facilities or equipment – to commercial or community activities. In doing this, they hope to attract people's attention and create a good public image for the company. Sponsorship doesn't necessarily make a direct contribution to profits.

In the leisure and tourism industry there are examples of:

- leisure and tourism organisations benefiting from the sponsorship of other organisations
- leisure and tourism organisations themselves sponsoring other activities.

The manager of a sports centre talks about this two-way sponsorship:

66 *We have a very good relationship with a local producer of bottled mineral water and other soft drinks. They have sponsored a number of events at the centre, including open days and competitions. In return we have sponsored them in other ways, by offering our facilities and staff at reduced rates for their events. We find it's a very profitable relationship – we work together very well, with our shared interest in health and well-being.* 99

Examples of different sponsorship activity:

- providing a minibus for a local community organisation
- paying for the printing of publicity material for a charity event
- providing staff for a fundraising event
- running a special event for a charity
- donating products for fundraisers to use as prizes in a competition.

Sponsors normally expect their name and logo to appear in any publicity material so that the public knows that it has given support.

Examples of sponsorship:

- McDonald's provides litter bins in town centres.
- Virgin sponsors the 'Tidy Britain' Campaign.
- BT sponsors an annual Swimathon.
- National Westminster Bank sponsors a national cricket knockout tournament.

Lobbying

Lobby groups represent particular interests. Charities lobby on behalf of their social or welfare interests. Businesses lobby on behalf of their commercial interests. Lobby groups have a range of aims – for example, more funding from government, a change of law or policy at national or local level, more public awareness. Sometimes, different lobby groups share a general interest or concern but more often they conflict with one another.

Lobbying is campaigning to influence politicians to take action.

ACTIVITY

Visit some local leisure and tourism outlets and facilities. Make a note of an examples you see of sponsorship. For example, posters for theatre and sports events will carry logos and brief details of any sponsor.

Lobbying activities

- The Ramblers' Association lobbies local and national government to persuade them to protect access to footpaths and common rights of way.

- National trade organisations lobby central government on behalf of the travel industry. For example, ABTA would lobby on such things as VAT on travel products, European directives that affect UK legislation on the sale of package holidays or any other matter that affects the industry nationally or internationally.

DISCUSSION POINT

If you were the public relations officer for a sports centre in your area, how would you ensure your organisation had good community relations?

Community relations

Most organisations like to support the local community. Local people are more likely to buy goods or services from an organisation which has a positive image in the community. Community relations are particularly important for an organisation which depends on the local community for its staff and trade.

Corporate communications

Large organisations use corporate communications as a type of PR for their staff. The aim is to provide information, bring everybody closer together and to create a good working atmosphere. Many produce 'in-house' magazines or newsletters which give news about the company and its activities, employees – who has joined the company, who has retired, who has had a baby, and so on – and how well products and services are selling. Some use specialist PR organisations to advise on or produce corporate brochures and magazines.

ACTIVITY

Collect some examples of in-house magazines or newletters produced by organisations in the leisure and tourism industry. What type of information do they contain? What messages do you think the company is trying to pass on to its staff? How well do you think they work as a public relations tool?

Sales promotion

Sales promotion is an important part of the marketing mix. Leisure and tourism organisations target sales promotions at consumers (the general public) and at trade (other companies). In both cases, the aim is to:

■ raise awareness of new products or services so they start to sell well

■ remind people of existing products and services so that they go on to sell even better.

Consumer promotions

Trundle Sportswear
Free Gift!

All you have to do to qualify for your free gift is to place your order within the next ten days. Order from our exclusive range of mix and max fashion sportswear to receive your free gift from the choices below. Just detach the sticker with your choice of gift, moisten, and stick to your reply-paid envelope enclosing your order. All orders that reach us within the next ten days will receive their free gift. Order now! Don't miss out!
Trundle Sportswear – First for fashion and quality.
Trundle Beach Towel   Trundle Sweat Bands
Trundle Sweatshirt   Trundle Kit Bag
Trundle Weight Scales

TASTON GARDENS OPEN WEEK
Taston Gardens are pleased to announce ▢▢▢▢▢ ng from the ▢▢▢▢ this year. Free ▢▢ f the Tastonian ▢▢▢▢ Prices for non-▢▢▢▢▢
Children £1.00
Everyone coming to see the gardens will be given a free packet of seeds for the newly bred and named Taston Poppy! All are welcome.

Visit Cambridgeshire's Wildlife Breeding Centre and discover a delightful zoo in a beautiful garden setting covering 16 acres. See a wealth of rare creatures from snakes and tarantula spiders to giant tortoises, tapirs, zebras, snow leopards, tigers and much more.
There's something for all the family here!
Linton Zoo, Hadstock Road, Linton, Cambs. CB1 6NT. Tel: 01223 891308
A B C D E
Not to be used in conjunction with any other offer or on Bank Holiday weekends
Valid at Linton Zoo only

(see page 69)

Sales promotions to consumers – the general public – include:

■ **samples**, which may be given away in magazines, sent through the post, or be on display at point-of-sale (see page 69)

■ **coupons**, which offer customers money off their next purchase, and may be
  – printed in newspapers and magazines
  – sent through the post
  – promoted at point-of-sale
  – included on packaging

  coupons can usually only be used for a limited period of time

■ **competitions**, which customers can only enter if they buy a product or service – many competitions include a tie-breaker, which asks people to think up a slogan; the company can then use this in future advertising campaigns

■ **special offers**, which are used to introduce new or improved products and services. A special offer will either offer more of the product (possibly for less money) or an extra service

■ **gifts**, which are usually offered at point-of-sale or on mail order, and may be free or at a specially reduced price. Customers usually have to prove they have bought the item before they receive the gift. Sometimes the gifts are themselves promotional material, e.g. sweatshirts, tea-towels or baseball caps with the company's name or logo on

■ **loyalty incentives**, which are offered to customers who can show that they use a product or service regularly. They are then given a discount so that they continue to buy the product or service.

Trade promotions

Similar promotional activities are directed at customers within the trade. Organisations use trade promotions to provide incentives for trade customers to use products or services or to encourage them to sell its goods:

- **discounts**, which are sometimes given to trade customers buying goods before, or at the time of, a special promotion. If an organisation is aiming a sales promotion at consumers, it may need to encourage the trade to buy in more stock so that there is enough for people to buy. In this case, the trade customers are usually offered a discount, which in turn encourages them to recommend the product to customers

- **allowances**, which are sometimes given on trade sales: some further purchases might be free if a high enough level of sales is achieved.

- **free products**, which may be given to trade customers when a new product is being launched

- **free gifts**, which may either be given to promote a brand name (e.g. travel bags or clothing), or may be offered if a shop sells more than expected

- **trade exhibitions**, which let organisations in the trade see what new products or services are available. They are useful for seeing what competitors are offering and picking up sales leads. They also give organisations a chance to demonstrate products and services and get feedback from potential customers . Large annual events involving hundreds of exhibitors are held at venues such as the National Exhibition Centre in Birmingham or the Earl's Court Exhibition Centre in London

- **educational visits** (also known as familiarisation trips), which are often used as a sales promotion by companies in the travel industry. Tour operators (like Thomson and Travelscene) offer free or cut-price holidays and visits to travel agency staff. As well as giving the staff a chance to go on the holiday or trip, the educational visit may include sales training.

Direct marketing communications

Organisations use direct marketing to sell directly to the general public rather than through shops or agents. The main advantage of direct marketing is that it can be cheaper; for example, a tour operator selling directly to the public will not have to pay commission to agents. However, they may have to spend a lot more on promotion in order to make the same number of sales.

Catalogues and brochures

Organisations use catalogues and brochures to describe and show pictures of their products and services. In this way, they are able to promote a complete range of products at a relatively low cost. Holiday brochures are one of the main costs or overheads for a tour operator. The large tour operators expect to sell one holiday for every twelve brochures they print – this is known as a conversion rate of 12:1.

The marketing executive of a small independent travel company explains their range of brochures and catalogues:

❝ *We produce a catalogue once a year which gives full details of our products and services along with prices and special offers. We send it out to all the customers on our database. We also produce a range of brochures to promote particular types of travel, holiday or destination. We target particular customer groups for these.* ❞

DISCUSSION POINT

Travel brochures need to catch customers' attention and stand out from the competition on the travel agency shelf. What makes you pick up a particular brochure? If you were producing a travel brochure, how would you make it stand out?

Direct mail

Promoting a product or service by post – direct mail – gives organisations an opportunity to target messages at a specific group of customers (for example, particular professions, geographical areas or age groups). Direct mail is now a very popular way to promote leisure and tourism products and services, and the number of promotional letters sent out to customers has increased dramatically over the years. Some organisations use direct mail as one of a range of promotional activities. Some use it as their only activity. Conversion rates (the number of sales produced from a mailshot) are low for direct mail but they can be increased by careful targeting. To keep people's interest, direct mail is often combined with other promotions such as special offers, prize draws and discounts.

A direct mail manager describes how she increased the conversion rates of enquiries to sales for direct mail promotions:

❝ *When I joined the company, their philosophy was the more people you mailed, the more likely you were to reach people who were interested. I had other ideas. My philosophy is 'If you don't want it, it's junk mail. If you do want it, it's information.' I wanted to concentrate on the people who did want to hear*

ACTIVITY

Imagine you are the marketing manager of a country hotel. To try to improve occupancy rates in the winter, you decide to run a direct mail campaign targeting customers who have stayed at the hotel before.

Design a one-page leaflet and write a direct mail letter to send to the hotel's customers. How will you catch their attention? Will you offer them incentives to keep them interested?

about us. I put a lot of work into analysing and updating our database and finding new markets for our product. It paid off – by carefully targeting the mailshots, the conversion rate of enquiries to sales increased from 25 enquiries to one sale to 14 to 1. 🟥

Telemarketing

Telemarketing is similar to direct mail but instead of sending information by post, the organisation uses the telephone to communicate with potential customers. Like direct mail, telemarketing works best if the calls are carefully targeted.

The telesales supervisor of an organisation specialising in sports and leisure clothes explains how they uses telemarketing to follow up sales campaigns:

🟥 *The sales team give the telemarketing team information on successful and unsuccessful sales leads and the telemarketers contact the people to ask them about their decisions to buy or not buy. The information we gather is useful for the sales team, who can concentrate on potential buyers. It's also useful for the marketing team. It helps them build up profiles of our likely customers and evaluate the success of their promotional activities.* 🟥

Media direct response promotions

Direct response promotions are carried out through the media – television, radio, newspapers and magazines – and also through direct mailing. As the name suggests, they aim to make people respond directly to the promotion by filling in a tear-off slip or order form or phoning or faxing an order.

Like advertising, the choice of media – TV, radio or publication – for a direct response campaign needs to be carefully considered and will depend on the target audience. These campaigns are normally run for a set period. The products or services are often available at a discount.

ACTIVITY

Direct marketing is meant to reach you the customer and encourage you to try or buy the goods and services on offer. In your experience, which sorts of direct marketing work and which don't? Collect examples of the different types of direct marketing described in this section. These could be media direct response in journals or newspapers, catalogues or brochures or a description of electronic shopping.

How successful do you think each one is? Does it reach its target audience and make an impact? Have you ever bought a leisure and tourism product as a result of direct marketing?

DISCUSSION POINT

Have you bought a product or service through direct response? If so, what benefits did you see in buying this way? If not, what put you off?

Electronic shopping

Electronic media – televisions and computers – are the marketplaces of the future. Customers can look through catalogues and price lists, and can even walk through realistic shopping centres which are shown on screen.

The technology for electronic shopping has only been developed recently. It started with Teletext-style promotions and now, with advances in microchip technology and telecommunications, can be linked either to a TV or a computer via a modem.

Suppliers of goods and services have to think carefully about how electronic shopping may affect their sales, and how to use the new technology to reach customers and promote services and products. But it is unlikely to be used widely until paying for goods or services is made easier and more reliable.

Personal selling

Personal selling is carried out through direct contact with the customer.

All leisure and tourism organisations do some personal selling, either to the trade or to the general public.

Product-orientated selling

In product-orientated personal selling, the technique is to persuade customers they want the product or service you have to sell. For example, a salesperson selling sportswear at a sports event aims to persuade people passing by that they need the product. This is a product-orientated approach.

Personal selling with a product orientation is used mainly for mass markets – goods which a lot of people will want to buy, such as food and drink.

Customer-orientated selling

In customer-orientated selling the technique is to find out what customers want then persuade them that your product or service fits their needs. For example, a travel agent tries to find out what type of holiday the customer has in mind, and then find a holiday that suits them.

Customer-orientated selling is used to sell goods or services to targeted people. Because it is expensive to target individuals in this way, the product or service being sold is often expensive, such as holidays or luxury goods.

Face-to-face sales

Most personal selling, whether product-orientated or customer-orientated, is carried out face to face. It is usually offered by trained sales staff – for example, travel agency desk staff. It is also carried out by people such as the receptionist at a leisure centre who talks to customers about facilities, classes and events and encourages people to use or attend them.

The managing director of a travel agency describes their view of selling:

66 *Selling is a responsibility of all staff here, not just the sales team. All staff are well-briefed on our products and services and they can all offer assistance to customers and find out what they want before passing them on to a relevant specialist sales team member. Picking holidays can be a big thing and the hard-sell approach wouldn't work with our customers. We like our customers to feel at ease and take their time over the choice so that they get it right and come back to us when they need their next holiday.* 99

Telesales

Personal selling may also be carried out over the phone. This can be either:
■ when a customer is contacted 'cold' by a representative of an organisation
■ when a customer contacts the organisation to talk about products or services they have seen advertised.

Many people think cold canvassing by phone is a nuisance and salespeople expect a low success rate. On the other hand, if a customer makes contact with an organisation, the telephone conversation can play an important part in helping them make up their mind whether or not to buy.

Evaluating and comparing marketing communications

Sections 3.3.1–5 look at the different ways in which leisure and tourism organisations communicate with their customers to market their products and services. With so many different ways to communicate, it is important for organisations to pick those which will work for their target customers – to choose the right 'communications mix'.

To evaluate the effectiveness of marketing communications, you need to know:
- the marketing objectives
- how to measure whether the objectives have been achieved
- who the targets were
- why the particular methods of communication were chosen
- details of the implementation plan (costs, timescales, resources).

Effectiveness can be measured by looking at:
- how many sales are made (volume of sales)
- how many customers buy from you again (repeat business)
- how many customers buy your products and services in preference to similar ones offered by your competitors (brand loyalty)
- how many customers buy from you because they trust your reputation (customer loyalty)
- how many new customers you attract (new business)
- how many people have heard of you (public awareness)
- what proportion of the total number of customers for a type of product or service buy from you (market share)
- whether the marketing activities kept within set budgets.

The sales and marketing departments in leisure and tourism organisations will evaluate the effectiveness of:
- all their promotional activities put together – for example, total promotional spending against total revenue raised through promotions
- individual promotional activities and projects – for example, expenditure on a single campaign and the revenue directly attributable to it.

ACTIVITY

Make a checklist of questions you would ask to evaluate the effectiveness of an organisation's marketing communications. Next, write a proposal for carrying out your evaluation which shows:

- how you would gather the information you needed
- who you would talk to at the organisation
- how you would present the information you gather.

Read through the following case study, which lists and describes the different ways one major airline communicates with its customers.

Marketing in action

British Airways is one of the world's largest and most profitable airlines. It uses a wide range of activities to make sure that it keeps its market share in the face of competition from other airlines:

- The airline advertises its products on television and radio, in the national press and on roadside billboards.

- British Airways Holidays is part of the tour operating division of the airline. It uses the British Airways logo as part of its brand image which features on the cover of its brochures.

- Most travel agents sell British Airways flights and large amounts of point-of-sale material are produced so that the public is aware of the services on offer.

- The airline has a large public relations division which promotes the company's corporate image to the media. As part of its activities, the airline sponsors national events, sporting personalities and charitable functions. It supports local community activities in areas which are affected by its flights and buildings.

- The public relations division also makes sure that any bad publicity is kept to a minimum. It lobbies individual politicians and the government to make sure that they are aware of how legislation may affect the company (e.g. airline fare increases, bans on night flights and noise legislation).

- Many thousands of employees receive regular information about the airline's activities through in-house magazines.

Sales promotion is an important part of its advertising and public relations activities. Air Miles is a subsidiary company of the airline, although it uses many different promotional techniques to support its sales activities. Within the travel industry itself, British Airways offers discounted travel and educational visits to travel trade employees. It attends most of the important travel trade fairs and offers free gifts and competitions to support its image (the same products are used in its point-of-sale promotions).

Most of the airline's sales promotions are carried out through the trade. Its direct marketing communications are therefore limited; however, the airline is now doing some research into ticketless sales via electronic shopping.

Personal selling is an important part of the marketing plan at British Airways. Sales representatives are employed to visit travel agents, other airlines and major business clients. The sales representative's job is not only to sell British Airways products, but also to provide sales support by getting in touch with other departments on the clients' behalf.

ACTIVITY

Produce a report on how two leisure and tourism organisations market their products and services. You can either choose:

■ large national organisations (use information from brochures, newspaper advertisements, and so on)

■ local organisations (interview people involved in marketing).

You should choose one organisation from the leisure industry and one from the tourism industry.

When producing your report, think about the following:

■ the objectives or purpose of each marketing activity

■ the marketing methods used

■ how well the activity works.

Important aspects to think about:

■ number of sales (or number of tickets sold, places booked, etc.)

■ repeat business: how many people come back to buy more, revisit, etc.

■ brand loyalty: do people buy the brand again because they think it is better than other brands?

■ customer loyalty: do people buy from the organisation rather than from another one selling similar products or services?

■ new business: are there many new customers?

■ public awareness: is the general public aware of the product or service?

■ increased market share: are more people buying the product or service? Are total sales high compared to other companies'?

■ keeping within budget: does the company spend too much on marketing, or does it spend as much as it planned?

How can you work out the answers to these questions? How can you work out whether a promotion is successful or not?

DISCUSSION POINT

Having read through the case study of British Airways, think about the following points:

■ Do you think British Airways uses suitable forms of marketing communications for its particular services and customer groups? Why?

■ What other forms of communication could the airline use to reach its customers?

Judging the effects of marketing

It is worth remembering that a change in sales may not be entirely down to promotional activity – sales may increase or decrease because of factors which have little or nothing to do with the organisation. For example, there is always an increase in the sale of tennis equipment and the use of tennis courts during and just after the Wimbledon Tennis Championships, and some brands of equipment are sponsors of leading players. Clearly, organisations offering tennis products and services do well because of Wimbledon, but they also have to work hard to make the most of the opportunity that the Championships provide.

In the same way, the number of holidays sold by a tour operator may not increase just because of a major advertising campaign – holidaymakers may choose where to go for other reasons. For example, the British holiday industry suffered after the bombing of Libya, the Chernobyl nuclear explosion and the Gulf war, as many American tourists decided that it was too dangerous to visit Europe.

Key questions

1 What things would you consider before choosing your advertising media?
2 What is meant by PR? Why is it so important to an organisation?
3 How can you encourage customers to respond to sales promotions?
4 What are the advantages and disadvantages of direct marketing communications?
5 What is the difference between product-orientated selling and customer-orientated selling?
6 How can you measure the success of promotional activities? Briefly describe what each of your examples involves.

Assignment

Pick two leisure and tourism organisations, one from the leisure and recreation sector and one from the travel and tourism sector. Find out as much as you can about:

■ what marketing communications are used by each organisation
■ why they use them
■ what they aim to achieve.

Write a report on your findings which describes marketing communications in the leisure and tourism industry. Use the organisations you've investigated as examples of how effective marketing communications are in practice. Make sure your report covers these different aspects of communication:

■ advertising
■ public relations
■ sales promotions
■ direct marketing
■ personal selling

ELEMENT 3.4

A marketing plan

In this element you'll look at how leisure and tourism organisations plan to market their products and services. They start by looking around them to see what their strengths and weaknesses are. Then they assess the opportunities in their particular markets and any threats from the competition, price wars and so on. After that they are ready to produce a marketing plan, showing how the marketing research will be done, what methods they will use to communicate with customers, the timescales and budget and how the success of the plan will be evaluated.

Organisational objectives

Leisure and tourism organisations usually have one or more of these three objectives:

- to succeed financially and make a profit
- to help the community by providing facilities and events for local people to use
- to develop their business and grow (this is often linked to making a profit).

The marketing plan is an important document in any organisation. It:

- summarises what the organisation aims to achieve by selling its products and services
- identifies and explains the marketing activities that will help achieve those aims.

The first step in developing a marketing plan is to identify the organisation's objectives. What it is trying to achieve in the long term will affect the type of marketing activities it carries out.

DISCUSSION POINT

What do you think would be the objectives (one or more) of these leisure and tourism organisations:

- an old people's club which runs activities in a local hall
- an out-of-town multiplex cinema
- a local authority leisure centre operating under competitive tendering
- a national hotel chain?

A marketing consultant explains how objectives affect an organisation's marketing activities:

66 *If the organisation's objective is to increase its profits, its marketing activities will focus on increasing sales by selling more to their existing market and finding new markets for its existing products and services. Its promotional activities will be directed at keeping its existing customers and attracting new customers.*

If an organisation's objective is to provide a community benefit, its marketing activities will focus on raising public awareness, encouraging people to make use of the products and services and encouraging funding bodies to provide financial support. Its promotional activities will be directed at publicising its activities, informing the public of the issues and highlighting the social or cultural benefits the products or services offer.

If an organisation's objective is growth, its marketing activities will focus on finding new markets for its existing products and services and creating new products and services that will get it into a new or different market. Its promotional activities will be directed at launching the organisation into new markets and launching new products and services.

Whatever the objectives, marketing activities will always include continuous market research to identify and anticipate the needs of the markets the organisation wants to be in. 99

ACTIVITY

Talk to the marketing manager of a local leisure and tourism facility about the organisation's objectives. How do they influence the marketing activities the organisation carries out? Does the organisation's marketing plan include a description of objectives?

The marketing environment

The second step in developing a marketing plan is to analyse the marketing environment in which the leisure and tourism organisation is operating. Where does it stand in the industry as a whole?

The results of a SWOT analysis show an organisation:

- strong areas to build on
- weak areas to overcome or eliminate
- opportunities to take advantage of
- threats to guard against or convert to an opportunity.

Most organisations analyse the marketing environment by carrying out a SWOT analysis of:

- Strengths – what the organisation is good at, the skills and expertise they have, successful business activities
- Weaknesses – where necessary skills and expertise are missing, unsuccessful business activities
- Opportunities – new markets, new needs in existing markets
- Threats – competitors, shrinking markets.

DISCUSSION POINT

Think of the section of the leisure and tourism industry that you'd most like to work in. What sort of opportunities and threats do you think exist for that section? What sort of strengths do you think are needed by organisations operating in that section of the industry?

ACTIVITY

A friend already runs one gym, and is thinking about opening another in a nearby town. She has asked you to analyse the marketing environment by carrying out a SWOT analysis. She gives you the following information:

- Membership of her existing gym has doubled in the past year and it's clear that fitness training is very popular with young people in particular.
- There is already one gym in the town. It is very busy and customers have complained that they have to queue to use equipment. It is located on the outskirts of town. Women have said that the facilities and classes for them are inadequate.
- There are still a couple of empty sites in a new shopping centre which has opened. One would convert well into a gym.
- A tennis club in the town is also building a gym complex for its members.
- Several new retirement homes are being built in the town and the area is developing a reputation as being for older people.

Use this information to carry out a SWOT analysis and recommend what your friend should do.

A dance studio prepared the following SWOT analysis of their marketing environment to look for ways to hold on to existing customers and find new ones:

- Strengths – a good team of fully qualified dance instructors

  dance classes are consistently popular and well-known forms of exercise

  school-age children make up a large and consistent segment of the market
- Weaknesses – dance is perceived as too technical and too demanding for some people

  dance is perceived as a girls-only activity
- Opportunities – an untapped market amongst older women and men of all ages
- Threats – competition from local fitness centres offering dance aerobics and other forms of dance-based exercise

On the basis of the SWOT, the owners of the studio decided on the following marketing objectives:

- to raise awareness of the benefits of dance
- to dispel the myth that dance was only for girls
- to increase the number of older and male customers.

They decided to run the following promotional activities:

- adverts in the local press
- posters in local schools, youth centres, the library
- dance displays in local schools.

All the promotional activities would present a fun image of dance. The press adverts would be used to send the message that dance can be enjoyed by all age groups and both sexes. The posters in the schools and youth centres would be aimed at young people. The poster in the library would be aimed at all age-groups.

Marketing objectives

Key marketing objectives of leisure and tourism organisations

- to analyse the needs of the market
- to satisfy customer requirements
- to manage the effects of change
- to manage the effects of competition
- to coordinate activities (relating to market information, customer requirements, competition, change)
- to maximise income
- to make a profit
- to improve people's lives
- to improve people's opinions of a product or service

The marketing objectives will tie in with the organisation's business objectives. An organisation needs to state its marketing objectives clearly in its marketing plan. It can then look back at the plan after carrying out activities and evaluate whether the objectives have been achieved, and whether they need to be changed.

Analysing market needs

To make sure it is producing the right products and services, at the right price and in the right place, an organisation has to know as much as possible about what the market is demanding. The information gathered from market analysis provides an organisation with criteria for assessing:

- how well it is meeting market needs
- new opportunities the market may offer.

Satisfying customer requirements

The marketing function isn't just about identifying needs. It's also about checking continuously that the products and services the organisation provides meet the customers' requirements and expectations. The marketing officer of a small cinema describes how they thought they'd provided what the customers wanted – but the customers thought otherwise:

66 *Our research showed that customers wanted the cinema to be seen as more than just a place to watch films. They wanted it to be more of a meeting place and a social venue. So we developed our snack bar into a licensed bar and offered a range of hot and cold meals. We thought we'd done well and we conducted customer surveys expecting they'd confirm what we thought. They didn't. Although the bar attracted new customers and the meals were popular, our cinema customers complained that the noise from the bar and the smell of the food was spoiling their enjoyment of the films. Additional sound-proofing and more effective extractor fans solved the problem. But if we'd just assumed our perception of the level of customer satisfaction was right without checking it, we'd have lost quite a few of our cinema customers.* 99

Managing the effects of change

All markets are subject to change. A key objective of marketing is to keep in close touch with their existing and potential markets. External factors like political, economic, social and technological changes must also be closely monitored. Keeping a continuous watch on all the likely causes of change enables an organisation to respond to and anticipate changes. It puts it in a stronger position for dealing with the effects of change and gives it a head start in developing its products and services to keep pace with the changes in customer demands.

DISCUSSION POINT

Think of a leisure and tourism organisation you know about. What sort of changes can you foresee in its markets? How might the organisation be affected and how might it respond positively to the changes?

Managing the effects of competition

All organisations need to keep a close eye on what their competitors are doing and evaluate the effects of their competitors' activities on the market. The fiercer the competition, the more effort an organisation has to put in to differentiate itself from its competitors. A key marketing strategy for differentiation is known as the unique selling proposition (USP). The organisation defines what is unique about its products and services that makes them more attractive and beneficial than those of its competitors. The managing director of a gym explains how they used their USP to hold on to their customers when a new competitor entered the market:

66 *Six months ago, a new gym opened in the town. Its membership fees were 10% cheaper than ours and it offered a wider range of exercise facilities. We saw that as a serious threat to our business. We couldn't afford to drop our fees without affecting the quality of the products and services we offered and, besides, we'd spent eight years building up the business to provide quality rather than quantity. That gave us our answer. In comparison with our new, cheaper and more diverse competitor, our USP was experience, quality and specialisation. So we focused on these aspects in our promotion and highlighted the additional benefits customers got from us – like the café and the crèche our higher prices enabled us to provide. It worked. We gained more customers than we lost.* 99

ACTIVITY

Collect some brochures and other promotional information from four or five organisations competing in the same leisure or tourism markets. What do they do to set themselves apart from each other and persuade customers to buy from them instead of their competitors? What would you say was the unique selling proposition of each organisation?

DISCUSSION POINT

Think about a swimming pool. How would these people contribute to its business success:

■ the promotions manager

■ the reception staff

■ the maintenance staff

■ the financial manager

■ the swimming instructors?

What would be the effect if any one of these people made a bad impression on a customer?

Coordinating activities

At the beginning of this unit, marketing was defined as 'the management process responsible for identifying, anticipating and satisfying customer requirements profitably' (Institute of Marketing). As this definition implies, marketing involves the whole organisation, from the directors who decide on the organisation's objectives to the staff who deliver the products and services to the customer. This means that everything an organisation does must be geared towards achieving its aims in a professional and effective way. Everybody in the organisation needs to have a clear idea of what the organisation is aiming to do and make sure their work contributes.

Maximising income

Maximising income is the result of carefully targeted spending. Everything an organisation does will cost them money so it needs to ensure that the money will be recouped from the income gained by selling its products and services.

A marketing consultant explains the principle:

> *It doesn't matter if you're generating a huge income or a modest one – it's being able to use it effectively that matters. It involves ensuring cost-effectiveness, planning and targeting spending and keeping within your budgets.*

Making a profit

To make a profit, an organisation needs to make sure its income is greater than its expenditure. The amount of profit an organisation wants to make will be part of its business plan. All its marketing activities will be directed at making the plan a reality.

Improving people's lives

In the 1960s, the American marketer Theodore Levitt stated that people don't buy drills, they buy holes. The hole is what they want, the drill is the thing that gives them what they want. So the benefit of buying the drill is that they can use it to make the holes they want. Effective marketing always promotes the benefits the product or service provides. This is particularly true of the leisure and tourism industry. For example, people don't buy holidays, they buy the benefits the holiday will give them – relaxation, a new experience, fun, adventure and so on.

Improving people's opinion of a product or service

All organisations work hard at presenting a positive image of themselves and their products and services. Marketing is the means for presenting an organisation's image, raising awareness of what it has to offer and encouraging customers to see the benefits they can gain by having the product or using the services.

ACTIVITY

Listed below are some typical leisure and tourism facilities. For each one, state the benefits its products or services offer the customer:

- a tour operator
- a theatre
- a swimming pool
- a ten-pin bowling alley
- a heritage site
- a nature reserve
- a theme park.

DISCUSSION POINT

Think of some well-known providers of leisure and tourism organisations. What sort of image do they present of themselves? What expectations would customers have?

ACTIVITY

A squash and badminton club is preparing its marketing plan for the year. The club is run by volunteers and its main aim is to provide facilities and events for the local community. However, it also needs to make enough money to cover its costs. The club's committee has carried out a SWOT analysis of the marketing environment, which identified the opening of a new leisure centre as a threat, but showed that the club still has plenty of strengths and opportunities to make the most of. The committee thinks it should investigate the possibility of offering new products and services to meet customer's needs.

What do you think the club's marketing objectives are? Look at the list above and write down those which you think the club should include in its marketing plan. Then suggest three ways you think the club could work towards achieving these objectives.

Marketing research methods

The fourth step in preparing a marketing plan is to decide which marketing research methods to use. As you found out in section 3.2, there are two main types of marketing research:

■ secondary research – which involves analysing published data and information about customers

■ primary research – which involves finding out about current and potential customers by observing and talking to them.

Secondary marketing research

When producing a marketing plan, organisations need to decide whether they are going to use:

■ internal secondary data sources – information collected from inside the organisation, such as visitor records

■ external secondary data sources – information collected from other organisations, such as national statistics.

The marketing manager of a theatre explains:

" *It's important to decide from the start what marketing research methods you're going to use, otherwise you tend to waste a lot of time. That's why we always state what research methods we're going to use in our marketing plan. Our latest plan concentrates on secondary marketing research using a combination of information provided by our box office on ticket sales, where customers live and our 'friends of the theatre' scheme; and data on national leisure trends published by leisure organisations. External data helps to give us the wider picture, while internal information gives us the current state of play.* **"**

Primary marketing research

A plan for carrying out primary marketing research might include:

■ qualitative research – looking in depth at customers' needs, wants and attitudes. This usually involves asking customers to fill in a questionnaire, or interviewing them

■ quantitative research – providing results which can be measured as statistics. This usually involves counting customers and watching the way they behave

■ interviews – with individuals or groups

■ surveys – face-to-face, over the telephone or in writing. These often involve questionnaires

■ observation – counting people and watching the way they behave

■ experiment – carrying out experimental trials by asking customers questions about a product or service, its price, packaging and so on.

The marketing plan should also say how the organisation is going to contact its customers to carry out primary marketing research. This may be:

■ by mail – using mailshots to send out questionnaires to a large group of people

■ by telephone – ringing up customers and asking them questions over the phone

■ personal contact – speaking to people face to face.

DISCUSSION POINT

Why do you think organisations might waste a lot of time if they didn't plan their marketing research activities carefully?

ACTIVITY

Imagine you are the marketing manager of an entertainments venue. You want to find out more about the needs of customers in the age range 16–21. Write a short section for the venue's marketing plan, explaining what primary marketing research methods you will use and how you will contact customers.

Marketing communication methods

**Marketing
communication methods**

- advertising
- public relations
- sales promotion
- personal selling
- direct

Communication is a vital part of successful marketing, and organisations need to say in their marketing plans how they intend to do it.

As you found out in section 3.3, leisure and tourism organisations use five main marketing communication methods.

A leisure and tourism organisation may decide to use any number of these communication methods as part of a marketing campaign. A large organisation with a lot of money to spend on marketing may run a coordinated campaign using all five; a small, local company with a limited budget may just run a sales promotion or concentrate on public relations. Whatever the organisation's size, their choice of method would be based on:

- the most effective ways of reaching their target audience
- the type of message they wanted to get across
- the organisation's image
- how much money they have to spend.

They would also ensure that:

- the methods were complementary
- the activities were coordinated in a way that strengthened the message
- they could cope with the predicted levels of response the activities generated.

The following extract is taken from the quarterly marketing plan of a national hotel chain. One of its main problems is under-occupancy in winter, and it is planning a campaign to counteract this by promoting winter breaks.

ACTIVITY

Choose two leisure and tourism organisations – one large, national organisation and one small, local organisation. Find out as much as you can about the marketing communication methods they use. Collect their marketing material and, if possible, interview people who work at the organisations about how they market their products and services.

Write a summary of the marketing communication methods used by each organisation, explaining why you think they use these methods.

Marketing communication methods

This is our major campaign for 1996, and we should try to get our message across to the public in as many ways as possible, including:

- *Advertising. We will place colour ads in style magazines, classified ads in broadsheet newspapers, and run a TV advertising campaign in early autumn. We will also update our winter breaks brochure*

- *Public relations. We will aim to get at least two features in national newspapers/magazines; plus coverage on a TV holiday programme. To create goodwill, we will organise special Santa Breaks for under-privileged children at selected hotels*

- *Sales promotion. We will offer three nights for the price of two during November, January and February. Guests will be able to enter a competition for a luxury week's summer break*

- *Personal selling. All reception staff will be briefed on the winter break offers, and encouraged to tell guests about what's on offer*

- *Direct communications. We will write to regular hotel guests, sending them a copy of the new winter breaks brochure and offering them a special rate if they book before the middle of October*

Implementing a marketing plan

ACTIVITY

Think of an objective you would like to achieve. Decide on your overall timescale and draw a chart to cover the number of weeks or days you've allowed. Now list all the activities you need to do to achieve your objective and give them start and end dates within your overall timescale. Fill them in on your chart. Now break the activities down into their component tasks, give them start and end dates, and draw them in on your chart.

Timescales

The timescales of a marketing plan state the whens. The plan should have:

- a start date and an end date for the plan as a whole – the overall timescale
- start dates and end dates for the individual activities within the overall timescale
- start and end dates for the individual tasks of each activity.

For example, an organisation whose objective is to increase sales over the year would plan a series of promotional activities throughout the year. Each promotional activity would have a start and an end date and each task involved in the activity would have start and end dates.

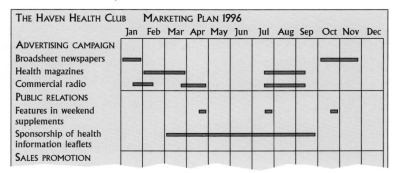

Costs

It's very important to estimate the costs of a project before the work begins. Like timescales, costs need to be worked out and allocated:

- overall
- for each activity
- for each task.

Sometimes organisations set a budget for implementing the marketing plan and choose activities that fit into the budget. Sometimes they work out what they would like to do, then estimate the costs, then decide if they have the money to do it or if they need to revise the plans.

Resources

Resources are things like equipment, space, information, materials and people. For example, a plan involving a direct mail campaign as part of a promotion for a new product would need:

- people to decide on the target customers, write the promotional literature, organise the design and print work
- access to information on customers
- office space and equipment
- mailing facilities
- paper for promotional literature
- envelopes
- telephones and faxes
- people to deal with the increase in customer enquiries and orders
- people to pack and send the product to customers
- sufficient supplies of the product to meet the predicted demand.

DISCUSSION POINT

What would be the effects of underestimating timescales, costs or resources?

191

Evaluating marketing

Evaluation tells you how successful you've been in achieving your objectives. It also gives you an opportunity to analyse what went well and what went less well, so that you know what to do and what not to do next time.

Evaluation techniques

There are two common evaluation techniques:

- comparison
- surveys.

Comparisons are useful when your objective can be measured by quantities, like increasing sales or bringing in new business. The important thing to do when making comparisons is to compare like with like. For example:

- sales figures for the month following the promotion with sales figures for the month preceding the promotion
- proportion of first-time buyers amongst all buyers.

Comparisons rely on the consistency and accuracy of record-keeping methods.

Surveys are also useful in collecting quantitative measures but they can also be used to get qualitative information – that is, information based on feelings, attitudes and perceptions rather than statistics. A survey would be a good way to evaluate how successful an organisation had been in activities to raise people's awareness, influence people's opinions or promote a cause.

It's often useful to use both techniques – for example, to compare current figures with past figures then use a survey to test the validity of any conclusions the figures suggest.

DISCUSSION POINT

Why is evaluation important? What does it achieve?

A **criterion** is a set standard (the plural form of criterion is criteria – one criterion, several criteria).

Evaluation criteria

To evaluate something, you need to have some way of measuring performance. Evaluation criteria provide those measures. The clearer the measures, the easier it is to show how well an activity has been performed. Evaluation criteria always relate to the objective and set the parameters for performance in specific terms of quantity or quality. For example, if your objective is to eat 40 biscuits in half an hour without leaving any mess, the criteria would be:

- the number of biscuits
- the timescale
- the tidiness of the area after you've eaten the biscuits.

The first two are quantitative criteria – they can be assessed by numerical measures. The third is a qualitative criterion – it can be assessed in terms of quality.

Common marketing criteria

- **Volume of sales** The number of sales achieved in a given period. Useful for judging if business has increased and for judging the success of promotional activities.

- **Repeat business** The number of customers who buy the product or service again. Useful for judging the hold on market share.

- **New business** The number of first-time buyers for a product or service. Useful for judging an increase in market share and growth.

- **Brand loyalty** The number of customers who choose the organisation's products or services in preference to similar ones produced by competitors. Useful for judging the hold on market share.

- **Customer loyalty** The number of people who buy from the organisation because they trust its reputation. Useful for judging perception of an organisation's image and the quality of products and services.

- **Public awareness** The level of recognition of or familiarity with an organisation's products, services, activities, name and image. Useful for judging market share and effectiveness of promotional activities.

- **Market share** The proportion of the total number of customers in a market who buy from the organisation. Useful for judging competitiveness and growth.

- **Keeping within the budget** Implementing the marketing plan within a set budget. Useful for judging staff performance, cost-effectiveness, marketing methods and processes and the levels of funding being allocated.

ACTIVITY

For each of the following, describe the evaluation criteria you would use. Say if your measures would be quantitative, qualitative or a combination of both. Explain why.

- a promotion aimed at increasing membership of a health and fitness club
- an advertising campaign using the national press and television to raise awareness of the benefits of keeping fit
- a launch of a new product to existing customers
- a strategy for attracting customers away from your competitors

Presenting a marketing plan

A marketing plan is a summary of all the different types of information covered in this section.

The following case study looks at one company's marketing plan, at a time when it was considering expanding its services.

Incoming Tourist Services is a small tour operator which specialises in organising guided coach tours for overseas visitors to Britain. During the first three years of operation it built up a reasonably large client base of American visitors and is now thinking of expanding into other markets.

1 Organisational objectives:

To grow at a rate of 15% a year, and make a return on investment of 30%

2 The marketing environment:

- Strengths – United Kingdom attracts a lot of overseas visitors thanks to its history and heritage.

- Weaknesses – it attracts mainly English-speaking people, particularly Americans.

- Opportunities – more people from the Far East (Japan, China, Indonesia) could be attracted to visit the UK.

- Threats – other European countries are now attracting visitors from other parts of the world.

3 Key marketing objectives:

- Look at the market needs of both existing and potential customers.

- Make sure that existing product meets needs of current market.

- Keep our product and service competitive.

- Maximise income by offering more services.

- Make a greater profit through increased sales.

- Promote quality rather than price.

4 Marketing research methods:

Secondary – British Tourist Authority statistics

– reports from tour managers

– British Incoming Tour Operators Association research

– briefing documents from Foreign Office for developing business in the Far East

Primary   – questionnaire survey of recent customers

– interview existing customers at end of tour

– experience a rival company's product by going on one of its tours

5 Marketing communication methods:

Advertising   – in Far East press

	– in airline 'in flight' magazines
	– produce small brochure in Japanese
Promotions	– travel bags and sweatshirts
Public relations	– develop links with Far East companies in the UK
	– sponsor restoration and conservation projects
Sales	– visit travel trade fairs in the Far East
	– employ local sales representatives
	– make contact with major Far East airlines.

6 Implementation:

■ Costs of marketing to be taken from existing budget.

■ Research to be carried out within next three months.

■ Campaign to run for six months (during winter period).

■ Use existing staff plus marketing consultant specialising in Far East markets.

7 Evaluation techniques:

■ Monitor sales figures for each year.

■ Compare statistics with those published by other tourist organisations.

■ Survey all customers.

Criteria for evaluation:

■ Maintaining or increasing number of US visitors.

■ Meeting target for new business from Far East.

■ Gaining repeat business from USA.

■ Marketing budget set and kept to.

The marketing director of the company explains the importance of the marketing plan:

❝ *The marketing plan details how we're going to achieve our business objectives. It's vital that it is based on thorough research of the markets and that all the resources needed for its implementation have been thought through. It's not a wish-list. It's a realistic plan of action and every member of the organisation will play a part in its success.* **❞**

ACTIVITY

Contact a leisure and tourism organisation and arrange to talk to someone involved in developing the marketing plan. Find out how they go about:

■ creating the plan

■ implementing the plan

■ evaluating the plan.

Key questions

1   How does a marketing plan relate to an organisation's objectives?
2   What are the main steps in developing a marketing plan.
3   Why is it important to have clear marketing objectives?
4   What is meant by:
    – primary marketing research
    – secondary marketing research?

Briefly explain the sort of information you would get from each type of research and the sources you would use.

5   What are the five main methods of marketing communications?
6   What would you take into consideration when choosing marketing communication methods for a promotional project?
7   What steps would you take to ensure that a marketing plan could be implemented successfully?
8   Why would you evaluate a marketing plan? What information would you expect to get from an evaluation and how would you use it?

Assignment

Prepare a marketing plan for one product or service in a leisure or tourism organisation of your choice.

The first step is to choose:

■   a leisure or tourism organisation for which you can prepare the plan – ideally, this should be an organisation that you know, but you can use a case study if it isn't possible to use a real organisation
■   a product or service – again, a real product or service would be ideal but you can make up a product for your plan, even if the organisation is real.

When you have chosen your organisation and product or service, start the marketing plan. To do this, you will need to collect information – about the organisation, the market, the product or service, the competition, etc. You should look closely at the following areas:

■   organisational objectives – what is the organisation aiming to do in general?
■   marketing environment – where does it stand in the industry?
■   key marketing objectives – what is it aiming to achieve through marketing?
■   marketing research methods – how should it carry out research?
■   marketing communication methods – what marketing activities should it carry out?
■   implementation – how will the plan be put into practice?
■   evaluation techniques and criteria – how will you judge whether the marketing plan is successful or not?

UNIT 4

Element 4.1
Financial performance

Element 4.2
Financial accounts

Element 4.3
Budgeting

Finance in the leisure and tourism industries

ELEMENT **4.1**

Financial performance

Any business, whether it is in the private, public or voluntary sector, has to cover its costs and make enough money to survive in the future. That's why it is important to keep track of how the organisation is doing financially. Making money isn't the only measure of success: many leisure and tourism organisations measure their success by the level of service they provide to the community or to visitors. But all leisure and tourism organisations work to a budget, have financial targets and need to assess their financial performance. In this element you'll be finding out how they do this and the reasons why monitoring financial performance is so important.

66 We sell souvenirs because it supplements the tourist information centre's budget. We also act as an agency, selling bus tickets for trips out, concert tickets and membership of organisations like the YHA, National Trust and English Heritage. We can sell almost anything as long as we can make 10% income on it! 99

manager of a tourist information centre

66 Very few swimming pools make a profit. We are one of the few that does, because the local authority pays us a fee to run the pool and we get an agreed percentage over and above that on our takings. To get the contract to run the pool we had to submit a tender suggesting how much we thought it would cost to do so and this gave us financial targets that we have to meet. Our teaching classes are now 60–85% full this term – which is excellent, as it means we are meeting targets. 99

development officer at a swimming pool

66 It's hard to define what my targets are because I started from nothing and we are now in our ninth year. One year we broke even, but on the whole we do better than that and make a small profit. My target is to have some decent money in the bank when I retire – I know that I have to make the organisations more efficient to end up with a real profit at the end of the year. 99

owner of an outdoor holiday centre

66 For us, running the guest-house is as much pleasure as business. We don't want to grow too much, so our financial target is to make as much as we can while staying below the level for VAT registration. That means we close during the week in winter for varying numbers of weeks each year, depending on how busy we have been in the summer. 99

owner of a guest-house

Reasons for monitoring financial performance

Sources of income could include:

- sales of products and services
- grants (for example, from local authorities)
- membership fees
- donations.

Expenditure could include:

- staff pay
- supplies and materials
- tax
- mortgage or rent.

Monitoring financial performance shows leisure and tourism organisations whether or not they are:

- staying solvent
- making a profit
- keeping cash flowing
- achieving their financial targets
- improving their financial performance
- keeping to budgets.

Monitoring financial performance means collecting information about, and watching carefully, the amount of money an organisation is earning, spending and saving.

Organisations monitor financial performance to answer two basic but crucial questions:

- do we have enough financial resources to do what we need to do?
- how effectively are we using our financial resources?

All organisations need to monitor their financial performance carefully, to make sure that their income (money coming in) is covering their expenditure (money going out).

In financial terms, if an organisation is performing:

well, it will probably:
- be making a profit
- have money in the bank

- be able to pay bills on time.

badly, it will probably:
- be making a loss
- owe money to the bank, and possibly other businesses
- have difficulty paying bills on time.

The financial manager of a travel agent explains why monitoring financial performance is important:

66 *Our business activities don't just happen. They're all part of a plan we've set out which defines what we are going to do, how we're going to do it and what we aim to achieve. As we put the plan into action, we need to check that we're following it and that it's working out in the way we predicted – that's the monitoring process. By checking what we do and the results against what we planned, we can identify any differences between the two. This gives us the information we need to decide on any adjustments to the plan or to our activities.* 99

Solvency

An organisation is **solvent** if it has the financial resources to cover its debts and costs.

A business adviser at a bank explains why monitoring solvency is important:

66 *An insolvent organisation is one that's going out of business. As all organisations want to stay in business, staying solvent is of immediate importance. Monitoring solvency levels is a continuous process for any organisation. To do it, they need to know:*

- *how much money they have*
- *how much money they have to pay out.*

If the money they have is equal to the money they have to pay out, they're solvent. If the money they have is less than the money they have to pay out, they're insolvent and need to find ways of making up the shortfall or face going out of business. 99

ACTIVITY

How do you monitor your own financial performance? What do you do to keep track of money that you:

- earn
- receive as a gift
- spend
- save.

If an organisation doesn't have enough cash to make payments, it may have to convert other things into cash – for example, by selling machinery, vehicles or property. These would be short-term, emergency measures which might create problems later. It could try to borrow money but few lenders would want to lend to an organisation bordering on insolvency unless the organisation could show that it could get back to a more secure and sustainable financial footing in the near future.

Monitoring solvency means looking ahead. Most organisations use cashflow forecasts to do this. A cashflow forecast predicts:
- when money will come into the organisation
- when money will go out of the organisation.

By forecasting, an organisation can identity in advance when money will be needed for expenditure and take action to ensure that money will be available at the right time.

Profitability

Many leisure and tourism organisations – mainly those operating in the private sector – aim to make a profit.

Organisations calculate their profit by subtracting their total expenditure from their total income:
- if total expenditure is less than total income, the organisation makes a profit
- if total income is less than total expenditure, the organisation makes a loss.

Monitoring profitability helps an organisation to identify the financial strengths and weaknesses of:
- its internal structures and processes
- the markets it operates in
- the business activities it's involved in.

The finance director of a leisure complex explains why she monitors profitability:

66 *Identifying reasons why the business is or isn't profitable helps us to improve our performance. For example, if we find that our profits have gone down because fewer customers are buying our products and services – a drop in income – we can investigate the reasons for the declining sales. Having identified the reasons, we can then decide if we can improve profits by renewing customers' interest, moving into different markets or changing the products or services. If we find that our profits have gone down because it's costing us more to produce our products and services – an increase in expenditure – we can find out where and how money is spent and look for ways of reducing spending or spending more efficiently.* 99

Cash flow

Organisations use cashflow forecasts to work out whether there will be enough cash to cover their predicted expenditure over a period of time. If there isn't enough cash, they will need to adjust their plans and activities to accommodate or make up for the shortfall.

An organisation is **profitable** when it consistently makes enough money to cover all its costs, and has money left over to spend, invest or save.

Cash flow is the movement of money in and out of an organisation.

200

The central diagram shows **ORGANISATION** at the centre with arrows connecting to: **Grants**, **Membership fees**, **Sales of products and services**, **Donations**, **Staff pay**, **Mortgage or rent**, **Supplies and materials**, **Tax**.

Financial targets are the amount of money which an organisation aims to make or spend over a period of time.

Cash flow is important to an organisation because it gives them their day-to-day spending money. Anything stopping the flow – like a shortfall in predicted sales, an increase in costs or a late payment of a large invoice – threatens the organisation's ability to operate efficiently and may stop it operating altogether.

Comparison with financial targets

By setting targets an organisation can:
■ define what it wants to achieve in financial terms
■ control how it works towards achievement
■ measure how well it has achieved.

There are two main types of financial target:
■ targets for making money
■ targets for spending money.

Targets for making money are based on what income an organisation thinks it needs to:
■ maintain business activities – survive
■ increase business activities – grow.

Targets for spending money are based on what expenditure levels an organisation can afford.

A financial adviser explains the benefits of targets:

66 *Knowing what it wants to achieve and knowing what financial limits it has helps an organisation to plan its activities. For example, to achieve a target of a 5% increase in profits over six months, an organisation could plan to increase income by increasing sales, decrease expenditure by reducing costs, or both. It could then identify and implement activities that would fit in with the plan. By comparing actual results against the target results, the organisation can measure how well its plan worked in practice.* **99**

Improving financial performance

Monitoring financial performance provides a record of:
■ how finances were used
■ whether the use was effective or not.

201

A small theatre wanted to increase its ticket sales by 10%. The management team considered having a few big-name stars in their stage productions to bring in more sales. But the finance manager pointed out that this would increase their spending on production costs so they would need to be sure that it would bring in sufficient sales to cover the increased costs and achieve the target 10% increase in sales. So the marketing department sent out a survey to all the customers on their database. The results showed that customers were less affected by who the performers were and more affected by what was being performed. The general response was that the theatre's concentration on stage-plays was too limited. On the basis of this information the theatre staged different types of production including comedy performers, concerts and bands. As a result, not only did ticket sales begin to rise but production costs went down as well.

ACTIVITY

Choose three leisure and tourism organisations in your area:

- one from the public sector
- one from the private sector
- one from the voluntary sector.

Talk to the manager or financial director of each, and find out how and why they monitor their organisation's financial performance.

This helps an organisation identify the strengths and weaknesses of its financial performance and identify ways of:

- building on the strengths
- overcoming the weaknesses.

Budget

Budgets are financial plans which show how an organisation intends to spend its money.

Monitoring financial performance provides the basic information for setting budgets. If you have a record of how much income and expenditure was involved in a past activity, you can use it as the basis for setting budgets for similar activities in the future.

Monitoring financial performance in the different sectors

Monitoring financial performance is important for all organisations regardless of which sector they belong to.

As a public-sector organisation, we need to monitor our financial performance to make sure we are making efficient and effective use of the money we get from our financing bodies – the county council and the Sports Council – the tax payers who provide funding indirectly through council tax and income tax. Because we are funded by public money, we measure financial performance in terms of the range of services we offer to the public while still keeping within budgets and minimising costs.

chief accountant for a large sports and recreation complex

As a private-sector organisation, we need to demonstrate an efficient financial performance to the board of directors for our parent company, our own board of directors and our shareholders. Because our primary aim is to make a profit, we measure our financial performance in terms of profit, levels of return on money invested, and growth of markets and activities.

financial director for a bowling alley

As a voluntary-sector organisation, we need to show a scrupulous use of the money we receive from the trust fund and other donations. Because our aims are to provide community and social benefits, we measure our financial performance in terms of sustaining or improving the service we provide and using our resources in a cost-effective way.

treasurer of a riding club for the disabled

DISCUSSION POINT

The representatives of the three sectors quoted in the box each use different words, but is there much difference between their reasons and aims for monitoring financial performance?

Criteria for evaluating financial performance

All organisations in the leisure and tourism industry evaluate their financial performance regularly. This means considering some or all of these questions:

- Is the organisation solvent?
- Is the organisation making a profit?
- Is the organisation meeting its financial targets?
- Is the organisation working within its budget?

Who needs to evaluate financial performance?

Who?	Why?
directors	to see if the managers are running the organisation efficiently
managers	to find out how well they are managing their resources
bank managers	to decide whether or not to offer loans or other financial facilities
Inland Revenue inspectors	to work out how much tax is due
Customs and Excise inspectors	to work out any VAT payments due
accountants	to advise about financial planning and control
auditors	to check the accuracy of the accounts
shareholders	to decide whether to buy or sell shares
tax payers	to see if their money is being spent appropriately

A bank manager explains why it is important to evaluate the financial performance of her business clients:

66 *When an organisation asks for a loan, I need to assess whether or not it can repay it. So I look at its financial performance. What level of profits has it achieved over the past few years? What are its cashflow forecasts? What kind of financial targets has it set? Is it operating within its budgets, or is it regularly overspending? Once I have this kind of information, I can make an informed decision about whether or not to approve the loan.* 99

Solvency

To stay solvent, an organisation has to have sufficient income to cover its expenditure. As a criterion for evaluating financial performance, it's a straightforward one and used to judge whether an organisation is surviving or failing. An organisation is either:

- able to match income to expenditure so therefore solvent and able to continue operating, or
- unable to match income to expenditure so insolvent and unable to continue operating.

In practice, if an organisation found itself heading for insolvency, it would try to raise its financial performance to a survival level.

Profitability

How much profit an organisation makes is important to its plans for continuation, growth and investment. As a criterion for financial performance, it shows an organisation's ability to succeed, its potential for growth and whether it's worth investing in. To be useful as information on performance levels, profitability would have to be monitored over a period to test if the profit levels were consistent.

Achieving financial targets

Generally, an organisation which consistently meets its financial targets is performing well and an organisation which consistently misses them is performing badly. In some cases though, it may be the targets that are at fault. They may be too low and therefore easy to achieve or too high and therefore impossible to achieve.

Operating within budgets

Operating within budgets shows that an organisation is good at estimating and using the amount of money it has to spend. Like financial targets, the budgets need to be realistic. It's easy to operate within a generous budget and impossible to operate within an inadequate budget. So to be an effective evaluation criterion, operating within budgets needs to include a look at how realistic the budgets are.

DISCUSSION POINT

You're looking at the accounts for the refreshment bar at a fitness centre. Your first impression is that it is doing well. The figures show that it has:

- made a profit
- achieved its sales targets
- kept within budgets.

When you look into how it set its budgets, you think they're over-generous – the organisation is paying a higher than usual price for some of its supplies and there's a high allowance for wastage. Does this information make you think differently about the bar's profitability?

ACTIVITY

One of your friends is going for an interview next week for a job in the accounts department of a travel agent. He's keen to impress the interviewer with his knowledge of finance in the leisure and tourism industry but is worried that his nerves will get the better of him and he'll muddle up the different criteria for evaluating financial performance. Prepare a summary of the criteria that will help to fix them in his mind.

Factors which affect financial performance

The financial performance of leisure and tourism organisations can be affected by:
- external factors – which the organisation has no control over; for example, recession and seasonal changes
- internal factors – which can be controlled by the organisation; for example, debts and wage bills.

UNIT

4

ELEMENT **4.1**

External factors

DISCUSSION POINT

Which types of leisure and tourism organisation do you think would suffer most from a recession?

External factors which affect the financial performance of organisations:
- recession
- boom
- local conditions
- seasonal changes
- the activities of competitors

Unemployment

Less disposable income

Manufacturers produce fewer goods

More people lose their jobs

Less job security

Less spent on luxuries and non-essentials

Fewer holidays are booked

Recession

A **recession** is a slump in the economy of a country, when unemployment rises and the public has less money to spend.

Leisure and tourism products and services – holidays, entertainment, eating out and so on – are luxuries rather than essentials. Because of this, they are one of the first things that people stop buying when they are short of money.

To keep their share of the market in a recession, leisure and tourism organisations set up schemes to encourage people to buy their products and services:
- a leisure centre might introduce reduced rates for unemployed people
- a tour operator might reduce the selling price of a holiday if the booking is made within a fortnight of departure
- a restaurant might introduce a 'two meals for the price of one' offer.

A **boom** is when the national economy improves and new jobs are created.

Increase in employment

More disposable income

Greater job security

More spent on luxuries and non-essentials

More spent on expensive holidays

Boom

An economic boom has a positive effect on the financial performance of leisure and tourism organisations. Unemployment falls; people have more money to spend; and start buying luxuries such as leisure and tourism products and services.

ACTIVITY

Ask friends, family or neighbours how the current state of the national economy has affected the amount of money they spend on leisure and tourism. Are they spending more or less money now than ten years ago? What would make them increase their spending on leisure and tourism?

Local conditions

Local conditions are factors which can change the economy on a local scale. For example, when a large factory opens or an employer moves to an area, new jobs are created and the local people have more money to spend. However, if a factory closes or an employer moves away, local people are made redundant and have less money to spend.

Because of local conditions like these, even if the leisure and tourism industry in the UK as a whole is flourishing, local facilities may still be struggling. For example:

■ the closure of a large, local employer would affect the financial performance of a provincial theatre, which relies on the local theatre-going population

■ the relegation of a football club to a lower division would affect its financial performance and that of hotels, bars and restaurants near the ground.

Seasonal factors

The leisure and tourism industry is seasonal – the demand for its products and services varies depending on the time of year. Because of this, the financial performance of organisations goes up and down from season to season.

Seasonal variations

Most people choose to take their holidays in the summer, rather than the winter.

Leisure and tourism facilities are busier at the weekend than during the week.

Leisure activities are in particular demand during school and national holidays.

Many leisure and tourism activities rely on the weather. For example, an open-air swimming pool is only popular in warm weather; a ski resort needs snow.

Internal factors which affect the financial performance of organisations:

- volume of sales
- level of credit
- level of debt
- wage bills
- fixed costs
- variable costs
- stock control

Leisure and tourism organisations need to be aware of the seasonal variations in their income, and plan how to counteract them. A tour operator explains how his company copes during the winter low season.

❝ *Like most holiday companies, we sell most of our holidays during the summer. As we have to cover our expenses throughout the year, we offer low cost and discounted holidays during the quiet, winter months. These special offers – loss leaders – might not even make a profit, but they ensure that the market is still aware of our name.* ❞

Competitor activity

The leisure and tourism industry is competitive and all leisure and tourism organisations have to be ready to respond to changes in their competitors' activities. But before deciding on its response, an organisation would have to think carefully about the financial implications any possible response could have.

A financial adviser explains the importance of making a considered response:

❝ *When competition is fierce and an organisation feels threatened by competitor activity, the management's response is sometimes to act first and think later. Financially speaking, that sort of response can be a disaster. Doing the first thing that come into your head is never the only possible response. And you can't decide if it's a valid response, let alone the best one, until you've considered the financial implications it involves and compared it with other options.* ❞

Internal factors

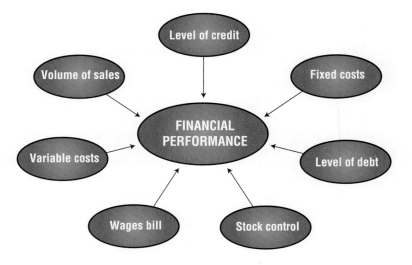

> **Volume of sales** is the total number of products or services an organisation sells over a certain period of time.

Volume of sales

Volume of sales is a crucial part of financial performance – most leisure and tourism organisations rely on sales for much of their income.

Organisations set themselves targets for the number of sales they want to make. To set the target, the organisation needs to take into account:
- the overall profit the organisation is aiming for
- what percentage of the overall target will be made up of sales
- what the break-even point is – the minimum amount of money an organisation needs to cover all its expenditure, overheads and running costs.

The sales director of a small mail order firm specialising in sportswear and equipment for the home explains their use of volume of sales targets:

66 *All our income is from sales. We know that to break even we need to make around £8,000 of sales a day. We're also aiming for a 10% increase in profits this year. The financial director prepares an annual forecast of sales. She then breaks this down into monthly targets which take into account the seasonal nature of our customers' buying habits. November to January are good months for us – Christmas presents and New Year resolutions prompt our customers into buying. April to September are also good months – getting fit seems to be more popular in the summer. Every day the financial director runs off a daily sales sheet which is given to all the sales staff. This lists every product we do and the amount of each we've sold. At the bottom of the list are three figures – the volume of sales for that day, the predicted monthly total based on an average of sales to date and the target number of sales for the month. This means we can see on a daily basis how much we've sold and how well we're doing towards the monthly target.* 99

To make a profit from sales, an organisation builds a profit margin into its prices. Basically, this means working out how much it costs to produce the product or service then adding an amount on top which will be the profit. The profit margin needs to be thought about carefully. If the organisation is operating in a market where sales volumes are high, but prices are low, the profit margin will be small – otherwise the overall price would be higher than the competitors. If the organisation is operating in a market where sales volumes are low, but prices are high, the profit margin will be big.

Many leisure and tourism organisations are affected by the seasonality factor. So they build in high profit margins when sales volumes are high and reduce the margins in less busy times when they need to offer cheaper prices or discounts to encourage sales.

ACTIVITY

Give an example from the leisure and tourism industry of:
- an organisation operating in a high-sales-volume/low-profit-margin market
- an organisation operating in a low-sales-volume/high-profit-margin market
- an organisation operating in a seasonal market and alternating between high-sales-volume/high-profit-margin and low-sales/low-profit-margin

> **Level of credit** is the amount of money that suppliers or loan companies are happy for an organisation to owe them.

Level of credit

Most leisure and tourism organisations use credit to help their financial performance. Credit can be:
- an amount of money – for example, a bank might give an organisation an overdraft so that it can borrow up to an agreed limit

■ a period of time – for example, a supplier might provide goods to an organisation and then give it a fixed period of time in which to pay (usually 30, 60 or 90 days).

Using credit gives organisations time to collect money they are owed, before paying out the money they owe themselves.

The accountant for a sports centre explains how he uses credit:

66 *Credit is a useful way to spread outgoings – for example, paying for expensive items in small chunks over a period of time. Another use is as short-term funding – for example, taking out a loan to buy a piece of equipment. Sometimes we use it to help our cash flow – when we know we've got money coming in but we need to spend on something before then. It also lets us hold on to money – the longer the money stays in our bank account before we settle for what we've bought on credit, the longer we've earned interest on it.* 99

A reasonable level of credit reflects a financially stable organisation. If the creditors are willing to give credit, they must trust the organisation's ability to pay it off under the terms agreed.

Level of debt

A high level of debt is all right if the organisation knows it can afford to cover it. For example, the costs incurred when developing a new product which will be covered by the income the product generates. But it can have a bad effect on an organisation's financial performance if the level isn't monitored and controlled. Most leisure and tourism organisations try to keep their level of debt as low as possible.

A high level of debt can cause problems with cash flow. If money isn't coming in on schedule, it can't go out on schedule and that can cost an organisation money – for example, interest charges on invoices or credit agreements it can't pay on time because money owing to it hasn't come in. It can also cost the organisation its reputation with existing and future creditors. Being labelled a bad payer can make it difficult to get credit again.

Wage bills

Leisure and tourism organisations spend large amounts of money on staff wages, and it is important that they monitor carefully the number of people they employ. If an organisation wastes money on unnecessary wages, it can have a bad effect on its financial performance.

This is particularly important because of the seasonal nature of the leisure and tourism industry. Leisure and tourism organisations need to keep a close check on wage costs and staff numbers during quiet times of the year, and consider:
■ whether they need to employ a different number of staff during different seasons
■ whether staff should be full-time or part-time

DISCUSSION POINT

What suspicions might you have of the financial health of an organisation with a very high level of credit? What would it suggest about their financial performance?

Level of debt is the amount of money owed to an organisation, often because they have given credit to their customers.

ACTIVITY

Get in touch with accountants at two or three leisure and tourism organisations – e.g. a cinema, a tour operator and a sports club – and ask them how they control debt levels in their organisations. What are the similarities in their answers?

- how staff numbers can be kept to a minimum during the low season without threatening heath, safety and efficiency levels.

Fixed costs

- rent
- insurance
- telephone-line rental
- vehicle and property insurance

Fixed costs

> **Fixed costs** remain the same, no matter how many products or services an organisation provides.

Because fixed costs stay the same regardless of the amount of business an organisation does, it makes financial sense to keep them as low as possible. For example, the rent on a hundred square metres of office space will be the same whether one person uses it or 20 people use it. It would probably be more cost-effective to rent a smaller space if only one person was needed for office work.

Variable costs decrease and increase, depending on an organisation's activities.

Variable costs

Because an organisation can control variable costs to some extent, it can use them to improve its overall financial performance. As with fixed costs, it's a matter of ensuring that the money is spent wisely and effectively – for example, ensuring that only necessary expenditure is made and using competitively priced supplies.

Variable costs

- stock
- wages (depending on the number of staff, whether they are full-time or part-time, overtime paid)
- advertising (depending on the number and type of advertisements bought)
- telephone calls
- petrol
- stationery and postage
- heating and lighting

DISCUSSION POINT
A moped-hire company lists certain spares and components – lamp bulbs, spark plugs, carburettors and oil filters – as variable costs. Why are they variable rather than fixed? How can the company control expenditure on variable costs during the low season when hire demand is down?

Stock control

Poor stock control can have a bad effect on an organisation's financial performance. For example:

- if an organisation buys too much perishable stock (such as food), it may have to be thrown away if it reaches its sell-by date without being sold
- if a manufacturing organisation buys too many raw materials, it will need to pay for them before using them. If it doesn't buy enough raw materials, production may be held up, affecting sales, income and customer goodwill.

Stock control is the control of the amount of stock – raw materials, or finished products and services – going in and out of an organisation.

Many leisure and tourism organisations buy stock in bulk, as suppliers give a discount to customers who buy a lot at once. This can have a positive effect on financial performance by reducing the amount of money an organisation spends on stock. However, the organisation must make sure:

- it has enough funds to buy the stock
- it is able to store large quantities of stock
- it is able to sell all the stock.

Sources of information and data about financial performance

Most leisure and tourism organisations produce balance sheets, profit-and-loss accounts and cash flow as part of their company accounts. Between them, they give a clear picture of an organisation's:

- forecast performance (what it expects to achieve in the future)
- actual performance (what it is achieving at the moment).

Forecasts

Financial forecasting – predicting the future pattern of income and expenditure – is an important part of running an organisation.

A management accountant explains the basics of financial forecasting:

66 *Good financial forecasting depends on using accurate information. The forecaster looks at an organisation's current: balance sheet; profit-and-loss account; and cash flow.*

From these, the forecaster identifies times when the organisation didn't have enough income to meet expenditure, the organisation's solvency was at risk or there was extra money available for additional staff, advertising, special promotions or other kinds of expansion. 99

The most common types of forecast are:

- the balance-sheet forecast
- the profit-and-loss forecast
- the cashflow forecast.

Balance-sheet forecast

A forecast balance sheet predicts what the organisation's financial position will be at the end of a given period of trading or operation. It shows where the organisation plans to get its money, how it plans to use it and any likely or known changes to the assets and liabilities.

Sources of information about financial performance

- balance sheet
- profit-and-loss account
- cash flow

A **balance sheet** is a statement of a company's financial position. It summarises what the company owns (its assets), and what the company owes (its liabilities).

SILVER SPLASH AQUATIC CENTRE AND HEALTH CLUB

Balance Sheet	Jan	Feb	Mar	Apr	May	Jun	Jul	Aug	Sep	Oct	Nov	Dec
Fixed Assets	1,000	1,100	1,100	1,150	1,150	1,150	1,175	1,175	1,175	1,175	1,190	1,190
Current Assets												
Stocks	50	51	52	52	53	54	55	55	56	57	58	59
Debtors	400	325	330	335	340	345	350	355	360	365	370	375
Bank & cash	100	170	225	183	203	122	8	21	138	259	274	207
	550	546	607	570	596	521	413	432	554	681	702	640
Current liabilities												
Trade creditors	150	246	294	299	309	217	118	114	212	317	327	235
Accruals	10	9	16	10	11	14	9	10	14	12	10	21
Taxation	12	12	12	12	12	12	12	12	12	12	12	12
Other	5	5	5	5	5	5	5	5	5	5	5	5
	177	272	327	326	337	248	144	141	243	346	354	273
Net Current Assets	373	274	280	244	259	273	269	291	311	335	348	367
Long term liabilities												
Loan	240	230	220	210	200	190	180	170	160	150	140	130
Net Assets	1,133	1,144	1,160	1,184	1,209	1,233	1,264	1,296	1,326	1,360	1,398	1,427
Capital & Reserves												
Share Capital	1,000	1,000	1,000	1,000	1,000	1,000	1,000	1,000	1,000	1,000	1,000	1,000
Profit & Loss a/c	123	144	160	184	209	233	264	296	326	360	398	427
	1,123	1,144	1,160	1,184	1,209	1,233	1,264	1,296	1,326	1,360	1,398	1,427

Profit-and-loss account forecast

> A **profit-and-loss account** is a summary of a company's income (money coming in) and expenditure (money going out) over a period of time (a month, quarter, half-year, or year).

A profit and loss forecast is a predicted calculation of how much profit or loss an organisation will have made at the end of the forecast period.

SILVER SPLASH AQUATIC CENTRE AND HEALTH CLUB													
Profit & Loss Account	**Jan**	**Feb**	**Mar**	**Apr**	**May**	**Jun**	**Jul**	**Aug**	**Sep**	**Oct**	**Nov**	**Dec**	**Total**
Sales	320	325	330	335	340	345	350	355	360	365	370	375	4,170
Cost of Sales	(192)	(195)	(198)	(201)	(204)	(207)	(210)	(213)	(216)	(219)	(222)	(225)	(2,502)
Gross Profit	**128**	**130**	**132**	**134**	**136**	**138**	**140**	**142**	**144**	**146**	**148**	**150**	**1,668**
Expenses													
Salaries	100	100	100	100	100	100	100	100	100	100	100	100	1,200
Light & Heat	3	2	4	2	3	1	2	3	2	4	2	3	31
Postage	3	3	3	3	3	3	3	3	3	3	3	3	36
Travel	2	2	2	2	2	2	2	2	2	2	2	2	24
Advertising			5			5			5			10	25
Other	2	2	2	3	3	3	2	2	2	3	3	3	30
Total	**110**	**109**	**116**	**110**	**111**	**114**	**109**	**110**	**114**	**112**	**110**	**121**	**1,346**
Profit	**18**	**21**	**16**	**24**	**25**	**24**	**31**	**32**	**30**	**34**	**38**	**29**	**322**
Tax													
Profit after tax	**18**	**21**	**16**	**24**	**25**	**24**	**31**	**32**	**30**	**34**	**38**	**29**	**322**

Cash flow

> **Cash flow** shows how and when an organisation is likely to spend money; and how much and when it expects to receive money. It identifies times when the organisation's solvency may be at risk, and when there won't be enough income to cover expenditure.

A cashflow forecast is a prediction of the amounts and times cash will flow into and out of the organisation over the forecast period. Some items will be easy to predict – for example, payment of annual, quarterly or monthly bills for things like phones, light and heating. Others will be less easy to predict and will have to be based on assumptions – for example, spending on the development and launch of a new product and income from the sales of the product after its launch.

DISCUSSION POINT

What sources of information would you use if you had to put together a financial forecast? What basis would you use for any assumptions you had to make about things you couldn't predict with certainty – for example, inflation levels, changes in the market or changes in funding?

SILVER SPLASH AQUATIC CENTRE AND HEALTH CLUB												
Cashflow	**Jan**	**Feb**	**Mar**	**Apr**	**May**	**Jun**	**Jul**	**Aug**	**Sep**	**Oct**	**Nov**	**Dec**
Cash received from sales	0	400	325	330	335	340	345	350	355	360	365	370
Other receipts												
Total receipts	**0**	**400**	**325**	**330**	**335**	**340**	**345**	**350**	**355**	**360**	**365**	**370**
Payments to suppliers	150	100	151	197	195	300	310	218	119	115	213	318
Salaries	100	100	100	100	100	100	100	100	100	100	100	100
Light & Heat	0	3	2	4	2	3	1	2	3	2	4	2
Postage	0	3	3	3	3	3	3	3	3	3	3	3
Travel	0	2	2	2	2	2	2	2	2	2	2	2
Advertising	0	0	0	5	0	0	5	0	0	5	0	0
Other	0	2	2	2	3	3	3	2	2	2	3	3
Payments for fixed assets		100		50			25				15	
Loan repayments	10	10	10	10	10	10	10	10	10	10	10	10
Total Payments	**260**	**320**	**270**	**373**	**315**	**420**	**459**	**337**	**239**	**239**	**350**	**438**
Surplus/deficit	**(260)**	**80**	**55**	**(43)**	**20**	**(81)**	**(114)**	**13**	**116**	**121**	**15**	**(68)**
Opening bank balance	**350**	**90**	**170**	**225**	**183**	**203**	**122**	**8**	**21**	**138**	**259**	**274**
Closing bank balance	**90**	**170**	**225**	**183**	**203**	**122**	**8**	**21**	**138**	**259**	**274**	**207**

Actual

Balance sheet

An actual balance sheet is a summary statement recording the real financial state of an organisation's assets and liabilities. Apart from the factual information it gives, it can be:

- compared with the forecast to see if the company performed as well as predicted over the given period
- used as a basis for the forecast for the next period.

Profit-and-loss account

An actual profit-and-loss account shows the real amount of profit or loss an organisation has made over the given period. Apart from the factual information it gives, it can be:

- compared with the forecast to see if the profit or loss was as predicted over the given period
- used as a basis for the forecast for the next period.

Cash flow

An actual cash flow shows how much cash came into and went out of the organisation and when. Apart from the factual information it gives, it can be:

- compared with the forecast to see how accurately income and expenditure levels were predicted
- used as a basis for the forecast for the next period.

Key questions

1. What are the characteristics of:
   - an organisation that is performing well financially
   - an organisation that is performing badly financially?
2. Who is likely to be interested in an organisation's financial performance?
3. What criteria are used to evaluate an organisation's financial performance?
4. Can you list four external factors and four internal factors which might affect financial performance?
5. What's the difference between a high profit margin and a low profit margin?
6. What documents provide information about a company's financial performance?
7. What is meant by:
   - an actual?
   - a forecast?

Assignment

Prepare for and give a presentation on the reasons why leisure and tourism organisations in the public, private and voluntary sectors monitor financial performance and how they do it. Make sure your presentation covers:
- the reasons for monitoring financial performance
- criteria for evaluating financial performance
- factors affecting financial performance
- sources of information and data relating to financial performance.

Include visual material to add interest for your audience – graphs and charts are a good way of showing changes in financial performance over time. You might also like to prepare a handout summarising the main points from the four areas of coverage listed above as evidence for your portfolio.

> 66 *As far as budgeting goes, I keep tabs on what happened in the year before and think: 'Is this year more or less?'. I tend to spend what I feel I need to spend. When I'm organising the figures to be sent to the accountant I have a good look at things and work out averages and whether something has gone up – I assess the situation then.* 99
>
> *owner of a riding school which also provides holidays*

> 66 *We work on a nil-basis budget system which means we start every year with a zero balance. I sit down with the managers and we work out what we are going to need to spend in different areas. Requests for extra funds – for example, to deal with repairs or special events – are dealt with regionally. There is a regional financial controller who runs the accounts department and helps us monitor our budget. In order to evaluate efficiency at different sites, the financial controller sets objectives. These obviously vary from property to property. We would usually be required to make an agreed surplus for the property. We have to set prices and then review whether these are right and are bringing in enough income.* 99
>
> *administrator of a heritage site*

> 66 *All the money is put back into the business. We just take what we can and spend what we feel we need to in order to be in profit. Our target is more a happiness and contentedness target than a financial one!* 99
>
> *owner of a guest-house*

> 66 *We usually have to negotiate a fee for each appearance. The amount we ask for depends on the size of the venue and whether or not they have sponsorship. We can go for a fixed fee, a smaller fee and a proportion of the profits or no fee and a larger share of the profits. Travel and accommodation are paid for on top of our fee. We either arrange to stay in small hotels or with friends. If we're lucky we get our fee straight after the concert, but it usually comes a month later in the post.* 99
>
> *leader of a band*

Financial accounts

All business organisations have financial accounts to keep track of the money coming in and going out of the business. As well as a record of all financial transactions, the accounts provide valuable information about how the business is doing. In this element you'll be finding out more about the kinds of information that the accounts provide. You'll also be looking at how owners and managers of leisure and tourism organisations use the information to monitor the performance of the business.

The purpose of financial accounts

ACTIVITY

Ask someone in the accounts department of:

■ a private-sector leisure and tourism organisation

■ a public-sector leisure and tourism organisation

■ what their financial year is and why it was chosen.

Financial accounts in leisure and tourism are used for:

■ analysing financial health

■ monitoring solvency

■ monitoring profitability

■ comparing performance with financial targets

■ accountability.

Financial accounts provide information about an organisation's financial performance and profitability. Organisations produce a range of financial information for internal use which provides information for making and monitoring finance decisions. They also have a legal duty to produce specific types of financial information for external users like the Inland Revenue, the VAT authorities (Customs and Excise), shareholders and auditors.

All organisations produce annual accounts showing their financial activities and performance over the year. The dates they fix as their financial year is up to them, though once they've stated their choice they have to stick to it. Common choices are:

■ to count the year as starting from the day they set up in business

■ 1 January to 31 December

■ 1 April to 31 March

■ 6 April to 5 April – which is the period the tax authorities use in their assessments of tax payments.

Analysis of financial health

An organisation's finances are a crucial part of its life-support system – it can't survive without them. Many words used to describe an organisation's performance come from the ideas of health – for example, thriving, flourishing, developing, failing, ailing, weakening.

The financial director of a museum describes the sort of information the accounts give:

66 Financial accounts give pictures of our financial health. They record past performance, show current performance and predict future performance.

By analysing the reasons behind financial performance, we can identify what makes us do well and keeps the finances flowing, and what makes us do badly and impedes or kills off finances.

Once we have that information, we use it to identify which activities are good for business and which are not. By frequent analysis, we can pick up unhealthy signs and take action to cure them or prevent them from developing into more serious problems. 99

Monitoring solvency

A solvent organisation is one that has enough money coming in (income) to cover the money they have to pay out (expenditure). All organisations monitor their income and expenditure to make sure they can meet their expenses when they occur and to spot and plan for temporary shortfalls.

Here are the views on the importance of solvency from two people with a financial interest in a restaurant:

66 If the restaurant was consistently failing to meet its costs, it could be heading for insolvency. I'd be worried that it was not a safe investment and probably withdraw the money I'd put in. 99

an investor in the restaurant

66 *I'd want to know that the restaurant was solvent before I agreed to supply it with fruit and vegetables. I wouldn't want to hand over supplies that they couldn't pay for.* 99

a fruit and vegetable supplier to the restaurant

Monitoring profitability

Profit is the amount of money an organisation has left from its income once all the expenses of running the business are paid. If the expenses are greater than the income, the organisation has made a loss, sometimes called a negative profit. Making a profit is important because it provides money for growth, savings and investment. Making a loss can threaten the organisation's existence. Organisations monitor their levels of profitability to:

- find out if their business activities are successful or not
- calculate how much tax they may have to pay
- plan for the future.

Existing and potential investors would also be interested in the levels of profitability to see if investment is worth their while.

Comparison with financial targets

Most organisations set themselves financial targets which state for a given period:

- how much income they want to generate
- what spending limits they want to keep to
- how much profit they aim to make.

An accountant explains how she uses the information she gets from comparing actual performance figures with target performance figures:

66 *I carry out comparisons at the end of each month. I compare the actual figures for income, spending and profit with the target figures. If there's a big shortfall between the two, I investigate to find out why and discuss actions we can take to improve performance with the management team. If there's a match between the two, I know that the organisation is performing well and I look for ways to sustain and improve performance. If we've exceeded the targets, I look for the particular strengths that led to the success so that we can build on them in the future.* 99

Monitoring financial performance

Monitoring financial performance is a continuous activity for all organisations. They need to know how well they are performing and how efficiently they're using their finances so that they can take action to:

- sustain their financial position
- improve it
- prevent or limit financial problems.

DISCUSSION POINT

All organisations should keep their eye on the financial ball by:

- analysing their financial health
- monitoring solvency
- monitoring profitability
- comparing targets with actual performance
- monitoring financial performance.

What do you think could happen if an organisation didn't keep up with these monitoring and analysing activities? What might the effects be:

- immediately
- in the short term
- in the long term?

Accountability is an organisation's obligation to account for how its finances have been gained and used.

Trading account for the year to 31 March 1996		
	£,000	£,000
Sales		1,200
Opening stock	200	
Purchases	500	
Closing stock	(300)	
Cost of sales		(400)
Gross profit		**800**

Accountability

The level of accountability an organisation has and the type of information it has to supply depends on:

■ what type of organisation it is

■ who is asking for the account.

To the tax authorities

All organisations are accountable to the Inland Revenue. They are legally obliged to give the Inland Revenue an account of their profits and to account for the income tax they have deducted from their employees' pay and paid to the Inland Revenue on their behalf.

All organisations registered for Value Added Tax (VAT) are accountable to the Custom and Excise authorities. They are legally obliged to pass on to the Customs and Excise department the VAT they've charged on the supplies, products or services they've sold. They are also entitled to claim back from the Customs and Excise the VAT they've paid out on supplies, products or services they've bought.

To providers of finance

Banks and other lenders are entitled to see that an organisation is using any finance they have provided for proper reasons.

To shareholders

As well as borrowing from banks, organisations often sell shares to raise finance. In return for their investment, shareholders are buying a share of ownership and expect to receive a share of any profit the organisation makes. The organisation has to demonstrate to shareholders that it is using their money honestly, efficiently and effectively.

To other stakeholders

Stakeholders are people who have an interest or stake in the organisation's performance and have to take it on trust that the organisation is operating honestly. Stakeholders are people like customers, suppliers and employees.

Trading account

The trading account is used to work out the gross profit or loss. It shows:

■ the revenue raised from sales of products or services

■ the cost involved in making the products or providing the services.

The difference between the two amounts is the gross profit or loss.

Profit-and-loss account

The profit-and-loss account is used to work out the final profit or loss. It shows:

- the gross profit
- the cost of overheads and other operating expenses like heating, light, rent, pay and the drop in the value of assets like machinery and vehicles (known as depreciation)
- the net profit (what's left when the overheads and operating costs are deducted from the gross profit)
- income from sources other than the main trading activity (for example, interest earned from money in bank or other investment accounts)
- interest payments on money borrowed
- the amount of tax payable
- the profit after tax
- the amount paid out of the profit after tax to shareholders
- the amount of profit the organisation has left to use for reinvestment (the retained profit).

Profit-and-loss account for the year to 31 March 1996		
	£,000	£,000
Gross profit		800
Expenses		
Salaries and wages	400	
Light and power	100	
Depreciation	20	
Rent	150	
Stationery	10	
Postage	10	
Travel and subsistence	15	
Repairs	10	
Marketing	50	
Total expenses		765
Net profit		35
Interest received		5
Interest paid		(10)
Net profit before tax		30
Tax		(7)
Net profit after tax		23
Dividends		(10)
Net profit retained		13

Balance sheet

A balance sheet gives an overview of an organisation's financial position at a particular time.

The balance sheet shows what an organisation owns – its assets – and what it owes – its liabilities – and is used to work out how much an organisation is worth in total.

Assets are usually:

- fixed assets like buildings, machinery and vehicles
- current assets like stocks of raw materials, semi-finished and finished goods, money held in the business and in bank accounts and money owed by debtors
- money invested in the business by the owners (capital).

Liabilities include:

- payments to be made for goods and services received
- loans
- leases.

Balance sheet for the year to 31 March 1996	
	£,000
Fixed Assets	
Fixtures and fittings	30
Plant and equipment	40
	70
Current assets	
Stock	30
Debtors	50
Bank and cash	20
	100
Current liabilities	
Trade creditors	40
Loans	10
Leases	10
	60
Net current assets	**40**
Long-term liabilities	
Five-year loan	20
Net assets	**90**
Capital	
Share capital	40
Share premium	20
Profit-and-loss account	30
	90

DISCUSSION POINT

Why do fixed assets and current assets count towards an organisation's financial value?

Annual report

An annual report gives the information about a limited company's finances, development plans and financial accounts that it is legally required to give to its shareholders. Members of the public can also ask for copies of a limited company's annual report.

The contents of an annual report:

■ the directors' report – directors have a legal obligation to give details on how the organisation has developed over the past year, its development plans for the coming year, its health and safety policy, donations to political or charitable bodies, directors' shareholding and share options, changes in board membership, the amount of profit to be allocated to shareholders and the amount to be retained by the organisation for reinvestment

■ the chair's or chief executive's statement – this isn't a legal obligation but large organisations often include in their report a statement on the organisation's past performance and future plans

■ the balance sheet – to show how the organisation has gained and used its finances over the year

■ the profit-and-loss account – to show the organisation's trading activities over the year

■ the cashflow statement – to show the amount of money coming into and going out of the organisation over the year

■ notes to the accounts – to explain what the accounts show and how they have been constructed

■ auditor's report – a statement from independent auditors stating whether or not the accounts give a true and fair view of the organisation's financial position and trading activities

Auditors are specialist independent accountants who are hired by an organisation to check the accounts before they are published.

Who uses financial accounts?

Who uses an organisation's financial accounts?

- people within the organisation itself, including:
  - directors
  - governors
  - owners
  - managers
- the Inland Revenue
- VAT authorities
- people who provide finance for the company
- shareholders
- other stakeholders, including customers

Boards

The board of directors of a private-sector company uses financial accounts to:

- prepare a summary of the accounts to present to shareholders at the company's annual general meeting
- prepare an annual report for shareholders
- decide whether a 'dividend' (share of the profit) should be paid to shareholders, and how much this dividend should be
- check that the organisation was operating in accordance with company and employment law.

The directors of a public-sector company use financial accounts to:

- prepare financial reports for committees.

For example, the director of leisure services for a local authority would prepare regular financial reports for the council members on the leisure services committee.

The governors or trustees on the board of a charitable or trust-funded organisation use financial accounts to check that:

- funds were being spent effectively
- business activities, funding sources and spending were in accordance with the organisation's aims.

For example, an organisation which promoted conservation would choose to buy stationery made from recycled paper.

Owners

Owners use financial accounts to:

- monitor the financial performance
- check that their investment is safe
- check that the managers are running the organisation efficiently.

Managers

Managers use financial accounts to:

- make day-to-day decisions
- understand how much the organisation has earned and spent in the past – this helps them to prepare budgets for the future
- check whether they are meeting their financial targets
- identify how their department's activities have contributed to overall financial performance.

Inland Revenue

The Inland Revenue uses an organisation's financial accounts to assess how much tax it has to pay.

Organisations are obliged by law to declare their profits to the Inland Revenue. The annual profit-and-loss account gives this information but organisations

---

ACTIVITY

Talk to a manager who works for a leisure and tourism organisation, and ask when he or she has used the company's financial accounts to help with decision-making. What sort of decisions were they? Which accounts were used? How did the information help?

usually give the Inland Revenue an annual trading account and a balance sheet to show that their statement of profit or loss is an accurate one. The Inland Revenue inspectors will investigate any inaccuracies they find.

VAT authorities

The VAT authorities have their own forms that organisations fill in to show how much VAT they've charged on the goods, products and services they've sold and how much VAT they've paid on goods, products and services they've bought. The VAT inspectors can call on an organisation at any time to check on its accounts to make sure that it is giving accurate information.

Providers of finance

Providers of finance – such as banks and loan companies – use an organisation's financial accounts to decide whether to lend money. They:

- look at the organisation's financial performance
- decide whether the organisation is a good investment
- decide whether the organisation can afford to repay the loan and make the interest payments.

In the public sector, the service providers have to account to the local or national government officials on how they have used the money allocated to them. The government officials have to account to the taxpayers who indirectly provide finance for leisure and tourism organisations. They can use financial accounts to see whether local government is spending their money in the way it promised.

When local councils send households details of the community charges for the coming year, they also issue financial summaries showing how they've spent the finances over the past year, what budgets they have set for the coming year and how their spending plans will be funded. Recreation and tourism is usually one of the headings on these accounts.

DISCUSSION POINT

If you had £1,000 to invest in a company, what sort of information would you want to find out before deciding which company to invest in? Would you want to know how they made their profit? Would you be able to get this information from their financial accounts?

Shareholders

Shareholders use financial accounts to decide whether to keep their shares in the company and remain a shareholder, or whether to sell the shares.

The organisation's annual report gives them the information they need.

	1993/94		Class of service administered by the District Council		1994/95	
Est. Gross Expenditure £000	Est. Gross Income £000	Est. Net Expenditure £000		Est. Gross Expenditure £000	Est. Gross Income £000	Est Net Expenditure £000
744	415	329	Planning and Economic Development	792	507	380
408	24	384	Recreation and Tourism	647	146	501
749	165	584	Environmental Health	721	154	567
710	120	590	Refuse Collection and Disposal	725	131	594
4,762	4,372	390	Housing	5,851	5,316	535
3,852	3,522	330	Other Services	3,813	2,738	980
11,225	8,618	2,607	Aggregate of above	12,549	8,992	3,557
		125	Provision for inflation			91
		435	Parish precepts			489
		252	Internal Drainage Board special levies			265
		768	Increase or (reduction) in reserves			(194)
		4,187	Budget Requirement			4,208

A district council's spending plans for 1994/5

Other stakeholders

Stakeholders are people with an interest in an organisation's financial performance.

stakeholders	what they would want to know
employees	■ how secure their jobs are ■ how the organisation is making and using profits ■ what contribution they and their departments are making to the organisation's financial performance
trade unions	■ that the organisation is using its finances to maximise its employees' pay and conditions
other organisations who buy from the organisation	■ whether the profit margins allow any room for negotiation over prices
individuals customers who buy products and services or use facilities	■ how the organisation uses the money it makes ■ whether they are getting value for money
suppliers	■ that the organisation is solvent and can pay for their products and services before entering into agreements to supply

Extracting information from financial statements

Financial statements – such as profit-and-loss accounts, balance sheets and annual reports – provide a lot of information.

Information provided by financial statements

- how much profit an organisation makes before deducting any costs
- how much an organisation is spending on heating, lighting, staff pay
- how much its assets are worth
- how much it owes to suppliers
- the dividend per share paid to its shareholders
- how much tax it has to pay
- how it earns its money
- how it spends its money
- how much it has to spend to make the products or services it sells

Sometimes, people may want to extract just one or two items of information from a financial statement; for example, the amount of money a company owes. At other times, they will need to look at the whole financial statement in detail to get a clear view of the company's financial performance.

In either case, people need to understand a range of financial terms in order to get information from financial statements.

Understanding financial terms

Term	Meaning
Assets	Items of value owned by the company, which it could sell to pay off a debt; e.g. buildings, vehicles, computers, desks, filing cabinets
Audit	An examination of a company's financial statements carried out by an independent auditor, accountant, solicitor or Inland Revenue tax inspector
Capital	Money which has been invested in the company by owners and shareholders
Capital expenditure	Money spent on capital assets such as buildings, vehicles, computers
Current assets	Items owned by the company which change value regularly; e.g. stock, raw materials, cash in hand
Current liabilities	Debts which must be paid within twelve months; e.g. bank overdrafts, unpaid bills
Debts	Money or goods which the company owes; e.g. a loan which can be paid over time
Deferred loan	A loan which doesn't have to be paid back until after a project has been completed
Depreciation	The amount of money which is deducted from the value of a capital asset for 'wear and tear'; e.g. if a company bought a car for £6000 in May 1995, it might take £800 off its value to allow for wear and tear after a year

Understanding financial terms (continued)

Term	Meaning
Dividend	A share of the company's profits which is paid to the shareholders
Fixed assets	Assets which the company keeps, rather than turning them into cash. Companies usually keep fixed assets for a number of years
Gross profit	The sales revenue minus the cost of making sales
Net current assets (also called working capital)	The difference between the value of current assets and current liabilities; e.g. if a company owns current assets of £10,000 and owes current liabilities of £3000, then it has net current assets of £7000
Net profit	Profit after tax has been deducted
Revenue	The income the company receives from its main, day-to-day business activities
Share capital	The money which shareholders invest in the company
Turnover	The total value of sales

The most important financial accounts are:

- the trading account
- the profit-and-loss account
- the balance sheet
- the annual report.

Getting information from the trading account

The trading account shows:

- the turnover
- the cost of sales
- the gross profit.

Turnover is the total amount of income an organisation has made through sales.

Turnover

Turnover can be used:

- to find out how many sales have been made
- in comparison with turnover targets
- in comparison with turnover for previous periods
- to set turnover targets for future periods
- to work out gross profit.

The trading account shows the turnover as a single figure at the start of the account.

DISCUSSION POINT

A health, beauty and fitness centre's revenue comes from membership subscriptions, sales of sports and slimming products, and so on. The owners of the club also give private Yoga lessons in members' homes. How would you work out the business' turnover?

Cost of sales

Sometimes the trading account shows the cost of sales divided into three parts:

- the opening stocks – the cost of stocks the organisation already has at the beginning to the accounting period

The total **cost of sales** is the amount of money an organisation has had to spend to make those sales.

- purchases – the cost of additional stock bought during the accounting period
- the closing stock – the cost of stocks unused by the end of the accounting period.

Gross profit

The gross profit is the figure at the bottom of the trading account.

Healthy Habits Ltd		
Trading account for the year ending 31st December 1995		
Turnover		**200,000**
Cost of sales		
opening stock	10,000	
purchases	55,000	
closing stock	(15,000)	
	50,000	
Gross profit		**150,000**

A financial accountant explains how her organisation uses the information from the trading account:

The **gross profit** is the amount of money an organisation has left over when the cost of sales has been deducted from the turnover.

66 *We use the trading account to monitor our turnover, cost of sales and gross profit. We compare current figures with past figures and with targeted figures. We also use the information to decide whether: the cost of making a product or providing a service is too high in relation to the gross profit it generates; sales levels are increasing or decreasing; the cost of making a product or service has increased or decreased; and stocks are being bought at the right time and at the right levels.* 99

Getting information from the profit-and-loss account

The profit and loss shows:
- the gross profit
- all the running costs and expenses incurred by an organisation during the accounting period
- the net profit, sometimes called profit before tax or the operating profit
- the amount of money paid in tax on its profits – organisations pay what is known as corporation tax
- the profit after tax has been deducted
- dividends paid to shareholders
- the profit retained for reinvestment into the business.

ACTIVITY

Use the following figures to work out the gross profit then write some brief notes to say what gross profit means and how it is worked out.

Turnover	200,000
Cost of sales	
opening stock	20,000
purchases	120,000
closing stock	(30,000)

Net profit

The two stages involved in reaching the net profit figure are sometimes shown separately as:
- net profit before taxation – what's left when expenses have been deducted from the gross profit
- net profit after taxation – what's left when taxation has been deducted.

Net profit is the gross profit minus the expenses of running the business minus taxation.

The figure for net profit before taxation is used by the Inland Revenue to decide how much tax the organisation must pay.

Expenses include all costs of running the business – for example, lighting and heating, wages and salaries, depreciation on buildings and equipment. The tax paid by organisations is called **corporation tax**.

THE WATERFRONT TOURIST CENTRE	
Profit-and-loss account: year ending 31.12.95	
Gross profit	**195,000**
Expenses	
Heat and light	5,200
Business rates	1,400
Telephone	2,000
Promotions	90,000
Wages and salaries	107,000
Bad debt provision	5,000
Depreciation	3,000
Net profit	**(18,600)**

Dividends are the portion of the organisation's profits that they pay to shareholders.

ACTIVITY

Look at the profit-and-loss account for the health club Healthy Habits Ltd shown on the right. Write a letter to the organisation's shareholders telling them what the dividends are for the year.

The figure for net profit after taxation is used by:

- existing and potential investors and financers to see how profitable the organisation is
- the organisation to
  - monitor its overall financial performance
  - compare with net profit targets it has set and with past net profit
  - assess how efficiently it is operating.

ACTIVITY

Look at the profit-and-loss account for Waterfront Tourist Centre. The net profit figure is in brackets which means it's a loss or negative profit. What course of action would you suggest to find ways of bringing the organisation back into profit?

Dividends funding

Private and public limited companies aim to pay a proportion of profits to their shareholders every year in return for their investment in shares. The dividends funding will depend on the amount of profit a company makes, and how much of this money it needs to reinvest in the company.

Dividends are paid after tax has been deducted from the net profit. The amount given tells shareholders how much has been set aside from the organisation's profit to be shared out amongst them in return for their investment in the organisation.

Healthy Habits Ltd		
Profit-and-loss account for the year ending 31st December 1995		
Turnover		**500,000**
Cost of sales		**150,000**
Gross profit		**150,000**
less expenses		
heating and lighting	10,000	
telephone	800	
stationery	3,000	
advertising	12,000	
wages and salaries	95,000	
business rates	1,800	
insurance	1,500	
depreciation	2,500	
Net profit		**23,400**
add income from bar	764	
less interest payments	980	
Profit before tax		**23,184**
less Corporation tax	5,790	
Profit after tax		**17,394**
proposed dividends	8,000	
retained profit for the year		**9,394**

DISCUSSION POINT

Angela recently inherited several thousand pounds and wants to invest the money so that it provides some income. A friend who works in the entertainment industry asks her to invest in his company.

Dave tells her that his company's turnover last year was £500,000, which Angela thinks sounds pretty impressive. As she hasn't done this type of thing before, she takes some advice from an independent financial adviser before buying shares. The adviser looks at the company accounts, and tells Angela that although the turnover was as Dave had told her, the company's net profit was only £3000 and dividends hadn't been paid to shareholders for the past three years.

On the basis of this information, do you think Angela should invest or not?

ACTIVITY

Look at the following profit-and-loss account, which is for a large leisure group.

		1994		**1993**
		£,000s		**£,000s**
TURNOVER				
Continuing operations		1941.7		1615.1
Acquisitions - LWT		156.0		
		2097.7		1615.1
DEPRECIATION				
Rental assets	83.2		84.8	
Other assets	43.5		42.6	
	126.7		127.4	
Staff costs	482.9		370.5	
Net other operating costs	1189.3		912.7	
		1798.9		1410.6
CONTINUING OPERATIONS	269.3		204.5	
Acquisitions - LWT	29.5			
Operating profit		298.8		204.5
Net interest		33.4		28.5
Profit before taxation		265.4		176.0
Tax on profit		73.2		49.3
Profit after taxation		192.2		126.7
Dividends on shares		70.1		53.1
Amount transferred to share reserves		121.9		73.2

Using the figures shown in the table, extract the financial information for:

■ total turnover in 1994

■ operating profit for 1994

■ profit after taxation for 1994

■ total staff costs for both 1993 and 1994

■ tax on profit for 1994

■ dividends paid on shares in 1993 and 1994.

Getting information from balance sheets

The balance sheet sets all the assets – the things an organisation owns – against all its liabilities – the things an organisation owes money on. It shows you how much an organisation is worth on the day the balance sheet was drawn up.

Assets

There are two types of asset:

■ fixed assets – things that will last for longer than a year and that take time to sell for cash if necessary, such as buildings, vehicles, computers and furniture

■ current assets – things that will last for less than a year and that can be sold quickly for cash if necessary, such as stocks of materials, stationery, and money owed to the organisation that it can reasonably expect the debtor will pay within the course of a year.

Assets are listed on an organisation's balance sheet and show how much the organisation's possessions are worth. The financial value of each asset is its estimated selling price.

Liabilities

There are two types of liability:

■ current liabilities – debts the organisation will have to pay within a year, payments for supplies bought on credit, tax debts, overdrafts, payments for expenses due within the period

■ long-term liabilities – debts it will have to pay in full after a period of more than a year, such as long-term loans.

Money invested in the organisation by the owners also counts as a long-term liability because although the organisation uses the money to finance its operations, it still strictly belongs to the owners and is in effect a long-term loan.

Liabilities are listed on an organisation's balance sheet and show how much the organisation owes in total.

The relationship between assets and liabilities

The total value of the assets should be equal to (balance) the total value of the liabilities. This means that, in theory, an organisation could pay off its liabilities by selling its assets.

DISCUSSION POINT

Look at the following list of assets and liabilities for a gym and decide which are:

■ fixed assets

■ current assets

■ long-term liabilities

■ current liabilities.

1 bank loan for changing room extension

2 sports equipment bought on twelve months' credit

3 gym mats

4 computer

5 gym premises

6 basket balls

7 bank overdraft

8 capital invested by owner

Explain why in each case.

ACTIVITY

Look at the following balance sheet. It is for a large leisure group organisation with many interests, subsidiary companies and shareholders. Its balance sheet reflects this. But if you look at the figures in bold, you can see that the balance sheet principle is the same – in both years, what the organisation owns is equal to what it owes.

		1994		1993
Fixed assets				
Tangible assets		862.1		786.8
Investments		123.1		208.1
		985.2		994.9
Current assets				
Stocks	184.4		128.4	
Debtors (due within one year)	248.7		189.7	
Debtors (due after more than one year)	194.7		215.5	
Cash & short-term investments	281.1		146.0	
	908.9		809.9	
Creditors (falling due within one year)				
Borrowings	107.5		274.9	
Other creditors	719.1		535.0	
	826.6			
	809.9			
Net current assets/(liabilities)		82.3		(130.3)
Total assets less current liabilities		1067.5		864.6
Creditors (falling due after more than one year)				
Borrowings	466.1		273.3	
Other creditors	46.8		50.2	
		512.9		323.5
Provisions for liabilities and charges		51.4		75.5
Net assets		503.2		465.6
Capital and reserves				
Called up share capital		162.7		134.5
Share premium account		157.7		175.6
Revaluation reserve		137.7		138.1
Merger reserve		(416.8)		(344.8)
Profit-and-loss account		461.0		360.9
Shareholders funds		502.3		464.3
Minority interests		0.9		1.3
		503.2		**465.6**

With the help of a friend or your tutor, work through the figures in the balance sheet for each year and check that the balancing totals are correct.

Pick out the following figures from the balance sheet:

■ the net assets for 1993

■ the fixed assets for 1994

■ the current liabilities (sums to be paid out within twelve months) in 1994.

Getting information from annual reports

An annual report is a summary of an organisation's business and financial activities for the year.

All limited companies (those with Limited, Ltd or plc in their company name) have to be registered with Companies House. Each year, they must publish their accounts and:

■ send a copy to the Registrar of Companies at Companies House

■ issue the published accounts to their shareholders at an annual general meeting (AGM).

Members of the public can ask to see any published annual account held by the Registrar of Companies or ask the limited company directly for a copy.

Public-sector organisations have to prepare a statement of accounts for their funding bodies.

Voluntary-sector organisations also have to prepare annual accounts for their financial supporters.

Any organisation earning an income would have to prepare annual reports for the tax authorities showing how its income had been made and used.

The following extract is taken from the 1994 annual report of a large leisure organisation.

	1994 (m)	1993 (m)	Change (%)
Turnover	2097.7	1615.1	30%
Operating profit	298.8	294.5	46%
Profit before tax	265.4	176.0	51%
Net cash inflow before investing activities	303.3	248.5	22%
Earnings per share	33.6p	25.6p	31%
Dividend per share	10.0p	8.75p	14%

The figures show that the organisation had a very successful year in 1994:

■ The company's turnover increased by 30% from £1615.1m in 1993 to £2097.7m in 1994.

■ The company's operating profit increased by 46% from £294.5m in 1993 to £298.8m in 1994.

As a direct result of this improved performance, the Board of Directors paid an increased dividend to shareholders.

Key questions

1 Why do organisations need accounts?
2 What does 'accountable' mean?
3 What are the purposes of:
   – a trading account?
   – a profit-and-loss account?
   – a balance sheet?
   – an annual report?
4 Can you list five types of people who use financial accounts, and explain why they use them?
5 What kinds of financial information do the following accounts give:
   – a trading account?
   – a profit-and-loss account?
   – a balance sheet?
   – an annual report?
6 What is meant by an organisation's turnover?
7 What is the difference between gross profit and net profit
8 What are:
   – assets?
   – liabilities?
9 If you were a tax inspector for the Inland Revenue, which item on the profit-and-loss account would interest you most?
10 If you were a shareholder in a company, which item on the profit-and-loss account would interest you most?

Assignment

Part 1

Pick two private or public limited organisations, one from the leisure and recreation sector, one from the travel and tourism sector.

Get hold of their annual published reports from the organisation itself, a public library or Companies House.

Look through the reports and see what information is given about the financial situation and performance of each organisation. Make a list of the items of information you extract and write an explanation of what each one means.

Part 2

Prepare a leaflet explaining in general terms the purposes of financial accounts in leisure and tourism organisations. Include a summary of who uses the accounts and what they use them for.

ELEMENT **4.3**

Budgeting

Budgets are the basis for monitoring financial performance. People use budgets to help them control their personal finances – for example, they might have a weekly household budget and an annual budget for clothes or holidays. Organisations use budgets for the same reasons. In this element you will be looking at the budgets used by leisure and tourism organisations to control costs and monitor their financial performance. You'll have the chance to investigate different types of budget and to draw up a budget yourself.

66 When it comes to budgeting we aim to keep as much money as possible circulating in the business – we don't take as much money out as we could. That's because we prefer to offer high quality at a high price rather than low quality at a low price. After ten years of business we can be fairly sure of the level of income we get each year and this gives us a base budget for the year. 99

owner of a guest-house

66 The budgets we get from the finance manager are very strict. To maximise the amount of profit we make, we have to keep our running costs down, offer competitive rates and run at a high utilisation rate on the vehicles. 99

car-rental manager

66 Although the local authority finance department monitors our figures closely, we have finance workers in each department and I have to manage the budget for our own team. The finance people set the budget, but it's up to me to make sure that we keep costs within it. 99

community play officer in a city council

66 Our costs include prizes, permission from the water authority to use the river, a donation to the St John's ambulance, rescue services, an affiliation fee for the Amateur Rowing Association, and so on. There are no labour costs because everyone works as volunteers. We also need to provide mobile toilet, premises for prize giving and serving food. We run the event to make a profit. This is used in the first instance to guarantee the event for other years, then if there is a surplus we advertise the fact and ask junior rowing groups to bid for it. We could help them buy a set of oars, for example. Any profit we make goes back into the sport. 99

organiser of a regatta

66 We had a big firework display as a finale to the festival. It was easy to work out exactly what work was needed for a self-contained event like that, so we could work to a fixed price. The subcontractors always knew the budget that we were working to. 99

festival organiser

The requirements of budgets

A **budget** is a plan which describes how an organisation or individual will obtain and use its money over a specified period of time.

Any individual or organisation with money coming in (income) and money going out (expenditure) needs a budget. Budgets are used to plan:

■ how much money will be available and when
■ how much to spend
■ what to spend it on.

The way organisations budget is similar to how you and your family might plan to spend money. On the left of the page is one family's monthly budget.

Budgets should be:

■ accurate and up-to-date
■ easy to understand
■ produced regularly
■ reviewed regularly.

Budget targets should be:

■ related to the organisation's financial objectives
■ realistic
■ achievable.

ACTIVITY

Draw up a monthly budget for your own income and expenditure. Allow enough money for different types of expenditure – clothes, travel, entertainment and so on. Then for the next month note down everything you spend and what you spend it on, and monitor your spending against your budget. At the end of the month, compare your budget with your actual expenditure.

■ Did you have to make any changes to ensure that you kept within your budget?

■ Did you spend on items not in your budget? If so, what effect did it have?

There are four main reasons why leisure and tourism organisations need to set budgets:

■ to monitor their performance
■ to control their performance
■ to control their cash flow
■ to forecast their future expenditure.

Monitoring and controlling performance

By monitoring their actual income and expenditure in comparison with their budgeted income and expenditure, leisure and tourism organisations can see whether they are:

■ keeping to financial targets
■ spending according to plan
■ getting as much income as they expected.

For organisations to do this effectively, they need to record accurate information about the amount of money they spend, and what they spend it on. If they see that they are spending more on an item than they budgeted for, they can control their performance by:

■ trying to spend less on the item
■ spending less on another item, to balance the budget
■ trying to increase their income.

The finance manager of a health club explains how he uses budgets to monitor and control the club's financial performance.

66 *We've set ourselves income and spending targets for the coming year that should help us to achieve an increase of 5% in profits. We've estimated the*

MONTHLY BUDGET FOR THE WALKER FAMILY	
Monthly income	£1660.00
Mortgage	£420.00
Community charge	£52.00
Telephone	£12.00
Electricity	£10.00
Gas	£15.00
Food	£400.00
Car repayments	£348.00
Car insurance	£32.00
Road tax	£11.25
Petrol	£85.00
Train fares	£58.00
Credit repayments for furniture	£21.75
Entertainment	£65.00
Clothes	£30.00
Holiday savings	£20.00
Savings	£40.00
Emergencies	£40.00
Total	**£1660.00**

levels of sales we need to aim for and the spending limits we need to keep to over the year. We've then broken it down into monthly targets. Each month, we review our performance against our monthly targets. We then look at the reasons for any difference, decide what effects the differences could have and make any adjustments necessary to targets for future months. **99**

ACTIVITY

A gym set itself the following budget.

Carlton Park Gym: budget as at 5 January 1996

	Amount allocated for the period 1 October 1995 to 1 January 1996	Actual expenditure
Wages:	£20,000	£22,000
Rent:	£9,000	£9,000
Heating and lighting:	£3,000	£2,700
Stationery:	£400	£423
Snack bar supplies:	£1,200	£1,300
Advertising:	£1,200	£1,475
Maintenance:	£1,500	£1,480

For each item (wages, rent etc.) work out whether spending has been kept within budget allocation, or whether there has been overspending or underspending.

■ Has the total amount spent on items exceeded the total budget?

■ In the light of the figures, which areas of spending would you want to investigate?

Cash flow is the flow of cash into and out of an organisation.

Controlling cash flow

A budget identifies:

■ the likely amounts and dates of outflows of cash – by identifying the resources, supplies and services needed, estimating how much they will cost and when they'll have to be paid for

■ the likely amounts and dates of inflows of cash – by estimating levels of income from funding sources or the sale of products and services and when they're likely to come in.

Identifying amounts and dates of inflows and outflows of cash gives the organisation:

■ a timetable for their spending

■ a limit to the amounts of money that can be spent at a time.

It can then organise its activities to fit in with the cash flow to ensure that cash is available at the right time and in the right amounts to cover the spending.

A marketing manager explains how she controls cash flow on promotional letters and leaflets mailed directly to customers.

66 *The most expensive bit is the cost of design work and printing. Two-thirds of the cost is covered by a budget allocation from internal resources like profits on previous promotions but there's also an assumption that the sales the promotion generates will cover the remaining third of the costs. Because we sell through direct mail, our customers can only see the product by sending for it. If they like it, they keep it and pay for it. If they don't like it, they send it back. This means that sales tend to be at their highest in the two weeks following the promotion, and returns are at their highest for the two weeks after that. To fit in with this pattern of cash flow, we schedule the printing so that the leaflets come in four days before the mailing date and the printer's bill comes in four weeks after the mailing date. That way we know we'll have the money to pay it.* 99

Forecasting

Forecasting aims to set a realistic budget for the year ahead. Previous years' budgets are a good starting point for preparing the coming year's budget. An organisation can look at how well previous budgets covered their year's activities. It can identify where the actual spending varied from the budget plan – these are known as budget variances. Then it can investigate why the variances happened – this is known as variance analysis. For example, there may have been an underestimate of costs, an unforeseen expense or a lack of proper spending controls. All this information will be used in preparing the forecasted budget.

Costs won't necessarily be the same in the coming year. So a budget forecast will take into account definite and possible increases and decreases so they can adjust their predicted expenditure levels accordingly. Income is also likely to be different so a budget forecast will also take into account things like predicted sales levels or changes in funding.

DISCUSSION POINT

What could happen to a business if:

■ it didn't have a budget?

■ the budget wasn't properly monitored?

Budget variances are the differences between the planned income and spending and the actual spending and income.

If the actual amount is better than the planned amount, it's called a **positive** or **favourable variance**. If the actual amount is worse than the planned amount, it's called a **negative** or **unfavourable variance**.

Investigating the reasons for variances is known as **variance analysis**.

ACTIVITY

The figures on the right are the budgeted total sales and actual total sales made by a tour operator over a twelve-month period. Use the figures to calculate:

■ monthly variances

■ quarterly variances

■ total annual variance.

Draw a graph showing the budgeted and actual figures for the year.

Touralot Limited
Sales budget performance for the year ending 31st March 1996

	Budgeted £,000s	Actual £,000s
Jan	55	56
Feb	50	48
Mar	65	68
Apr	70	72
May	85	80
Jun	120	111
Jul	200	210
Aug	250	290
Sep	190	175
Oct	160	175
Nov	100	105
Dec	75	69

The limitations of budgets

As you probably know from your own experience, setting a budget is one thing, keeping to it is another. This may be because the information used to set the budget wasn't accurate, or because unexpected things happened and interfered with the plan.

Organisations need to bear in mind two main limitations of budgets:

■ the quality of information used – good budgeting depends on information which is accurate, reliable, consistent, and sensitive to factors within the organisation which might affect spending and income (e.g. sales forecasts)

■ the quality of assumptions made – good budgeting needs to take into account factors outside the organisation which might affect spending and income (e.g. recession).

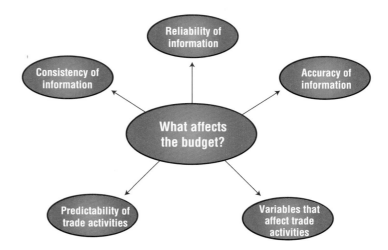

DISCUSSION POINT

If you have problems with your personal budget, are they caused by poor quality information, or poor quality assumptions?

Quality of information

When setting budgets, organisations need to make sure that the information they use is:

■ accurate and well researched

■ from a reliable source

■ used consistently (for example, taken from a similar period in previous years)

■ sensitive to factors within the organisation which might affect income and expenditure. For example, budgets should take into account issues such as projected incomes, sales forecasts and resourcing requirements.

The finance manager for a sports centre describes how she ensures the quality of the information she uses to set budgets:

66 *The records I have of our past performance give me a lot of accurate, reliable and consistent information. I can look back over a number of years and see what sort of spending and earning patterns our activities have shown in the*

past, what sort of things knocked us off course and how we responded. Some of the information I have about the future can be reasonably certain – for example, the levels of staff pay for the year. Some things I may have to take a reasoned guess at – for example, likely rises in the cost of heating or supplies. I also have to build in an element of flexibility so we can respond to changes along the way – for example, setting aside money in case of an unexpected rise in interest rates. Gathering and using information is a continuous process not a one-off activity. I work with the information I have at the time. If the information changes over the course of the budget period, I look at how the changes affect the plan and adjust the plan accordingly. **"**

Quality of assumptions

As budgeting is about looking into the future, it involves making assumptions about what is going to happen. It is important that these assumptions are as accurate as possible, so that the budget is realistic.

Good-quality assumptions:

- are well researched
- take into account factors beyond the control of the organisation which may affect budgets.

For example, a travel company setting its budgets would need to bear in mind the following factors when making assumptions about the future:

- a competitor might start selling a new product or offer discounts
- a foreign currency might be devalued
- the summer might be particularly hot, or the winter particularly cold
- major unexpected increases in the price of food, which could affect the price of hotels
- what the pattern of demand for their products or services tells them about the level of stability of their markets.

ACTIVITY

Talk to someone involved in budgeting for a leisure and tourism organisation. Find out:

- what sort of information they use when putting together budgets
- how they ensure that the information is
  - accurate
  - reliable
  - consistent
  - sensitive to possible change factors
- what sort of assumptions they make.

Types and structure of budgets

An organisation has a hierarchy of budgets. At each level of the hierarchy the organisation's budgets are divided into separate areas of income and expenditure and become more specific and more detailed. For example, the master budget will show amounts predicted for total sales. A number of departments in the organisation may be involved in making sales and they will each have their own budget showing the proportion of total sales they are expecting to make. The organisation may offer a range of different products and services and there will be a target number of sales set for each product and service in the range.

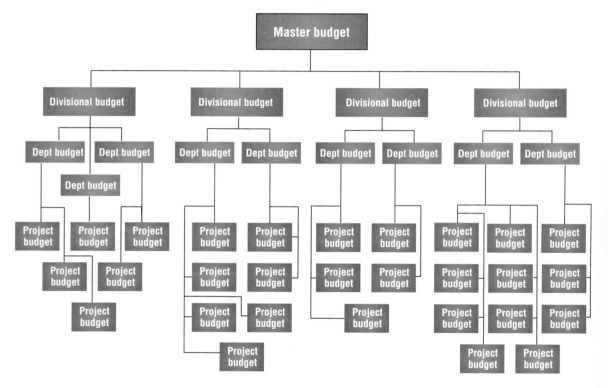

Master budgets

Preparing a master budget is part of the normal accounting procedures for an organisation. It incorporates the financial budgets of all divisions or departments, and is used to control spending across the whole organisation.

Senior staff within an organisation – such as financial directors and heads of accounts – are responsible for setting and monitoring the master budget. By looking at income and expenditure from the past year, and the planned activities for the year ahead, they decide how much money the organisation can spend over the coming year and what resources they will need to provide. They then work out how to divide this total budget between different departments in the organisation.

An accountant who works for a theme park explains the process for doing this:

> 66 *I look at how much money we've got, the forecast for income and spending for the period ahead, how much money we spent last year and how it was allocated. Department heads give me information on their proposed spending plans for the period. I decide on the best way to divide up the money and make sensible allocations to each department's budget. In some areas, there can be a certain amount of negotiation involved. For example, the marketing department may want to increase their spending on a certain type of promotional activity because their research has shown that it's likely to increase sales. Other areas may be fixed and not open to negotiation. For example, a department head may want to take on more staff but the forecast level of income for the organisation as a whole isn't enough to allow an increase in staffing levels.* 99

Dreamworld Theme Park – master budget for the year to 31 March 1996

	£,000	£,000
Trading account summary		
Sales		1,200
Opening stock	200	
Purchases	500	
Closing stock	(300)	
Cost of sales		(400)
Gross profit		**800**
Total expenses		**765**
Net profit		**35**
Balance sheet summary		
Fixed assets		70
Current assets		100
Current liabilities		(60)
Long-term liabilities		(20)
Net assets		**90**
Capital and reserves		**90**

Divisional budgets

A divisional budget is the portion of the master budget allocated to particular areas of an organisation's activities. Having agreed to their divisional budgets, the division or department heads are responsible for monitoring and controlling them.

The head of catering at a large public-sector arts centre explains her responsibilities for the catering budget:

66 *Our divisional budgets are set by the finance department and we don't have much room for negotiating. My responsibility is to make sure that the activities involved in providing the catering service stay within the budget. I decide how to allocate money from the budget to the resources we need – food, supplies, equipment and so on. My aim is to keep the costs down as far as possible without impairing the quality of the service we provide. So I have to look around for the best prices, check that the way we prepare food involves only the minimum of wastage and so on. I monitor the budget constantly throughout the year to make sure we're keeping to the spending plan and to identify any adjustments we need to make. I have to keep a careful eye on spending. Overspending in one area means cutting back in another. If I do overrun on the budget, I look very carefully into the reasons why it happened. That gives me the information I need either to keep a stricter control of spending in the future or to justify asking for an increase for a future budget period.* 99

DISCUSSION POINT

If one department overspends on its budget, what might be the effects on:

■ its future plans

■ other departments' budgets

■ the organisation's financial targets?

Dreamworld Theme Park – divisional budget for the year to 31 March 1996

	£,000
Division A – Accommodation services	200
Division B – Rides and amusements services	600
Division C – Food outlet services	100
Division D – Music and visual entertainment services	300
Total sales	**1,200**

Trading budget for divisions for the year to 31 March 1995

	A	B	C	D	Master budget total
£,000	£,000	£,000	£,000	£,000	
Sales	200	600	100	300	1,200
Opening stock	15	100	40	45	200
Purchases	100	220	30	150	500
Closing stock	(65)	(75)	(60)	(100)	(300)
Cost of sales	50	245	10	95	400
Gross profit	**150**	**355**	**90**	**205**	**800**
Profit-and-loss account					
Gross profit	150	355	90	205	800
Expenses					
Salaries and wages	50	200	50	100	400
Light and power	10	35	5	50	100
Depreciation	1	15	2	2	20
Rent	50	50	20	30	150
Stationery	1	1	1	7	10
Postage	2	5	2	1	10
Travel and subsistence	5	5	3	2	15
Repairs	2	5	1	2	10
Marketing	2	35	5	8	50
Total expenses	**123**	**351**	**89**	**202**	**765**
Net profit	**27**	**4**	**1**	**3**	**35**

Project budgets

Project budgets are for one-off projects which are not part of an organisation's regular activities. For example:

■ a hotel might set a project budget if it wants to renovate its reception area but didn't allow for it in the refurbishment budget

■ a theme park might set a project budget if it decides to build a new restaurant

■ a local sports club might set a project budget if it decides to resurface its football pitch.

Most organisations allow money for projects like these in their master budget and divisional budgets. Project budgets can then be prepared at any time in the financial year, depending when the project is due to start. The person managing the project may be:

■ given a total budget for the job, and asked to decide how it should be spent

■ asked to prepare a budget to estimate how much the project is likely to cost.

Either way, it involves thinking through what the project will require in terms of:

■ what needs to be done

■ time

■ people

■ money.

Budget structure

Although organisations may have their own style of presentation for budgets, they basically consist of four components:

■ the budget title

■ the budget period

■ expense headings

■ elements within headings.

Budget title

This identifies what the budget is for. For example:

■ the master budget

■ the marketing budget

■ the promotions budget.

It should also state whether it is a budget forecast or an actual budget.

Budget period

The budget period is the time the budget covers. Some budgets are set for a year. Some are set for parts of the year – for each quarter or each month. Some are set on a week-by-week or even day-by-day basis. The budget period

You work for a travel company which is keen to promote sales of holidays to India. The marketing manager has decided to hold an evening event which will involve a talk on holidaying in India and information about the holidays available through the company. Your part in the project will be to arrange for food and drink for the customers. The budget allocation for this is £400. A hundred customers are expected to attend and the evening will last about three hours.

Draw up a spending plan for the food and drink service for the marketing manager to approve. Make notes on how you found the information you needed on costs for providing the food and drink service.

chosen will depend on the type of budget – for example, master budgets are usually set for a year, project budgets are set for the time the project is expected to take.

Expense headings

The total amount of money allocated to a budget is divided up into different areas of spending. For example, a budget for the production of a holiday brochure would show how much would be spent on individual aspects involved in producing the brochure. Each area would be identified by a heading to make clear what type of expense it was – for example:

- design
- copywriting
- printing.

Elements within headings

Each area of spending will be made up of a number of elements – smaller, specific items of expenditure. For example, the design aspect of producing a holiday brochure could include the elements of:

- artwork
- photography
- typesetting.

Each element will then be allocated an appropriate amount of the overall spending on design.

ACTIVITY

Think of the domestic budget for your family. If you were to start with the total income as being your master budget, how would you divide it into divisional budgets for your family's expenditure. What headings and elements would you include in each divisional budget?

DISCUSSION POINT

Look back at the example of budgets given in this section. How do the components of a budget structure help to control, monitor and evaluate the way the budget is implemented?

Preparing a simple budget

Preparing a budget involves thinking through every detail of the activity you're budgeting for. It's a bit like doing a jig-saw in reverse – you start with the whole picture then you take it apart and look at each component piece. In the case study below, two colleagues talk about how they went about preparing a budget.

Andrea and Michael work in the personnel department of an organisation which owns a number of outdoor activity centres in your county and the two neighbouring counties. As part of a recruitment drive, the organisation is planning to visit six schools and colleges in their catchment area to raise students' awareness of the career opportunities available in the outdoor activity sector. Andrea and Michael have been given the task of estimating the costs of making the visits and drawing up a budget for expenditure.

Andrea explains their first steps:

66 *Michael and I got together and discussed the information we'd been given about the project. The marketing department was putting together a plan for displays and would provide leaflets and brochures about the centre's facilities. The personnel director was planning a presentation which would involve overhead projector slides, a video film and some question-and-answer sessions. The organisation owns a number of overhead projectors and a video film projector but the projector screen we have here is fixed to the wall in the board room. So we needed to find out about hiring or buying a screen. We also need to find out about hiring or buying display boards. The organisation does have some of its own but they're constantly in use around the centre. We also needed a means of transporting the people and equipment to each of the schools and colleges.* 99

Michael took on the task of finding out the costs of both hire and purchase of the equipment and Andrea contacted a number of vehicle hire firms in the local area.

Michael found out that it was cheaper to hire the screen and display boards than to buy them. While he was thinking about equipment needs, Michael came up with another consideration:

66 *It occurred to me that we didn't know anything about the facilities the schools and colleges were offering us. We knew they were arranging for a room we could use but I thought it would be useful to suss out what the rooms were like before the actual event. This meant one of us would have to make a visit to each venue. We decided that I would take on that role and costed out the travelling expenses involved so they could be added into the budget. I have my own car and if I use it for company business I'm entitled to claim expenses. The organisation pays 35p per mile. The total mileage I'd do in travelling to each venue would be 200 miles so that was quite a straightforward costing exercise.* 99

245

The next aspect Michael and Andrea considered was staffing. Andrea explains:

    There was quite a lot of equipment when we thought about it. Also, we needed to be able to set up and pack up as quickly as possible. So we decided that three people would need to be involved – Michael and I made two and we asked a colleague, Tim, to be the third.

Michael explains the cost implication for staffing:

    In all, four of us would be involved – me, Tim and Andrea as the 'crew' and the personnel director, Jan, as the 'performer'. Although each visit was relatively local, by the time we'd got back from each one, unpacked the van and returned to the hire firm, we estimated it would be after 6.00 p.m. when we finished for the day. Andrea, Tim and I are eligible for overtime payment for work outside the normal office hours of 9 to 5. Jan isn't because she's senior management and extra input is expected from them. So that meant working out likely overtime for me, Tim and Andrea and adding payment for that into the budget.

Bringing in Tim as part of the crew also had implications for the travelling arrangements, as Michael explains:

    The van we were hiring only seats three. We were proposing to take four staff members. This meant one would have to travel separately. It made sense for it to be Jan. She has a company car and her use of it wouldn't affect our project budget.

Michael and Andrea's budget was almost complete. Andrea explains the final element:

    Like any plan, a budget can go wrong. So Michael and I thought through some possibilities. We identified two that could realistically happen. Either we could get held up in traffic or have a flat tyre and get back too late to return the van in time – this would mean paying for a two-day rather than a one-day hire and extra overtime. Or equipment could get damaged and have to be replaced.

We then discussed a reasonable level of contingency funding to add to the budget. We decided that it was unlikely that both things would happen and over the six visits we were making neither would happen more than once. So we decided that adding an amount equivalent to an extra day's van hire and half an hour's overtime per person would cover us for an emergency.

Having assembled all the information they needed and costed out all the resources, Andrea and Michael drew up the budget and submitted it to Jan for approval.

ACTIVITY

The outdoor centre staff in the case study are making a visit to your school or college and others in the area. You've been asked to organise a poster advertising the visit that will be put up around all the participating establishments.

Draw up a design or a written brief describing the aim and effect you want the poster to achieve. Contact a couple of local designers and discuss with them how much it would cost to produce the artwork from your design or design brief. Then contact a couple of printers and discuss with them how much it would cost to print the poster. Finally, work out your distribution costs. Use all the information you have gathered to put together a budget for producing and distributing the poster.

ACTIVITY

The six visits the outdoor activity staff made to schools and colleges were so successful that they are thinking of doing the same thing again the following year. This time, they're proposing to make two trips to each of the schools and colleges they visited last year and two trips to your own school or college which is 80 miles away from their head office.

The trips to your establishment will mean two overnight stays for three people in a hotel in your area. Tim won't be taking part this year as they decided that the setting up and packing up can be managed by two people. They also know that it takes an hour to set up, an hour to pack up and an hour to unload the van and return it to the hire firm. The presentation takes two hours.

When they visit your establishment, any overtime will be calculated from 5.00 p.m. until they get to the hotel. For each visit, the starting time for the presentation is 1.30 p.m.

Your task is to draw up the budget. Here's last year's actual expenditure budget:

RECRUITMENT PROMOTIONAL VISITS, JULY 1995
ACTUAL EXPENDITURE

Inspection visits
Expenses: 200 miles @ 35p per mile   £70.00

Van hire
6 one-day hires @ £45 per day
plus petrol: 25 litres @ 55.9p per litre   £283.97

Equipment
Projection screen: 6 one-day hires @ £20 per day   £120.00
Display boards: 6 one-day hires of 4 boards @ £3 per   £72.00
board per day

Staff
55 hours overtime @ £4.40 per hour   £242.00

Total   £787.97

Here are some other considerations for you to build into your budget:

- The cost of equipment has gone up by 5%.
- The organisation has increased car usage expenses to 37p per mile.
- Overtime payments have increased by 1.5%.

Key questions

1 What is a budget?
2 Why is it important to have a budget?
3 What is the purpose of monitoring a budget?
4 How can organisations make sure good quality information is used when budgeting?
5 What do organisations need to consider when making assumptions for budgets?
6 What are the differences between a master budget, a divisional budget and a project budget?
7 What expense headings might you find in a leisure and tourism budget?

Assignment

Part 1

Use a leisure or tourism organisation you know about as the basis for a case study on the theory and practice of budgeting. Your case study should:

■ explain what the organisation expects to achieve from its budgeting activities
■ say what limitations it has to take into consideration
■ describe the types and structure of the budgets the organisation uses.

Part 2

Prepare a checklist of the things you need to include when preparing a budget. Use the checklist to help you prepare the budget for the event you are organising as part of your work on Unit 8, Event management.

UNIT 5

Element 5.1

Administration systems

Element 5.2

Communications systems

Element 5.3

Information-processing systems

Business systems in the leisure and tourism industries

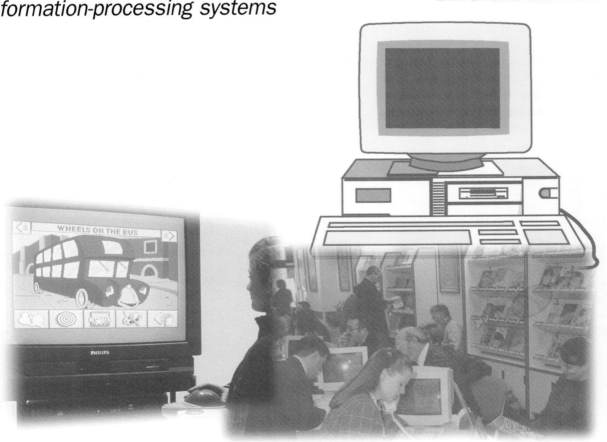

ELEMENT **5.1**

Administration systems

Think of the things that happen every day in any leisure and tourism organisation: customers coming in and out, goods and services being bought and sold, all the daily operations of running a facility. It all has to be done efficiently, safely and to the right quality. Many areas of the leisure and tourism industry have quality standards and kitemarks so that customers know the standards to expect and staff are clear about the standards they are working to. In this element you'll be looking at these standards and what they are for. You'll also be finding out how leisure and tourism businesses use administration systems to organise their work efficiently.

❝ We have various systems to ensure information is up to date and accurate. We have a stock-control system for our leaflets – we write down in a diary when leaflets come in and what their expiry date is, usually the end of the year. We also put events in the diary. We sometimes have problems because we are sent hundreds of leaflets by national distributors. Sometimes they update the leaflet but don't change the cover, so it's hard for us to work out which is the most up-to-date version of a leaflet. ❞

manager of a tourist information centre

❝ Two years ago the company decided to go for the Investors in People award. Our main aim was to make sure that we provide a good environment for people to develop their skills. We took the view that it would benefit the company as well as the individual – people would learn more and be better motivated if they had the opportunity to train. Our branch managers say that the award has helped staff become more aware of the company's training policy. ❞

training manager, national hotel chain

❝ I used to think administration was just a lot of unnecessary paperwork. Since I've been running this guest-house I've come to realise it's essential. I have to record bookings, plan ahead for the new leaflets, organise the cleaning and cooking rota and a thousand other things. I've become a lot more systematic – and more efficient too. ❞

owner of a guest-house

Quality standards

Quality standards are the levels of quality which a product or service must reach. Standards allow organisations to assure and control the quality of a service or product regardless of the individuals or methods involved in producing or providing it.

There are three different kinds of quality standards:

- internal
- external and voluntary
- external and compulsory.

Organisations in the UK operate to different levels of quality standards:

- international – issued by different countries or groups of countries, mainly to control the quality of imports and exports. For example, camera films which satisfy the International Standards Organisation (ISO) standards can carry the ISO mark
- European – mainly established by the European Commission (EC) and controlled through the issue of directives. For example, seaside resorts which meet the EC standards of beach quality are awarded a Blue Flag
- British – mainly set by the British Standards Institution (BSI). For example, products such as riding hats or cycle helmets which meet BSI standards can carry the BSI Kitemark.

Internal standards

are set by an organisation for itself. Many organisations have their own customer codes or charters which set out the kind of service that customers can expect to receive. For example:

- a restaurant owner has a rule that customers should not have to wait longer then ten minutes for their meals
- a hotel has a policy that all calls to the reception desk from outside should be answered within six rings.

External and voluntary standards

are set by an outside body and are not compulsory. An organisation can decide itself whether it is going to follow all, some or none of the standards. An example is the British Code of Advertising Practice which provides a system for the control of press advertising.

External and compulsory standards

are also set by an outside body, but this time the organisation has to follow them. They may be covered by government legislation. For example, in the Health and Safety at Work Act 1974 the safe handling, storage, use and transport of dangerous substances such as chlorine is the responsibility of the employer.

DISCUSSION POINT

Why do you think some quality standards are voluntary and others are compulsory?

THE BLUE FLAG FOR BEACHES

Below you will find the criteria for the award of the European Blue Flag for beaches in 1995.

The European Blue Flag is awarded annually and thus it is only valid for one year at a time, and during the time of the year when all criteria are fulfilled.

To be eligible for the Blue Flag a beach has to fulfill all " **i** " -requirements.

In addition, the fulfilment of a maximum number of "**g**"-criteria is taken into account.

WATER QUALITY

1. Compliance with the requirements of the EU Bathing Water Directive concerning the parameters of total and fecal coliform and fecal streptococci.

   Water samples must be taken fortnightly during the entire bathing season and must commence within a fortnight of its beginning but no later than five working days from the first date of the season.

   Moreover, in the case of the two coliform parameters at least 80% of the sampling results must be below guideline while for fecal streptococci 90% must be below the guideline value. At the same time no more than 5% of the samples can be above the imperative value for the two coliform parameters. During the season updated information on the bathing water quality must be posted on the beach.
2. No industrial or sewage related discharges may affect the beach area. (i)
3. Local and regional emergency plans to cope with pollution accidents. (9)
4. Beach and immediate hinterland to comply with official development plans and planning law. (i)

Extract from the Blue Flag criteria

Quality assurance

Quality assurance is the process which enables organisations to claim that a product or service is reaching the required standard. For example, a large hotel chain will have quality standards for every aspect of its business. Staff responsible for quality assurance make sure that those standards are kept, using a set of procedures to assess and monitor other staff, suppliers and products.

Where an official standards body is involved, they audit and approve these procedures before the kitemark is awarded. Organisations which gain the kitemark are required to document the procedures regularly and keep a record of how they are being observed.

The catering manager of a chain of hotels describes how they make sure their hotels are keeping to the quality standards:

❝ *My job is to maintain the food hygiene standards in all our hotels. We have produced a standards guide for all our chefs, and it's their responsibility to make sure their kitchens follow those standards. I do spot checks unannounced to make sure that they are up to standard. With this system there shouldn't be any problems with the environmental health people. But if there are I follow them up immediately and make any changes necessary.* ❞

Quality control

Quality control is the process for controlling the quality of a product or service, using particular methods and techniques. For example, a hotel might have a system of checking that rooms were being cleaned to standard.

The housekeeper of a hotel describes how their quality control process for rooms is carried out:

❝ *Our staff are fully trained in the procedures for cleaning a bedroom but I do a random check once a week to make sure everything is being done correctly. We have particular ways of folding the sheet corners and placing the hotel information literature on the desks in each room. We also lay out the towels and toiletries in the bathroom in a particular way. They're all small details but they add up to an attractive effect and they show the customer that we care enough to take the extra trouble.* ❞

Quality standards in leisure and tourism

Three quality standards are particularly relevant to leisure and tourism organisations:

■ BS EN ISO 9000

■ BS 7750 Environmental Management

■ Investors in People.

BS EN ISO 9000

An international standard which organisations are awarded when they have proved that they have introduced quality systems throughout their operations. The manager of a leisure centre describes how they have just introduced the standard:

❝ *We spent a year or more working towards the standard. We've introduced clear levels of quality in all our departments – plant management, lifeguarding, teaching, reception, catering and so on. All the staff are aware of these standards and work to them. Some of the systems were used before but we didn't have them written down and set out in the same way. An outside body audited us to check that the systems were up to the correct standard. We were then awarded the kitemark. The certificate's up in the reception area so that the public know that we're working to high standards all the time. But the biggest benefit is to us – all the staff say it's better to have clear quality standards.* **99**

DISCUSSION POINT

Why do you think it's important that an organisation such as a leisure centre works to quality standards such as ISO 9000? How might it help:

■ the day-to-day running of the centre?

■ its marketing?

Which organisations in leisure and tourism have a significant impact on the environment and could benefit from registration to BS7750?

BS 7750 Environmental Management

The first environmental management standard in the world, which will lead to the publication of the ISO 14000 series of environmental standards. It provides organisations of all sizes a framework against which they can:

■ look closely at their own environmental performance

■ make improvements where necessary so that the environmental impact of their operations is minimised.

Using the standard as a model they can set up and shape their own systems, review them and have them audited and registered. Registration to the standard demonstrates to customers the quality of the organisation's control and management of environmental effects.

Investors in People

An award sponsored by the UK government and administered by Training and Enterprise Councils (TECs). Organisations which wish to be registered as Investors in People are required to satisfy a number of criteria relating to staff development and training.

The managing director of a medium-sized company providing specialist holidays explains the value of being an Investor in People:

66 *It's a sign that we're committed to our staff. All staff have appraisals twice a year with their managers, where they discuss the job and any training needs they have. At the end they agree a training action plan for the next six months. Sometimes staff go on training courses, but more often it's a chance for them to learn new aspects of the job, or a new job altogether. It works both ways – we get the best out of our people and they get the chance to develop their jobs.* **99**

INVESTOR IN PEOPLE

ACTIVITY

Contact your local Training and Enterprise Council (the telephone number is in the front of your local Thomson Directory). Find out:

■ what criteria they set for organisations wishing to be registered as Investors in People

■ whether any local leisure or tourism organisations have been registered.

Administration systems

Administration systems are concerned with the collection, storage and distribution of information.

Organisations use their systems to support routine tasks and functions like dealing with customer enquiries or recording cash transactions. Most organisations also have administration systems for dealing with non-routine functions such as accidents and emergencies, or producing information which is only needed occasionally.

There are four main areas of administrative activity in leisure and tourism:
- finance – paying wages, sending out invoices, paying bills
- human resources – recruiting staff, administration of holiday and sick leave
- customer services – collecting customers' opinions, after-sales service
- quality assurance – monitoring standards.

There is often overlap between these areas. For example, the manager of the reception area of a large facility might use all four types:
- finance – keeping summaries of money received
- human resources – keeping staff time sheets
- customer services – training staff in customer relations
- quality assurance – carrying out customer surveys.

Most administration systems are now computer-based but some are still paper-based – for example, an accident log book.

Efficient administration systems help the organisation to run smoothly. They also create a good first impression for customers.

DISCUSSION POINT

What do you think are the main advantages of computer-based administration systems over paper-based ones? Are there any disadvantages?

Compare what happens in these two hotels, when a customer rings to make a booking for a room with a sea view:

HOTEL 1

The receptionist confirms on the telephone that a room is available but is unable to confirm whether it will have a sea view or not. She writes the details of the customer's name and date down on a piece of paper and leaves it on the reception desk to deal with later.

HOTEL 2

The receptionist is able to use the computerised booking system to confirm that a room is available and that it has the sea view the customer wants. She enters the customer's name, phone number, address and expected time of arrival on the computer. At the end of the day a computer print-out of new bookings is circulated to all reception staff. Once the booking has been entered on the computer, an address label is generated automatically and the customer is sent confirmation of the booking together with a copy of the hotel's brochure with a map and other details.

DISCUSSION POINT

Hotel 1 in the case study can't afford to buy a computer. How could its booking system be improved, even without a computer?

Each type of organisation in the leisure and tourism industry has its own administrative needs and methods. A member of the sales staff in a high-street travel agency explains what systems they use for routine business:

❝ *Our systems are quite easy, and they really help keep things in order. We use customer profile sheets where we write down what they want and keep a record of the services and products they have bought. Every night I go to the shelves and fill in brochure control sheets, to find out the most popular holiday brochures and keep stocks at the right level. My supervisor does the cash receipt books to record any payments we've had in over the counter. Then there are the usual filing systems for customer details and holiday information.* ❞

The same travel agency will also occasionally have to deal with non-routine tasks. For example, it may have to make a special announcement in the form of a poster that it is no longer dealing with a particular tour operator.

ACTIVITY

Think of three different facilities. Identify:

■ four routine administration systems that each would need

■ one non-routine system for each one.

How should the routine systems be set up?

How should the organisation handle its non-routine system?

<table>
<tr><td>**Section 5.1.3**</td></tr>
</table>

Evaluating the effectiveness of administration systems

What makes an administration system effective?

Fitness for purpose

There is no point in having an administration system that doesn't serve its purpose. For example, if someone needs information about current demand for a service, the system used should be concerned only with the collection and distribution of current information. Any out-of-date information will be irrelevant, unhelpful and even misleading.

Value for money

All administration systems should be cost-effective. This means that the financial return or saving on other expenses as a result of using the system should make the cost of setting it up and using it worthwhile. For example, buying an expensive computerised system will give value for money if it saves time and resources previously spent on a paper-based system. If it takes longer, it's not good value.

Accuracy

Information generated by an administration system has got to be accurate and reliable. For example, airlines have to to be able to collect, store and retrieve accurate information about the numbers of passengers on each of its flights. 'Guesstimates' aren't good enough if there's an accident or emergency.

Efficiency

Administration systems should work with the minimum waste of effort. For example, information that is needed constantly by a number of different people in a department could be stored in a central point in the office in an easily accessible format, like a wall planner.

Security

Confidential or sensitive information should be stored in a secure place and access to it should be restricted. For example, personal details about staff or customers should be stored in files with restricted access, not on an open-network computer system.

Ease of use

The best systems are simple to use, easily understood and accessible by the people who need to use them. They are also likely to be accurate and good value for money. For example, it may be possible to simplify a highly complex accounting system – or at least parts of it – so that staff without any accountancy training can use some of it.

User opinion

The people using an administration system need to be happy with it, especially if it's new or different from what they are used to. Some people are more resistant to change than others, but if people are encouraged to take an active part in change they are usually more likely to accept it.

Anyone evaluating the effectiveness of a system should take all these factors into account, as the case study illustrates.

Mena is a marketing assistant in a city council arts and leisure department. Her job is to maintain the organisation's mailing list. She uses a computer-based system which stores customer details and prints them on address labels. Her supervisor has asked her to look at how well the system is working, as there have been complaints from customers. They  say they are receiving details of forthcoming attractions too late or that they are getting two sets of details.

Mena draws up a list of questions which she will use to check how well the system is working.

Fitness for purpose

■ Is the system set up to collect and store the details that are needed – for example, does it have a prompt to include post codes in addresses? (items sent without postcodes can take longer to arrive)

■ Is it easy to update and amend customer details if they change?

Value for money

■ Are we saving time on this system, or does it take as long to enter details on the computer as it would to enter them on paper?

■ Is the system out-of-date – maybe there's a newer system on the market which would be better value for money?

Accuracy

■ Some customers are receiving details late because of inaccuracies in the mailing list itself – are these human errors or a problem in the system?

■ What checking devices are there in the system to make sure that details entered are accurate and that customers' details are not entered twice by mistake?

Efficiency

■ Is the system used efficiently – for example, can anyone in the box office change customer details or does this always have to be done by a particular person, who may not always be available?

■ Can we speed up the system in any way?

■ Is everyone who uses the system properly trained?

Security

■ Are customer details kept confidential?

■ What security measures are taken to make sure that only authorised people have access to the computer records?

Ease of use

■ Is the system easy to use – do some people find it more difficult to use than others?

■ Is it too difficult for people who are not used to computers – how could it be made easier?

■ Is it fast to use?

■ Are there problems such as computer crashes which make people reluctant to use it?

User opinion

■ What do people in the department think of the system?

■ Do they think it is helpful to them and to the organisation?

■ When it was introduced, did people think they were given enough back-up – training, support, encouragement?

Improvements to the system

This section started by looking at the reasons why leisure and tourism organisations have quality standards. Continuous improvement is part of quality. It means that everyone is looking for ways of improving what they do. They may only be small improvements – like having a notepad and pen on the reception desk or counter so customers don't have to scrabble in their bags or pockets for pen and paper. But a hundred small improvements are just as good as one big one.

Procedures

When you have worked out how well a system is working you may be able to suggest ways in which it could be improved. Before you start, it's a good idea to review the procedures, like Mena did in the case study on page 257. For example, you might be able to suggest ways in which procedures could be:

- simplified – are procedures unnecessarily complicated, is there a lot of paperwork or labour involved?
- streamlined – are they logical?
- updated – were they developed some time ago to match a set of requirements which no longer apply?
- formalised – are they too informal or do you need to be more specific about how they should be carried out?

Once you are satisfied that the procedures being used are as efficient as possible, you can think about two other main areas in which you could improve the system.

DISCUSSION POINT

What do you think will happen if systems are introduced or changed and staff don't get proper training? How could that affect the way they feel about their job and the organisation they work for?

Staff skills and expertise

You may decide that the system is not being used as well as it might because of the level of staff skills or expertise. For example, a new system might have been introduced without enough training for staff. You could:

- suggest some internal training sessions
- recommend that staff are funded to go on an outside training programme.

Equipment

Options for improving equipment can range from something quite simple and inexpensive such as an additional filing cabinet or computer software to a major purchase such as a completely new computer system. If you do suggest buying new equipment you will need to be satisfied that it will:

- lead to the improvement you are looking for
- be cost-effective – are there cheaper ways of achieving the same improvement such as simplifying a procedure or providing more staff training?
- be compatible with existing equipment – if you are buying new software for your computer it needs to work on the same operating system
- be flexible – if requirements change in future, will you have to change equipment again or will you be able to adapt what you have?

Mena's supervisor asks her to suggest ways for improving the mailing system. Mena's memo first reviews the procedures used for her mailing list, then goes on to consider staff skills and expertise and the actual equipment used.

Procedures

• Introduce a standard procedure to include the postcode in every address.

• Reduce the time interval between printing address labels and dispatching information to customers – three days should be the maximum.

• Introduce a system so that all staff check that a customer is not already on the mailing list before entering their details.

• Check customer details once a year to make sure all addresses are complete and that no address is repeated.

Staff skills and expertise

• Provide training in computer skills for staff who need to improve their accuracy on the keyboard.

• Suggest that two members of staff who are skilled in and confident about using the computer are nominated to provide back-up to other staff and deal with any minor problems.

• Introduce a monthly meeting for all staff to discuss any problems or difficulties with using the system.

Equipment

• Buy one additional computer terminal so that another member of staff can get involved in keeping the mailing list up to date.

• Buy additional computer software to speed up input of customer details.

• Get extra memory for the printer to speed up printing of address labels.

DISCUSSION POINT

Put yourself in the shoes of Mena's supervisor.

Which improvements is she likely to agree to?

Which might she turn down because they are too expensive or time-consuming?

Key questions

1   Why do leisure and tourism organisations need quality standards?
2   What's the difference between quality assurance and quality control?
3   What are the three main quality standards which apply to leisure and tourism organisations?
4   What functions do administration systems support in leisure and tourism organisations?
5   What's the difference between routine and non-routine functions?
6   Which seven criteria should you use to evaluate the effectiveness of an administration system?
7   What are the three main areas in which improvements can be made to administration systems?

Assignment

A leisure centre has recently expanded its business. The managing director has asked you to be part of a team investigating the administration systems and evaluating how well they are coping with the increase in business activities.

Write a three-part report for the managing director. In the first part:
■   outline in general terms the main purposes of quality standards
■   identify the administration systems supporting:
   – the routine functions – finance, human resources, customer service and quality assurance
   – the non-routine functions – emergencies, accidents, one-off or occasional needs
■   give an example of one administration system supporting each of the four routine functions
■   give an example of one administration system supporting one of the non-routine functions.

In the second part, pick a system that supports one function and evaluate its effectiveness. Base your evaluation on these questions:
■   Is it fit for its purpose?
■   Does it give value for money?
■   Does it ensure accuracy?
■   Is it efficient?
■   Does it meet security requirements?
■   Is it easy to use?
■   What do the users think of it?

In the third part, suggest any improvements you think could be made to the system you've evaluated. For example, you might be able to recommend:
■   improved procedures
■   improved equipment
■   training to increase staff skills, confidence or expertise.

ELEMENT **5.2**

Communications systems

People who work in leisure and tourism organisations have to be good communicators. They communicate with customers, colleagues, suppliers and many others. Think of a day in the working life of any employee in a travel agency, leisure facility or hotel: communicating with others is likely to be a big part of their job. Some of the communication will be with other people directly – face to face, on the telephone or using electronic communications. Some of it will be indirect – making signs and posters, writing and designing leaflets and so on. These days much of the communication in travel agencies and in large organisations is done electronically, by fax or using computers attached to networks. Increasingly, smaller organisations are starting to use these newer ways of communicating too.

❝ We deal with about two-thirds of our customers face to face and about a third on the phone. We don't tend to do mailings because of the time factor. People usually come in and want to book up there and then or they might ring up and pay by credit card over the phone. We use PCs to print out all our standard letters, and flight bookings these days are all done using a centralised computer system. **❞**

travel consultant in a travel agency

❝ We use personal computers in our office and are now using e-mail to communicate with other venues and with organisations like the regional arts bodies that fund us. The box office is also computerised, so we can keep information about customers on the database and mail them regularly with the new season's leaflet. We work quite closely with other venues and try to keep in regular touch with them. We want to keep up a constant flow of information with them, so we can all keep up to date about what's going on. **❞**

press and publicity officer at an entertainments venue

❝ As we all work within a few feet of each other we can obviously communicate with each other by talking. I don't have a PC because our receptionist also types all the managers' letters. Most of my contact with customers is face to face, when I deliver and collect cars, or over the phone. **❞**

car-rental manager

❝ As we are part of the council, we're part of the leisure services department and under the authority of the director of leisure services. In our office my staff are in the room next to me and I have a very hands-on style – helping out in the shop and so on. We have access to the council's computer system and use it regularly to create documents and collect statistics. **❞**

manager of a tourist information centre

Functions and purposes of communications systems

Communication is the process of exchanging messages – information, ideas or feelings.

All organisations need communications systems to be able to function effectively. It's particularly important in a service industry like leisure and tourism.

❝ *In a multinational organisation like this, we need to be able to keep all staff up to date. We use electronic mail to issue memos worldwide to all our offices so that everyone knows what is happening.* ❞

communications manager, international cinema group

❝ *We send a standard letter to all our users to let them know about forthcoming events.* ❞

marketing officer, sports centre

❝ *We have regular team meetings to discuss what we are doing and any problems we might be facing.* ❞

customer reservations manager, international airline

There are probably as many different types of communications systems as there are types of organisation. But they all have one or more of these functions and purposes.

DISCUSSION POINT

The managers quoted on this page work for a cinema group, a sports centre and an international airline. Think of four examples of tasks involving communication which they might have to carry out to:

■ support the management and operation of their organisations

■ make connections or links with another organisation

■ make connections or links between individuals

■ provide channels for giving or exchanging information.

Functions

■ to support the management and operation of an organisation – distributing department, sales information or responding to an enquiry from a customer

■ to make connections or links between organisations – making a written application for funding, paying a bill or sending information for a brochure to an advertising agency.

Purposes

■ to make connections or links between individuals – confirming a travel booking on the telephone, introducing members of a holiday group to each other

■ to provide channels for giving or exchanging information within an organisation or between organisations – faxing information to another department about a new service, reserving an airline seat on the telephone.

Section 5.2.2

Types of communications systems

Communications go on between people inside and outside an organisation. Internal systems are used by members of an organisation to communicate with each other. External systems are used when they are communicating with people outside their own organisation.

Internal systems

■ memos

■ meetings

■ notice boards

■ bulletins or newsletters.

External systems

■ instruction leaflets

■ advertising

■ interactive computer systems

■ radio and television broadcasting

■ sales conversations with customers.

DISCUSSION POINT

Look at the list of internal and external systems given in the box to the right. For each one, list at least two advantages and two disadvantages.

Communications systems can work one way, or both ways.

One-way systems

When a message is communicated in one direction. You need:

■ a sender – the person transmitting the message (information, ideas or feelings)

■ a method of transmitting the message – letter, fax, advertising, display board, e-mail

■ a receiver – the person on the other end receiving the message.

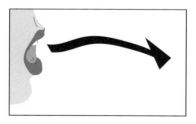

Examples of one-way communication

■ signs, signposts, notices, interpretation panels, display panels

■ written correspondence – letters, faxes, memos

■ public-address systems

■ computer-generated speech

■ instruction leaflets

■ books, newspapers and magazines

■ radio and television broadcasting

■ guided tours on cassette.

DISCUSSION POINT

From your own experience, think of different examples of one-way communication in local leisure or tourism facilities. Use the list above to get you started.

Why do you think one-way communication was used in your examples?

In one-way communication there's no immediate response to the message given. So it's hard to tell if it has been received and understood. To avoid misinterpretation and misunderstanding in one-way communication you need to take extra care in deciding what to say and how to say it.

Mena, the marketing assistant in the city council arts and leisure department, explains how important it is that leaflets about events give the right information in a style that will suit the reader:

❝ *I have to make sure that all the information people need is on the leaflets – things like the date and venue and ticket price, and also details of concessionary prices and parking. For children's events, I give a suggested age range. When I describe the event itself I have to think about who is likely to attend and what they will be looking out for. For example, if I'm writing the copy for a classical concert, I try to fit in as much detail as I can and keep the style formal. But if it's for a children's circus, I'll write in a much more informal style which children could understand and which makes the event sound fun.* **❞**

Two-way systems

When there's communication in both directions. You need:

- a sender – the person transmitting the message
- a method of transmitting the message – telephone, intercom, sign language
- a receiver – the person at the other end receiving the message
- feedback – a response to the message from the receiver.

Examples of two-way communication

- face-to-face discussions
- telephone conversations
- intercom systems
- mobile radio
- video conferencing
- interactive computer programs
- sign language.

DISCUSSION POINT

Think of four examples of two-way communication in local leisure and tourism facilities. What do you think are the main advantages and the main problems of two-way communication in these examples?

Unlike one-way communication, two-way communication allows the sender to find out immediately whether or not the message sent has been received and understood. It also gives the receiver an opportunity to respond. One disadvantage of two-way communication is that complex messages can get distorted in transmission, particularly if more than two people are involved. In many situations, two-way communication often involves a lot more than two people. There is plenty of scope for mixed messages and confusion. To avoid this, you need to make sure you understand and are understood.

UNIT

5

ELEMENT **5.2**

A customer assistant in a travel agents explains how she makes sure she understands the customers and they understand her:

❝ *I always check with the customers that I've understood what they've said by saying it back to them using my own words. I also summarise what's been said so far from time to time, just to make sure we're all still talking about the same thing. I use questions too, such as 'Am I right in saying that you're looking for a watersport holiday or are you looking for something that offers a wider range of outdoor activities?' and I prompt them to check they've understood me with questions such as 'The pricing options are a bit complicated – would you like me to go over them again?'* ❞

Communication isn't always spoken or written. Non-verbal communication – body language – can also send its own messages. For example:

- you can show you agree with something by nodding your head
- you show you are interested in something someone is saying by leaning towards them.

Body language can influence or distort spoken messages. Sometimes people indicate non-verbally that they do not really mean what they are saying. For example, they can pretend to be angry with someone but continue to smile at them, letting them know that the anger is not real.

ACTIVITY

Get together with six or seven other people. Stand in a line about three feet apart from each other. The first person in the line whispers a fairly complex message to the next person. This person then whispers the message to the next person and so on until the last person in the line has received the message. The last person then says the message out loud and the first person says what the original message was.

Are the two messages the same?

Discuss how difficult it was to pass on a message if you didn't understand it and couldn't ask the sender to say it again or explain it more clearly. What has the exercise shown you about one- and two-way communication?

DISCUSSION POINT

Decide which of these methods of communication are one-way and which are two-way:

- two people using sign language
- a no-smoking sign
- a public-address system informing people that a concert begins in five minutes
- a memo
- a telephone call
- a video conference
- a daily bulletin for counter staff at a travel agent
- a notice board in a head office
- two memos, one in reply to the other
- three people discussing which film to go and see together.

Where is there the most potential for messages to be confused or distorted?

266

ACTIVITY

Keep a diary or log of the different communications systems you use during the course of a week. For each one say whether it is:

■ internal or external

■ one-way or two-way.

Every time you make a note of the system, write down in your diary or log:

■ how likely you think it is that the message will be confused or distorted

■ how you can try to clarify the message.

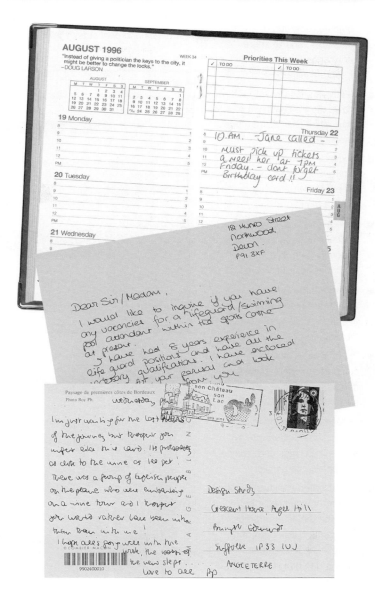

Section 5.2.3

The impact of electronic technology

Electronic technology in leisure and tourism

- computer reservation system – databases containing information about availability and prices of services, customer details, passenger lists and so on

- computer network – allows different people to have access to one central computer or group of computers, and to share information like the number of seats available on a flight

- electronic mail (e-mail) – allows the transmission of information directly from one computer to another

- modem – allows computers in different places to send information to each other using a telephone link

- fax – allows the transmission of documents on the telephone line, like confirmations of bookings

- answering machine – automatically answers telephone calls and records messages

- the Internet – allows computer users to access databases and networks such as the World Wide Web

- speech comprehension and generation – understands simple messages and creates an appropriate answer

- touch screen – allows people to control a computer by touching the screen rather than using a keyboard or mouse, like information 'kiosks' in shopping centres or interactive displays in museums and visitor centres.

Electronic technology is everywhere:

- in a supermarket where laser barcodes are used to price products
- at home, using a remote control to change television channels
- in a library where information about all the books is held on a central computer system, and newspapers are stored on CD-ROM.

The technology makes it easier and faster to store and exchange information, as an experienced assistant at a travel agency explains:

66 *I remember working here in the 1960s, just when the travel boom started. We were very busy – the office was full of files, papers, letters, index cards, timetables, booking charts, telephones, telex machines, typewriters and carbon paper. Nowadays, we're just as busy but there's a lot less mess – just computer terminals and print-outs.* 99

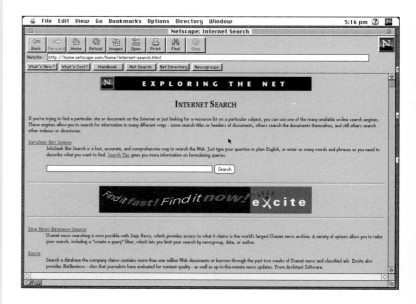

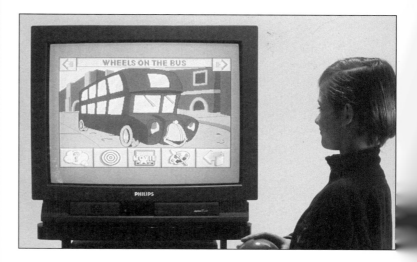

ACTIVITY

Visit or call a leisure or tourism facility in your area. Ask to speak to someone about what forms of electronic technology they use. Make a list which you will use in the next activity.

ACTIVITY

Go back to the list of electronic technology you drew up in the previous activity. Find out how using the technology has improved the facility's communications systems. Make notes under the headings in the list above.

Other recent forms of telecommunication include mobile telephones, electronic pagers, touchtone telephone systems and freephone telephone systems. These are all used a lot in tourism and leisure.

Thomas Cook began business in 1841 with an excursion train from Leicester to Loughborough and back. In 1869, he set up his first tour of Egypt and the Holy Land. Imagine the organisational difficulties he would have experienced in organising a foreign excursion like this with no telephones, no aeroplanes to deliver mail or transport his customers, no computers to make bookings and no faxes to confirm them.

The effect on communications systems

Electronic technology affects organisations and individuals because of its:

- speed – messages travel at the speed of light
- accuracy – financial packages produce accurate bills with just a few keystrokes
- reliability – the message on an answering machine doesn't go to sleep or get confused
- productivity – a gym with computerised equipment means that fewer coaching staff are needed
- access to information – a customer's credit rating can be checked automatically before payment is accepted.

For example, a computerised reservation system allows an airline reservation office to give customers information about flight availability over the telephone, making the service they provide faster, more accurate, more reliable and more cost-effective.

Electronic improvements

Computerised reservation systems

- fast, accurate and reliable information
- access to information for all computer users
- costs reduced and productivity improved through use of a single computerised system rather than several paper-based systems.

Computer network

- access to centrally stored information for all users with terminals
- fast, accurate and reliable.

Electronic mail (e-mail)

- fast and accurate transmission of information directly from one computer to another
- can replace other slower – and potentially less reliable – forms of transmission such as letters
- messages can be left rather than waiting for someone to answer the phone
- productivity is improved because people are not tied up on the phone.

Fax

- fast and accurate transmission of documents
- allows speedy written confirmation of conversations.

Answering machine

■ way of receiving messages when you are busy or out

■ caller does not have to wait for someone to answer the phone.

The Internet

■ improves both the range of computerised information accessible and the speed of access

■ improves quality and quantity of desk-based research.

Speech comprehension and generation

■ automatic interpretation of simple requests or commands, for example giving access to information held on computer

■ automated generation of information such as telephone numbers.

Touch screen

■ improves access to information by people who are not keyboard-users.

  I use a laptop computer when I'm travelling. With a fax-modem card in the computer I can get all the data I need from the company's main computer, wherever there's a telephone socket.

sales representative, package holiday company

  I get e-mail messages every day from colleagues all over the world. It's made talking to each other much easier – I don't have to make work phone calls to the States in the middle of the night any more!

customer services manager, international hotel group

  Without the fax we'd be lost. This way we can confirm a booking within minutes at a very low cost.

travel clerk, travel agency

  The Internet lets me communicate with other people in the same line of business as me. It's amazing what information you can pick up on the World Wide Web.

freelance tourism consultant

New skills and expertise

Whenever a new technology is introduced, people have to learn new skills and acquire new expertise, as a training manager in a local authority points out:

  Using the new computer-based equipment can mean learning a range of new skills – from basic keyboard use to writing or customising software programs. More and more people have now had experience of computers and related technology at school, but some still suffer from 'technophobia'. We give anyone who wants it training in how to operate computer-based systems, which usually overcomes their fears. The extent of the training needed will depend partly on the existing level of skills and expertise and partly on the individual's level of resistance to change.

Evaluating communications systems

Good communications systems are essential for exchanging information or ideas. A good system should provide opportunities for communication at all levels of an organisation:

- between individual members of staff – including part-time, temporary and seasonal staff
- between different departments, sections or divisions.

Hierarchical communications systems in which information is in one direction only – usually from the top downwards, from managers to employees – can cause divisions, frustration and other sorts of damage to an organisation.

What makes a good communications system?

Here are some of the factors which influence how well a communications system works.

Fitness for purpose

Communications systems should be carefully selected for their purpose. For example, if you need an instant response from a colleague, none of the one-way systems such as letters, faxes or answering machines will be suitable.

Value for money

New systems should be introduced if they are cost-effective. For example, investing in the Internet to gain access to databases will be worthwhile if you can make significant savings in terms of staff time previously spent using traditional research methods.

Accuracy

All systems need to transmit information accurately and reliably. For example, an answering machine which makes an unclear recording is unhelpful and could lead to misunderstanding.

Efficiency

Systems should function effectively and with the minimum waste of effort. For example, a computer reservation system which is constantly crashing will be impossible to use in the long term. They should also enable people to make a more efficient use of their own time, for example by freeing them from routine telephone calls so they can attend to customers face-to-face.

Security

One of the concerns about computer-based systems is that it can be difficult to restrict access to information. This is especially important in a service industry like tourism and leisure which involves storing information about customers. It is essential for new forms of technology to store information securely.

Ease of use

One of the main criteria for selecting a communications system should be that it is simple to use, easy to understand and accessible to those who need to use it.

User opinion

New forms of technology can be overwhelming for some people. They think there is too much to learn and they will never manage it all. Communications systems should be readily accepted by the people who will be using them – staff, customers and suppliers.

When you are evaluating how good a system is you will need to take all these factors into account. Here's how Jon, the curator of a small railway museum, manages to run the museum by himself with the help of a reliable group of volunteers.

The museum has just been awarded a grant to update the communications system. Before he receives the grant, Jon has been asked to do an audit of the systems already in place to:

■ work out how they can be improved

■ make recommendations about which new technology the museum should invest in.

At the moment the museum has:

■ leaflets about different services, displayed on a table in the entrance

■ a noticeboard for posters and notices

■ an old computer for wordprocessing

■ a telephone with an answering machine.

Jon writes down a list of questions which he feels he needs to answer.

Fitness for purpose

■ Do the posters and leaflets give the information clearly enough and do they attract the attention of the visitors?

■ Is the computer able to do the tasks I would like it to do?

Value for money

■ Am I spending too much having the leaflets and posters designed and produced by an outside agency? Could I produce some of them myself if I had the system to do it?

■ Is the computer out-of-date? Is there a newer one on the market which would be less time-consuming to use and able to do tasks which I am currently paying other people to do?

Accuracy

■ Are the notices as up-to-date as I would like? Could they be updated more quickly when needed?

Efficiency

■ Can I produce leaflets, posters and notices as quickly as I would like? Could I do it some of it myself and cut down the time it takes?

■ Is the computer fast to use?

■ Do I know how to make use of all the computer's functions?

■ Am I able to send correspondence to arrive as soon as I would like?

Security

■ Are my computer files confidential?

Ease of use

■ Is the computer system easy to use?

■ Could I ask the volunteer helpers to use it?

User opinion

■ What do customers think of the leaflets and posters?

■ What do my volunteer helpers think of the computer system?

■ Do agencies and organisations I regularly communicate with want to send documents by fax? Would I benefit from having a fax machine?

On the basis of answers to these and other questions, Jon writes a report for the grant-awarding body summarising his findings.

Possible improvements

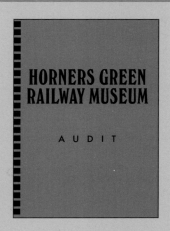

After Jon has completed his audit of the communications systems in the museum, he has to write a short report for the grant-awarding body recommending improvements.

Based on the audit that Jon carried out, write a report using the headings discussed above:

- staff expertise – volunteer helpers as well as Jon
- equipment
- access.

Once you have looked at the effectiveness of a system you may be able to suggest ways in which it could be improved in these three areas:

- staff expertise
- equipment
- access.

Staff expertise

The communications system may be fine, but staff need the skills and expertise to use it properly or appropriately. Often extra training or encouragement is all that's needed to boost skills and confidence in using a new system. In some organisations, a mentoring system is used where one member of staff gives guidance to anothers less experienced colleague.

Equipment

New or different equipment might be needed to improve the communications system you have evaluated. For example, you might be able to improve access to the system through a series of simple measures such as:

- increasing the number of computer terminals in an office
- upgrading a telephone system to take direct-dial lines so everything doesn't have to go through the switchboard
- buying a fax to speed up operations and improve communications between departments.

Or maybe the whole system needs to be replaced – for example, buying a computerised reservation system to replace a paper-based one.

Access to communications

You might decide after evaluating a communications system that the system itself is adequate, but that the level of access is insufficient or too restricted. For example, a video-conferencing facility that does not include a principal member of staff may mean that important questions cannot be answered despite the sophisticated technology available.

Key questions

1   What are the four main functions or purposes of communications systems?
2   What is the difference between internal and external communications systems?
3   What are the main disadvantages of
    ■   one-way communications systems
    ■   two-way communications systems?
4   In what ways can the introduction of electronic technology improve communications systems in leisure and tourism?
5   What are the main criteria to use when evaluating the effectiveness of a communications system?
6   What are the three main areas in which improvements can be made to communications systems?

Assignment

A large chain of hotels has contracted a team of consultants to help improve their communications systems. As a member of the team, you have been asked to write a case study on leisure and tourism communications systems and their applications in one of the hotels. The case study will be used as part of a training programme to improve communications in all the hotels in the chain.

The case study will be in four parts. The first two parts will set the context for parts three and four by looking at communications systems in general in the leisure and tourism industry.

Part 1

Explain in general terms the communication systems used in leisure and tourism organisations. Focus on:
■   functions
■   purposes
■   types of systems.

Support your explanations with examples and visual illustrations of:
■   two one-way communications systems
■   two two-way communications systems.

Part 2

Explain how the development of electronic technology has affected communications systems. Give examples of how the new technology is used – for example:
■   computer reservation systems
■   computer networks
■   electronic mail (voice, written)
■   enhanced telephone systems (fax machines, modems, the Internet)
■   voice comprehension and generation
■   touch screens.

Describe the effects of the technology on:
■   the organisation
■   individual employees.

Part 3

Summarise the findings from an evaluation you have carried out into the effectiveness of two communications systems:
■   one one-way system
■   one two-way system.

For each system, your evaluation will need to answer the following questions:
■   Is it fit for its purpose?
■   Does it give value for money?
■   Does it ensure accuracy?
■   Is it efficient?
■   Does it meet security requirements?
■   Is it easy to use?
■   What do the users think of it?

Part 4

Suggest any improvements you think could be made to operation of the systems you've evaluated. For example:
■   training to increase staff skills, confidence and expertise
■   improved equipment
■   improved access to communications.

66 The national legislation which most affects us is the Data Protection Act. This means that we must be very careful who we give information out to. We can't, for example, give anyone who rings in details of who is on a flight. All the files have to be locked away at night and we use passwords to enter the computers. **99**

travel consultant in a travel agency

66 We are looking at computerising the administration of the play centres so that the information we need is more easily available to us. We have one personal computer for the use of the play team and four in total in the department. **99**

community play officer in a city council

66 We are building up our own database and we mail everyone on it every six months. This is definitely the most successful way of getting an audience. The direct contact is very effective. I write a first draft of the leaflet and then circulate it to all the other members of the band for their comments. But it's the database that makes all the effort of writing and producing leaflets worthwhile – it means we can send information direct to the people most likely to come to our concerts. **99**

band leader

Information-processing systems

Think about the last time you made an enquiry about an event in a leisure and tourism organisation or bought a ticket from a travel agent. The chances are that the information you asked for was provided by someone using an information system. The system could have been anything from a filing cabinet to an on-line system providing up-to-the-minute information on the number of seats left and the prices available. In this element you will see how these information systems work and what they are used for in leisure and tourism. In particular, you'll be looking at the effects of electronic technology, which has made information more up-to-date and accessible.

Section 5.3.1

Functions and purposes of information-processing systems

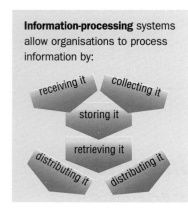

Information-processing systems allow organisations to process information by:

receiving it

collecting it

storing it

retrieving it

distributing it

distributing it

Information may not be very useful in its raw, unprocessed state. It may have to be processed before it can be used. The systems manager of a national coach company describes what processed information the company uses:

66 *We have a huge system at our head office which our branches can all log into. The central computer processes all sorts of information which we use constantly. We have a system for scheduling travel times, which we update twice a year. We store information about our coach drivers and of course about our customers so that our marketing department can send them details about coach trips. The system also gives us access to an information service on roadworks likely to cause delays round the country. I don't know how we managed before we had computers – it would have been impossible to process all this information.* 99

Systems used to process information range from a simple card index to a sophisticated, expensive computer network.

All organisations need to be able to process information about the organisation itself and customers. For example, a sports centre may have systems for processing:

■ information about running the organisation – staff rotas, staff wages, training records, equipment inspection, admission levels, accounts

■ information about customers – timetables, membership status, bookings, participation in special offers, mailing lists for special events, offers and so on.

DISCUSSION POINT

What sort of information would another type of leisure and tourism facility, such as a tour operator or guest house, receive, store and distribute?

DISCUSSION POINT

Think of occasions when you have been a customer of a leisure or tourism organisation and you have needed information.

■ Who or what provided the information?

■ What form did you get it in?

Customer service information

Information provided by someone in an organisation to someone else outside it – an external enquirer. For example:

■ a travel agent provides information about holiday resorts

■ a tourist information centre provides information about bed and breakfast facilities in an area

■ a railway station provides train timetables.

Management information

Information provided and used by people who run the organisation. For example:

■ a sports centre supervisor uses daily timesheets to help organise staff rotas

■ the sales director of a travel firm uses monthly bookings statistics to decide next month's special offers

■ a sportswear manufacturer uses the annual sales figures to work out long-term trends in buying habits.

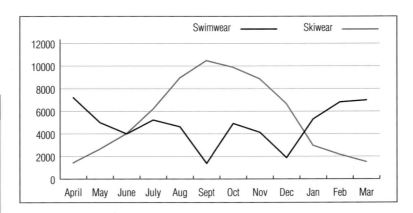

Information is also needed by management for statutory purposes such as producing the organisation's annual accounts or VAT returns.

Information can be processed so it's useful for customer service and management purposes. In this case, the information is likely to be presented and distributed in different ways. The manager of a leisure centre explains how information about peak booking times can be useful to both customers and management:

66 *We know from our computer records when we are likely to be busy. I get a print-out every week showing the take-up rate on all the facilities in the centre. One of my staff makes a chart every month which we put up in reception so customers can look at. It gives the off-peak times for court bookings, the solarium, the fitness room and everything else we have here. Some people are able to take advantage of these off-peak times and the discounts that come with them. I use this information from the weekly print-outs to work out staffing levels. We know that at certain times of the week we are going to need more instructors in the fitness room. The catering manager can also predict when she's going to be busy in the cafeteria.* 99

AFTERNOON BOOKING CHART 12/3/96										
FITNESS	12.00	1.00	2.00	3.00	4.00	5.00	6.00	7.00	8.00	9.00
ROOM 1	Jones	Smith		Kingsley	Knight		Patel	Hobort	Blake	Cook
2	Brown	Cole					Jones	Ohno	Moon	Mason
3	Fagan	Dixon					Bootard	Pearce	Colyn	
4	Gibson						Green	Looge	Jonaba	
5							Babcock	McKernan	Ramigan	
6							Lewis	Peel		
7							Dean	Pugh		
8							Ruffell			
Comments	Treadmill on the blink — Mechanic in at 8.30pm this evening									
SQUASH										
Court 1	Churchill	Darrell	Allen				Page	Ruffell	Oiley	Jackson
Court 2							Jeffrey	Black	Ian	
Comments	Jackson already paid for two.									
BADMINTON	Mitchell							Majors	Kerry	Kinross
Comments	Pete Mitchell is coaching session for 5 people – all to pay on arrival. Khinari cancelled this morning.									
STEP							Gill		Gill	

Types of information-processing systems

Most organisations use two types of systems for processing information:

- manual
- electronic.

Some systems can be either manual or electronic. Others have to be one or the other.

Manual systems

Until recently, almost all operations in leisure and tourism were carried out manually – and some still are. For example:

- customer reservations were made by writing details on a form and then sending the reservation by letter to the supplier
- financial records were kept in a system of cash books and ledgers, filled in and analysed by accounts clerks.

> **Manual** means something that is done by hand rather than mechanically, automatically or by computer.

Some manual systems – paper filing systems, card indexes, daily staff rotas – may be quicker than electronic ones. The manager of a sports and social club explains why they use a manual system for booking the pool tables:

We have a membership of about 300 people. The pool tables are used by about 50 people on a regular basis. There's a weekly booking sheet at reception which members fill in themselves. It seems to work well enough – the tables are usually busy, anyhow. We don't need this on our computer system yet. Perhaps in the future we'll give it some thought.

Electronic systems

> **Electronic**, in relation to information-processing, usually means a system controlled by computer.

The use of electronic technology has revolutionised the information-processing potential of all sectors of industry, including leisure and tourism. Personal computers enable staff to perform a wide range of functions accurately, efficiently and easily.

Computers are based on a combination of:

- hardware – the physical equipment used, like the computer's hard disc and the printer
- software – computer programs (also called applications) which enable users to perform functions.

DISCUSSION POINT

Think of two or three examples of manual and electronic information-processing systems that you have seen in leisure and tourism organisations – for example, when you have booked a seat at the cinema or theatre or a court at a leisure centre. Why do you think these different systems are used?

The manager of the sports and social club goes on to talk about the computer system:

We do have a computer in the office which we use for correspondence, accounts and membership details. All our members are on a database. Whenever we need information we can simply call them up by name or postcode. We send out membership renewal forms, details of price increases, special offers – all by using mail-merge. We use it for all correspondence and our bookkeeper uses a spreadsheet package for the accounts.

Hardware

- central processing unit (CPU) – controls and coordinates the operations of the computer

- visual display unit (VDU) – displays the data on a screen, which can be monochrome or colour

- keyboard – user inputs data into the computer and gives instructions

- mouse (manually operated user signal encoder) – another way of inputting data

- printer – prints out the hard copy

- scanner – copies images (text, photos, illustrations, logos, etc.) directly from source documents to the computer memory.

Software

Wordprocessing

The most commonly used software. Wordprocessing on a computer has replaced the use of typewriters in most organisations and is used to produce letters, reports, minutes, price lists, memos and so on. As well as the basic typewriting facility they provide, wordprocessing packages usually have other features such as mail-merge, spell-checking and grammar-checking.

Desktop publishing

Special software used to produce documents like leaflets, posters, advertisements and reports. Like wordprocessors but more powerful, allowing skilled users to lay out documents in different ways, using a variety of typefaces and other typographical features. DTP packages also enable users to incorporate images in text.

Spreadsheets

Software packages used to process and present numbers in a set format, usually rows and columns. They allow users to make rapid calculations, enabling organisations to make financial projections and forecasts quickly and accurately. In most spreadsheets, the information can be presented in the form of a graph or pie chart.

Databases

Used to store information such as names and addresses of customers and suppliers, contacts, records. Database programs can also sort data and present it in a range of formats.

Graphics

Special drawing or painting programs used by graphic designers to produce illustrations and diagrams.

The main features of electronic systems

Electronic systems have six main features which make them attractive to leisure and tourism organisations.

Speed

Electronic systems allow users to sort, store and retrieve information quickly and easily. Tasks which might have taken days to perform or organise using a manual system can now be performed in minutes – making complex calculations, sorting information and printing. A skilled operator can perform a range of tasks at the same time, accelerating the process considerably.

Accuracy

If the input into a computer is accurate, the output will also be accurate. (The opposite is also true – 'garbage in, garbage out'.) Computers might sometimes crash but they don't make mistakes. Only the people using them do that.

Reliability

Most computer systems are generally reliable although they do sometimes crash. Reliability can be improved by using software packages such as anti-virus devices. Big organisations usually have back-up service or support staff to maintain equipment and sort out any software problems. Wherever there's a network, there's a network manager. Smaller organisations may have to fix the problems themselves or get in outside help from a computer firm.

Costs

The cost of installing a computer system can be high. But the savings made in terms of reduced staffing levels and increased productivity should mean that the system will pay for itself in a short time.

DISCUSSION POINT

66 Computers don't always speed things up. Sometimes they cause more problems than they solve. 99

- What do you think of this sceptical view of electronic systems?
- Do you have any personal experience of computers causing more problems than they solve?

Productivity

Electronic systems can help to improve productivity in three main ways:
- by the speed with which computers can carry out complex tasks and operations
- by taking highly skilled and trained staff away from everyday information-processing functions to work on more complex tasks
- by making it possible for an organisation to function 24 hours a day, 365 days a year.

Access to information

The volume of information that can be stored and handled by a computer means that access to information need only be limited by the capacity to input it. This has opened up many possibilities for all sectors of industry, particularly in sales and marketing.

The Data Protection Act 1984

WHAT THE ACT COVERS

The Act only applies to automatically processed information – broadly speaking, information which is processed by a computer. The Act does not cover all computerised information but only that which relates to living individuals. It does not cover information on individuals which is held and processed manually – for example, in ordinary paper files.

The Act uses some unfamiliar words and phrases and it is important to grasp their meaning because they define how the Act works. Guideline 2 defines these words and phrases more fully but the following broad descriptions will be helpful:

Personal data

Information recorded on a computer about living, identifiable individuals. Statements of fact and expressions of opinion about an individual are personal data but an indication of the data user's intentions towards the individual is not.

Data subject

An individual to whom personal data relate.

Data users

People or organisations who control the contents and use of a collection of personal data. A data user will usually be a company, corporation or other organisation but it is possible for an individual to be a data user.

Computer bureaux

People or organisations who process personal data for data users or who cause – even indirectly – personal data to be processed for data users, or who allow data users to process personal data on their computer.

As electronic information-processing systems became more widely used in the 1980s, there was a growing concern that confidential, personal or sensitive information could be abused or acquired by those who were unauthorised to have it. The Data Protection Act was introduced in 1984 to safeguard against these kinds of potential problems. The Act gives individuals the right to:

- know what computerised records are held about them by an organisation
- correct any information that is incorrect.

The purpose of the Act is to 'restrict the possibility of living individuals being harmed by the abuse of personal information or data.' All organisations which store personal data on computers are required to comply with the Act and to register with the Data Protection Register.

The Act does not apply to:

- information stored on a manual system
- lists of names and addresses which are only used for distribution purposes – provided the people listed have agreed to disclosure.

Examples of the abuse of information could include:

- personal customer information displayed on a computer screen where anyone can see it
- computer print-outs with confidential information left on a desk in an open-plan office
- sensitive sales information acquired by someone who is unauthorised to have it, such as a competitor.

The effects on leisure and tourism

Leisure and tourism organisations often keep information about people – staff and customers – on their computer systems. To stay within the law, they must:

- make sure that personal information about individuals is kept secure so that it cannot be abused
- restrict access to that information
- make sure that records are accurate, up to date and maintained only for valid commercial reasons.

DISCUSSION POINT

Do you think the Data Protection Act should be amended to include data stored on manual systems as well?

DISCUSSION POINT

A member of staff in a facility regularly has to:

- give customers information about the organisation's services and products – some of the information is only available on computer
- take details about customers and put them on to the company's database
- produce a weekly analysis of customer enquiries for head office.

How do you think the requirements of the Data Protection Act would affect her work?

Evaluating and improving systems

Good information-processing systems are essential if an organisation is to operate efficiently. Most people have had some experience of dealing with inefficient organisations:

- the computer is 'down' when you ring for information
- the bookings clerk does not have up-to-date information about timetables
- the leisure centre double-books a tennis court.

These things are not good customer service. Many of them can be solved by looking at the systems in place, working out how well they are used and making improvements where necessary.

What makes a system effective?

As with other systems, there are seven factors which make an information-processing system effective – or not.

Fitness for purpose

As with all systems, information-processing systems should meet an organisation's requirements as closely as possible. For example:

- there is no point in investing in a complex graphics software program without also purchasing a good-quality laser printer capable of printing the graphics produced
- an organisation with only a small customer base will probably be able to function just as efficiently with a manual record system as with a computerised database.

Value for money

There is a huge range of information-processing systems on the market but not all of them represent value for money. Most organisations will need advice from specialists about which systems are cost-effective.

Accuracy

It almost goes without saying that an information-processing system needs to be accurate if it is to be useful. In fact, most errors in information-processing are generated by humans. For example:

- a print-out of customer details is only as accurate as the original information put in to the database
- if a vital piece of information – like the date – is left off a poster advertising an event, it's not the desktop-publishing package that's made a mistake.

Efficiency

An efficient system will make people's jobs easier, improve the level of service to customers and help the organisation to meet its objectives. An inefficient system will produce errors, delays and misunderstandings.

The management committee of a voluntary organisation has been thinking about improving the way in which information about members, supporters and staff is stored by the club. A local business has offered to sponsor the club by paying for a new computerised system, if the committee can prove it would help.

Produce a short report for the managing director of the business suggesting ways in which you think the effectiveness of the club could be improved if a computer system is used.

Security

The Data Protection Act requires all organisations to maintain the security of personal information stored electronically. Organisations also need to protect information that may be confidential because it is commercially sensitive.

Ease of use

Information-processing systems should be simple to use, easy to understand and accessible to those who use them. People who are familiar with manual systems may be resistant to changing to electronic systems and may require support, encouragement and training to enable them to make the transition.

User opinion

Information-processing systems in leisure and tourism will be used by a range of different people including staff, customers and suppliers. All of these people should be asked occasionally what they think of the systems they are using.

Key questions

1 What are the five main ways in which information can be processed?
2 What are the two main purposes of information-processing systems?
3 What are the main differences in the types of information provided for these two purposes?
4 What are the main differences between manual and electronic information-processing systems?
5 What are the five types of software which are most commonly used in computerised information-processing systems?
6 What is the purpose of the Data Protection Act 1984?
7 What has been the main effect of the Data Protection Act on ways in which personal information about individuals is processed?
8 What are the seven main criteria to use when evaluating the effectiveness of an information-processing system?
9 What are the three main areas in which improvements can be made to information-processing systems?

Assignment

Write a feature article for a Sunday supplement magazine about information-processing systems and their use in leisure and tourism organisations. The aim of the article is show the benefits of effective information-processing systems and the importance of choosing the right types of system.

Start the article with a general explanation of the functions, purposes and types of information-processing systems in leisure and tourism organisations. Support your explanation with examples of:
■ two manual systems
■ two electronic systems.

Point out what benefits electronic technology can bring to leisure and tourism organisations:
■ speed
■ accuracy
■ costs
■ productivity
■ access to information.

Comment on the types of skill staff need to make good use of new technology.

Highlight the effects of the Data Protection Act 1984 on:
■ individual rights
■ access to information
■ security
■ ownership.

Explain how the Act affects the users and operators of information-processing systems.

End your article by summarising the results of an evaluation you have conducted into the effectiveness of one manual and one electronic information-processing system used by a leisure and tourism organisation.

For each system, your evaluation will need to answer the following questions:
■ Is it fit for its purpose?
■ Does it give value for money?
■ Does it ensure accuracy?
■ Is it efficient?
■ Does it meet security requirements?
■ Is it easy to use?
■ What do the users think of it?

Draw out any improvements you think could be made to the systems. For example:
■ improved procedures
■ training to increase staff skills, confidence and expertise
■ improved equipment.

UNIT **6**

Customer service

ELEMENT 6.1

Investigating customer service

You'll probably know from your own observations that leisure and tourism organisations are very customer-orientated. Whether you're investigating a local gym or a national airline you will find that they have positive attitudes about their customers. Staff in the leisure and tourism industry are trained to look after their customers well and communicate with them effectively. The aim is to have customers who are happy with the service they received, keen to come back for more and likely to go and tell their friends about it. You might also have come across the term 'internal customers' – the other people within the organisation who should be treated in some ways like customers. In this element you'll be looking closely at the services provided to both internal and external customers

66 You have to be helpful, cheerful and interested in what people want. You need to have a wide knowledge of the country and the region. One young person working here is taking COTIC – the Certificate of Tourist Information Competence – which involves having a vast knowledge both of the area and the UK. It means she has to know about things like bus and train timetables – being able to tell someone the best way to get to Scotland and other far-away places is all part of the service we provide to visitors. *99*

manager of a tourist information centre

66 This is a 24-hour-a-day job because that's the kind of attention a business like this requires. In this sort of service industry you can't expect to lock up at 6.00 p.m. and put your feet up. The phone can go at any hour and I always have to know what's going on. The welfare of the horses and riders is always top priority. *99*

owner of a riding school which also provides holidays

66 It's important to create a good first impression by being smartly dressed – in a suit – if we are going to meet someone, and turning up in a good car. Most of our business comes from repeat orders – if customers like us the first time they tend to stay with us. I'll go out of my way to make sure that a regular customer is well looked after. Sometimes it means delivering or collecting cars at odd times of the day or night, but it can mean the difference between keeping them or seeing them go off to one of the other rental companies. *99*

car-rental manager

66 The skills needed in this work are mainly to do with customer care – you have to know how to deal with all kinds of customers: parents and small children, people who want to do Aquafit, people who need coaching. You have to be very caring, but at times very firm about how things are run. *99*

swimming development officer

Types and components of customer service

Good customer service means really caring for customers. It is a high priority for all leisure and tourism organisations. Every member of an organisation contributes to providing customer service, not just those who deal with customers directly.

Staff roles in providing customer service fall into three categories:

- front-of-house staff – those who are constantly in direct, regular contact with customers
- backroom staff – those who have indirect or irregular contact with customers, but provide services which are directly used by customers
- support staff – those who are rarely in direct contact with customers, but support both front-of-house and backroom staff.

Support staff → Backroom staff → Front-of-house staff → Customers

Front-of-house staff

Front-of-house staff such as receptionists, customer advisers, salespeople, waiters and bar staff come into contact with customers throughout the day. They expect customer contact at any time, and are always ready to meet, greet and help customers.

The manager of a travel agency explains how his staff are prepared for dealing with customers:

66 *Our front-of-office staff know how important it is for them to be cheerful, friendly, efficient and professional at all times. They've all been trained in good customer care and how to use the computer systems so they can always find the information customers need. They also wear a uniform which not only makes them look smart but also means that customers know immediately who they are.* 99

Backroom and support staff

Backroom staff and support staff may not have regular, direct customer contact, but they still play an important role in providing customer service. The manager of a hotel explains:

66 *The receptionists and porters, waiters, waitresses, bar staff and room service staff come into contact with the customers throughout the day. They are our front-of-house staff. The backroom staff – the people who work in accounts, the housekeepers and chambermaids, the chefs and kitchen staff – don't meet the customers as much, if at all. But the customers would know if they weren't doing their job – there'd be nothing to eat, their rooms wouldn't be cleaned and they wouldn't receive their bill at the end of their stay! And then there are the support staff such as maintenance staff, kitchen porters and storekeepers, who don't normally meet the customers at all, but we rely on them to keep the hotel running smoothly – the maintenance staff, for example, mend equipment that's not working, touch up the paintwork round the hotel when it gets damaged, and that sort of thing.* 99

DISCUSSION POINT

How do these people contribute to customer service? Are they front-of-house staff, backroom staff, or support staff?

- a reservations agent with a travel agency
- housekeepers and room-cleaning staff in a hotel
- a chef in a restaurant
- a security officer at a theme park

ACTIVITY

Think about a leisure and tourism organisation you know of and draw a diagram to show how staff contribute to providing customer care.

DISCUSSION POINT

Think of a time when you have felt an organisation hadn't made an effort to meet your needs as a customer. How did it make you feel about the organisation as a whole?

ACTIVITY

With a friend, roleplay the scene described under 'Achieving customer satisfaction' so that the salesperson not only meets the customer's needs, but also achieves customer satisfaction.

After the role-play, discuss what it was like to be:

■ the satisfied customer

■ the helpful salesperson.

The components of customer service

All staff working in leisure and tourism, whether providing customer service directly or indirectly, do so by:

■ caring for customers
■ meeting customers' needs
■ achieving customer satisfaction
■ meeting customers' expectations
■ maintaining security
■ maintaining safety.

Caring for customers

The main goal of customer service is to look after customers and make sure that they are happy with the services or products provided. It means treating them with consideration and courtesy.

Meeting customer needs

Meeting customers' needs means giving them the products and services which suit them. This means the organisations have to put time and effort into finding out what their customers need and then make sure the products and services meet those needs.

Achieving customer satisfaction

Achieving customer satisfaction is not the same thing as meeting customer needs. Read through the following scene.

A customer walks into a travel agency and approaches a salesperson.

Customer: *Hello. I wonder if you could help me. I want to find out about holidays to Greece.*

Salesperson: (Without looking up from computer screen) *Rack on the left, top shelf.*

Customer: *Oh, OK. Thanks.*

The customer's needs have been met – she leaves the shop with a pile of brochures about holidays in Greece – but is she satisfied?

Meeting customer expectations

Customers buying leisure and tourism products and services go to an organisation with some expectations of what they are going to get. These expectations may be created by advertisements, brochures, leaflets, posters, word of mouth or even the way a building is decorated. If the service fails to live up to these expectations, it can be frustrating and annoying.

A customer whose meal at a restaurant failed to live up to her expectations describes her reaction.

❝ *From the outside, the restaurant looked extremely plush – with menu prices to match! It had recently taken out a series of advertisements in local newspapers, billing itself as 'the best restaurant in town'. Well, we certainly didn't agree. The service was slow, the food bland and the atmosphere unmemorable. I don't think we'd have felt so cheated if we hadn't been led to expect great things – we certainly won't be going back there again.* **99**

Maintaining security and safety

Creating a secure, safe environment is an important part of providing good customer service. Customers need to know that safety and security standards are met so that they can feel confident about visiting a facility, or using a product or service.

Maintaining security and safety might include:

- installing closed-circuit TV or employing security guards
- providing a secure place for customers to leave belongings
- ensuring health and safety procedures are followed
- ensuring fire extinguishers are working and fire escapes are clearly signposted
- arranging for trained first aiders and first-aid equipment to be on hand
- giving information and advice to customers on how to use equipment properly or what to do with personal belongings
- checking that staff are well trained in safety and security matters.

CRANDOWN LEISURE CENTRE

Following the opening of a swimming pool at a local school, the Crandown Leisure Centre lost a regular group booking from the school for Thursday mornings. The leisure centre manager asked the marketing team to carry out some market research to see if the pool could attract new customers to fill the gap. They devised a questionnaire that reception staff gave to customers.

When they analysed the results, they found that a lot people would be interested in coming to an adult-and-child swimming class on a Thursday morning. The manager then put together a planning team to investigate the idea further. They looked into what would help make the class a success and identified the following:

- instructors with experience of teaching adult-and-child groups
- facilities for babies like nappy-changing areas in the changing rooms
- toys, armbands and other equipment
- raising the water temperature to 30° C for these sessions
- installing a ramp and a secure parking area in reception for pushchairs
- a special children's menu in the restaurant
- a crèche for parents who had other younger children who would need looking after while they were in the pool.

They decided that they had all the right people on the staff to run the class and the crèche. The restaurant chef was happy to put together sample menus which they approved; the site manager confirmed that getting the temperature up was no problem; the finance manager worked out costs for the additions and adaptations needed for the facilities and reported back that the scheme seemed viable. So they all agreed to try it out as a ten-week course.

It was a big success and was enjoyed by staff and customers alike. A survey at the end of the course showed that parents thought it was better than expected and they would recommend the course to other young parents in the area. The 'icing on the cake' came when a local newspaper published a letter praising the efforts of all the members of staff. As a result of the good publicity, the next three courses were fully booked. Managers also noticed that the pool was busier at other times than it had been before.

ACTIVITY

1 The case study of Crandown Leisure Centre describes a successful response to a new need from customers. Go through the six aspects of customer service described on pages 288–289 and note down how the centre covered them.

2 Using the same case study, give examples of employees who took front-of-house, backroom and support roles.

ACTIVITY

Think of an instance when you've been an internal customer – for example, during a work placement or job, or at college trying to find help or information for your coursework. Describe:

■ what your needs were

■ who was involved in meeting those needs

■ how well they met your needs

■ the effects it had on your ability to perform your own role effectively.

Internal customers

The customer service manager of a city art gallery believes that good customer care relies on teamwork.

66 *Good customer care is achieved by a team effort. As with any team, each person must play their role to the full because the rest of the team is relying on them to do so.* 99

Think about what happens inside an organisation to get a product or service to a customer. It's like a chain of demand and supply with each person being a vital link in that chain. To make the chain a strong one, each person has to think about what their colleagues need from them and then make sure they fulfil that need. So in effect they see their colleagues as customers and themselves as internal suppliers. All the components of customer care given on pages 288 to 289 apply to the internal customer as well as the external customer.

A waiter in a hotel restaurant describes the internal customer chain involved in serving a meal to a customer:

66 *My role is to give the customer information about the food available – the menu – and then bring them what they choose. To do this, I rely on the chef and the restaurant manager to keep the menu up to date and include any specials for the day. So I'm their internal customer.*

Once I've taken the order, I need the chef and his staff to supply the food. So now I'm their internal customer. But to fulfil my needs, they need to know exactly what I want. So now they're my internal customers and I have to supply them with the right information about what the customer has ordered. 99

   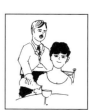

A training officer for a large chain of travel agencies demonstrates the importance of being a good supplier to your internal customers with what she calls the 'multiplier effect':

66 *Suppose there are four stages in getting a product or service to an external customer and the person involved at each stage only gives the next person 90% of what they need. If you multiply that, it's 0.9 x 0.9 x 0.9 x 0.9 which is 65%. So the customer is getting only 65% of what they ought to have.* 99

The importance of customer service

Successful leisure and tourism organisations make good customer service a high priority in the way they operate. They understand that without customers there would be no leisure and tourism organisations.

> *"Let us do the worrying for you"*   *"Put your feet up and let us do the rest"*
>
>   *"Let us take care of you"*   **"For professional service and personal attention"**
>
> *"Personal service from a family business"*   *"A better service, the best result"*

Customer satisfaction

Effective customer service is about caring for customers, meeting their needs and expectations and achieving customer satisfaction. Customers who feel they have been well treated leave happy and are likely to return. So good customer service makes good business sense – satisfied customers mean more customers, and more income for the organisation.

As this keen swimmer explains, satisfying customers can be even more important than meeting their needs:

66 *I go swimming every day, and was delighted when I heard a new pool was opening near my home. The pool is modern and large, and a big improvement on existing facilities. I went at the first opportunity, but left very disappointed. The pool was great, but there weren't enough staff on duty and I had to wait ten minutes to get in, the changing rooms and toilet areas were dirty, and somehow the whole place was unwelcoming. I'm back at the old pool now – the facilities may not be as good, but it's very friendly and I feel at home there.* **99**

The new swimming pool had missed out on a good opportunity. Achieving customer satisfaction by providing good customer service can:

- create repeat business
- help an organisation keep customers
- help an organisation attract new customers
- improve an organisation's competitive advantage
- enhance the image of an organisation and its products.

DISCUSSION POINT

Think of the words people use to praise or complain about customer service. How much of it describes intangible things like feelings, perceptions and emotions? What pictures of an organisation come into your mind when someone tells you about good or bad experiences they've had as customers?

Repeat business and customer retention

Customers remember how they have been treated by an organisation. If they feel they have been treated well and leave satisfied, they are likely to return. If they feel unwelcome, have to wait too long or find that they are not getting what they expected, they are likely to go elsewhere.

DISCUSSION POINT

Why do you choose to go to one leisure centre over another? Or to one restaurant rather than another?

Effective customer service can help organisations to:

- gain repeat business – by encouraging customers who have used a product or service to do so again
- keep customers – by encouraging customers to feel a sense of trust in the organisation, or loyalty to it, so that they come back again and again.

New customers

Satisfied customers not only return to an organisation, they can also take new customers with them. Leisure and tourism organisations should never underestimate the power of word of mouth. Happy customers tell their friends, families and colleagues, and the general good reputation of the organisation attracts new customers.

ACTIVITY

Over the next two weeks, make a note of every occasion that someone recommends a facility or product to you – for example, a shop, a CD, a restaurant or a book. How many of these word-of-mouth recommendations do you act on? You will probably find that a large number of the things you choose to do have been influenced by other people's opinions.

Competitive advantage

Customer service is a form of added value – it is what makes the difference between simply having your needs met and feeling completely satisfied. Good customer service can be an important selling point for organisations, giving them an advantage over their competitors.

A customer explains how, faced with six high-street travel agents, she chose which to use when booking her holiday:

66 *There were a mixture of travel agents in the high street, some branches of national chains, others independent traders. Some were smart, with bright modern furniture, while others were quite scruffy. I was automatically drawn to the shops with bright, tempting offers in the windows – one travel agent lost my custom straight away because its windows were dark and unappealing. I cut the options down to three, and went in to chat with counter clerks. Two knew a lot about different holidays, flights and services, but one was a lot more helpful and friendly than the other. That's the one I chose. I was very pleased with the service I received. I'll definitely use the travel agent again and I've recommended it to friends and relatives.* 99

Enhanced image

All leisure and tourism organisations want to present a good image of themselves. The way that they treat they customers is a crucial part of this. It would be pointless to put time and money into creating first-class products and services and then put the customers off by treating them badly.

DISCUSSION POINT

In their advertising, many leisure and tourism organisations try to create a positive image by talking about the quality of their customer service and their friendly, welcoming and efficient staff. Discuss how organisations create positive images in this way, giving examples from television, radio, newspapers and magazines.

ACTIVITY

Think about the customer service you've had from leisure and tourism organisations.

1   Make a note of a service which particularly impressed you.

2   Make a note of a service which you thought was poor.

3   What was it about each of these services that gave you these impressions? Think about your needs and expectations at the time and how they were met or exceeded.

4   Write two letters, one a letter of praise to the organisation which provided a good service, the other a letter of complaint, suggesting improvements which might be made to customer service. Make sure you emphasise how the customer service you have received has affected your perception of, and attitude to, the organisations.

CASE STUDY

The managing director of a fitness centre describes his organisation's view of customer care:

66 *We see customer care as an integral part of what we offer. We fulfil our customers' needs for fitness facilities through our gym equipment, exercise classes, swimming pool and squash courts. But the customer service we offer provides for their personal needs – the feel-good factor, the personal touch that makes the customers feel they're seen as people not numbers. It makes people feel good about the organisation and trust it to fulfil their needs and expectations. Once we've given people the image, we work hard to make it a reality.* 99

Paul is one of the reception staff at the centre. He clearly recognises the effect his attitude towards customers has on their perception of the organisation as a whole:

66 *Customers come here to relax and enjoy themselves. So they expect that to start happening from the moment they come in the door. I'm one of the first people they see. The way I treat them can colour their experience of our facilities. If I'm unwelcoming or off-hand, they'll feel irritated or disappointed. And no matter how brilliant our facilities are, that feeling will stay with them. So instead of enjoying themselves, they'll be thinking 'He was rude. What sort of an organisation staffs its reception with people like that?'* 99

Many organisations use quotes from their satisfied customers in their promotional materials. These are known as endorsements; they help project a positive image of the organisation and their products and services. They also use pictures of people enjoying their products, services and facilities. The aim is to build up the expectations and trust of potential customers.

TOPSY TWISTER!!

Try it if you dare! These people did

"Brilliant! I can't wait to go again!" – John Wade, 18 yrs old.
"Wow! What an experience! – Sue Older, 43 yrs old.
"Roller-coaster heaven!" – Kevin Healey, 25 yrs old.

Effective communication

Customer service is all about meeting customers' needs and matching – or, better still, exceeding – their expectations. To do these, you need to be absolutely sure you know what the customer wants. The best way to find out is by talking to them and listening to them. So effective communication is crucial to good customer service – for both external and internal customers.

Effective communication means giving:

- the right message
- to the right people
- at the right time
- in the right way.

Dealing with individual customers

Communication with individual customers gives staff in leisure and tourism organisations the best opportunity to find out what the customer needs and to explain to the customer how the organisation can meet those needs. It also helps to build up good one-to-one relationships with customers. This is important – customers who feel they are valued and recognised as individuals are more likely to return. A regular customer at a gym explains how the staff's skills in individual communication has gained them her customer loyalty:

66 *I'd tried a number of different exercise programmes at a number of different gyms and fitness centres but I always ended up dropping out after the first session or two. The classes I'd tried seemed to be run on the principle of 'keep up or keep out'. The instructors didn't seem interested in helping you improve and one or two seemed to be there to show off how fit they were. When I first contacted my current gym by phone, I was amazed at how much information the receptionist gave me in response to my general enquiry. Right from the start I felt they made it their business to find out what I was looking for. And the individual treatment continued from there. I booked in for an assessment session with one of the instructors and from that he devised an exercise programme just for me. He made sure I knew how to do the exercises and how to use the equipment and he worked through them with me until I felt confident to do them on my own. At every session, we would talk about how I was getting on and we'd work out any adjustments to the programme we felt were necessary.* 99

Dealing with groups of customers

Many staff working in leisure and tourism organisations need to communicate with groups, as well as on a one-to-one basis. Group communication can either be:

- face-to-face – for example, a tour guide describing attractions to a party of tourists, or a fitness coach teaching an aerobics class
- written – for example, signs, notices, promotional materials, memos, letters.

A guide in an art gallery explains some of the skills he uses in talking to groups:

66 *In an average day, I do between eight and ten gallery tours. I have to be fresh and enthusiastic for each one. Luckily for me, I love the gallery and the exhibits are all like old friends to me. So I think of the tour as a way of*

introducing people to things I love. I know a lot about the exhibits and the artists who created them. But I have to tailor the information to suit the groups I'm taking round. For example, knowledgeable art enthusiasts have different needs and interests from school parties. I've been on guided tours of galleries myself all over the world and quite often the guides treat you like a herd of sheep to be got through the gallery as quickly as possible. I like to make every group feel I'm doing the tour just for them. Talking to a group of people can be quite difficult. I make sure everyone feels included in the group by looking around at them while I'm talking. I talk a bit more slowly than I would in normal conversation and take care to speak clearly. I always encourage people to ask questions and make their own comments on the exhibits. My proudest moment was when a woman came up to me after a tour and told me she now felt she knew the artists personally and that their work had really come alive for her. **99**

Making a good impression

As soon as customers come into contact with a leisure and tourism organisation, they form first impressions. They notice:

- the decor and tidiness of the reception area
- how staff dress and how they present themselves
- whether there is a warm and friendly welcome
- the quality of the organisation's leaflets or brochures and the helpfulness of any information provided
- the service they receive on the first telephone conversation or when they receive a reply to an enquiry.

These first impressions can have a lasting effect on how a customer views an organisation.

In most organisations there are some staff who are usually the first point of contact with customers, such as receptionists, switchboard operators, box-office staff, front-of-office staff or sales staff. These people are particularly well placed to create a good first impression. It means they have to communicate professionally and efficiently and be positive, whatever happens or is said. This may mean dealing with difficult questions, or even awkward customers, calmly and politely.

DISCUSSION POINT

You will have a lot of experience of being a customer of different leisure and tourism organisations, for example:

- going to a cinema or theatre
- using a sports or leisure centre
- getting information from a travel agent or entertainment centre.

Think about your first impressions of these and similar leisure facilities you have used. What things helped form your impressions? Discuss your experiences of using these facilities with other students in your group.

How did the organisations and their staff communicate with you as a customer? Which of the organisations you discussed would you be most likely to visit or use again? Why?

Presenting a positive image

The personal image of staff can communicate strong messages about an organisation's attitude and image.

Whenever people meet for the first time, they assess each other according to their:

- appearance – dress, physical appearance
- actions – handshake, voice, body language
- attitudes – to other people, to situations.

How does this employee's personal image play a part in the way the organisation provides customer service?

This is why people dress up for interviews and greet and speak to the interviewer in a friendly manner – they are presenting a personal image that they hope will create a good impression.

Talking to customers on the phone

DISCUSSION POINT

Here's the experience of a potential customer ringing to find out about the classes run at a dance centre:

Receptionist: *Hello?*

Customer: *Hello. Is that Julienne's Dance Studio?*

Receptionist: *Yes.*

Customer: *I wonder if you can help me. I'd like to know what sort of classes you run, the times and the prices.*

Receptionist: *Classes, times and what, dear?*

Customer: *Classes, times and prices.*

Receptionist: *Classes, times and prices. Hang on, I'll put you through to someone who'll tell you. Now, what's her extension? 62. Oh no, that's the wrong one – 63, that's it. (a minute of silence)*

Receptionist: *Hello? Caller, are you still there?*

Customer: *Yes.*

Receptionist: *Oh, hello dear. I was trying to put you through but I can't find her. Hold on . . . Janice, where's Julie? . . . Oh, is she? . . . Are you taking the post down? Take these letters for me – I'm on the phone. Thanks. Hello, caller?*

Customer: *Yes?*

Receptionist: *Hello dear, yes . . . um . . . the person you need to speak to has just popped out. Can you call back in about – ooh, I don't know – ten minutes or so?*

Customer: *Um, well, yes, but couldn't you, er . . .*

Receptionist: *Thank you, dear. Goodbye.*

What sort of impression has the receptionist given of the organisation? What sort of customer service has the receptionist provided? If you were the customer, would you call back? What should the receptionist have said and done?

Telephones are a vital communication method in any organisation. They mean that people can contact each other quickly and directly and they allow immediate two-way communication. Although most people have telephones at home, using a telephone effectively for business needs a certain level of thought and skill. A trainer who runs training courses in telephone skills explains why:

66 *As with other forms of business communication, telephone calls should be conducted in an efficient and professional way. A sloppy approach can damage an organisation's image. When customers contact an organisation by phone, they expect the same courtesy and helpfulness as they would face to face. They expect the person who answers the phone to greet them in a friendly but business-like way, give them the information they need or put them through to the person who can help them. It's all part of providing a customer service that meets the customer's needs.* 99

Dealing with customers face-to-face

Face-to-face communication brings customers and staff members into direct and personal contact. In this situation, making a good impression and presenting a positive image of the organisation all rely on your personal skills. A face-to-face encounter with a customer gives you many advantages. For example:

- the communication between you is two-way
- you can see your customer's reaction
- you can check on the spot if you have understood the customer.

> **Body language** means the non-verbal signals you give out through your posture, facial expressions, gestures and eye-contact.

When dealing with customers face to face, you need to be aware of the messages you send through your body language. This includes:

- facial expressions – frowning, smiling and so on
- eye contact – keeping or avoiding it
- body position – sitting or standing close to people, or moving away from them
- body posture – sitting or standing upright, slumping or leaning back
- gestures – pointing, shrugging, nodding and so on.

Your body language should be in tune with your verbal message. For example, to make a customer feel welcome, you'd give your greeting with a smile.

DISCUSSION POINT

Think of some situations in leisure and tourism when face-to-face communication is the main means of communication. What skills and attributes must a staff member have to be an effective communicator?

Without speaking to these people, what can you tell about their attitudes?

ACTIVITY

Carry out research into body language. You may find it helpful to look in books on communication or psychology textbooks. Make a chart listing as many types of positive and negative body language as you can. Think about your own behaviour – is your body language good?

Using the results of your research, produce a set of guidelines for receptionists on how to use positive body language when dealing with customers face-to-face.

Written communications

Visit any leisure or tourism organisation and you'll see a lot of written information. Some will be for external customers and some will be for internal purposes. Here are some examples:

- letters
- memos
- reports
- forms
- staff handbooks
- posters.

- instruction manuals
- signs
- notices
- leaflets
- brochures

Whatever the format, written communication should:

- be easy to understand
- be clearly laid out
- use accurate language, grammar and spelling
- include all the right information
- give details of who to contact with queries or for more information.

Here is an extract from a notice in a hotel, explaining what customers should do if the fire alarm goes off. How well does it work as a piece of written communication? Write an improved version.

NOTICE TO CUSTOMERS

On hearing the fire alarm being sounded, the correct procedure to follow is to pass with all necessary haste to the nearest emergency fire exit which can be found at either end of all corridors. The lifts must never be used in the course of an evacuation procedure. Personal belongings should not be collected before making an exit from the building. Having vacated the premises, customers should make their way to the assembly point which can be found situated in the car park to the fore of the hotel where hotel staff should be reported to for names to be recorded.

Verbal and non-verbal communication

All the kinds of communication described so far break down into two types:

■ verbal – using words

■ non-verbal – not using words.

Some communication uses only one type. For example:

■ a telephone conversation uses only spoken words (vocal communication)

■ a letter uses only written words

■ road signs use symbols to direct or warn drivers (visual communication).

More often, communication is a combination of the two types. For example:

■ a face-to-face conversation would be a combination of spoken words and body language signals

■ a brochure would be a combination of written words and pictures or photographs.

Whichever type is used, the important thing is that it is the appropriate and most effective way of communicating with the customer.

Feedback loop

Good communication often depends on having a good system for getting feedback:

■ from external customers – through direct or indirect comments, letters of praise or complaint, customer surveys or questionnaires

■ from internal customers – information from other departments. For example, data about number of sales, occupancy or usage figures from the sales department, or summaries of customer feedback from the customer services department

■ on the spot to check if information given vocally has been understood.

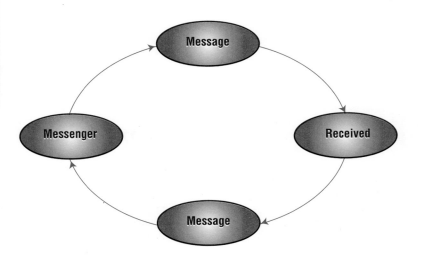

Customer feedback can help an organisation improve customer service by telling it what it is doing well and how it could improve its performance. The marketing officer of a concert hall explains:

66 *The box office assistants have direct contact with customers. If the prices for a particular concert are more than we normally charge, the box office manager may tell me at our weekly meeting that people are booking seats for the lower-priced tickets and not booking the better, more expensive seats. I would have to think about doing a special promotion in the local paper or advertising the concert more widely. I would also know for the next time that I should keep the ticket prices at the normal rate. We also give out a simple questionnaire with every ticket asking customers for their comments on the venue, its facilities and the concert programmes.* 99

QUESTIONNAIRE	
Name	Is this decision based on who is playing, ticket price or a combination of both? ....
Address	
Male/Female	Do you ever take advantage of our multiple booking discounts? ....
Single/Married/Partnered/Divorced/Separated	
Profession	How far in advance do you usually reserve your seats? ....
Do you have any children? If so, how many and what ages?	What form of payment do you usually use to pay for your reservations? ....
Have you been to the Devere Concert Hall before?	In general, do you think that the price of seats is fair? ....
If so, which performance/s? – name up to three.	Do you use the Concert Hall Restaurant prior to a concert? If so, how often? ....
On average, how many times a season would you expect to come to the Hall?	
Would you normally book for yourself only, come with a friend, or with a group?	Do you use the Concert Hall Bar? ....
Do you normally reserve the same seats? If so, which ones?	Do you pre-order interval refreshments? ....

On-the-spot feedback can help you check that your listener has understood what you've said. An assistant in a tourist information explains how he uses questions to check that customers have understood the information he's providing:

66 *Nearly all my customers are visitors to the area, many from abroad, and I have to make sure that they understand all the information I give – details about tourist attractions, events, places of historical interest, route directions, places to stay and so on. I ask questions such as 'Would you like me to go over that again?' or 'Is there anything you're not sure about?' to check that I've made myself clear.* 99

The benefits of effective communication

Effective communication creates good relationships with customers – both internal and external. It also creates a happy working environment and satisfied staff. When communication is good, the organisation becomes:

■ more efficient – because everyone has the information they need
■ more effective – because information is getting to the right people, in the right way, at the right time.

Good communication creates:

- customer satisfaction
- staff satisfaction
- increased organisational efficiency
- increased organisational effectiveness

Here are some quotes from customers and staff in the leisure and tourism industry which illustrate the importance of effective communication:

66 *The staff at the gym I go to always treat me in a friendly way. They greet me by name when I arrive – that always makes me feel special. They have all the information about the facilities at their fingertips. And the instructors take a lot of time to show me how to use the gym equipment and work out exercise programmes to suit me personally. I wouldn't go anywhere else.* 99

customer at a gym

66 *Helping customers find the holiday they want means I have to really listen to what they say and be up to date with all the products, prices and offers. We're all well trained in customer service and product knowledge so I feel confident that I know what to do and what to say in any situation with a customer. It's a demanding job but I really enjoy it. When customers call back to say how much they enjoyed their holiday it really makes my day, because I know I helped them to make the right choice. It shows me that I've done my job and done it well.* 99

customer adviser in a travel agency

66 *From our staff appraisal system, we realised that staff morale was low. The heart of the problem was poor communication. People felt they weren't being given enough information about the important things like product information, how well they were doing and the company's future plans, and spending too much time bogged down in masses of paperwork and meetings. So we got everyone to think of themselves as internal customers and suppliers and suggest improvements to our communication systems and procedures. As a result, we developed more efficient and realistic ways of communicating, staff morale is high and productivity is up.* 99

managing director of a watersports centre

66 *Our direct-mail campaigns weren't pulling in as much business as we'd hoped. We needed to improve their effectiveness but we weren't sure how to go about it. We bought in some outside help from a corporate communications consultant. It was money well spent. Having an outsider's view helped us to recognise that we'd slipped into set patterns of thinking – about the organisation's image and our customers – and it was costing us business. We analysed our target customers more closely and carefully defined their information needs. Then we created promotional materials to match those needs. The result was an instant improvement in business – and a lesson that being effective means keeping in touch with the customers' needs.* 99

marketing manager of a seaside marina

ACTIVITY

Devise a booklet and accompanying poster for staff in a leisure or tourism organisation you know about that would help them to understand the role of good communication in customer service

Types of customers

People working for leisure and tourism organisations deal with two types of customers:

- internal customers – their colleagues who need information, support and other internal services
- external customers – people outside the organisation who use or buy the organisation's products or services.

Internal customers

Within leisure and tourism organisations, employees often have roles that are similar to those of customer and supplier. An individual or team supplies a product or service – for example, accounts information or computer support – and these are used by other individuals or teams.

A marketing manager in a local-authority-run theatre describes the following situations in which she is either an internal customer or an internal supplier.

66 *The marketing director – my direct boss – is my major internal customer. I supply services for her which include writing press releases and brochures, making contacts with clients and organising marketing events. In turn, I have an assistant who helps out with administration and uses the marketing database to print envelope labels for mailshots. I am her customer, because she supplies services for me – she is my customer because I have to make sure I supply her with interesting work to do.*

As a department, one of our major internal customers is the city council's Leisure Services Division which we are part of. For example, we supply the Leisure Services Director with a lot of information about attendance and finance, and they often use us as a venue for Leisure Services events such as receptions. We are also customers of other council departments, such as the design and print section which produces most of our posters and leaflets, and the finance section which deals with all our salaries, expenses and so on. 99

As this marketing manager's experience shows, internal customers may include:

- colleagues who see and talk to each other on a daily basis
- management
- staff teams in the same and other departments
- employees
- other functional departments within the organisation.

It is often a good idea to take a formal approach to communicating with internal customers. For example, it can be helpful to write a memo stating clearly what service one colleague will provide to another. This is similar to writing to an external customer saying what they can expect from the organisation.

External customers

Organisations providing leisure and tourism services and products depend on external customers for success. Commercial organisations need their customers' money to carry on trading and to make a profit. Organisations that provide free or subsidised services still rely on their external customers' interest in, and continued use of, their products and services.

All leisure and tourism organisations need to decide who their customers are – what the market is for their particular goods or services. This is harder for some organisations than for others. For example, a multiscreen cinema showing the latest big-budget films attracts a wider range of people than a cinema showing mainly foreign, less commercial films.

A tour operator explains why his company invests a lot of time and money in researching who its customers are:

66 *We need to know who our customers are so that we can give them what they need, want and expect from our holidays. We send out questionnaires to find out who the typical customers are for different products – we ask questions about age, cultural background, specific needs (mobility problems, languages etc.) and whether people travel alone or as a group. We then use this information to tailor holidays to meet their needs and expectations, and target our marketing to attract the 'typical' customer.* **99**

Different age groups

Different age groups have different needs and tastes. Some organisations cater for a range of age groups. Some target particular age groups.

ACTIVITY

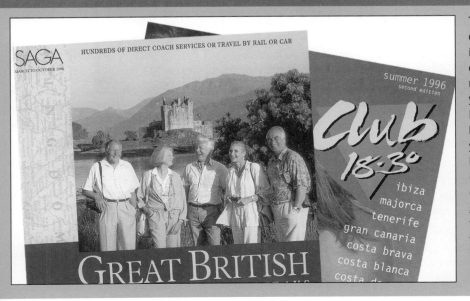

These two tour operators have identified target customers by age range. How can you tell just by looking at their brochures? Why do you think they have decided to identify their customers by age group? How do you think this helps them provide a better customer service?

ACTIVITY

Visit your nearest tourist information office. Ask the staff there about the contact they have with people from different cultural backgrounds. Find out what the staff do to make sure any special customer needs are met.

What specific needs are these organisations meeting?

```
HARRY'S BAR
MENU
STARTERS  £3.50
Cream of vegetable soup     Avocado and prawn salad
Roll mop herrings with rye bread
Melon and parma ham
Smoked salmon pate with granary toast
MAIN COURSES  £7.50
Beef stroganoff with rice     Half chicken roast
Pork schnitzel     Poached salmon     Grilled herby trout
VEGETARIAN  £6.00
Stuffed baked red pepper
Spinach and ricotta cannelloni
'Everything' salad     Mushroom moussaka
Four cheese pizza

All served with a selection of fresh vegetables or
salad with a choice of potato dishes
DESSERT & COFFEE  £2.50
Brandy walnut cheesecake     Chocolate mousse
Fresh fruit salad     Flambé banana surprise
```

ACTIVITY

Visit a travel agent and ask about the products and services they offer for these types of customer:

- people travelling alone
- families
- groups – for example, school parties, special interest holidays like painting holidays, and so on.

Collect examples of brochures and other information the travel agent provides for each type.

Different cultural backgrounds

Many leisure and tourism organisations have to cater for a wide range of cultural needs. Here are some examples:

- language
- diet
- religious observances
- dress codes
- social conventions.

Specific needs

To provide good customer service, leisure and tourism organisations must make sure that everyone has the same opportunities to use their products and services. This means catering for customers with a range of specific needs, including:

- difficulties in seeing (visual impairment)
- difficulties in moving or getting about (restricted mobility)
- difficulties in hearing (hearing impairment)
- problems with reading or using numbers (literacy or numeracy problems)
- having a first language different from the majority of the population (in the UK, this means people with English as a second or foreign language).

ACTIVITY

The conference manager for a hotel has been asked to arrange a conference on the environment for 80 delegates from around the world. To make sure she provides good customer service, she sends out a questionnaire in advance to find out more about the delegates' needs and wants. She finds out that one is in a wheelchair, and another has hearing difficulties. Over half don't speak English as their first language and 25 don't eat meat.

She asks your advice on how to provide good customer service to the delegates. Write a short memo summarising different points she needs to bear in mind when planning the conference.

What would have been the repercussions if she hadn't found out in advance about her customers' special needs?

Individuals and groups

Many leisure and tourism services and products are intended for use by individuals. Others are aimed at groups (families, large parties and so on). This influences the type of customer service an organisation offers.

Catering for groups is often more cost-effective than for individuals, which is why many facilities offer group discounts or appeal to families by offering cut-price, or even free, places for children.

Investigating customer service

Customer service is made up of:

- direct contact with customers
- indirect contact with customers
- products and services
- policies and procedures
- systems and processes.

To provide a high standard of customer service, organisations have to make sure that everything they do contributes to ensuring customer satisfaction.

The case study below describes the customer service offered by a travel agent.

TRAVEL OPTIONS LTD

Travel Options has been in business for 17 years. The managing director, who founded the company, describes some of the things they do to give a good customer service.

❝ First impressions count so it's important that we give the right impression. Our offices are always bright and cheerful and there are lots of posters and displays around. We want our customers to feel relaxed and at home while they're here. There are plenty of comfortable chairs around and we're happy for customers to gather up a bundle of brochures and sit down for an hour browsing through them.

We offer our customers an individual service that ensures that they get the holiday they want at a price they can afford. This means spending a lot of time talking to customers and discussing their needs until we're absolutely sure we understand what they want

We make a lot of arrangements on the customer's behalf – for example, travel, hotel bookings, car hire, insurance and currency exchange. We take great care to ensure that all details are recorded and then checked, double-checked and treble-checked. A slight error on our part could ruin a customer's holiday and damage their confidence in us. We also give them advice and information on things like health precautions, social or cultural conventions in different countries, personal safety and so on.

All our staff are given thorough training in good customer care – for both external and internal customers. Whether they're customer advisers, administrative, promotion or finance staff, they all have a part to play in our customer service. For example, in-depth product knowledge is the speciality of the customer advisers and the promotion staff, but the administrative and finance staff need some knowledge, too, to help them in their work. The customer advisers and promotion staff have to understand the administrative and finance procedures so they give and get the right internal information.

The travel business is a highly competitive one, so we're always looking for ways to improve our service. We welcome feedback and comments from staff and customers alike. We're always asking ourselves and our customers 'How well are we doing and how can we do better?' ❞

ACTIVITY

You and a friend are thinking of going into business in the leisure and tourism industry. Pick a sector of the industry you'd like to work in and select two organisations operating in that sector. Investigate the customer service they offer. Use your findings to write a report explaining the sort of things your business will need to do to ensure it offers a competitive customer service. Make sure your report covers these aspects of customer service in your chosen sector:

- the types of customer service offered
- the components of the service
- external and internal customers
- the way communication is used in the service.

Key questions

1 What is the difference between external customers and internal customers? Give examples of some internal customers in a large leisure and tourism organisation.

2 What are the roles of front-of-house staff, backroom staff and support staff? Give examples of where their work may overlap in a leisure and tourism organisation of your choice.

3 Why is customer service important from a 'business' point of view?

4 What differences are there between communicating with individuals and communicating with groups? What different approaches would you use?

5 What is the difference between verbal and non-verbal communication? Give some examples of each.

6 What 'specific needs' are you likely to come across in a leisure and tourism organisation? How can these needs be met?

Assignment

Part of your evidence for this element is a summary of your findings based on one organisation from the leisure and recreation industry and one from the travel and tourism industry. Working through the following steps will help you plan and organise this work.

1 Make a list of possible organisations you could use. (These could be the same organisations as those you use for Unit 3 on marketing). Decide how easy it will be to get information about the organisation. If it is a local organisation, will you be able to visit it? Could it be an organisation where you do a work placement or some part-time or voluntary work?

   Choose two of these organisations.

2 What types of customer service does each organisation provide? Which staff members are front-of-house, which are backroom and which are support staff? Give examples of how different staff come into contact with customers. Is there a clear difference between the ways they provide customer service?

Investigate the different components of customer service and how each organisation achieves them. How well does each one:

■ care for customers – both external and internal
■ meet customers' needs
■ satisfy the customers
■ meet customer expectations
■ care for the security and safety of customers.

What evidence is there that customer service is provided throughout the organisation?

3 Who are the organisations' customers? Think about both external and internal customers. What efforts do the organisations make to collect and look closely at information about their customers? How will you find out this information? Who will be the best people to talk to?

4 In what ways do the organisations communicate with customers? Where possible, collect examples of written communication and describe examples of other sorts of communication.

5 When you have gathered all this information, compare the ways in which the organisations provide good customer service. Look at the similarities and differences between the organisations and the different ways they deal with customer service.

Decide how you will present your findings. You could write up a report or you may prefer to give a presentation. If you give a presentation, you should also prepare some handouts summarising the information you have found. Your report or presentation should include examples of any 'good' or 'poor' customer service which you noticed.

> **66** I'm always selling to people, really. It's what I like most about the job – being able to go away from a customer knowing that you've made a sale and there's an opportunity for more business later. It's especially satisfying with companies which may make several rentals in a week. **99**
>
> *car-rental manager*

> **66** I don't think of what we do as selling. Our aim is to give the people who stay here a high standard of food and accommodation, and to get the atmosphere right for them to relax. That's why I put so much into the look of the place. I think if guests come in and feel at home straight away they are much more likely to enjoy themselves. In a way I suppose that is selling, but it comes naturally to me! **99**
>
> *owner of a guest-house*

> **66** We are here to sell tickets – that's what our business is about. Often it's quite straightforward; customers know what they want and our job is to tell them whether it's available and how much it will cost, and then go through the booking procedures as quickly as we can. Sometimes, though, we are conscious of selling to customers, for example if they come in to enquire about different sorts of holidays. The brochures are a great help, but we know that customers can get the same brochures in the travel agency down the road, so it's the way we treat customers that counts in the end. **99**
>
> *travel consultant in a travel agency*

ELEMENT **6.2**

Investigating sales and selling

Selling is part of customer service. People expect to pay for the goods and services they receive and selling is one of the ways for staff to meet their needs. Many jobs in leisure and tourism involve selling even if it's not their main function. For example, a receptionist in a hotel might ask newly-arrived guests if they wish to dine in the dining-room – it's good customer service and it's also good for business. You will know from your own experience that there are good and bad ways of selling: nobody likes to be put under pressure to buy, but at the same time customers often want information and advice. In this element you'll find out about the need for people in leisure and tourism organisations to sell and the things that make selling a rewarding and profitable activity.

The functions and objectives of selling

Many jobs in leisure and tourism involve sales and selling. Providing an efficient sales service can make a major contribution to good overall customer service.

Selling is the most important role of some leisure and tourism employees:

- a travel agent's main aim is to sell holidays
- a concert promoter's main aim is to sell tickets.

For other leisure and tourism employees, selling is not their main role, but it is still important:

- wardens at a country house open to the public are there to help people visiting the house, but may also become involved in selling guidebooks, postcards and other souvenirs
- reception staff at a leisure centre deal mainly with enquiries and bookings, but are well placed to sell other services, such as subscriptions, party bookings or the centre's restaurant facilities
- holiday resort representatives are there to help clients by providing information and dealing with problems, but they may also be encouraged to sell excursions to their clients.

The functions of selling

In simple terms, selling means persuading a customer to part with their money for a product or service. In practice, this can involve:

- giving customers information about products or services
- creating and keeping good relationships with customers
- dealing with customers' queries or problems
- dealing with customers' complaints.

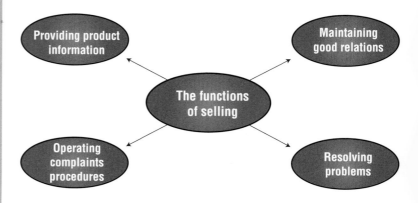

DISCUSSION POINT

How could each of these leisure and tourism employees make a contribution to good customer service by efficient selling?

ACTIVITY

Interview two people who work in different sales roles for leisure and tourism organisations. They may be people whose main job is to sell or who sell as part of their job. Talk to them about how they fulfil the four selling functions. Do they feel that their selling role is part of customer service?

Based on your findings, write a report on the sales functions of both jobs and how they relate to customer service.

Objectives of selling are:

- securing repeat business – encouraging existing customers to continue dealing with the organisation
- increasing sales – finding new customers and encouraging existing customers to buy more
- achieving customer satisfaction – making sure customers are happy with their purchases and the service they receive
- increasing profitability – finding cost-effective ways of maximising income
- securing competitive advantage – keeping ahead of the competition.

The objectives of selling

Selling lies at the heart of customer service. The objectives of selling are very similar to those of giving good customer service.

A telephone salesperson working for a travel company that books flights and car-hire describes selling roles in his company:

66 *Our customers come to us after seeing ads on Teletext or in papers and magazines. All our sales are made by telephone, so it is the telesales staff who do most of the selling. We have to create a good impression and show that we will do anything to get them the best flight at the best price. I try to get on well with my customers, so that they know they won't get a better deal or get a better service anywhere else. You have to judge the best way to do this from listening to their voices and from the little clues you get from what they tell you.*

Of course, everyone in the organisation has their own part to play in selling. For example, the finance staff deal with queries about invoices or receipts – although if a customer rings me direct with a problem, I like to deal with it for them. Details of customers are passed to the administration staff who then make sure they go on the mailing list and get our leaflets, plus details of special offers and stuff like that. That's an important part of selling, too, as it keeps us in people's minds. 99

ACTIVITY

Make a chart showing the different ways in which the organisation's sales methods help it to achieve its sales objectives of:

- securing repeat business
- increasing sales
- achieving customer satisfaction
- increasing profitability
- securing competitive advantage.

Section 6.2.2

Sales techniques

Selling requires knowledge, skills and techniques. People whose jobs involve a lot of selling usually receive training from their employers in these skills and techniques, but they can also be useful for people working in jobs where selling is only a small part of their responsibilities.

Preparing for a sales interview

When a salesperson and a customer talk, it is not like an ordinary conversation that takes place, say, between friends. In this situation (sometimes called a sales interview) both people have their own aims. The person selling has the main aim of making a sale – persuading the customer that buying a particular product or service is the right thing to do. Customers may want to find out information, but don't want to agree to buying the product or service until they are quite sure about it.

Preparing well for sales interviews can help employees to meet their aims and make a sale. A travel agent provides these four golden rules for sales clerks before opening for the day:

Approaching the customer

How customers meet sales staff depends on the type of product or service being offered. At one extreme are the timeshare touts in holiday resorts, hassling people to show them an apartment or new holiday complex. At the other extreme are the fans of a rock band who queue up for hours to buy tickets for a concert.

As these examples show, it can be either the customer who approaches the person selling or vice versa. It is often easier for the sellers when customers make the first move, as they know they are dealing with people who are already interested in the product, and should be willing to buy, provided the product or service is right.

When the person selling makes the first move, they need care and sensitivity to make sure they don't put the customer off. A sales assistant working in a museum shop describes how she approaches customers:

66 *Working in a shop, I've quickly learnt to tell what customers want and what they expect me to do. It's never a good idea to pounce on customers – that would put most of them off – but some do want you to take the lead, perhaps because they're not sure what they want or don't know where to find something. I try to use body language rather than approaching them too enthusiastically – I make eye contact and give them a welcoming smile to attract their attention. If they smile back, I usually give a friendly greeting to make verbal contact. Sometimes a queue builds up at the till in the summer, and I'm too busy to help a customer immediately. When this happens, I make sure I let the customer know I've seen them by explaining that someone will be with them as soon as possible.* 99

Be prepared!

- Be ready to make a good impression on everyone who walks in the door – think about the shop's appearance as well as your appearance and attitude.

- Make sure you're up to date on destinations, offers, flights, insurance and so on.

- Have brochures, leaflets and other information to hand, and switch your computer on.

- Decide with other members of staff who will answer phone enquiries while you are busy. An unanswered phone can put off both the customer in the shop and the one on the other end of the line.

TICKETS

DISCUSSION POINT

As a customer, how do you feel when approached by a salesperson? How do you tell a member of sales staff that you want help, or that you'd rather be left alone? If you were in a selling role, what hints would you look for to tell whether or not to approach a customer?

1 Give the customer your full attention.

2 Use good communication skills, friendly body language and a welcoming approach.

3 Ask the customer a few questions to find out about their needs and expectations.

- who is the customer?

- what type of holiday do they want (active, peaceful, etc.)?

- when might they want to go on excursions?

- where might they want to go to?

- why do they want to go – is it something they definitely want to do, or just a possibility?

You may also need to find out how much the customer is prepared to pay.

4 Listen carefully to the customer.

5 From the customer's answers, decide what trips and excursions would best meet the customer's needs. A customer may have several needs – you may have to find out which one(s) the customer considers most important.

6 Summarise the customers' needs to make sure that you have understood them all.

Identifying customer needs

Leisure and tourism organisations use marketing research to find out in general which products and services to sell. Members of staff involved in selling then need to find out, and meet, the specific needs of individual customers.

This is straightforward if customers know what they want: a simple 'I would like. . .', or 'Do you have. . ?' tells a salesperson straightaway what a customer's needs are. If customers don't know what they want, or don't understand exactly what products or services are available, then selling skills are needed.

A tour operator realised that it wasn't making the most of the potential to sell excursions to holidaymakers through resort representatives. As it was difficult to organise sales training with reps scattered around the world, it produced a set of guidelines for them to follow. The extract shown on the left gives advice on how to identify customers' needs.

Identifying customer needs will probably involve asking two types of question:

■ closed questions, which restrict the answers that can be given to 'yes', 'no', or one of a limited number of answers

■ open questions, which give the customer the chance to give views, opinions or preferences.

DISCUSSION POINT

Below are six questions which a travel agent could ask a customer. Which of them are open and which of them are closed?

1 Do you want to go to Madeira, the Canaries or the Azores?

2 Do you have any particular islands in mind?

3 Can you go during the first week of September?

4 When do you want to go away?

5 What sort of holiday do you want?

6 Would you prefer a beach holiday or a lakes and mountains holiday?

Think of a situation in which each of these questions would be appropriate.

Sales negotiating

For a product or service to be sold, the buyer and seller have to agree on price and the conditions of the sale. Not all selling situations are simple:

■ A customer buying in bulk or paying a large amount of cash may ask for a discount.

■ Services may not be available at the time required.

■ The make or model of a product may not be available and other similar products need to be considered.

The manager of a hotel reports on how he filled rooms when business has been slow:

❝ *During the recession of the early 1990s, we knew that we had to be flexible about room prices. People were spending less money on leisure and taking fewer holidays, and customers became precious! Many customers realised this and tried to get a cheaper price for a hotel room, especially if they were offering cash. If we had refused to negotiate, then they would have looked elsewhere. As far as I was concerned, an occupied room at a cheap rate was better than an empty room!* **99**

Not all the staff within an organisation are allowed to negotiate like this. If a customer tries to haggle with sales staff who don't have the authority, they should fetch a more senior member of staff for the customer to speak to.

If a customer wants to negotiate about price or conditions, staff members should:

- keep within the limits of their authority
- find out how far they can negotiate – what the lowest price is they can accept, for example
- make offers confidently
- never be grudging or rude when agreeing to a reduction or different conditions
- be prepared to be assertive and to say 'no', but always do so politely.

Overcoming objections

Customers usually make objections when they are uncertain whether or not to buy a product or service. They may not be sure whether the goods or services on offer actually meet their needs, or they may be unsure about the price or some of the conditions of the sale.

The seller needs to find out why the customer is making objections and work out how serious they are. Customers may make objections as a way of saying that they have changed their mind and don't want to buy a product or service any more.

If customers have a real concern, the seller needs to find a solution, e.g. by suggesting another similar product or by finding a way of changing the service to suit the customer.

When there is no suitable solution, it is better to tell customers that and stop selling, rather than to try to persuade them to accept something that would be unsuitable. That is much more likely to make an impression of good customer service, and may make the customer come back to the organisation at a later date.

Handling complaints

Handling complaints is an important part of an organisation's after-sales service.

The complaints an organisation receives are the tip of an iceberg. Only 5% of dissatisfied customers complain about the goods or services they receive. This means that 95% of dissatisfied customers don't bother to complain. So what do they do instead? They stay dissatisfied, but rather than try to get their money back with a formal complaint, they are likely to take their custom elsewhere.

Find out what the complaint is – listen carefully to what the customer has to say.

If, after listening, you are still not sure what the complaint is about, ask furher questions.

If you cannot sort out the complaint on the spot, take written details and pass the matter on to your supervisor or manager.

Reply to written complaints promptly, even if the organisation needs more time to look into the matter further.

Keep records of the complaint, any investigation carried out and copies of letters sent.

What does a sales report include?

- details of sales interviews or contacts with customers
- figures describing actual sales
- an analysis of whether sales are to regular or to new customers
- information about which goods or services attract particular interest, which are selling well and which are only selling slowly
- comments on the quality and standard of goods
- comments on after-sales service

This means that if a company receives only five formal complaints in a year, there could be 95 dissatisfied customers who do not return. These customers may tell their friends about the poor service they received. Their friends may also take their business elsewhere.

If a customer shows signs of dissatisfaction, an organisation should take prompt action to put matters right. This will help prove its commitment to customer care, as well as improving its reputation. All complaints should be handled professionally.

Closing the sale

When a customer agrees to buy a product or service, the seller is said to 'close the sale'.

There are situations where customers can't or won't make up their minds on the spot. They may need to consult others or spend a bit more time thinking. Some customers may simply need a little reassurance or some gentle persuasion to make a decision – good sellers can provide it, without putting too much pressure on the customer.

Before actually agreeing to buy a product or service, many customers show that they are ready to buy in other ways:
- through positive, open body language
- by asking more questions: 'How can I pay?' 'Can I pay in instalments?'
- by speaking positively about products or services: 'Yes, I really would like to try that.'
- by inviting the seller to reassure them: 'So you think my children would really enjoy this?'

Sales reporting

The sales techniques covered so far in this section are about relating to customers and trying to meet their needs. But there are other aspects of selling that are more concerned with meeting the needs of the organisation and providing the products or services being sold.

The organisation needs information about sales and records of what customers do or don't buy. This helps them to find out what their customers need, so that they can work out if there are better ways to meet them.

One way in which employees of leisure and tourism organisations can provide this information is through sales reports. A sales report is a written summary of sales.

Supplier	Code	Price	Description	O/Bal	Reorder Level	Stock Level	Total
TrundleWear	1573	39.36	Jogger Bum Bag	9	5	9	
TrundleWear	1574	43.62	Jogger Pants	8	6	6	
TrundleWear	1575	63.19	Jogger Jacket	8	6	8	
Mercury	1583	86.60	Jacket	5	5	10	
Mercury	1584	171.28	Boots	5	2	5	
Mercury	1585	90.85	Salopettes	6	6	10	
Mercury	1586	254.68	Skis	3	2	4	
Mercury	1587	63.19	Sunglasses	6	2	8	

Sales reports are mainly used by managers of organisations. It helps them to look at goods and services as actual and future sales. Organisations generally have guidelines for their staff on to how to write sales reports, what figures to include, and so on.

Sales recording

Sales records, like sales reports, contain important information which managers use to work out the success of individual products and services.

Employees involved in selling write down the numbers of sales achieved over a period. This information may then be used by different departments within a leisure and tourism organisation:

SALES ANALYSIS

INV NO	DATE	SALES PERSON	DAY SOLD	PROD CODE	PRICE	QTY	P/PRICE	VAT	TOTAL
4029	2.2.96	Marsdon	FRI	1127	638.30	1	638.30	111.70	750.00
4029	2.2.96	Marsdon	FRI	1133	127.66	1	127.66	22.34	150.00
4028	1.2.96	Kelly	THU	1402	126.81	4	507.24	88.76	596.00
4030	3.2.96	Marsdon	SAT	1403	637.45	2	1279.40	223.10	1502.50
4027	1.2.96	Kelly	THU	1553		1	414.47	72.53	487.00
4033	4.2.96	Kelly	SUN	1553		1	414.47	72.53	487.00
4027	1.2.96	Kelly	THU	1554	131.92	2	263.84	46.16	310.00
4032	3.2.96	Clark	SAT	1554	131.92	2	263.84	46.16	310.00
4031	3.2.96	Clark	SAT	1583		1	850.21	148.79	999.00
4031	3.2.96	Clark	SAT	1585	382.98	2	765.96	134.04	900.00
4031	3.2.96	Clark	SAT	1586		1	339.57	59.42	398.99
TOTAL									**5366.01**

The owner of a firm that manufactures and sells leisurewear explains how he uses sales records and reports:

66 *We produce a wide range of leisure products – sweatshirts, trainers, polo shirts and so on. Many of these products have brand names or logos attached to them, but the problem is that these logos or names might not stay in fashion for long. Something that is worth £75 one day can suddenly go out of fashion. Even if you reduce it to a tenner, it won't sell, because no one wants something so unfashionable. I have to look at sales reports and sales records every week to see which brands are in and which are definitely out. The information I get from my sales teams is important for me to check that we are producing clothing and footwear that customers want to buy and that our sales people can sell.* 99

Time management

Most people involved in selling are aware how long it takes to make a sale. Time is money – so an hour spent trying to persuade someone to buy something they don't want is time wasted. It also means no money! Managing time well is difficult. It means working out how much time to give to a particular customer to close a sale. Where there is clearly no hope of making a sale, it is best to stop selling as quickly as possible.

Other aspects of sales work take up time – tasks such as completing sales records and sales reports. Managing time means writing up these records as efficiently as possible. One way of doing this is by writing up records of sales as they happen – keeping on top of paperwork so that it never gets out of hand.

Sales presentation

Talking to customers individually makes sure of a personal touch, but it is not always the best way to sell products or services. It is often more cost-effective to sell to large numbers of customers in one go.

This can be done through sales presentations. These are situations where an organisation wanting to sell a product or service brings together a group of customers who are interested in buying the same product.

Sales presentations are often arranged with an inducement to get customers to attend. The owner of a company selling holiday flats in Greece explains:

66 *We run a series of presentations every year in towns and cities all over the UK. We are careful to hold them in very good hotels and we always offer them a Greek-style buffet. We invite people who we know have holidayed regularly on the island or who are in the higher income brackets and may be considering a second home abroad. Of course only a small number of them may be interested in really buying a home in Greece, but we stand a good chance of catching the ones that are really interested.* 99

Giving sales presentations requires a range of specialist skills:
■ public speaking
■ giving a carefully prepared sales speech
■ being totally familiar with the product and believing in it
■ being able to project the voice and use aids such as microphones
■ being able to use visual aids and sales support material
■ nerves of steel!

Duties, responsibilities and qualities of sales staff

The duties and responsibilities of sales staff are closely linked to their overall role in providing good customer service. Sales staff may need to do some, or all of, the following:

- provide point-of-sale service
- provide sales information and help
- know about the products or services they are selling
- deal with payments
- give refunds when necessary
- promote the organisation they work for and its other products and services.

To do this well, they need certain qualities and personal characteristics. The manager of a travel agency explains what the organisation looks for when taking on a new counter clerk:

66 *The sales staff we employ need a range of qualities to succeed. They must be friendly – able to chat with customers and make them feel welcome. They must be enthusiastic and honest – any hint of lack of sincerity and they're not in the running. Our customers value our honesty as a company above all else. Sales staff also need to be intelligent, so that they can remember all the information customers want to know and take the initiative sensibly. Judgement and consistency are very important qualities – they need to be able to make the right decisions and treat all customers fairly.*

We don't expect sales staff to come to us with an enormous amount of knowledge, as they learn a lot on the job. But we do expect them to be show an interest in the industry, our organisation, the job and the products and services we sell. It's always impressive if interviewees have made an effort to find out about us and what we do in advance. Once they're in the job, it's vital that they know the trade inside out. **99**

ACTIVITY

Prepare a person specification for any two of the following:

- a counter clerk in a travel agency
- an airline sales representative
- a resort representative
- a hotel receptionist
- a membership secretary of a national sporting association
- a customer services manager in any of the above.

DISCUSSION POINT

Look through the following key words. Which do you think are essential qualities for sales staff? Which do you think are most important? Are different qualities important for different jobs?

enthusiastic	resourceful	friendly	conscientious
consistent	approachable	reliable	accurate
informed	honest	attentive	inquisitive
presentable			

Customer service

Providing excellent customer service is the main responsibility of people involved in selling. Sales people aim to:

- find out what the customer wants and needs
- meet those needs
- make the customer feel valued.

Point-of-sale service

Many leisure and tourism organisations sell their products and services directly to the customer. For example:

- holidays
- sports equipment
- rail tickets
- souvenirs.

Point-of-sale service involves face-to-face contact with customers.

DISCUSSION POINT
What advantages does a point-of-sale service have over telesales or direct mail? What skills and attributes would a sales person need in this type of sales situation?

Sales information and assistance

Sales information may be either:

- written – leaflets and brochures
- verbal – with the customer asking the salesperson questions and relying on their knowledge and expertise.

When sales staff give assistance, their main aim should be to help customers to take their own decisions about the goods and services on offer. Salespeople should not be pushy; they should give advice in a professional way.

Product knowledge

Sales staff must have a thorough knowledge of the products and services they are offering to customers. Customers are never impressed by sales assistants who can't provide basic information about the things they are selling.

The box office assistant at an arts centre explains how she keeps her product knowledge up to date:

66 *I sell tickets for our events both over the phone and face-to-face at the counter. Some people are not sure whether an event really suits them and they ask me for more information so that they can make their minds up. I go to most of our events so if the band, the theatre group, or whatever, return to the centre – which many of them do – I know what they're like and I know the sort of people that they appeal to. A lot of shows are new to us, but our marketing officer tells us as much as she knows about them, which is normally more than we have room for in our leaflets. So I do help people make a choice. Obviously, I wouldn't recommend a heavy rock band to a senior citizen just because I think they're good!* **99**

After-sales services

The responsibilities of sales staff don't stop once a sale has been closed. When customers buy goods or services, they expect (and have a right to) good after-sales service. After-sales service includes things like:

■ maintenance and repair services for sports and exercise equipment
■ contacting customers who've bought holidays to check that everything went smoothly
■ monitoring gym-users' progress and offering advice on further exercise programmes
■ keeping customers up-to-date on new products and services.

Payments

Processing payments is a day-to-day task for sales staff. Customers may make payments:

■ in cash
■ by cheque
■ using a credit, debit or charge card.

Sales staff need to know the procedures to follow for each of these different types of payment. For example, if a customer wants to pay by credit card, the sales assistant may need to get authorisation from a more senior member of staff or a central credit office.

Accuracy is essential when processing payments. Nothing annoys customers more than feeling their money is not being handled properly, or – worst of all – feeling that they are being cheated.

Refunds

Refunds may be made in cash, by cheque or on a credit transaction. Most organisations have their own policies for offering refunds. These should give staff clear guidelines about when they can give refunds and what form refunds can take. Like payments, it is essential that refunds are processed accurately.

Promoting organisation and related products

Sales staff usually sell particular products or services. But in doing so, they may also be able to promote their organisation as a whole, or other related products.

The receptionist at a leisure centre explains:

❝ *I mainly sell admission tickets for the swimming pool and squash courts, but in doing this I chat to customers and have a chance to promote other products and services we offer. I tell them about our fitness centre, and how they can get cheaper admission by taking out membership. If they hire equipment, I let them know that we also sell sportswear and equipment in our shop. And when they come off court or out the pool looking exhausted, I point them in the direction of the health food restaurant!* ❞

Sales administration systems

Section 6.2.2 looked at the importance of sales records and reports for organisations selling products and services. These records are examples of sales administration systems, or put more simply, ways of handling information about sales.

Sales administration systems used in leisure and tourism organisations include:
- customer accounts
- booking forms
- membership lists
- tickets.

All of these help make the selling of goods and services a smoother process.

Computer-based and paper-based systems

In the past, sales administration systems meant a lot of paperwork, but today more and more sales administration is being done on a computer.

In practice, sales are often processed on a computer, with information then given to customers on paper. For example:
- Customers' records are often stored on a database, so that when a customer buys something or has a query, the record can be updated by sales staff. If necessary, a paper-based account can then be printed out regularly for the customer.
- Clients of holiday companies are often asked to fill out a booking form in a brochure, but the details on the form are then transferred to a computer database. Again queries can be dealt with quickly, as any staff member can call up the details of the booking on their computer screen.
- Membership lists can be created either as a separate list in a computer file, or by combining individual customer records. Membership cards can then be printed for customers from these computer-based lists.
- Many venues operate computerised ticketing systems, where tickets are printed out by the computer operator. In a venue with numbered seating, for example, the computer will automatically update the seating plan as tickets are sold, so that staff can quickly see which seats are sold and which are still for sale.

The box office manager of a concert hall with 1,200 seats remembers how they used to sell tickets:

66 *Before the computerised ticketing system, selling tickets was pretty laborious. Because all seats are numbered we had to use large diagrams of the auditorium, on card, with a complete plan of all the seats. When seats were sold, these were crossed off using one colour of pencil – we had different colours representing sales, reservations, complimentary seats, reserved seats, and so on. Because we had three staff selling seats, they often had to pass the plans across to each other and if two customers at different windows wanted to buy tickets for the same concert, one had to wait.* 99

DISCUSSION POINT

Security of information is an important consideration for leisure and tourism organisations. Lost or damaged sales information can be expensive in terms of time, money and customer goodwill. How can organisations ensure the security of computer-based information? And of paper-based information?

Customer accounts

Some leisure and tourism organisations let customers have products and services before they pay for them. The organisation will keep records of the orders the customers have made and then send them an invoice showing them how much they owe. The customer then pays the invoice. Invoices are usually issued on a monthly or quarterly basis.

JANE HOBART SPANGLIES WINE BAR 127 CATHCART ROAD LONDON NW3 5HIP	INVOICE NO	218
	OUR REF	TS51809
	DATE	30.4.96

FOR 12 T-SHIRTS SUPPLIED BY THE FEELGOOD FACTORY HEALTH CLUB SHOP. 3 X LARGE 8 X MEDIUM 1 X SMALL	£ 59.97 £159.92 £ 19.99
SUB TOTAL	£239.88
VAT 17.5 %	£ 41.98
TOTAL	£281.86

Booking forms

All sorts of leisure and tourism organisations use booking forms. For example:

■ hotels to book rooms

■ travel agents to book transport and accommodation

■ sports centres to book sports facilities.

Booking forms show details of the product or service the customer wants and helps the organisation to make the necessary arrangements and to keep records.

Membership lists

Many leisure and tourism organisations offer membership – for example:

■ sports and fitness clubs

■ holiday clubs

■ golf clubs.

■ charity organisations

■ special interest organisations

■ arts societies.

They usually record details of their members on a database. Members pay a subscription fee, usually once a year. Some organisations are strictly 'members-only' – they only offer products, services and facilities to members. Others are also open to non-members who have to pay higher prices than members.

Tickets

Tickets have two main purposes:

- they allow the customer the right to enter and use a facility or service
- they act as records of bookings or sales for an organisation.

Registering

Many large leisure and tourism organisations register customers to keep their sales records up to date. For example, most large hotels either ask new guests to register in writing in a book or add their details to a computerised register.

The manager of a large hotel describes how his computer-based register records information about customers:

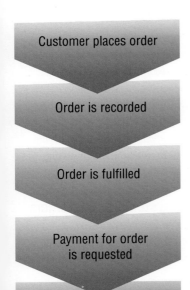

Customer places order

Order is recorded

Order is fulfilled

Payment for order is requested

Payment for order is made

66 *We have a computerised register. Details of guests are entered into it when they check in – or we may already have their details on computer if they have booked earlier. This file is then used to record details of their spending – bar, restaurant, room service and so on. It then produces the bill at the end of their stay.* 99

Order processing

Customers' orders are recorded in a standard format and processed by administrative staff. Order processing can be done using a paper-or a computer-based system. Most organisations give each order its own code or number. Customers are often given numbers or codes, too. Both help to make it easier to trace and keep track of orders as they are processed, fulfilled and paid for.

Credit clearance

Before a customer is allowed credit – particularly for large amounts – organisations need to check that the customer can keep to the credit agreement terms. This sometimes means the customer has to fill in forms including details of salary and financial status.

The value of sales administration systems to an organisation

Sales administration systems have several purposes:

■ to make the process of selling and buying easier for both the organisation and the customer
■ to reduce the possibility of errors
■ to help organisations gather information they can use for other purposes, such as marketing and sales analysis
■ to help organisations keep an edge over their competitors.

For example, a hotel could gather all of the following information from a hotel registration system:

■ how many guests are in the hotel – essential in case of fire
■ where guests come from, their occupations, the newspapers or magazines they read, the credit cards they use
■ what additional services are most often requested (useful for special offers and promotions)
■ information useful for public relations (for example, whether there are any celebrities staying at the hotel)
■ data for a mailing list.

The box office manager of the concert hall which has installed a computerised ticketing system explains the value of the new system:

66 *The computerised ticketing system has enormous value to the organisation. It makes selling tickets easier – once a customer has bought one ticket, they have a personal record. Box office staff can call up records whenever a customer wants to book a seat. We also keep records of all the tickets individuals buy over the years, which is useful for the marketing department. If we are putting on, say, a country and western show, we can ask the computer to create a list of all customers who have bought C&W tickets in the past and print out address labels just for them. Then we send them the leaflet on the show by post. It is so much easier and quicker to work with the marketing department in this way.* 99

The value of sales administration systems to customers

Efficient administration systems also have value for customers.

■ The process of buying is made as smooth and trouble-free as possible.
■ Knowing that there are good administration systems gives customers confidence in an organisation.
■ Comments from customers can be fed back to the relevant department and used to improve products and services.
■ Efficient systems for processing payments improve security and reduce the number of complaints.
■ When customers have queries or complaints, they can be dealt with quickly and efficiently.

DISCUSSION POINT

Can you think of occasions, from your own experience, when sales administration systems have been particularly efficient or inefficient? What difference did it make to the overall quality of customer service you received?

The special nature of selling leisure and tourism products and services

The products and services sold by leisure and tourism organisations have their own special qualities and particular features. Selling a leisure service, such as an aerobics session, or a tourism product, such as a holiday, is very different from selling items like clothes or electrical appliances. Why is this?

Intangible products and services

Most leisure and tourism products and services – from holidays to membership of a sports club – are intangible. This means they can't be handled, tried and tested like an item of clothing or an appliance. Customers can't examine a holiday for quality before buying it. When selling intangible products and services, sales people often focus on the benefits they will bring the customers and spend a lot of time encouraging the customers to imagine themselves enjoying the benefits.

The element of trust when buying

When customers buy a leisure and tourism product or service, they are taking a risk. They are paying for something without being able to test its quality. For this reason, they rely heavily on the knowledge and advice of:

- sales staff
- sales material, such as brochures and leaflets.

Their decision to buy is based on good faith and trust in the honesty and knowledge of the sales team. This is particularly true in the travel industry, where holidays are usually paid for well in advance. The manager of a travel agency explains how his staff are given training to ensure customers can trust their opinions and advice:

66 *We realise how important it is that customers can trust what our sales staff say. If sales staff are dishonest or give bad advice, customers won't come back. To make sure that staff really know what they're talking about, we send them on as many training days as we can where they learn about the holidays offered by different tour operators. They also go on holidays and weekend trips offered by different operators themselves, so they experience the holiday and service personally. We also have a lot of directories, maps and guides in the agency, which we make sure are up to date and accurate.* 99

Enjoyment is hard to quantify

One of the difficulties facing leisure and tourism sales staff is that customers' opinions of products and services such as a holiday or a film usually depends on how much they have enjoyed it, and enjoyment is very hard to quantify – particularly when the product is intangible.

Often, customers may enjoy one aspect of a product or service but not another. For example, a holidaymaker may have a good flight, be disappointed with service in the hotel, hate the food in the restaurant and be delighted by the excursions organised by the resort representative. So did they enjoy their holiday?

Sometimes a customer's enjoyment of a product or service can depend on factors beyond the control of the provider. For example, if a customer buys a

- Leisure and tourism products and services are often intangible.
- Products and services are often bought on trust, through information in brochures.
- It is hard to quantify customers' enjoyment of an intangible product or service.
- Customers have different expectations and standards.
- Leisure and tourism products and services can't be stored like goods in a shop. They are provided at specific times and do not have a shelf life.

ACTIVITY

Collect examples of promotional materials for leisure and tourism products and look out for adverts on the television. Analyse the selling techniques the organisations use and make notes on what they do and how effective it is.

DISCUSSION POINT

Think of the last three leisure or tourism products or services you bought. These might be a ticket to a concert or play, a game of squash, a meal in a restaurant, or a holiday. Which did you enjoy most? What are the difficulties of trying to compare how much you enjoyed different leisure and tourism activities?

ticket for the final of an important tennis tournament and it pours with rain, they are not going to enjoy the event.

Varying levels of customer expectation and satisfaction

All customers have different expectations when buying a leisure and tourism product, and are satisfied by different things. Here two families compare their opinions of visiting a theme park on the same day:

66 *We were really looking forward to our day out at the theme park and had heard good things about it in advance. We're big fans of exciting, scary rides, and spent a week at Universal Studios in the States over the summer. We were so disappointed when we got there. The rides were tame, there was no atmosphere, we had to queue for up to half an hour to get on to rides, and the food was dull.* 99

66 *We had a brilliant day out at the theme park. We'd never been to one before, and had just expected glorified swings and slides. We were very wrong! The rides were exciting and worth the short waits. There were actors in costume, lots of different food stalls and games, and everyone seemed to be enjoying themselves. We'll definitely be going back.* 99

The salesperson as part of the service

In some cases, the salesperson is actually part of the leisure or tourism product on offer. For example, sports coaches often sell their own services to customers. This means that, as salesperson and organiser, they have greater control over the product or service provided.

The owner of some stables explains how she tailors her horseriding holidays to match the needs and experience of riders:

66 *I organise weekend riding holidays where a group of two or three riders stay in a nearby bed-and-breakfast and ride with me on Saturday and Sunday. I find out on the phone in advance how experienced they are and how many hours' riding they want to do. Some groups want to ride all day quite fast and cover a lot of miles. Others want a shorter ride with a longer lunch break, and some ask for a lesson as well as a ride out into the country. Most people who come here enjoy themselves, but some people find it difficult keeping up with the rest of the group or they want to go further and faster, and I have to find a compromise.* 99

The customer as part of the service

Many leisure and tourism sales staff use endorsements from past customers as a sales aid when selling to existing or potential customers. For example, a leisure centre's sales material might include quotes from satisfied customers, or a travel clerk might talk about past customers' holiday experiences when selling a holiday to the same place.

Services cannot be stored

Because most leisure and tourism products are intangible, they cannot be stored like goods in a shop. For example, if a nightclub doesn't sell all the tickets for a party, it can't save them up for the following week.

Investigating sales and selling

The best way of seeing how selling works in leisure and tourism is to look closely at sales in a typical organisation. This might involve finding out about:

■ the functions of selling at the organisation

■ the organisation's sales objectives

■ sales techniques used by staff

■ the duties and responsibilities of sales staff

■ the qualities needed by the organisation's sales staff

■ the value of sales administration systems used to the organisation and its customers.

Here are some checklists to help you make an investigation, along with some quotes from salespeople in the leisure and tourism industry to show how the theory works in practice.

The functions of selling

■ to provide product information

■ to maintain good relations with customers

■ to provide an effective complaints procedure

■ to resolve customers' problems

❝ The function of my job is to make help our customers make the right choices about the classes they choose. I advise them on the different exercise programmes we offer and help them to choose the ones that best suit their needs. I tell them all about the facilities at the club, subscription fees and club rules. I treat every customer as an individual and work hard at making them feel they're in professional hands all the time. If customers have any complaints, we identify how and why we've failed to come up to their expectations and look for ways of improving our performance. ❞

fitness instructor at a health club

Sales objectives

■ to secure repeat business

■ to increase sales

■ to achieve satisfied customers

■ to increase profitability

■ to secure competitive advantage

❝ We want our customers to enjoy their day here. If they go home happy, not only have we got satisfied customers, but they're likely to come back again. They are also likely to tell other people about how much they enjoyed themselves and that could lead to new customers for us. We're in a competitive market so we do all we can to get people to choose to spend their money with us, rather than with our competitors. ❞

customer service manager at a theme park

Sales techniques

- preparing for a sales interview
- identifying customer needs
- overcoming objections
- closing the sale
- sales recording
- sales presentation
- approaching the customer
- negotiating sales
- handling complaints
- sales reporting
- time management

 *I deal with customers by phone. Most of my leads are people who have responded to our mailings. Before I call them, I check their details on our database to see if they've got a customer history or are new customers. My first aim is to establish what the customer needs. Then I can give them information on the sort of products we have that could meet those needs. Some customers are already interested in our products and have a good idea of what they want. Some need more advice. Some just aren't interested – but their reasons for not wanting to buy can help us to identify any improvements we could make to our range or tell us that we're directing our efforts at the wrong person. Both sorts of information are useful. The most difficult part of my job is dealing with complaints. Some people can be really rude. But I've learned to take it in my stride and if I handle them with tact, they calm down and recognise that I want to help resolve their problem.*

telesales person for a sports equipment mail-order company

The duties and responsibilities of sales staff

- customer service
- sales information and assistance
- after-sales service
- giving refunds
- promoting related products and services
- point-of-sale service
- product knowledge
- taking payments
- promoting the organisation

As a receptionist, I'm right on the front line of the selling process. I take bookings, welcome customers when they arrive, help them to register and give them all the information they need about the hotel. I also promote the other services we offer – the restaurant, the gym, the swimming pool, car-hire arrangements and so on. Because I'm dealing with customers face to face, it's vital that I always make the right impression. I'm often the last person our customers see as well as the first. I prepare their bills and take their payments. While I'm doing that, I always take the opportunity to ask them if they enjoyed their stay. I pass on their comments to the relevant staff members.

receptionist in a city-centre hotel

Qualities of good sales staff

Personal:

- friendly
- enthusiastic
- honest

Capabilities:

- intelligent
- uses initiative
- confident in own judgement
- consistency

Knowledge:

- of industry
- of organisation
- of job
- of products and services

66 *Bar work's really demanding on your energy. You're on the go – and on your feet – all the time. But I really love the work – it's great to be working in a place where everyone's having a good time. I need a memory like an elephant's – prices, new drinks, cocktail recipes, guest beers, food menus – I have to know it all so I can give the right information to the customers. When I started working here, serving big rounds was a bit of a challenge – specially when the customers changed their minds half-way through while I was trying to add up the prices in my head. But I'm good at it now. My old maths teacher would be amazed. Handling money is a big responsibility. When everything's busy and I'm rushing to get people served, it's easy to make a mistake with someone's change – but those sort of mistakes are bad for business, so I have to concentrate really hard no matter how busy I am. Being a pub, customers are here to drink and sometimes a customer has a bit too much and gets out of hand. But we're all trained to deal with those sort of situations. When I'm not at work, I go out with my mates. Whenever we're in a pub or a club, I have a good look at the sort of service they give and the drinks and things they stock to see how it compares to ours.* **99**

bartender

The sales administration system

System:
- computer-based
- paper-based

Procedures:
- registering
- order-processing
- invoices and payments
- credit clearance

Sales information:
- customer accounts
- booking forms
- membership lists
- tickets

Benefits:
- value to customer
- value to organisation

ACTIVITY

Pick an organisation from the sector of leisure and tourism you'd like to work in and find out how sales and selling is used as part of their customer service. Use your findings to write a brief induction guide for staff involved in customer services that will help them understand:

- the functions of selling
- the objectives of selling
- appropriate sales techniques
- the duties, responsibilities and qualities of staff
- the value of the sales administration systems used.

66 *Our administrative system is a mixture of computer- and paper-based. All the information ends up on the computer but when we're taking bookings from customers face to face we write out booking forms. This allows the customer to check the details more easily. Also, it allows us to give the customer a more personal service. It's hard to build up rapport with a customer when there's a computer screen looming at you both. The computerised part of the system is a godsend though. We can keep masses of information on it and it's so easy to keep everything up to date. It also helps make the order processing procedure more efficient. The accounts staff can get all the information they need straight from the order records and use it to produce invoices and financial statements. Payment details also go straight onto the computer. We also use the computer to generate mailing lists. The customer details on the database mean we can select different sorts of customers for different sorts of mailings.* **99**

customer adviser in a travel agency

Key questions

1 What are the six functions of selling? What are the six objectives of selling? How can good customer service contribute?

2 What open and closed questions would you ask to establish a customer's needs?

3 How should you overcome objections? How should you handle customer complaints?

4 What are the purposes of sales reports and sales records? What is the main difference between the two?

5 How do organisations use customer accounts? How do they use membership lists? What is the value of sales administration systems to customers?

6 What makes selling a holiday different from selling a washing machine?

Assignment

Part of your evidence for this element is a summary of your findings based on an investigation of one leisure and tourism organisation of your choice. Working through the following steps will help you plan and organise this investigation.

1 Choose one of the organisations you investigated in element 6.1 for your investigation.

2 During your investigation you will need to find out about the functions and objectives of selling in the organisation. Who will be able to provide information about these?

3 What sales techniques are used by staff selling the organisation's goods and services? Think about how you will find these out. You may be able to discuss techniques with sales staff or even have the opportunity to watch sales staff in action. If so, draw up a checklist of techniques to look out for.

4 What are the duties and responsibilities of staff involved in selling? Again, think about how you would find this information.

5 What personal qualities are particularly important for staff working in this organisation? Are they typical of that area of leisure and tourism?

6 What administration systems does the organisation use in selling and sales? How do they benefit customers and the organisation?

When you have completed your investigation, you may find it interesting to compare your findings with students investigating other organisations in a similar area of leisure and tourism. Prepare a short report summarising common features of the selling process in the organisations covered. Highlight any differences between the different organisations.

> " We monitor complaints as a way of improving our customer service. When handling complaints we take notes of the details and liaise between the customer and the operator. We then pursue the matter until an outcome is reached that is satisfactory to the customer. In some circumstances we might refuse to deal with an operator again. "
>
> *travel consultant in a travel agency*

> " The skills you need in this job are face-to-face skills, and the ability to understand the needs of children and young people and to relate to them. What I most enjoy about my work is looking at lots of different activities and seeing which ones are the most successful. It's a challenge to meet all the needs of the children. But if we get it right, there's a tremendous feeling of satisfaction that we are providing a valuable service. "
>
> *community play officer in a local council*

> " For two weeks every year I ask guests if they are prepared to fill in a short questionnaire about various aspects of the service we offer. I choose different weeks each year so there's no bias because of the weather or the state of the garden. Most people are happy to fill it in and quite a few want to talk about what they like most and how they think we could improve the service. I listen carefully to them and add the information to a list that I make from reading the questionnaires. It takes time but I think it's worth it to find out what our guests think. "
>
> *owner of a guest-house*

Analysing customer service quality

Leisure and tourism organisations have to provide a high level of service to customers in order to survive and do well. How do they measure the quality of service? This element gives you the chance to find out about the different ways in which quality is measured, including how the service is delivered and the role of staff. You'll be seeing how leisure and tourism organisations find out what customers think and what use they make of the information. You'll also be looking at how organisations compare themselves with each other and set standards for the industry as a whole.

329

Assessing the quality of customer service

DISCUSSION POINT

As you saw in section 6.1.1, customer service can be broken down into a number of components:

■ caring for customers (internal and external)

■ meeting customer needs

■ achieving customer satisfaction

■ meeting customer expectations

■ maintaining security

■ maintaining safety.

Give one example of how the arts centre manager provides each of these components of customer service. Then for each example suggest one way he could assess the quality of the customer service provided (he might assess the quality of fire-safety procedures by asking for advice from the local fire prevention officer).

Customer service in leisure and tourism is about caring for all customers – that is, anyone who needs the services of a person working for a leisure and tourism organisation.

The manager of an arts centre explains what he means by customer service:

66 *We aim to show our customers that we care for them and are aware of their needs and wants. We conduct regular surveys asking them what they have liked, what they would like to see more of and what sort of activities they want us to hold here. We have a very good idea of what most people want and need, and we try to satisfy that with the events and activities we put on. Safety and security are important when events are attended by the public. We follow health and safety standards carefully, make sure qualified first aiders are always on hand, and offer facilities such as a staffed cloakroom to ensure customers' possessions are safe.*

Internally, we realise the importance of maintaining a good working atmosphere by providing a good service to each other. We hold regular staff meetings to check that all is running smoothly, and try to solve any problems or communication breakdowns as quickly as possible.

Overall, we make sure that the customer service we provide is consistently high – in the box office, the restaurant, the cloakroom – in everything we do. Basically, we are trying to meet customer expectations, if not exceed them. Quality service is our aim. 99

Warwick Arts Centre

Many organisations claim that they provide a quality customer service. But how can they be sure that what they are providing is of a high quality?

Some leisure and tourism organisations set standards of customer service quality (benchmarks) which they aim to achieve. They then give these standards to customers – often in a leaflet or on a noticeboard in the reception area – so that customers know what sort of service to expect.

The manager of the Jubilee Arts Centre decided that it would be a good idea to give customers a service guarantee leaflet, listing the quality of service customers can expect.

JUBILEE ARTS CENTRE SERVICE GUARANTEE

Customers are entitled to expect the following service standards from the Jubilee Arts Centre.
We will assess these standards regularly, to ensure they are being met and to see whether they need revising. If you have any comments
or complaints, please fill in a customer response form (available from the box office).

Reliability of service
All telephone calls to the box office will be answered within 45 seconds.
All customer letters will be answered within five working days.
Seats will never be overbooked – if customers buy tickets, they will get the seat they want.

Health and safety
The centre will be clean, safe and comfortable at all times.
Public toilet facilities will be inspected hourly.
Health and safety checks on all equipment will be made weekly.
Fire safety standards will be adhered to at all times.
Catering facilities will meet health and safety standards

Accessibility
Wheelchair access will be provided.
Six free wheelchair spaces will be available for registered disabled.
Car parking spaces will be available for 50 cars.

Availability
The box office will always be open at the hours stated.
500 seats will be available for every performance.
Customers will be able to choose where they would like to sit within each price bracket.
If their chosen position is not available, they will be offered an alternative.

Consistency
Staff will treat all customers with equal courtesy and care.
Customers can expect the same reliable service whenever they contact the Arts Centre.
All staff will be trained in every aspect of the Arts Centre's events, so they can all help equally well with customer enquiries and problems.

Price
Seats will always be available in at least three different price brackets.
Concessions will be offered to pensioners, students and the unemployed.
Seats for matinees will be offered to children at half price.

Staffing levels
At least ten members of staff will be on duty whenever the Arts Centre is open.
There will always be three people helping in the box office in the hour before a performance, to keep queuing to a minimum.

Qualities of staff
All staff will be polite, helpful, efficient and fair.
All staff will wear Arts Centre T-shirts or sweatshirts and name badges, so they are easy for customers to identify.
All staff will receive regular training, to ensure they have up-to-date knowledge on every aspect of the centre.

Timing of service
All telephone calls will be answered within 45 seconds.
All letters will be answered within five working days.
The box office ticket booking service will be open from 9.30 to 6.00 on weekdays, and 10.00 to 5.00 at weekends.

Value for money
The Arts Centre will endeavour to keep ticket prices as low as possible.
Some tickets for every performance will cost under £6.
Concessions will be offered, as listed.

Enjoyment of experience
The Jubilee Arts Centre aims to ensure all customers enjoy their visits to the centre. If you are disappointed,
please let us know so we can endeavour to improve our service in the future.
All customers should feel relaxed, safe and able to enjoy the event.

Provision for individual needs
Wheelchair access will be provided.
Disabled people and people with visual impairment who need to bring a companion to assist them
will be entitled to two seats for the price of one.
Audio links will be provided for people with hearing impairments.
Events programmes will be printed in English, French, German and Japanese.

Service levels
Customers can expect a high level of service at all times – whether they visit the centre at 11 am, or 11 pm.
Service levels will be high in every area of the centre; from box office to bar.

Establishing quality standards – often known as 'quality criteria' – is the first step in assessing the quality of customer service. Once standards are in place, it is important to be able to measure how well the organisation is achieving them.

■ Quality criteria for direct contact with customers need to be measured by asking customers whether standards are being met – customer feedback.

■ Quality criteria which are not directly related to customer contact need to be assessed in another way, such as staff appraisal or regular internal reviewer observation.

The arts centre manager realised he needed to find ways to assess how well the organisation was meeting the different quality standards it had set in its service guarantee document. After talking to other staff at the centre, he drew up the following list.

Area of customer service	Method of assessment
Reliability of service	Customer survey
Health and safety levels	Observation, staff checks
Accessibility	Observation
Consistency of service delivery and staff	Observation and customer survey
Price	Monitoring pricing system
Staffing levels	Internal review
Qualities of staff (appearance, knowledge, behaviour, judgement)	Staff appraisal, customer survey
Timing of service	Internal review
Value for money	Customer survey
Enjoyment of experience	Customer survey
Provision of individual needs	Customer survey
Service levels	Observation, customer survey

ACTIVITY

Look at the arts centre's service guarantee leaflet. List the individual quality criteria in each area of customer service and make notes on exactly how you think the manager could measure whether they are being achieved. For example, how could the manager use observation and staff checks to ensure that public toilets are kept clean and equipment is checked regularly?

Write a customer survey questionnaire which the centre could use to assess whether it is meeting the different service standards it has set.

More and more leisure and tourism organisations are now required to achieve levels of performance based on national, European and international standards. For example, a growing number of organisations are assessed to BS EN ISO 9000 – the quality systems standard. To reach the standard required, an organisation must set down how all its systems operate and prove that it is running according to these prescribed systems at all times.

ACTIVITY

Research the BS EN ISO 9000 quality systems standards and write a summary of what it covers. How do you think it would help leisure and tourism organisations assess the quality of customer service?

Appraising customer service quality criteria

It is very easy for leisure and tourism organisations to decide what customer service quality criteria to set without really considering the needs and concerns of those involved – the customers. Before setting customer service quality criteria, organisations should spend time:

- talking to customers to find out what aspects of service are most important to them
- analysing the customer service provided by other organisations.

When appraising their quality service criteria, leisure and tourism organisations need to consider:

- the perceived importance of different aspects of service to customers
- how the customers would rank different customer service quality criteria.

Perceived importance to the customer

All customers are different and their ideas on quality of service can vary considerably depending on:

- their attitude, which is often influenced by other people's opinions
- their personal needs
- their past experiences of a product or service.

What represents quality from a departmental manager's perspective may not correspond with the customer's view. Organisations need to carry out regular customer surveys to find out what is most important to customers and what they would like to see changed or improved.

The manager of a fast-food restaurant explains how a customer survey helped the organisation understand what customers saw as quality service:

66 *We're a 'fast-food restaurant', and as our name suggests our overall aim has always been to provide food fast. In the past we saw this as the most important part of our quality service – once a customer reached the serving counter, they should have their meal in front of them within one minute. But a recent customer survey showed us that although customers wanted quick service, ours was so quick that it had become completely impersonal. They would rather it took a little longer and they were treated with more care and respect. So we changed our approach to match. Waiting time is now two minutes, and the staff have time to talk to customers and make them feel welcome.* 99

Ranking based on customer perceptions

Once a leisure and tourism organisation has found out what aspects of service are most important to customers, it needs to rank them in order to decide which are top priority.

AN AIRLINE'S CUSTOMER SERVICE

An airline carried out a survey among its travellers over a few weeks one summer. The survey revealed the following areas, ranked in order of importance, where service could be improved:

- aircraft
- more regular services
- punctuality
- seating
- in-flight service
- special offers for large families
- duty-free goods
- check-in.

The airline management considered the different areas from the point of view of cost and practicality, and produced a ranking of improvements and changes which could be made in the short, medium and long term.

Short-term improvements

- special offers for large families
- duty-free goods
- in-flight service

Medium-term improvements

- seating
- punctuality

Long-term improvements

- check-in
- more regular services
- aircraft

Once the short-term improvements had been made, the levels of customer loyalty increased and the airline made more profit. It then used this to improve seating in the aircraft. The remaining problems required long-term planning and investment, but the levels of customer service had improved significantly.

ACTIVITY

Choose a local leisure and tourism facility that you use regularly; for example, your local cinema, leisure centre or swimming pool. What do you think its customer service quality criteria should be?

Look again at the Jubilee Arts Centre's service guarantee leaflet, and produce a chart with the same headings for different areas of customer service. Under each heading, list two or three customer service quality criteria which would be important to you as a customer. From these criteria, choose the five which you feel are most important and rank them in order of importance.

Visit the facility, and using your criteria as a checklist appraise how well the organisation is meeting the customer service standards you have set.

Section 6.3.3

Analysing the quality of customer service

Analysing the quality of customer service can be difficult for organisations. Staff who realise they are being observed and assessed are unlikely to behave normally and provide the usual level of customer service.

As a result, many organisations monitor their customer service quality by carrying out:

■ spot checks – staff don't know in advance that service is to be assessed, and don't have time to make any special preparations. For example, a hotel receptionist who doesn't know about a spot check won't have time to spend longer than usual tidying up

■ checks by mystery customers – the organisation hires someone to visit the facility as a mystery customer and report back to the management on their findings.

INCOGNITO INSPECTIONS

Inspections are also carried out by outside organisations to produce guidebooks and handbooks. For example, the Automobile Association (AA) uses inspectors to visit hotels all round the country and sample the services on offer. The service which they receive is then graded, and this grading is published in the annual members' handbook.

The Travel Trade Gazette has a weekly feature called 'Top Shop'. Each week four travel agencies from a town are visited and given the same enquiry to deal with. The quality of customer service is graded in four categories: service, shop appearance, use of material and customer reaction. Agencies which receive 80% or more are then awarded a certificate of excellence.

The manager of the Jubilee Arts Centre was finding it difficult to make a fair assessment of whether the centre was meeting its customer service quality criteria. Although a system was in place for internal reviews and checks, he felt some staff were getting complacent and only meeting quality criteria when they knew they were being observed.

To counteract this, he decided to hire customer care consultant Jessica Palmer. She agreed to be a mystery customer so she could visit the centre and observe customer service. He asked Jessica to focus on the quality criteria for:

■ health and safety levels

■ consistency of service delivery and staff

■ qualities of staff.

He also asked her to comment in general on the quality of customer service at the arts centre, in particular how well she felt it:

■ cared for customers

■ met customer needs

■ achieved customer satisfaction

■ met customer expectations

■ maintained security and safety.

After visiting the centre twice to observe customer service and talk to fellow customers, Jessica submitted the following report to the manager.

ASSESSING CUSTOMER SERVICE AT THE JUBILEE ARTS CENTRE

I was asked to assess the quality of the customer service at the Jubilee Arts Centre using the following criteria:

HEALTH AND SAFETY
The centre will be clean, safe and comfortable at all times.
Public toilet facilities will be inspected hourly.
Fire safety standards will be adhered to at all times.
Catering facilities will meet health and safety standards.

CONSISTENCY
Staff will treat all customers with equal courtesy and care.
Customers can expect the same reliable service whenever they contact the Arts Centre.
All staff will be trained in every aspect of the Arts Centre's events, so they can all help equally well with customer enquiries and problems.

QUALITIES OF STAFF
All staff will be polite, helpful, efficient and fair.
All staff will wear Arts Centre T-shirts or sweatshirts and name badges, so they are easy for customers to identify.
All staff will receive regularly training, to ensure they have up-to-date knowledge on every aspect of the centre.

The quality criteria in relation to the actual level of service
The following chart summarises the quality criteria I was checking, and the actual level of service I observed.

QUALITY CRITERIA	ACTUAL LEVEL OF SERVICE
Cleanliness, safety and comfort	On my first visit all areas of the centre were clean and comfortable. On the second occasion the centre seemed short-staffed, and cleanliness had suffered. Rubbish was under seats in the auditorium and the reception area was untidy.
Public toilet facilities inspected	Again, the first time this had been done (a chart on the wall monitoring hourly checks was up to date and facilities were spotless). But on my second visit the toilets hadn't been checked for three hours and were dirty.
Fire safety standards adhered to	As far as I could see, all was well. Fire exits were well signposted and kept clear, extinguishers in place.

Catering meeting health and safety standards	As far as I could see catering met health and safety standards. Food preparation and serving areas looked clean and hygienic, staff were smart and wearing clean overalls with hair off their faces.
Treating customers with equal courtesy and care	I was extremely impressed by the attitude of staff. They seemed relaxed, happy and had time for every customer. I played the difficult customer on a couple of occasions, and was treated with care and respect each time. I observed staff dealing with children, elderly people, disabled and large groups of visitors, and felt that they treated everyone with the same courtesy.
Reliability of service	I felt this suffered at times because of low staffing levels. The second time I visited the centre I had to queue for ten minutes to pick up my tickets. I tried ringing the centre a few times, and the response time for answering the telephone was unreliable — ranging from two seconds to two minutes.
Knowledge of staff	This seemed good. I asked several awkward questions about facilities, forthcoming productions and current events, and the staff were able to answer knowledgeably in each case. On the one occasion when the member of staff didn't know the answer, she called her manager over.
Politeness and efficiency of staff	On the whole excellent — although a little more fraught on my second visit due to pressures of low staffing, I presume.
Appearance of staff	This left a little to be desired. Not all the staff were wearing their Arts Centre tops, and were hard to identify. I only saw one member of staff wearing a name badge. This is an area where I think there is room for improvement.

Overall, I feel the Jubilee Arts Centre is providing a good quality customer service. It seems to care about its customers, and staff go out of their way to make people feel welcome and at ease. There seemed a good rapport between staff, so presumably internal customer care is working well.

The quality criteria in relation to customers' expectations
Talking to customers and observing audience reaction, the centre appears to be meeting customer needs and expectations. The programme of events is varied and the people I spoke to were all satisfied by the service and return to the centre regularly. Security and safety procedures seem adequate, but the centre needs to take care that they are not compromised by pressures of staffing.

ACTIVITY

Now its your turn to pose as a mystery customer. Make a list of leisure and tourism organisations in your area which you could visit without being recognised. You will need to be able to test their services against prescribed quality standards, so contact the organisations to find out whether they publish a leaflet or charter.

How will you work out whether these standards are being met? Think of ways that you can test the organisation's quality criteria promises. Consider the areas that are not easily measurable, as well as those that are.

Visit the organisation on two or three occasions and make observations and checks. Then following the format of Jessica's report on the Jubilee Arts Centre, write a report analysing the quality of customer service provided by the organisation.

Analysing customer service in related markets

As well as analysing their own customer service, many leisure and tourism organisations find it helpful to analyse other organisations' customer service in order to review and improve their own. This may include considering:

■ direct competitors
■ other organisations in the same business
■ related service organisations
■ unrelated service organisations.

Direct competitors

All organisations need to know what their competitors are doing.

The managing director of a company which organises walking tours in the Lake District carried out an appraisal of the customer service offered by other companies offering similar holidays:

❝ *I wanted to see what sort of customer care was being offered on walking holidays elsewhere in the country and other kinds of holidays in the Lake District, such as riding and cycling tours. I looked at things like standards of accommodation and meals, picking-up arrangements, insurance, refunds – the sorts of things that can make one operator just that bit better and more attractive than another. I learnt quite a lot. I know now where I can get excellent lunchtime meals and snacks which are real value for money, and I learnt from a company in Wales how I can manage cancellations and refunds. The service we offer now has definitely improved and regular walkers with us have commented on it.* ❞

Other organisations in the same business

It can also be useful to analyse the services offered by organisations who are in the same business but not in direct competition. There may be things to learn. For example, a heritage site could look at the facilities like shops, cafés and car-parks in heritage sites around the country to check that the facilities it offers are up to the same standards.

Related service organisations

Related service organisations can learn from one another. The manager of a sports centre explains how they looked at the reservations and customer information services offered by a large hotel to help them improve their own services in those areas:

❝ *We were planning on expanding our premises and offering more facilities. This would mean more customers and we needed to expand our customer services to match. We needed to upgrade our computerised reservations system and we wanted to produce a better range of leaflets and brochures about our new facilities. I contact the manager of a nearby hotel and asked for her advice. She was only too happy to help and invited us to spend a morning at the hotel talking to the right people. We were shown their reservations system and we also talked to the publicity manager about cost-effective ways of producing and distributing leaflets and brochures. During the visit, I noticed the closed-circuit TV system they used to keep an eye on the public areas of the hotel and the lifts, stairs and corridors. It struck me that a similar system could be useful at our centre and I'm going back to the hotel next week to talk to their security officer.* **99**

Unrelated service organisations

Leisure and tourism organisations can also draw on good customer service practice from unrelated business organisations.

DISCUSSION POINT

Can you think of any examples of good customer service which could be borrowed and introduced by leisure and tourism organisations?

For example, banks and building societies introduced 'hole-in-the-wall' cash and information machines to cut down queues and provide a more efficient customer service. Leisure and tourism organisations could also use this technology to improve their customer service:

■ travel companies could provide foreign currency service by machine

■ leisure centres could provide tickets or booking services by machine.

ACTIVITY

Look back at the analysis of the quality of customer service in one leisure and tourism organisation which you carried out at the end of the last section. Make a list of organisations which you could use to draw a comparison of customer service practice. These might be:

■ direct competitors

■ other organisations in the same business

■ related service organisations.

Again, find out if they have published customer service quality criteria. Assess their services against the standards. Are the quality criteria being met?

339

Comparing analyses

DISCUSSION POINT

Here are the criteria used by Jessica Palmer in section 6.3.3 to assess the customer service offered by the Jubilee Arts Centre:

Health and safety

- The centre will be clean, safe and comfortable at all times.
- Public toilet facilities will be inspected hourly.
- Fire safety standards will be adhered to at all times.
- Catering facilities will meet health and safety standards.

Consistency

- Staff will treat all customers with equal courtesy and care.
- Customers can expect the same reliable service whenever they contact the Arts Centre.
- All staff will be trained in every aspect of the Arts Centre's events, so they can all help equally well with customer enquiries and problems.

Qualities of staff

- All staff will be polite, helpful, efficient and fair.
- All staff will wear Arts Centre T-shirts or sweatshirts and name badges, so they are easy for customers to identify.
- All staff will receive regular training, to ensure they have up-to-date knowledge on every aspect of the centre.

What types of organisation would you suggest she use to provide the centre's manager with the sort of comparisons he'd find useful?

In comparing the customer services of different organisations, you need to ensure that your comparisons and contrasts are fair. It helps to have one set of criteria that can be used as a measure for all the organisations you are looking at. Sometimes, you may want to draw parallels with unrelated organisations because you think there are ideas and practices which could be useful for the leisure and tourism organisations you are investigating. In these cases, you need to be sure that it is realistic and practicable for the examples you give to be adapted from one industry sector to another.

In section 6.3.1, there is copy of a leaflet called 'Service Guarantee' issued to customers of an arts centre. The leaflet sets out the standards of services customers can expect. In section 6.3.3 there is a case study describing how the manager of the arts centre hired customer care consultant Jessica Palmer to act as a mystery customer to check if the centre was meeting its standards for customer service. The report Jessica produced highlighted the strengths and weaknesses of the centre's customer service as measured by its own quality criteria. The manager thought it would be useful to find out how the centre's standards of customer service compared with that of other organisations. But he wanted to make sure that the findings of the comparison would be relevant to the business he was in:

66 As a result of the mystery customer exercise, I now have a good idea of how well the centre is doing from three angles: measured against our own criteria, measured against our customers' perceptions and Jessica's direct experience. I could see that there was room for improvement in places but before deciding what to do, I thought some broader comparisons would be useful. I was very interested in how we compared with our direct competitors and also with organisations in similar lines of business but not actually in competition with us. I was also interested in any tips or models of good practice from organisations outside the leisure and tourism industry – so long as they were applicable to our circumstances. The reason I decided to produce the service guarantee leaflet for our customers in the first place was because I'd read the Customer Charter leaflet produced by the Post Office to explain their customer care standards and thought a similar thing would be useful to my customers. 99

ACTIVITY

Use the results of the analyses you did in sections 6.3.3 and 6.3.4 to make comparisons between the organisations you investigated. Make sure that:

- you use the same criteria for all related organisations so that your comparisons are fair
- any examples from organisations outside the leisure and tourism industry can be realistically adapted.

Write a report summarising your comparisons.

Recommendations for improving customer service

Organisations committed to good customer service are always on the lookout for ways to improve their standards. They will actively encourage comments and suggestions from customers and staff and have all sorts of ways for gathering feedback. Staff members may be given a 'watching brief' to look out for new ideas they come across in other organisations, the media, publications, conferences and so on. They may buy in outside help such as consultants. Training programmes to help staff develop and update their customer care skills will also be a high priority.

UNIT

6

ELEMENT **6.3**

Any recommendations for improvements would need to be carefully considered. The organisation would want evidence that the improvements suggested would be:
- practical
- realistic
- cost-effective.

The organisation would expect the recommendations to
- be professionally presented
- be based on a thorough analysis of its existing service
- describe benefits the improvements would achieve.

Sections 6.3.1 to 6.3.5 included quotes and examples from an assessment of the customer service offered by the Jubilee Arts Centre carried out by customer care consultant Jessica Palmer. Following the assessment, Jessica presented a report to the centre's manager and staff outlining recommendations for improving customer service. Here's the manager's response to some of the recommendations she made:

66 *Overall, Jessica felt the centre offered a very high standard of customer service. This pleased me as my staff and I believe in good customer care and we work hard to please our customers. By mentioning what we were doing well at the start of her report, Jessica got us in the right frame of mind for responding positively to her suggestions for improvements. Some of the things she mentioned we agreed with and resolved to take action on immediately – for example, always wearing the Art Centre tops and our name badges. Jessica had a slight concern that we were understaffed from time to time. She suggested increasing staff numbers and reviewing the rota system. I think we do need more staff but our funds are being squeezed at the moment. I decided I needed to think further about this recommendation but we could definitely review the rota.*

In her comparisons with other organisations, again Jessica felt we did well. She'd looked at the customer services offered by another arts centre, a sports centre, a museum and a restaurant. She felt we matched and in many cases bettered various aspects of comparable service. One area she criticised was our facilities for children. She felt we could attract more customers by providing a few more family-friendly services. For example, the sports centre she'd visited offered a crèche and the arts centre's restaurant offered a children's menu. We

Making recommendations

Recommendations must be:
- explained
- practicable
- realistic
- justified.

could certainly do a children's menu but I felt a crèche would be beyond our financial means at the moment. But when Jessica was talking about the museum, she mentioned that they had special exhibitions for children. This gave me an idea. When we run exhibitions which mainly appeal to adults, we could put on some children's events at the same time in different areas of the centre. That way, parents could relax and enjoy the exhibitions designed for them while their children enjoyed events designed for them. We could afford one-off supervised events for children even though we couldn't afford permanent facilities like a crèche. 99

ACTIVITY

Add a section to the report you did in section 6.3.5 which makes recommendations for improvements the organisation could make to its customer service. Think carefully about the recommendations you want to suggest. Make sure they are realistic, practicable and suitable for the organisation you have been investigating. To give your report a professional look, produce it on a DTP system and present it in some kind of binder or cover.

Key questions

1 What is customer service? List five main areas it should cover.
2 Which areas of customer service could be assessed?
3 What are customer service quality criteria?
4 Why is it important for organisations to take into account customers' views when setting service quality criteria?
5 Why would an organisation find it useful to compare its customer service with that of:
   - direct competitors
   - related service organisations
   - unrelated service organisation?
6 What should you bear in mind when making recommendations for improvements?

Assignment

Part 1
Devise a leaflet for leisure and tourism staff which explains how the quality of customer service is assessed in leisure and tourism organisations.

Part 2
Prepare and give a presentation on the customer service provided by a leisure and tourism organisation of your choice. Your presentation should include:
- an analysis of the quality of the service
- an explanation of the criteria you used to assess the quality
- comparisons between your chosen organisation and at least two other organisations in related markets
- recommendations for improvements your organisation could make to its customer service.

ELEMENT **6.4**

Delivering and evaluating customer service

This element gives you the chance to demonstrate your own skills in customer service and evaluate how well you did. You'll be making use of the knowledge from previous elements in this unit and your own experience as a customer. The things to watch out for in your own performance include the way you relate to customers, how you communicate with them, your dress and appearance and your knowledge of the products and services you are selling or providing.

66 I try and look at the service we offer through the eyes of our customers. It means I'm always looking for ways of improving what we do – researching new routes or different accommodation where riders can stay. People need to be made to feel looked after and at their ease. Organising accommodation depends on what people want to spend: some people are quite happy camping and others want to stay in smart hotels. It depends who they are. 99

owner of a riding school which also provides holidays

66 Every year we have to produce a report at the end of the year to go to the committee. This evaluates our work on the basis of feedback from parents from the summer programme, amongst other things. We also use responses from a questionnaire sent out to the voluntary sector to find our what their needs are and to see whether these are being met. 99

community play officer in a local council

66 We don't generally have to deal with complaints – this would be more the job of the front-of-house manager. But we listen to what people have to say, try to get it sorted out, and apologise if there is a problem. Our general attitude is that we want people to go away happy and there is a lot we can learn from customers who aren't happy for any reason. 99

press and publicity officer at an entertainments venue

The objectives of evaluating customer service and quality criteria

Customers need service in a range of different situations. They might:

- be satisfied – happy with the products and service they are receiving
- be dissatisfied – unhappy with the products and service they are receiving, and perhaps making a complaint
- need information
- need help with problems
- need sales help
- need advice.

In each case, it is important that staff provide a prompt, efficient and polite service which meets the customer's needs as closely as possible. A hotel receptionist describes the different situations in which she provides customer service:

66 *In my job, I handle all sorts of customers every day. The important thing is to provide good customer service to everyone – whether they're laughing and happy or throwing a temper tantrum. More often than not, customers are satisfied with our facilities and service, and I find it easy to provide good service to satisfied customers. But sometimes they are unhappy about something and want to complain. In this case my aim is to remain polite and calm, and solve their problem as efficiently as possible – to turn a dissatisfied customer into a satisfied customer.*

Often providing customer service is about meeting people's needs for information on the area or advice on how to travel into town. Sometimes they come to me with specific problems, such as a broken heater in their room, and I contact the maintenance department to make sure it's fixed as soon as possible. I also provide sales service, booking rooms and answering customers' enquiries about prices and availability. 99

Whatever the customer service situation, leisure and tourism organisations need to keep evaluating the service they are providing. This helps them to:

- assess how good the service is
- identify ways of improving the service
- identify new needs that can be added to the service.

An evaluation must include:

- objectives – to establish what is being evaluated and why
- quality criteria – the means to measure how effective the service is.

Objectives of evaluation

Some common evaluation objectives for leisure and tourism organisations are:

- to find out how satisfied customers are with the service
- to find out if the service is encouraging repeat business
- to check that they are keeping up with or bettering the services offered by their competitors
- to identify ways of attracting new customers.

345

The manager of a travel agency explains why she thinks it is important to evaluate customer service:

> 66 *In my experience, customers who receive good customer service and feel cared for are satisfied customers. So evaluating customer service can be an effective way to measure levels of customer satisfaction. Satisfied customers are good for the business – they return and bring new customers, meaning more income for our agency. We are one of several travel agencies in the same shopping centre and get a lot of people in here who have also been to the other agencies or may go there afterwards. Therefore we have to try to satisfy customers by providing better service than our competitors.* 99

Quality criteria

To evaluate a customer service, you need a means of measuring its quality. These are known as quality criteria. The table below lists some common quality criteria used in the leisure and tourism industry and gives examples of questions organisations could ask themselves and their customers to find out how good their services are.

Criteria	Questions
level of service	Is the service adequate? Is it covering all the customers' needs?
reliability of service	Is the service reliable? Are there any weak points? Do customers feel they will get a high standard of service every time?
timing of service	Are customers' needs being met at the right time? Is the service available to the customers when they want it?
accessibility	Are we making our customers feel welcome and at ease? Do they know what sort of services we offer? Are the right staff always on hand for the customers?
availability	Is the service always available? Are all the customers' needs being met?
consistency	Is the service of a consistently high standard? What expectations are we creating in our customers?
price	Is the price right for the customers? Is the price a competitive one?
staffing levels	Are there enough people to carry out and support the service? Are they properly trained?
qualities of staff	Are the staff presenting the right company image? Do they behave in an appropriate way at all times? Do they have all the knowledge and information they need? Are they confident in their own abilities to provide a good service? Do they know what's expected of them and how well they're meeting those expectations?
enjoyment of experience	Is the service enjoyed by the customers? Do staff enjoy providing the service?
provision for individual needs	Is the service flexible enough to meet the needs of individual customers? Are staff able to identify and respond to differing needs?
value for money	Are customers getting what they expect for the money they spend? Is the organisation getting a good return on its investment in customer care?
health and safety standards	Are health and safety standards being fully and consistently followed?

ACTIVITY

You have been appointed customer service manager at a leisure centre and have decided to carry out an evaluation of the customer service provided. However, there is resistance to the evaluation among staff, who feel they are going to be judged and are anxious.

Prepare a short talk explaining to the staff:

- what an evaluation of customer service is

- the areas of customer service to be evaluated

- why it is important to evaluate customer service.

DISCUSSION POINT

Get together with two or three people. Look at the customer situations listed below and decide the objectives and quality criteria you would use to evaluate the service given in each situation:

1 A group of friends are celebrating the end of their exams. They are having a meal at their favourite restaurant. They're enjoying their food and having a good time.

2 Two customers have come to play squash at a sports centre. Their court has been double-booked. The same thing has happened to them twice in three months. They are complaining angrily to the receptionist.

3 A tourist visits a tourist information centre to find out what attractions there are in the area.

4 A woman sitting in a hotel bar is being pestered by a couple of men who have had too much to drink. The woman complains to the bar steward.

5 A customer in a sports shop is interested in buying an exercise bike. The shop stocks twelve different models.

6 An instructor at a fitness centre is advising a customer about a fitness programme.

Delivering customer service

Whatever the situation, leisure and tourism employees delivering customer service should:

- consider the needs and characteristics of customers
- prioritise customer needs
- use appropriate communication methods
- record necessary customer information.

Considering customer needs

The first step in delivering customer service is to consider the customer. The extract on the left is taken from a hotel's customer service booklet issued to all staff.

THE FIRST RULE OF CUSTOMER SERVICE

The customer comes first! Look at who your customer is, and evaluate their particular needs and concerns so you can provide an appropriate service.

DISCUSSION POINT

What sort of needs might these customers have? What order of priority would you give them?

1 A first-time customer in a fitness class.

2 A customer ringing to find out about golfing holidays in Northern Ireland.

3 A family arriving at a bed-and-breakfast hotel for a week's holiday.

4 A business executive wanting to travel by air to New York and then on to Seattle two days later.

5 A party of people with hearing difficulties on a guided tour of a museum.

6 A couple with a small baby who want a hotel room for that night.

7 A customer who's just had their wallet stolen.

Is it an internal customer?
- Make sure service is appropriate for the level of customer. (Is the customer your manager? Or a colleague?)
- Should you take a formal approach to customer service (e.g write a memo)?

What is the customer's cultural background?
- Is your customer's first language English? If not, seek help with translation/ use leaflets in different languages.
- Does your customer have different dietary needs?

Are you dealing with a group?
- How many people are you catering for?
- Are there any individual specific needs within the group?
- Do we offer any concessions which apply to the group?

Who is your customer?

Is your customer an individual?
- Are there any special facilities we can provide for individual customers?

How old is the customer?
- Does your customer have special needs because of age? (e.g children's menus and play facilities)?
- Do we offer any concessions likely to be of interest to the customer (e.g mid-week breaks for pensioners)?

Does the customer have specific needs?
- Does your customer have difficulty seeing (visual impairment)?
- Does you customer have difficulties moving about (restricted mobility)?
- Does your customer have hearing difficulties?
- If the answer is yes to any of these questions, provide appropriate service.
- Is your customer vegetarian?

Prioritising customer needs

Delivering good customer service to customers with more than one need involves:

- identifying the different needs
- prioritising them
- dealing with them in order of priority.

Using appropriate communication methods

Good communication is at the heart of good customer service. It's through communication that:

- staff find out what customers' needs are
- customers find out about the products, services and facilities an organisation offers
- staff can check on how satisfied customers are with the service provided.

Good communication is appropriate communication – where information is given:

- to the right people
- in the right way
- at the right time.

A waitress at a café in a museum describes how she uses communication as part of customer service:

❝ *We get all sorts of people in the café. As I'm dealing with customers face-to-face, most of the communication is through speaking. I always greet customers with a smile. That's very important. I quite often deal with customers from abroad who speak only a little English. I make sure that I speak more slowly and clearly and I check that they've understood me and that I've understood them. It takes a little longer to get their order but not as long as it would take if I didn't bother properly, brought them the wrong things and had to start all over again.*

The way I look and behave is also an important part of the communication process. I'm serving food so I have to be clean and tidy. I'm dealing with people and I have to be polite, cheerful and welcoming at all times.

I'm also a useful means of gathering feedback from customers. My supervisor encourages all the staff to ask customers how they've enjoyed their food and drink. I also watch the customers as I can see by their faces and gestures if they're happy or not. **❞**

As the quote from the waitress shows, face-to-face communication involves verbal elements – speech – and non-verbal elements – gestures, facial expressions, personal appearance and so on. In good communication, both elements should give out the same message. For example:

- a smile shows that a greeting is sincere
- a clean and tidy appearance reflects a professional attitude.

The quote also shows that communication styles have to be adapted to suit the customer situation and the customer type.

Some forms of customer service involve other forms of communication. For example:

- letters
- memos
- brochures
- notices
- signs
- telephone calls.

DISCUSSION POINT

Think of times when you've been a leisure or tourism customer. How did the organisations communicate with you? How appropriate to the situation were the methods they used?

Some forms of customer service involve a combination of forms of communication. For example:

■ a demonstration of emergency procedures for plane passengers involves spoken instructions and mimed actions – verbal and non-verbal communication

■ taking a booking for a theatre production involves spoken communication, either face to face or on the phone, and written information in the form of tickets

■ showing a customer how to use a piece of exercise equipment involves spoken communication, gestures and facial expressions and practical demonstrations.

Recording necessary customer information

Many customer services are supported by some kind of record-keeping procedure. Here are some examples:

■ customer accounts to create a record of a customer's orders and payments

■ booking forms to note all details relevant to a booking

■ membership lists giving details of members

■ order forms to record details of customer orders

■ tickets showing details of entrance fees, fares and seat reservations

■ registering systems to record who is using the facilities.

ACTIVITY

Pick two different types of customer service you know about or can find out about. Analyse what is involved in each then write up your findings using these headings for guidance:

■ The needs the customer service meets

■ How customer needs are prioritised

■ The communication methods used in the service

■ How customer information is recorded.

Get together with some friends and prepare to roleplay delivering customer service in situations you've found out about through your analysis. Before you deliver the service, discuss and agree ways in which you'll evaluate your own and each other's performance. Sections 6.4.1 and 6.4.3 give information on evaluation objectives and quality criteria. You could use it to help you devise objectives and criteria for this activity. Arrange to have your roleplays video-taped and ask your tutor to watch you perform.

Evaluating delivery of customer service

Evaluating how well service is being delivered is an important and regular part of good customer care. It means that organisations can make sure that the services they provide are meeting customer expectations and keeping pace with any changing customer needs.

It also helps staff members to improve their skills and knowledge and develop new competences.

An evaluation must include:

■ objectives – to establish what is being evaluated and why
■ quality criteria – the means to measure how effective the service delivery is.

A trainer in customer care explains what she looks for when evaluating trainees' abilities in delivering customer service:

66 *Because dealing with customers involves contact – direct and indirect – good communication skills are a high priority. Customer situations can be face-to-face conversations, telephone calls, letters, with individuals, with groups and so on – all rely on the person's ability not only to communicate well but to choose the right type of communication according to the situation. Appearance is another high priority – seeing someone who is neat, tidy and appropriately dressed gives a customer confidence in the person and the organisation. It reflects a high professional standard which is vital to any organisation's image. The ability to identify and prioritise customer needs is another key aspect of good delivery. This also involves the ability to adapt your approach according to the customer. People in the leisure and tourism industry have to deal with more types of customer than in any other industry. Customers from different age groups, different cultural backgrounds, with special needs and so on are all an everyday occurrence – and of course most people will also have their internal customers. A good knowledge of the organisation's products and services is crucial and so is the confident and correct use of any related administrative procedures such as taking bookings, processing orders, keeping records and so on.* 99

Common objectives of customer service

■ to satisfy customers' needs and wants
■ to gain repeat business
■ to gain competitive advantage
■ to attract new customers.

Common quality criteria for customer service

■ reliability
■ consistency
■ health and safety standards
■ appearance of staff
■ behaviour of staff
■ knowledge of staff
■ judgement of staff
■ timing of service
■ value for money
■ enjoyment of experience
■ providing for individual needs.

ACTIVITY

Get together in the same group you worked with in the activity on page 350. Give each other feedback on how well you delivered your selected customer services. The box on the right gives some tips on how to give constructive criticism. Read through them before you start your feedback session. If you recorded your roleplays on video, play back the video to help you check your evaluation and to give examples to support the points you make. Ask your tutor for feedback too.

Constructive criticism

■ Start with comments on the things that went well.
■ Make your comments specific.
■ Give examples to support your comments.
■ Don't get personal.
■ Offer suggestions on how performance could be improved.
■ Ask the person if they agree with your comments.

Comparing evaluations and recommending improvements

DISCUSSION POINT

How do you think it would help your evaluation of your performance at work if you were also evaluated by your:

colleagues

supervisors

managers?

What perspectives would you gain?

Being evaluated can be a daunting experience. But if you think of it as a means of helping you to improve, you can see how useful it can be. Being evaluated by a number of people can be especially valuable because it gives you different perspectives. In section 6.3.5, the customer service given by an arts centre is evaluated from three different perspectives, using:

■ their own criteria

■ their customers' perceptions

■ the direct experience of a consultant acting as a mystery customer.

The manager of the centre felt that it was a good thing to have feedback from more than one source because it allowed different views to be compared.

Here's part of a report Mark, a Leisure and Tourism GNVQ student, produced on his own evaluation of his performance:

As part of my work for Unit 6.4, I spent an hour in the simulated travel agent's office we have at college, roleplaying a customer adviser. In preparation for the exercise, I had been fully briefed by my tutor about the products and services the travel agent offered, the office procedures and paperwork, the computer and the telephone system. We use the office quite a lot in our course and we had practised a number of different roleplays. I also prepared by making sure I was familiar with the products and services and how to get information from brochures and so on.

In the course of an hour I dealt with the following customers:

* a man coming into the office to ask about walking holidays in Scotland

* a woman with two small children interested in Disney holidays in Paris and Orlando

* a telephone call asking for brochures on the South of France

* a girl with a hearing impairment who wanted to book a weekend break to Eire.

I was nervous to begin with because I knew I was being assessed and my performance was being recorded on video. As a result, I sounded a bit rushed when I dealt with my first customer.

I thought the woman with the children might be difficult as the children were quite lively. To keep them occupied while I went through various holiday options with the mother, I gave them some Disney brochures, paper and pens and they settled down to draw pictures. This meant that the mother and I could talk without distractions. The mother thanked me for my 'children-friendly' attitude before she left.

While dealing with the customer on the phone, I had to leave the desk and collect up some brochures I wanted to discuss with the customer. I put the customer on hold and when I got back to the desk I had a little difficulty retrieving the call. The customer sounded a bit irritable when I got back to her and I apologised for keeping her waiting. She took my apology very well and I was pleased that I had pacified her.

I had no trouble dealing with the customer with a hearing impairment. In my spare time I help out at a local residence for the elderly and I am used to speaking to people who are hard of hearing. It is important to let your face be seen, not to cover your mouth when speaking, to speak slowly and clearly, and to check with the person that you are not speaking too fast or too quietly. I used this knowledge to help me communicate appropriately with the customer.

Here's what Mark's tutor had to say:

I thought Mark did very well. He had clearly prepared very thoroughly as he had no trouble explaining products and services, finding brochures and other details or in retrieving and recording information using the paper-based and computer-based administration systems.

He had four very different customers and he was quick to pick up on their individual needs. He did get a bit flustered with the first customer, but I think that was nerves getting the better of him. I was very impressed with the way he got over his difficulty in retrieving the customer call he had to put on hold. This would have thrown many people, but Mark didn't panic and his apology to the customer was very good. It's the sort of incident that can happen in real working life and Mark responded in a realistic and professional way.

I was also very impressed in the way he used his initiative with the customer with children. Giving the children something to occupy them while he and the mother discussed holiday details was a real brainwave.

His skill at dealing with the customer with the hearing impairment was first-rate. I understand that Mark knows of the considerations to make from his voluntary work with the elderly. It was good to see him bring in knowledge he has acquired from his experience outside the course and from contexts outside the leisure and tourism industry.

One area I noted for improvement was Mark's body language. He tended to wag his hands about a lot while talking and he avoided making eye-contact. I think again this was nerves.

Mark and his tutor compared and discussed their evaluations. Mark explains how he felt:

66 *I felt that my tutor's assessment was a fair one. I was nervous and it showed. I was pleased that she felt I'd done well and the examples she gave were things I felt I had done well too. She commented on my body language and we looked at the video recording so I could see what she meant. I know I wave my hands about when I'm nervous but seeing it on video made me resolve to get rid of the habit. I wasn't sure what she meant about eye-contact. But she showed me on the video and I could see that I was doing things like looking down at the desk or looking away when I talked to customers when I should have been looking at them. My tutor particularly praised the way I'd dealt with the customer with the hearing impairment and we discussed ways of helping me to be as confident in my abilities in other situations as I was in that one.* 99

Mark and his tutor agreed that it would help him to find out more about body language and then do a series of roleplays recorded on video to help him practice his skills and build up his confidence. Mark was happy with this:

66 *The experience of being evaluated has been a good one. I now know what I'm good at and what I need to improve on. I also know how I can make the improvements. I want to bring my skills up to a higher standard before I do a work placement planned for later this term. I'll be assessed during the placement by more people and I want to feel confident and fully prepared. The evaluation process I've just been through has given me the opportunity to do that and I've drawn up an action plan to show how I'm going to do it.* 99

The case study about Mark shows that he benefited from evaluation because it:

- showed him his strengths and weaknesses
- gave him an opportunity to develop his skills.

How would an organisation benefit from evaluation and recommendations for improvement? What does an organisation gain by developing the skills, knowledge and competence of its staff?

Mark Fuller

ACTION PLAN FOR BODY LANGUAGE SKILLS DEVELOPMENT

Action	Date to be achieved	Date achieved
Visit library and carry out research into body language (NB Training video 'Look who's talking' recommended by tutor)	3/5/96	
Discuss and agree possible roleplay situations with tutor	8/5/96	
Plan and prepare for roleplays	17/5/96	
roleplays and review session with tutor	20/5/96	

22nd April 1996

Compare the evaluations and recommendations for improvements you received on your customer service in the activity on page 350 with your own evaluation and recommendations. Write a brief summary of what you have learned from the evaluation process and how you are going to follow the recommendations. Draw up an action plan to show how you are going to make the improvements. Be specific about the improvements you are going to make and give details and dates of any training and development you are going to undertake.

If you delivered customer service as part of a work placement, make a note of any recommendations you have for the organisation which would improve the way it delivers customer service.

Section 6.4.6

Presenting evaluation findings and recommendations

A presentation is a way of communicating information to groups of people face-to-face. Presentations are often used in the workplace. Here are some examples:

■ sales presentations to explain and promote products and services to potential customers

■ presentations to explain new ideas the organisation could adopt

■ a consultant's report on findings of studies into practices and procedures

■ presentations on the results of market research

■ presenting a business plan to potential financiers such as bank managers or investors

■ presenting information about an organisation's activities and performance to a meeting of shareholders.

Many people working in the leisure and tourism use presentation skills in their everyday work:

■ guides showing visitors around galleries and heritage sites

■ instructors explaining how to use gym equipment

■ staff showing customers around facilities like conference venues, hotels and leisure complexes

■ a staff member making a report to a supervisor on the progress of a special project

■ a meeting where heads of department report on departmental targets, activities and achievements.

A trainer who helps people develop presentation skills in a number of different leisure and tourism organisations explains how to make successful presentations:

66 *The most important thing is to prepare thoroughly. You need to appear confident and knowing that you've prepared well will give you confidence. Practising your presentation before you give it is vital. Get friends or colleagues to watch and give you feedback. Seeing yourself is also a good idea. Practise in front of a mirror or better still record yourself on video.* 99

Good presentation techniques

■ Give your talk a beginning, middle and end. Make sure that your introduction and conclusion are particularly strong.

■ Practice giving your presentation in front of friends, your tutor or on video.

■ Say at the beginning what you are going to talk about, and as you move on to each new area say something like, 'Now I'm going to look at . . .'

■ Use simple words in short sentences.

■ Speak clearly and too loudly rather than too softly.

■ Do not rush, and use pauses so that points you make can sink in.

■ Dress appropriately.

■ Use eye-contact with your audience. Don't look at just one person all the time.

■ Limit any mannerisms you may have.

■ Stand upright with both feet firmly on the ground.

■ Don't fiddle with your pen, notes, or anything else.

■ If you use visual aids, practise before hand so that there are no technical hitches or delays.

Key questions

1 Why is it important to have objectives for an evaluation of a customer service?
2 What objectives could you set for an evaluation of a customer service?
3 Why is it important to define quality criteria for an evaluation of a customer service?
4 What quality criteria could you use for an evaluation of a customer service?
5 Why is it important to prioritise customer needs? Give an example of how you have prioritised customer needs when delivering customer service.
6 When assessing your ability to deliver customer service, what can you gain from:
   ■ self-evaluation
   ■ evaluation by others?

Assignment

Make arrangements to deliver customer service in three different situations – your tutor may be able to help you set this up. Your performance will be assessed. Design a form that you can use to keep notes on what you did in each situation and how well you think you performed against the evaluation objectives and criteria.

Prepare and give a presentation on the customer service situations you found yourself in. The presentation should include:
■ a description of the quality criteria you used in each situation
■ your evaluation of your own performance
■ a comparison between your evaluation of your performance and the evaluations made by other people
■ recommendations for improvements
■ an explanation of how you are going to make improvements.

UNIT 7

Element 7.1
Health, safety and security

Element 7.2
Health and safety at leisure and tourism events

Element 7.3
Security at leisure and tourism events

Health, safety and security in leisure and tourism

ELEMENT **7.1**

Health, safety and security

By their nature, leisure and tourism organisations deal with a lot of different people. Whenever there are people around, it is important to protect their health, safety and security and there is a range of laws whose purpose is to safeguard customers and staff. In this element you will find out which laws and regulations apply to leisure and tourism facilities and what facilities do to comply with the laws. It isn't usually necessary to know the laws and regulations in detail, but you do have to know where to get more information about them. So you'll also be investigating sources of information.

> We have a health and safety officer and adhere to all the rules concerning things like fire exits, putting bright tape onto things so people don't trip over them, ensuring electrical equipment works and having first-aid procedures. We also have a designated first-aider on the premises all the time.
>
> *manager of a tourism information centre*

> We had our regular visit from the environmental health inspector this year. Although there are regulations which everyone preparing food has to observe, we don't have to have big stainless-steel surfaces everywhere because we are not a restaurant and are considered to have a domestic kitchen.
>
> *owner of a guest-house*

> We are affected by health and safety legislation, particularly on the technical side – the stage and lighting. Also we have to observe the fire regulations which can be extremely rigorous. We maintain security through alarms and closed-circuit TVs, as well as by extensive locking.
>
> *press and publicity officer in an entertainments venue*

> The main national legislation which affects us is the Children Act. This requires that we maintain a ratio of staff to children of one to eight. It means that staff don't have unrealistic demands made on them, and the children benefit from better safety standards and more attention.
>
> *community play officer in a city council*

Section 7.1.1

The importance of health, safety and security

The best way to understand the importance of health, safety and security issues in the leisure and tourism industry is to think about what could happen if they are ignored.

These may be extreme incidents, but they show that health, safety and security problems can seriously affect customers using leisure and tourism services, as well as staff and organisations.

The leisure and tourism industry is very conscious of health, safety and security. In fact, it has an excellent record: most visitor attractions and facilities like hotels, fairgrounds and sports stadia are generally safe; serious hazards are rare; the number of accidents per passenger mile on public transport systems is low; and violent incidents at tourist resorts are very rare.

Health, safety and security issues aren't just the ones that make the headlines when things go wrong. The vast majority are simple, everyday things requiring common sense, sensible precautions and consideration for others.

Health, safety and security are important to:

- the organisation
- individual employees
- staff as a whole
- customers
- customer care
- public relations
- the environment.

Health, safety and security affect all areas of leisure and tourism. Many of the units in the GNVQ include health, safety and security aspects:

- Legislation (Unit 2) – there are many laws relating to health, safety and security. Leisure and tourism organisations must take care to follow them.

- Marketing (Unit 3) – Health, safety and security measures are important features of many products and services, especially for companies offering courses in hazardous activities like bungee jumping or parachuting. The company's safety record may be a major selling point for marketing campaigns. Incidents where health, safety and security measures fail can create bad publicity – organisations may need to deal with it through public relations.

- Costing (Unit 4) – the costs of health, safety and security measures need to be taken into account when costing products and services.

- Business systems (Unit 5) – Health, safety and security should be included in organisations' quality standards and codes of practice. Administration systems need to include procedures covering accidents and emergencies. If companies use electronic information-processing systems, they are governed by the Data Protection Act and must have procedures designed to ensure security.

- Customer service (Unit 6) – Health, safety and security are important to customers; they may be high on customers' lists of priorities. A high level of service proves that an organisation really cares for its customers.

DISCUSSION POINT

Discuss the daily health, safety and security issues for these leisure and tourism organisations:

- a premier division football club
- an amusement park
- a coach operator
- a teashop
- an art gallery
- a cinema.

How many are common to all of them?

ACTIVITY

Any leisure or tourism activity consists of these components:

- land and premises
- materials, equipment and/or machinery
- staff
- activities involved in providing products and/or services
- customers.

For each component listed, ask yourself these questions:

- What health, safety and security issues might affect this?
- What could happen if the issues were ignored?

Note down your ideas.

The organisation

No organisation wants to have a reputation for bad health, safety or security practices. Apart from the ethical issues, it can cost them serious or even complete loss of business. For example:

- A facility with a poor reputation for security will quickly lose customers and could face insurance problems.
- A restaurant repeatedly prosecuted by environmental health officers for low hygiene standards will find it hard to shake off the image of being a dodgy place to eat.
- Owners and directors may have to pay large sums in compensation to injured parties which may lead to financial ruin.

DISCUSSION POINT

Think of two or three different incidents in leisure and tourism where the health of customers was harmed or their safety or security affected in some way. For each one, discuss:

- how far the organisation providing the service should be held responsible for the harm done to customers
- what steps the organisation could have taken to avoid the incident or minimise the risk of it.

A health and safety expert who advises leisure and tourism facilities comments:

66 *No organisation offering a service can be absolutely sure that all possible risks are removed. Some are outside their control – for example, if a hurricane damages the hotel where a tour operator's customers are staying. Some problems may be the result of customers' mistakes, like when someone travelling abroad ignores health or hygiene advice and catches a tropical disease. But customers should expect organisations do everything they reasonably can to reduce the risks of incidents. Measures to ensure the health, safety and security of customers and employees should be a high priority in the organisation's management plan.* 99

Health, safety and security affect all aspects of an organisation. The programmes director of an outdoor activity centre explains why health, safety and security issues are an integral part of everything the organisation does:

66 *Whatever we do has a health, safety or security link. For example, the facilities we offer have to be inspected and maintained. So we have to have staff to do that and we have to ensure they're properly trained. They need tools, equipment and in some cases protective clothing. All of these are costs which have to be built into our budgets. We can't just bolt on the health, safety and security aspects. We have to think them through, cost them out, resource them and work them into our systems and procedures.* 99

Individual employees

Individuals working in leisure and tourism have a right to expect that, while at work, their personal needs for health, safety and security will be met by their employer.

Rights imply duties, and employees also have a duty to take reasonable measures to protect their own health, safety and security. They must observe all health, safety and security measures laid down by the organisation. They must also avoid placing others at risk, including both customers and fellow workers.

Health and Safety Policy

The board of directors wishes to pursue a policy to promote health and safety at work and seeks the cooperation of all staff members, trainees and visitors for that purpose. The company will provide working conditions which comply with the statutory requirements of the Health and Safety at Work, etc., Act 1974, and other approved codes of practice as appropriate. These standards are intended to provide adequate or more than adequate standards of health and safety.

We have concern for company staff members, and also for the many freelance contractors, temporary staff and visitors who use these premises. It is considered vitally important that this policy and all health and safety facilities and procedures, are in operation and adhered to; that they are monitored and reviewed regularly; and that everything possible is done to maintain an environment where full consideration is given to health and safety in all the company's activities.

1   The employer ensures, as far as reasonably practicable in the current state of knowledge, the health, safety and welfare at work of all staff members, trainees, clients and visitors to the premises. This is achieved by:
    • providing adequate working conditions with facilities and procedures intended to safeguard health and safety
    • providing information, instruction, training and supervision to create a safe and healthy environment for all employees and visitors.
2   The employer encourages staff members to cooperate with management in all health and safety matters.

Extract from Health and Safety Policy

Staff

Staff are responsible for making sure that health, safety and security procedures are put into practice. As employees, they have a duty to make sure that visitors to the facility are not placed at risk. They should expect to receive training in aspects of health, safety and security. They should also be made aware of what could happen if they don't pay attention to these procedures.

The receptionist at a swimming pool explains how the staff carry out their responsibilities for health, safety and security:

66 *We're all given a very thorough training in the company's policies and procedures as well as general health, safety and security training. This helps us all to keep our eyes and ears open for breaches of good practice – actual or potential. If we see something that could be a hazard or risk, we know we have a duty to do something about it. In some cases, we can remove the risk ourselves – for instance, mopping up a puddle of water in a changing room. In other cases, we may need to get someone else to take action – for example, getting a senior member of staff to deal with a troublesome customer or notifying the maintenance crew of damaged equipment. Because we've been trained, we know what to do, what our authority to act is, who else to involve, and where to find any staff or equipment we need.* 99

DISCUSSION POINT

Think of any jobs you've had in the leisure and tourism industry or elsewhere. How aware were you of the health, safety and security aspects of what you did?

Customers

Customers expect certain standards from the organisations where they buy products and service. They expect that:

■ health, safety and security measures meet the standards required by law

■ members of staff with whom they have contact have been trained in health, safety and security procedures

■ they will be told about any aspect of the facility which may present a risk to their health, safety and security.

ACTIVITY

Visit a leisure or tourism facility and look around for evidence of health, safety and security measures aimed at protecting the customers – for example:

■ notices and signs

■ fire escapes

■ security staff

■ cleaning and maintenance work

■ facilities for disabled people

■ information in publicity leaflets.

Make a list of everything you notice.

Criteria

The national tourist boards for England, Scotland and Wales operate a national ACCESSIBLE scheme to identify and acknowledge those places to stay that meet the needs of wheelchair users. There are three Categories of accessibility:

Category 1
Accessible to an independent wheelchair user.

Category 2
Accessible to wheelchair user with assistance.

Category 3
Accessible to wheelchair user able to walk a few paces and up at least three steps.

The minimum requirements for each of the three Categories are shown in this leaflet. It is emphasised that these are the minimum requirements. If an Access inspection reveals that there are other aspects, not dealt with in the criteria, that prohibit access or present serious obstacles, the awarding of an Accessible Category may be withheld until such time as it is confirmed that the situation has been remedied.

Please note:
The measurements included in these criteria are those acceptable to meet the requirements of the three Categories of accessibility. They are not, necessarily, recommended or Ideal measurements. Details of recommended measurements are given in the 'Providing Accessible Accommodation' guide published by the English Tourist Board and Holiday Care Service. Copies, price £5, can be obtained from the Holiday Care Service, 2 Old Bank Chambers, Station Road, Horley, Surrey RH6 9HW or from your regional tourist board.

Notes

1 Ramps, where present, should not have a gradient at any point of more than 1:12. Removable ramps, unless permanently in situ, are not acceptable for Category 1.

2 Single steps: For Category 2 there can be a succession of single steps, provided there is sufficient space after each step for a wheelchair to sit comfortably and safely, with all four wheels on the ground.

3 Steps to be used by a disabled guest should have risers no more than 19cm, treads no less than 25cm deep and 75cm wide.

4 For Category 1, thresholds to rooms to which the wheelchair user requires access must be no higher than 2 cm.

Extract from 'the 'National Accessible Scheme' published by the English Tourist Board

DISCUSSION POINT

What would you do as a customer if you felt you were at risk because of an organisation's bad health, safety or security practices?

Public relations is a system of establishing and maintaining good relationships and effective communication channels between an organisation and the general public.

Customer care

All leisure and tourism organisations want their customers to use their facilities, products and services safely. It's part of their legal responsibilities and part of their ethical responsibilities. The manager of a fitness centre explains why they see health, safety and security as a duty they owe to their customers:

❝ *Our customers come to us because they see us as fitness experts – both in the instruction we give and the facilities we provide. They trust us to provide a healthy, safe and secure environment. If we fail to live up to that trust, we're failing to do our jobs properly and we shouldn't be in business.* ❞

Public relations

Organisations use public relations to present their image to the outside world. For leisure and tourism organisations, demonstrating to the public that they take the health, safety and security of their staff, customers and the local environment seriously is an important part of their public relations activities.

When something goes wrong, like an accident, an organisation uses its public relations activities to:

- explain its side
- acknowledge any responsibility it has
- reassure the public it is taking preventative measures to stop a similar accident happening in the future.

A public relations officer for a theme park describes how important it is for organisations to take into account the power of public opinion:

❝ *A failure in health, safety or security measures in one organisation puts the whole industry sector under public scrutiny. It makes the public think 'If it happened at that facility, it could happen at others.' So we don't just have responsibility for the image of our own organisation. We also have responsibility for the industry sector as a whole. This means our public relations department has to be geared up to respond to the wider picture, not just our own part of it.* **❞**

The environment

Some leisure and tourism activities are a possible threat to the environment. Health, safety and security measures play an important in avoiding or limiting environmental damage.

The manager of an outdoor swimming pool at a seaside resort describes how they are aware of environmental hazards:

❝ *We thought about setting up another business hiring out motor boats and jet-skis. Local conservationists were worried about the effect the extra noise and activity would have on the wildlife. We also thought about other damage to the environment – for example, the fuel tank of a boat might leak. So we didn't go ahead with the expansion. We built a second swimming pool instead.* **❞**

It's not just leisure and tourism facilities that create an impact on the environment – their visitors do too.

Sidebar

Public relations activities include:

- dealing with the media
- organising public awareness events
- issuing press releases and statements
- coordinating publicity events
- organising and controlling the way information about the organisation is passed to the media and general public.

English Tourist Board **20 TIPS FOR**

VISITORS

☑ Always remember you are the guest: show consideration for residents and their environment. Respect local laws and customs.

☑ Leave beaches, parks and public places as you would like to find them.

☑ Put litter in a bin or take it home: don't expect others to clean up after you.

☑ Keep noise levels down, especially at night or in quiet places like churches and the countryside.

☑ Show respect for nature: keep to proper footpaths, don't feed wildlife and don't pick flowers or shrubs.

☑ Remember that many people find smoking offensive, and careless smokers may cause countryside fires.

☑ Don't carve your initials on trees and historic monuments or spoil them with graffiti.

☑ Complain if you have just cause, but do it politely.

☑ Don't argue with staff who seek to enforce rules: they are only doing their jobs.

☑ Avoid the temptation to touch valuable objects such as paintings, tapestries and vases.

☑ Keep an eye on your children to see they don't indulge in destructive or annoying behaviour.

☑ If you want to photograph other people, ask them first.

☑ Behave toward others as you would wish them to behave towards you: don't push, shove or jump queues.

☑ Good manners are always appreciated: don't forget to say please and thank you.

☑ Dress properly to visit places of worship: remember they are not holiday playgrounds.

☑ Wear suitable footwear to visit historic buildings: high-heeled shoes can cause a lot of damage.

☑ Be enterprising: visit parts of the country off the usual 'tourist trail'.

☑ If you live in Britain, try to visit our popular attractions in off-peak periods: you'll enjoy them much more.

☑ Use public transport whenever possible. If you take your car, park in a designated space, not just where you please.

☑ Help the local economy: buy locally grown or made goods wherever possible.

ACTIVITY

Design a leaflet which could be given to customers at a leisure and tourism facility you know of to help raise their awareness of the impact they may have on the local environment. Give them some guidelines on positive actions they can take and standards they can keep.

Ensuring health, safety and security

Organisations ensure health, safety and security through a range of measures. These measures may be:

- obligatory – which means you have to follow them
- voluntary – which means you can choose whether to follow them or not.

Obligatory measures

All organisations offering goods and services must meet minimum standards of health, safety and security. These standards are set at local, national or international level. They are described in various documents.

Organisations which do not meet the standards may be prosecuted in court. Many of the laws, regulations and directives affecting the leisure and tourism industry are described in Section 7.1.3.

- Laws – Rules made by Parliament which all individuals and organisations have to follow. Laws are enforced by the courts and local authorities.
- By-laws – Regulations made by local authorities which residents and businesses within the area covered by the local authority have to follow.
- Regulations – Official rules or orders, usually made by a government department, and authorised by law. They are different from laws in that they do not always apply to everyone.
- EU Directives – Regulations which apply to all member states of the European Union. The way they are put into practice, e.g. by law or regulation, is left to the individual state.

Voluntary measures

Laws, regulations and directives set minimum standards of health, safety and security which organisations have to meet. Some sectors of the industry have voluntary measures as well, such as:

- industry codes of practice – voluntary procedures laid down by organisations which represent an area of the industry. For example, travel agents follow guidelines set down by the Association of British Travel Agents (ABTA)
- organisational codes and procedures – procedures adopted by individual organisations.

These voluntary codes may:

- describe how laws and regulations – the obligatory standards – should be put into practice
- set standards that are higher than the legal minimum

HSC
Health & Safety
Commission

In 1994 the Activity Centre Advisory Committee (ACAC) drew up a voluntary code of practice for outdoor activity centres. The Committee took this action largely in response to an incident at Lyme Bay where four teenagers on a school trip died during a canoeing activity.

The code covers these areas:

■ general conditions (such as statutory obligations and insurance)

■ safety, welfare and care of people using and working in activity centres

■ staffing

■ facilities

■ management of activities

■ environmental considerations.

Centres who follow the code are eligible for accreditation by the Committee if they:

■ can demonstrate that they are implementing the code's guidelines

■ are open to independent inspections

■ have an effective customer complaints procedure.

The Government has incorporated much of the code in a new law on the operation of outdoor centres called the Activity Centres (Young Persons' Safety) Act 1995.

■ lay down additional health, safety and security measures relevant to a particular area of the industry – for example, a company offering diving lessons may have a code of practice relating to procedures all divers must follow and for using diving equipment safely.

Organisations can send copies of their voluntary codes of practice to the Health and Safety Commission (HSC) for approval.

ACTIVITY

Ask to see the health and safety policy statement of a facility you know. Make a copy of the checklist below and tick off each item you find in the policy statement.

☐ a general statement of policy

☐ a list of responsibilities, including named people who are responsible for some area of safety

☐ accident arrangements, including details of first aid

☐ general fire safety

☐ the address of the local Health and Safety Executive (HSE)

☐ special training arrangements

☐ the organisation's rules for outside contractors and other visitors

☐ notes of hazards

☐ housekeeping arrangements, including waste disposal

☐ rules for electrical safety

☐ dangerous equipment and necessary precautions

☐ dangerous substances and relevant precautions, for COSHH and flammable substances

☐ other important hazards such as on-site vehicles.

When organisations introduce their own procedures, they generally base them on laws, regulations and industry codes of practice.

A lifeguard talks about the voluntary measures that apply at the pool where he works:

❝ *In our normal operating procedures we have a ruling that the maximum number of people in our large pool is 100. As soon as we reach that figure we let the receptionist staff know, and they stop any more people coming in until it quietens down. There's also a ruling on how long a lifeguard is allowed to work on the pool side. No one works longer than 50 minutes at a stretch – we go off and do other duties and return later. That way we are fresh and more observant, and the public is safer.* ❞

ACTIVITY

Many leisure and tourism facilities are run by the leisure services departments of local authorities. Standards may be set out in local charters. Contact a local leisure services department near you (it may use a slightly different name) and ask for a copy of any standards or guidelines available to the public.

Individual facilities should also have their own guidelines. Contact one and ask for copies of any that exist.

DISCUSSION POINT

In what ways might an organisation ensure that health, safety and security procedures are understood and followed by staff and customers?

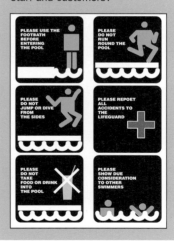

Many professional bodies and trade associations produce their own codes of practice on customer care. These often include health, safety and security procedures. Local authorities and government departments may produce statements relating to health, safety and security in their Citizens' Charters.

Implementing measures

Setting standards is one thing. Making sure they are kept to is much harder. It's up to everyone to make sure that the measures described here are put into practice.

- Individual employees must be aware of and follow relevant guidelines – whether obligatory or voluntary.
- Departmental managers are responsible for making sure that the procedures are used.
- Where security of information is concerned, organisations may have an information technology (IT) manager responsible for laying down procedures.
- Large organisations may employ a health and safety officer to oversee and coordinate health and safety regulations and procedures.
- In situations where health, safety and security is subject to laws and regulations, enforcement officers may visit premises to check that measures are being followed. If they're not, the officers can take action against the owner or directors.

Customers are also important pieces in the health and safety jigsaw. They should be made aware of any health, safety or security procedures which they should observe when using a facility. Customers ignoring the rules in force may put into danger the health, safety or security of themselves and others, and should be asked either to follow the rules or to leave.

The lifeguard at the swimming pool continues:

66 *We have signs on the walls asking bathers not to dive or run along the side. We warn people if they do go against this ruling, and if they continue to do it – which quite a lot of people do – we ask them to leave the pool. They're causing a danger to others as well as themselves. If they can't recognise that, we don't want their custom.* 99

Laws and regulations

Laws are rules that allow governments to set down standards of conduct and behaviour which everyone has to follow – including individuals and organisations. Laws also aim to protect people against the negligence and wrongdoing of others. Legislation is the process of establishing law.

The main purposes of laws and regulations

- To raise individuals' awareness of their responsibility in keeping health, safety and security standards
- To raise individuals' awareness of their responsibility to other people
- To reduce risks and dangers – to themselves and other people
- To set standards which organisations and individuals can follow
- To make sure that advice is available to organisations and individuals.

Purposes of laws and regulations

Here is a legal adviser's summary of the purpose of health, safety and security laws and regulations:

66 *Laws and regulations provide a framework which organisations and individuals can use to make sure they work in a way that promotes health, safety and security. As well as setting standards, they also describe actions that may be taken against organisations that don't follow the rules laid down.* 99

Most laws relating to health, safety and security aim to provide a better work and leisure environment. They apply equally to employers and employees.

Employers have a duty to:	**Employees have a duty to:**
■ cooperate with employees	■ cooperate with employers
■ take reasonable care of employees	■ follow guidelines laid down by their organisation
■ obey the law.	■ take reasonable care in their work
	■ obey lawful orders.

ACTIVITY

Pick one of the groups listed below and design a poster to get across to them the message that health, safety and security laws and regulations are there for a purpose:

- employers
- employees
- customers.

DISCUSSION POINT

Following health, safety and security laws and regulations means taking responsibility for yourself and for others. As an employee in the leisure and tourism industry, who would you count as 'others'?

Enforcement officers are employed to make sure that laws and regulations are followed and to look into cases where the regulations have been broken. They also have a duty to assist organisations to comply with the regulations, by giving information and advice.

The fire officer from the local fire service makes regular checks on all the public entertainment venues in the area. She describes some of the checks she makes:

66 *I go round the venues making sure that all the fire exits can be used. Sometimes I've found chairs in front of them, or that the aisle leading up to them has been narrowed. I also look at the number of people the venue can safely hold, and quite often I've had to reduce it as I didn't feel it was safe. That doesn't go down well with the management as they want to sell more tickets not fewer – but it has to be done.* 99

Sources of information

National organisations

- The Royal Society for the Prevention of Accidents (RoSPA) produce a number of leaflets relating to health and safety.

- Government publications on health and safety can be bought from Her Majesty's Stationery Office (HMSO)

- The Trading Standards Office provides information and leaflets about consumer protection.

- The Health and Safety Executive has an extensive library and information service. They produce leaflets and information sheets. They have three public enquiry points in Bootle, London and Sheffield as well as 21 regional offices.

- St John's Ambulance and the British Red Cross are able to provide advice on first aid. They also run first aid courses.

- Professional bodies and trade organisations provide information on issues which affect their members. Many of them also provide information services which are available to the general public.

- Some voluntary organisations, like charities and pressure groups, provide information on aspects of the law.

There's an enormous amount of legislation relating to health, safety and security. Keeping abreast of the most up-to-date information can be hard. So it's important to know where to get hold of the information.

For people working in the leisure and tourism industry, a good place to start is within the organisation. Try:

- a company safety representative or other officer whose role is to ensure that guidelines about health, safety and security are followed
- trade union representatives – all unions provide comprehensive information to their members on health, safety and security.

National and local sources

The main national organisations that can provide good information are listed in the first box. Some of them may have local or regional branches. The second box lists local sources.

ACTIVITY

Create a database of sources of information on health, safety and security relevant to the leisure and tourism industry. If you are interested in a particular area of leisure and tourism, find out what sources of information are relevant to that area. Include:

- addresses and telephone numbers of national organisations
- addresses and telephone numbers of local branches
- an outline of what information they can provide.

Using a database will make it easier to add to the directory, update information in the future and extract the information you are looking for.

Local sources

- Reference libraries can provide general information about laws and regulations. Many libraries are now equipped with on-line electronic information services which provide information and additional contact points.

- Citizens Advice Bureaux can give individuals information on their rights.

- Local authorities may have a centralised service which can provide information or they may provide information and advice through their departments.

- Most district councils have an Environmental Health Department which provides information and leaflets relating to health and safety – particularly on matters covered by the Offices, Shops and Railway Premises Act.

- Advice on fire regulations may be obtained from the local Fire and Rescue Service.

- Advice on crime prevention and security is available through the Crime Prevention Office at local police stations.

Key laws and regulations

UNIT

7

ELEMENT **7.1**

If they are not available in your local library, copies of Acts of Parliament may be obtained from:

> Her Majesty's Stationery Office
> Holborn Viaduct
> London WC1V 6HB

It's not much fun reading the whole of an Act. You may find it better to read a summary. Relevant directories often contain summaries – ask in your library where you can find them. The summaries given here are a start.

Many different laws and regulations govern health, safety and security in leisure and tourism industries. Neither employers nor employees need to know every single piece of legislation word for word. But they do need to know:

- which laws are relevant to their work
- what duties the laws place upon them.

Employers in particular need to know how to get hold of relevant information about health, safety and security.

The information in this section applies particularly to England and Wales. Most Acts of Parliament apply throughout the whole of the United Kingdom, but there are often separate provisions dealing with Scotland – the same laws apply, but the way in which they are put into practice may vary. This is because the structure of the legal system in Scotland is different from the rest of the UK. Although closely linked, the laws of Northern Ireland also vary; where there are any significant differences the relevant legislation which applies is mentioned.

Health and Safety at Work Act 1974
Health and Safety at Work (NI) Order 1978

The Health and Safety at Work Act is commonly referred to as HASAWA or HSWA. It applies to England and Wales. In Northern Ireland, the corresponding legislation is the Health and Safety at Work (NI) Order 1978.

The purpose of HSWA is to increase the protection of people at work. It applies to everybody at work – employers, employees or the self-employed. It also protects people who are affected by work activities – neighbours, passers-by and customers. It applies to people rather than premises.

The main points to note are Sections 2, 3, 4, 7 and 33.

DUTIES OF EMPLOYERS

Section 2

- provide and maintain equipment and appliances and systems of work which are safe and without risk to health
- arrange the safe handling, use, storage and transport of articles and substances
- provide information, instruction, training and supervision to ensure the health and safety of employees
- keep places of work in a safe condition without risk to health
- provide safe access to and exit from working premises
- provide and maintain a working environment that is as safe as possible and free of risks to health and safety, and in which the facilities and arrangements are adequate for the well-being of employees at work

Section 2 (continued)

- provide a written statement of the general health and safety policy and bring it to the attention of all employees (this does not apply to organisations where there are less than five employees)
- consult the safety representatives of recognised trade unions about making and maintaining health and safety and to set up a safety committee, if two or more safety representatives request it.

Section 3

- make sure, as far as possible, that people other than employees (clients, visitors, etc.) are not exposed to risks to their health and safety.

Section 4

- make sure that premises, equipment and machinery may be used without risks to health and safety.

DUTIES OF EMPLOYEES

Section 7

- take reasonable care for the health and safety of themselves and persons who may be affected by what they do or don't do at work
- cooperate with their employers about any duty placed on them relating to health and safety

Section 8

- not to interfere intentionally or recklessly with or misuse anything provided for health, safety or welfare (e.g. fire extinguishers)

Section 33

Section 33 describes what constitutes an offence under the Act. Offences include:

- failing to carry out duties laid down by the Act or by other health and safety regulations
- obstructing inspectors in their work or interfering with the inspection process – for example, by preventing employees appearing before an inspector
- failing to comply with improvement orders, prohibition notices and other court orders
- posing as a Health and Safety Inspector.

DISCUSSION POINT

A waiter employed in a country house hotel was carrying a tray from one of the guest rooms down the service staircase to the kitchens. To save himself two journeys, he had loaded a lot of things on the one tray, but it was still light enough to be carried. The staircase was poorly lit and some of the carpet was badly frayed. The waiter missed his footing and fell down to the bottom. He broke his ankle and received several bad cuts from the broken glass.

- Which sections of the HSWA are relevant to this incident?
- What did the owners of the hotel do wrong?
- What did the waiter do wrong?

Enforcing the HSWA

There are two government-funded bodies whose job it is to make sure that th HSWA is understood, followed and used:

- The Health and Safety Commission (HSC) – consists of a full-time chairma representatives from industry and local authorities. Its duty is to promote the objectives of the Act and to develop health and safety policies, provid guidance, codes of practice and proposals for regulations.

HSC
Health & Safety
Commission

HSE
Health & Safety
Executive

■ The Health and Safety Executive (HSE) has a duty to carry out the day-to-day work of the HSC and to put into force the legal requirements of the Act.

The HSE appoints inspectors who have the power to enter any premises, at any time, if they believe that there is a dangerous situation. They have the power to interview anyone who may have information relevant to their examination or investigation.

An inspector explains the action he is entitled to take if he finds any breaches in health and safety laws and regulations:

❝ *I can do one of four things:*

– *issue a prohibition notice which bans the activity causing the risk until action is taken to put the problem right – particularly if there's a risk of a serious personal injury*

– *issue an improvement notice which gives the organisation a specified time for putting the fault right*

– *prosecute so the matter is dealt with by the law courts – if the circumstances demand it, I may do this in addition to, or instead of, issuing a prohibition notice*

– *arrange to have the source of the danger made harmless or removed – particularly if it threatens to result in serious personal injury or damage to property.* **❞**

Under the Health and Safety at Work Act people guilty of an offence may be fined up to £20,000. Anyone failing to comply with a notice or court order faces a similar fine and up to six months in jail.

Workplace regulations

New laws made under HSWA – the Workplace (Health, Safety and Welfare) Regulations 1992 came into force for all premises on 1 January 1996. They were published by the HSC together with an approved code of practice (ACOP) which gives more precise guidelines on some topics.

These regulations set out the minimum working conditions for all workers in fixed permanent workplaces – including all offices, shops and similar premises. They also cover hospitals and schools.

Cleanliness

Premises, furnishings and fittings must be kept in a clean state. Dirt and rubbish must not be allowed to collect. Floors and stairs must be cleaned at least once a week.

Overcrowding

No room in the premises should be so overcrowded as to cause risk of injury to the health of persons working in them. The Workplace Regulations say that there should be enough floor area, height and unoccupied space to ensure health, safety and welfare. The ACOP states that this means at least eleven cubic metres per person (any space above three metres from the floor should not be included in the calculation).

Temperature

A reasonable temperature must be kept in every room in which people are employed to work. The minimum temperature should normally be 16 °C. Equipment used in workplaces, such as photocopiers and computers, must not cause discomfort or danger through fumes – temperatures of up to 32 °C have been found in rooms containing several pieces of electronic equipment.

Ventilation

A constant flow of clean, fresh, draught-free air should be provided.

Lighting

Lighting should be of the right quality and brightness, and, wherever possible, should be natural light. There should be no glare and black shadows.

Sanitation and water

Toilets should be provided for employees. There should be separate toilets for both sexes. Clean running hot and cold water, soap and towels (or suitable alternatives) should be provided. These facilities should be kept clean, properly looked after, properly lit and ventilated. There should be drinking water which employees can easily get to.

Seating

Where employees have to sit down to carry out their duties, suitable seating must be provided. Seating must be safe, of suitable design, construction and size.

Floors, passages and stairs

Floors, passages and stairs must be of sound construction, properly looked after and free from obstruction. Handrails should be provided on the open side of staircases.

Dangerous machinery

Dangerous machinery must be securely fenced and adequately guarded against all possible injuries.

The Shops, Offices and Railway Premises Act 1963

Sections 1, 7, 8, and 14 of an earlier Act, the Shops, Offices and Railway Premises Act 1963, cover similar areas to the Workplace Regulations. Section 3 of the Act excludes workplaces used for less than 21 hours a week by one staff member or a total of 21 hours between two or more staff members. Section 15 requires organisations to provide a suitable eating place for staff who have to eat on the premises.

ACTIVITY

What does eleven cubic metres look like? If you were working in a room three metres high with several desks in it, how much space would have to be left between the people sitting at each desk? Calculate how much floor space each person can expect as a minimum. Do you think this is a reasonable minimum?

EXTREMELY/HIGHLY FLAMMABLE

ENVIRONMENTAL HAZARD

CORROSIVE

OXIDISING

VERY TOXIC/TOXIC

EXPLOSIVE

HARMFUL/IRRITANT

The Control of Substances Hazardous to Health (COSHH) regulations

COSHH has two main purposes:

- to increase awareness of the hazards posed by chemicals and other substances
- to promote their safe handling and storage.

All employers and self-employed people must follow the COSHH regulations.

All substances are potentially hazardous – even water can burn when it's hot – but the regulations are designed to cover:

- substances which are labelled as dangerous – toxic, harmful, irritant or corrosive
- agricultural pesticides and other chemicals used on farms
- a range of other substances for which exposure levels have been set.

The regulations also include harmful microorganisms, substantial quantities of dust and any other material, mixture or compound which can harm people's health as a result of breathing it in, swallowing or skin contact.

No work which could expose anyone to hazardous substances may lawfully be carried on unless an assessment has been made and necessary precautions have been taken.

COSHH precautions

- control exposure to exclude or minimise risk
- check that the measures taken work
- ensure that the substances are properly looked after
- monitor substances to maintain proper limits
- keep records of monitoring
- train and instruct employees about the risk and precautions

COSHH has important implications for some areas of the leisure industry – for example, water in swimming pools is treated with chlorine. A farmer describes what he did to observe COSHH when he rented out cottages on his farm to visitors:

> 66 *I converted an old barn into some cottages, so families could see what it was like living on a working farm. I consulted my professional body, the National Farmers Union, and the local tourist board. I was particularly worried about some of the equipment and chemical fertilisers on the farm that could be very dangerous. I already had strict guidelines for my farm workers about storing and handling these substances. These were tightened to make sure that all these substances were well out of the way of the visitors. I also produced a leaflet for all the visitors on health and safety – a friend who was an artist added illustrations to make it easier for children to understand.* 99

How to have a safe holiday
1. Around the farm

Lorem ipsum dolor sit amet, consectetuer adipiscing elit, sed diam nonummy nibh euismod tincidunt ut laoreet dolore magna aliquam erat volutpat. Ut wisi enim ad minim veniam, quis nostrud exerci tation ullamcorper suscipit lobortis nisl ut aliquip ex ea commodo consequat. Duis autem vel eum iriure dolor in hendrerit in vulputate velit esse molestie consequat, vel illum dolore eu feugiat nulla facilisis at vero eros et accumsan et iusto odio dignissim qui blandit praesent luptatum zzril delenit augue duis dolore te feugait nulla facilisi. Lorem ipsum dolor sit amet, consectetuer adipiscing elit, sed diam nonummy nibh euismod tincidunt ut laoreet dolore magna aliquam erat volutpat. Ut wisi enim ad minim veniam, quis nostrud exerci tation ullamcorper suscipit lobortis nisl ut aliquip ex ea commodo consequat.

Duis autem vel eum iriure dolor in hendrerit in vulputate velit esse molestie consequat, vel illum dolore eu feugiat nulla facilisis at vero eros et accumsan et iusto odio dignissim qui blandit praesent luptatum zzril delenit augue duis dolore te feugait nulla facilisi. Nam liber tempor cum soluta nobis eleifend option congue nihil imperdiet doming id quod mazim placerat facer possim assum. Lorem ipsum dolor sit amet, consectetuer adipiscing elit, sed diam nonummy nibh euismod tincidunt ut laoreet dolore magna aliquam erat volutpat. Ut wisi enim ad minim veniam, quis nostrud exerci tation ullamcorper suscipit lobortis nisl ut aliquip ex ea commodo consequat. Duis autem vel eum iriure dolor in hendrerit in vulputate velit esse molestie consequat,

```
┌─────────────────────────────────────┐
│          FIRST AID KIT              │
│            Contents                 │
│        Guidance Leaflet x 1         │
│    Assorted Adhesive Dressings x 20 │
│  Sterile Eye Pad with attachment x 1│
│   Individually Wrapped Triangular   │
│             Bandage x 1             │
│     Safety Pins - Assorted x 6      │
│    Sterile Medium Unmedicated       │
│            Dressings x 3            │
│     Sterile Large Unmedicated       │
│            Dressing x 1            │
│   Sterile Extra Large Unmedicated   │
│            Dressing x 1            │
│       Moist Cleansing Wipe x 2      │
└─────────────────────────────────────┘
```

ACTIVITY

Find out who among the staff at your college or school has responsibilities for first aid. Talk to them about what their responsibilities involve and any training they have to do.

The Health and Safety (First Aid) Regulations 1981

These set down the legal requirements for employers. They are supported by an Approved Code of Practice which recommends one first aider for every 50 members of staff during working hours.

Workplaces should also provide first-aid boxes and kits. Each first-aid box should contain standard items including adhesive and other dressings, a triangular bandage, at least one sterile eyepad and a guidance card or leaflet giving first-aid advice.

Many leisure and tourism facilities have large numbers of people visiting them, and the arrangements for first aid should take account of this. One first-aid box is not enough on a large site or in a large building where there are going to be a lot of customers on busy days.

HSE
Health & Safety
Executive

Health and Safety at Work etc Act 1974
The Reporting of Injuries, Diseases and Dangerous Occurrences Regulations 1995

Report of an injury or dangerous occurrence

Filling in this form
This form must be filled in by an employer or other responsible person.

Part A
About you
1 What is your full name?

2 What is your job title?

3 What is your telephone number?

About your organisation
4 What is the name of your organisation?

5 What is its address and postcode?

6 What type of work does the organisation do?

Part B
About the incident
1 On what date did the incident happen?
/   /

2 At what time did the incident happen?
(Please use the 24-hour clock eg 0600)

3 Did the incident happen at the above address?
Yes ☐ Go to question 4
No ☐ Where did the incident happen?
☐ elsewhere in your organisation – give the name, address and postcode
☐ at someone else's premises – give the name, address and postcode
☐ in a public place – give details of where it happened

If you do not know the postcode, what is the name of the local authority?

4 In which department, or where on the premises, did the incident happen?

F2508 (01/96)

Part C
About the injured person
If you are reporting a dangerous occurrence, go to Part F.
If more than one person was injured in the same incident, please attach the details asked for in Part C and Part D for each injured person.

1 What is their full name?

2 What is their home address and postcode?

3 What is their home phone number?

4 How old are they?

5 Are they
☐ male?
☐ female?

6 What is their job title?

7 Was the injured person (tick only one box)
☐ one of your employees?
☐ on a training scheme? Give details:

☐ on work experience?
☐ employed by someone else? Give details of the employer:

☐ self-employed and at work?
☐ a member of the public?

Part D
About the injury
1 What was the injury? (eg fracture, laceration)

2 What part of the body was injured?

Continued overleaf

Notification of accidents and dangerous occurrences regulations 1985

Dangerous incidents, including all those where the injured person is in hospital as a result of an accident or incident in the workplace, should be reported to the Health and Safety Executive. Whenever a report is received, the HSE inspectorate will decide whether further investigations are needed.

In Northern Ireland this is covered by the Reporting of injuries, diseases and dangerous occurrences regulations (NI) 1986.

Fire Precautions Act 1971

This act details the regulations concerning lighting, heating, means of escape, and precautions to take in case of fire. Regulations are checked up on by inspectors working together with the local authority.

Occupiers Liability Act 1957

'Occupiers' have a duty to protect the lawful visitor who comes on to the premises. The Act applies to the occupier of land and buildings and to those who have furniture and fittings – shelves, cupboards, carpeting, floors and so on – under their control.

Consumer protection

Several laws offer protection to the consumer. The ones which apply to leisure and tourism organisations offering goods or services are:

■ The Consumer Protection Act 1987
■ The Fair Trading Act 1973
■ The Trade Descriptions Act 1987
■ The Sale of Goods Act 1979.

These Acts are controlled and regulated by the Office of Fair Trading (OFT) and are administered locally by trading standards officers. The main aim of these Acts is to look after the rights of customers when they buy goods or services:

■ they must be of a suitable quality
■ they must be what they claim to be – in other words, they should match the description given to customers
■ customers have a right to return goods which are faulty, damaged or don't match the description.

Data Protection Act 1984

One important aspect of security is security of information. With the increasing use of computers, it has become much easier to store and move information about individuals. The Data Protection Act is designed to protect individuals' rights in relation to computer-held personal data.

The Data Protection Act 1984:

■ forbids organisations or individuals from holding personal data unless they are registered with the Data Protection Registrar

■ gives individuals the right to know whether a data user is holding personal data and the right to look at that personal data

■ gives individuals a right to compensation where personal data held is inaccurate

■ gives the right to have inaccurate data corrected or removed.

ACTIVITY

Devise your own quick reference resource to help you make use of the information on the key laws and regulations given in this section. For example, you could:

■ use a desktop-publishing system to draw up a chart with the laws and regulations listed down one side and 'area of organisational activity', 'customers', 'employers', 'employees', specific regulatory bodies and so on as column headings along the top. Then for each law or regulation, put a tick in the relevant column to show:
– what and who the law or regulation applies to
– which regulatory body is involved

■ list the laws and regulations, summarise the main points you need to know about each one and then devise a colour code to help you see at a glance the people and organisational areas each one affects.

Relevance of laws and regulations

Many of the laws and regulations are relevant to particular types of leisure and tourism facilities. For example, COSHH is more important for swimming pools, which use substances such as chlorine, than for museums where the most hazardous materials are likely to be cleaning fluids.

CASE STUDY 1: SWIMMING POOL

Following a regular Saturday morning swimming session at the local swimming pool, Jamie Carter slipped on a pool of water in the changing area and fell, cracking his head on the floor. The lifeguard gave him first aid and called an ambulance. Jamie was taken to hospital. A gash on his head needed several stitches and he was kept in overnight with mild concussion.

CASE STUDY 2: OUTDOOR CONCERT

The town orchestra was staging its annual open-air concert. This was its Silver Jubilee and it was decided to stage something really special. Tchaikovsky's 1812 Overture was performed with cannon-fire, smoke and a fireworks display.

CASE STUDY 3: HEATWAVE

Sally Palmer was the supervisor in the Hollies Travel Agency. She was always concerned about working conditions in the back office. On cold days during the previous winter, it would take as long as two hours before the office reached 16 °C.

In the summer the office got incredibly hot. She complained to the owner when the temperature reached 32 °C, even though there was a large fan circulating the air. The manager said he wasn't going to do anything because the regulations did not mention maximum temperatures.

CASE STUDY 4: MAILING LIST

A sports club bought a computer and transferred their membership list on to a database. The club registered with the Data Protection Registrar even though they were only using the database as a membership record and as an address list for newsletters.

Following an inquiry by the Data Protection Registrar it was discovered that a rival sports club had got hold of a copy of the membership list. The membership secretary had a good idea who had handed the list over.

DISCUSSION POINT

Read through the four case studies again.

■ What laws and regulations are relevant in each situation – either because they have been broken or because they need to be considered to protect customers and employees?

■ What do you think should be the next steps in each situation?

What actually happened

CASE STUDY 1

The lifeguard had to make a full report to the Health and Safety Executive. The health and safety inspector visited shortly afterwards and issued an Improvement Notice requiring non-slip matting to be provided in the changing rooms within 14 days.

CASE STUDY 2

The local fire officer provided the orchestra with advice on fire safety during the performance and also arranged for a firefighter to be on duty during the performance. Special arrangements were made for storing the smoke canisters and the stage manager was given special instructions on their use. The fireworks were provided by a specialist firm with an excellent safety record. The company was a member of the Association of Firework Manufacturers who produced a code of conduct which met both health and safety and fire regulations.

CASE STUDY 3

After showing her manager a copy of the Workplace (Health, Safety and Welfare) Regulations, the owner had installed a very efficient convector heater which meant that the temperature in the back office was kept at 16 °C. Sally asked for advice from the local Environmental Health Department who contacted the owner and suggested that although no laws were being broken, it would be in the best interests of the staff and a part of her 'duty of care' to hire an air-conditioning system until the heatwave was over.

CASE STUDY 4

In this situation the Data Protection Act was clearly broken, but after discussions between the club chairman and the local crime prevention officer, it was decided that a police investigation would create too much bad publicity and would be unlikely to prove who had broken the regulations. The crime prevention officer suggested a number of security measures which could be taken. While on his visit he carried out a security inspection of the premises and made several recommendations about the security of the cash, locks and protection against vandalism.

ACTIVITY

Working with two or three friends, pick one of the laws or regulations described in this section. Prepare a storyboard for a five-minute training video for the relevant staff at a leisure and tourism organisation you know about.

Induction booklet

Induction – a planned series of activities to help new recruits:

■ feel welcome

■ find their way about the premises

■ get to know other staff, especially those they'll be working with directly

■ understand the organisation's processes and procedures

■ make a confident start to their new job.

When new staff join an organisation, they should be given clear information about health, safety and security. The best way to do it is as part of an induction programme.

The personnel manager at a cinema complex describes their way of explaining health, safety and security procedures to new recruits:

66 *The full induction process takes place over a week. Health, safety and security issues are part of that process. On their first day, we give the new recruits a guided tour of the premises. The health, safety and security aspects of this are showing them things like fire escapes and fire extinguishers, explaining the fire drill, explaining security practices and so on. Later in the day, we show them a health and safety video which is specially tailored for cinema employees. It's a very funny film but it does get the messages across. We also give them a copy of our health, safety and security handbook which includes our safety policy and describes the health, safety and security responsibilities of the organisation and all the staff. To help them take in the information, we give them a quiz sheet – a very light-hearted one – which we ask them to fill in. If they get a high score, they win free tickets for themselves and up to two friends to any film shown that month along with all the trimmings like popcorn, an ice cream and a snack from our snack bar.* 99

FILMSCOPE CINEMAS LTD HEALTH AND SAFETY HANDBOOK

Introduction

Reading this handbook will help you understand:
• the company's health and safety policies, standards and procedures
• why they are important
• how you can help to maintain them.

If you have any questions or need further explanation, your line manager will be happy to help.

What you can expect from us

The Board of Directors of Filmscope Cinemas Ltd has a duty of care towards you, your colleagues and our customers.

Our policy is to ensure that:
• your health, safety and welfare is protected
• the customers' health, safety and welfare is protected
• no employee's activities at work causes danger to colleagues or customers
• all parts of the workplace, equipment and work systems are safe and properly maintained
• all materials and substances used in the workplace are handled, stored and transported in accordance with approved safety procedures.

We will provide:
• all appropriate safeguards
• proper supervision, instruction and training.

What we expect from you

Whilst at work, we expect you to:
• always act in a safe and responsible way
• take reasonable care of your own health and safety
• take reasonable care of the health and safety of others
• have respect for the working premises and property
• follow all the health and safety standards set out in this handbook.

Here's what one of the new recruits thought about the induction:

66 *When I started here and they told me about the induction programme, I wasn't looking forward to the bits on health, safety and security. But actually it was brilliant. They made it really lively and I could relate all the laws and regulations I'd learned about at college to something real. The handbook is really clear and gives me something to refer to whenever I need to remind myself of processes and procedures. I see a cinema as something much more than somewhere you watch films now. So much goes on behind the scenes to make sure it's a safe place to be.* 99

CASE STUDY

Thorpe Park in Surrey is a leisure park offering a range of indoor and outdoor family entertainments and activities including:

- lakes
- rides
- a shop and a craft centre
- food outlets
- a working farm
- nature and conservation areas
- a collection of scale models of world-famous buildings
- special events such as jousting competitions, water-ski championships, airship displays and open-air drama productions. They employ around 1,000 people and have up to 18,000 visitors a day. Safety is a top priority and their safety policy aims to ensure:
- safe working conditions for employees
- a safe environment for visitors.

All staff are made aware of their responsibilities for safety. They're given guidance from their supervisors and also written information in the Terms and Conditions Handbook.

Staff are expected to:

- take care over the use and maintenance of equipment
- keep their own working areas clean, tidy and hazard-free.

All staff are aware of the procedures for emergencies such as fire or bomb alerts.

Security staff can be contacted by radio from many points throughout the site.

Security responsibilities for all staff include:

- always carrying their security passes
- knowing where to report incidents such as theft or damage
- making sure lost property is passed on to the Information Point.

ACTIVITY

Read through the case study on Thorpe Park. Write a brief report for the staff magazine that would help new recruits to understand the importance of health, safety and security issues at the park.

Key questions

1 Why are good health, safety and security procedures important to:
   – organisations?
   – staff?
   – customers?

2 What is the difference between:
   – obligatory measures?
   – voluntary measures?
   Give an example of each type.

3 Where can you go to find our more about health and safety legislation?

4 Can you summarise the responsibilities the Health and Safety at Work Act 1974 gives to:
   – employers?
   – employees?

5 Who appoints health and safety inspectors? What actions can inspectors take against an organisation failing to meet legal requirements for health, safety and security?

6 How many firstaiders do the Health and Safety (First Aid) Regulations 1981 recommend for every 50 members of staff during working hours?

7 Why is COSHH important? What incidents might occur if a swimming pool ignored its recommendations?

8 A small fitness centre has put all its customer details onto a computer database. Which Act will it have to stick to and what will it entail for them?

Assignment

Get together an information pack on health, safety and security in leisure and tourism. Use four different organisations – two from leisure and recreation and two from travel and tourism – and collect documents that illustrate what the health, safety and security laws and regulations mean in practice.

Prepare an induction booklet for new members of staff in one of the leisure and tourism facilities you used to gather the documents for your information pack. Include sections on:

■ the relevance of key laws and regulations to each organisation

■ the importance of maintaining health, safety and security

■ how health, safety and security are dealt with

■ sources of information about the key laws and regulations.

HAPPY DAYS *Holiday Park* **Staff training**

HEALTH & SAFETY STAFF CONDUCT GUEST WELFARE DRESS CODES

Key points to bear in mind:

■ Your booklet should clearly describe health, safety and security policies, and procedures within the organisation.

■ Bear in mind that your booklet is aimed at new members of staff who will be unaware of the people, systems, resources and layout of the organisation.

■ The document should be easy to use as a quick reference guide.

■ Use plain language and avoid jargon – if you have to include jargon words, explain them.

■ Don't describe procedures in a lot of detail – it's more important to describe who to contact and how, and where to find out more information.

66 *I have to be especially aware of health and safety issues when we run an event like a gymkhana. Our outside electricity supply has to be checked and we have to have a certificate for it. Any substance or chemical used by anyone on the premises that might be hazardous or dangerous in some way has to be covered by the health and safety legislation. With so much equipment, we also have to make sure things aren't left lying around so people can't fall over them.* 99

owner of a riding school which also provides holidays

66 *The main safety problems when we put on an outside show in summer are to do with the power supply for the stage lights and the seating. We get professional companies to set them both up for us and they ensure that all the regulations are being met. We also brief our stewards beforehand on what to do if there's an emergency and make sure that there is always someone with a first-aid certificate on the site throughout the performance.* 99

manager of a theatre group

66 *One of the jobs is to organise catering for the teams and spectators on the day of the regatta. We hire a marquee and set up a simple kitchen at one end producing sandwiches and things like hot dogs and hamburgers – nothing too difficult. We make sure that all the environmental health regulations are observed and we go through a checklist of procedures with the people who will be working in the kitchen during the day.* 99

organiser of a summer regatta

Health and safety at leisure and tourism events

Health and safety are especially important when leisure and tourism organisations are running events. This is because events attract many people and are often held on premises or sites that are not permanent and may need to be specially modified for the event. Anyone organising events must plan carefully in advance, anticipate the health and safety hazards that might arise and put in place measures to deal with them. In this element you will be investigating the potential hazards of a leisure and tourism event and describing what is done to safeguard customers and staff.

Identifying health and safety hazards

Many leisure and tourism organisations run events such as:

- a medieval banquet at a stately home
- an outing for a group of senior citizens
- an air show
- a concert staged in one of the local museum's galleries

. . . and many more.

Any event presents potential risks to health and safety. Avoiding the risks means:

- careful planning
- looking at the possible hazards
- checking legal and regulatory requirements
- taking measures to protect customers and staff.

Current and potential hazards

Health and safety hazards can take many forms – for example:

- a large piece of advertising hoarding swinging loose over a pavement
- a post supporting the hoarding that has rotted inside and is about to give way.

The first of these is a current hazard – it could cause injury to anyone passing by at any time. The second is a potential hazard – it will become a risk when the supporting post gives way and makes the hoarding unstable and likely to fall on someone.

Responsibility for health and safety at an event is usually given to one person as health and safety officer or coordinator. The same person may be responsible for security as well. It is the task of the health and safety coordinator at an event to look out for all sorts of hazards – actual or potential – so that steps can be taken to deal with them.

Hazards may be related to:

- materials
- substances
- activities
- equipment
- the environment.

SUMMER EXTRAVAGANZA

Every year a community organisation runs a charity event. All profits made from the event go to local charities. This year the organisers have decided to run a 'Summer Extravaganza'. The event will be held in the grounds of a local hall.

The day will includes stalls, activities for children, displays, catering (food and drink) and an all-day disco in a marquee. Based on the experience of previous years, people will come from a wide area. The event is run by volunteers and local charities are invited to set up stalls. The disco, drinks tent and refreshments are provided by outside companies.

At their first planning meeting, the team putting on the event draws up a site plan.

Notes

- The site is generally secure with high fencing between the area and the main road. A public footpath runs east to west from the lake to the main road, where there is a stile.
- There are two vehicle entrances from the A1234 suitable for use by emergency vehicles.
- The lake has a maximum depth of 1.5 m.
- There is public car parking for 160 cars on the south-west edge of the site.

ACTIVITY

Identify hazards for the event. Look at all aspects of the event, then list the hazards under these five headings:

- materials
- substances
- activities
- equipment
- the environment.

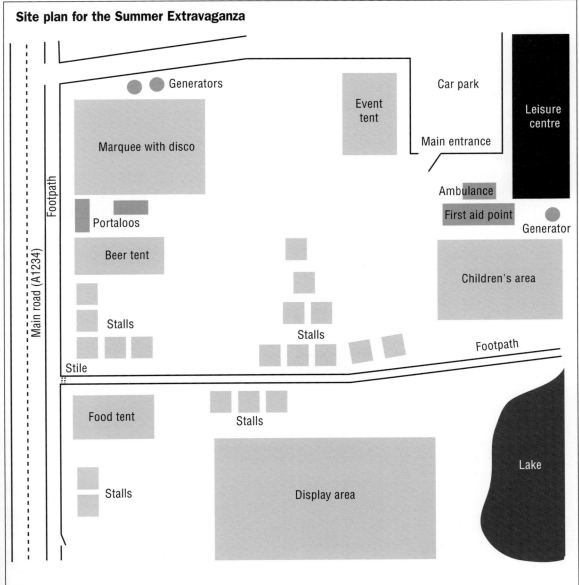

Site plan for the Summer Extravaganza

Generators

Event tent

Car park

Leisure centre

Main entrance

Marquee with disco

Ambulance

First aid point

Generator

Portaloos

Beer tent

Children's area

Footpath

Stalls

Stalls

Footpath

Stile

Food tent

Stalls

Stalls

Display area

Lake

Main road (A1234)

Key

- ■ Stalls – new and used goods, bric-a-brac, jumble, tombolas, bottle stalls.
- ■ Children's activities – bouncy castle, face painting, competitions, clowns.
- ■ Refreshments – hot and cold food stalls, tents, ice-cream vans, hotdogs, soft drinks.
- ■ Beer tent – beer, wines and spirits, glasses, tables and chairs.
- ■ Disco – marquee with portable floor, generator, sound system.

- ■ Event control – tent where organisers will be available with help, information, etc.; will include a personal announcement (PA) system, cables.
- ■ Displays – fire eating, juggling, exotic pets display and similar entertainments (may need room for vehicles and equipment).
- ■ Litter – waste bins.
- ■ Toilets – mobile portaloos.

Section 7.2.2

Evaluating health and safety hazards

Some health and safety hazards are relatively minor. Others can be highly dangerous. In severe cases, they can result in death – or even many deaths such as a transport incident or fire. Even less serious situations can result in unpleasant problems: injury, pain, financial loss, prosecution by the police and bankruptcy, and so on.

Probability and severity

When event organisers have drawn up a list of actual or potential health and safety hazards, the next step is to think about:

■ how likely they are to occur
■ how serious their effects would be if they did occur.

DISCUSSION POINT

The team planning the Summer Extravaganza listed these potential hazards and evaluated their probability and severity:

	Probability	Severity
■ people tripping over cables	high	medium
■ a child falling in the lake	medium	high
■ the marquee collapsing on top of dancers	low	high
■ an explosion in one of the generators setting fire to one of the tents	low	high
■ someone being bitten by one of the exotic pets	low	medium
■ someone cutting themselves on a broken glass in the drinks tent.	high	low

Do you agree with their assessment of the risk?

A safety officer gives her view:

❝ *Some hazards are very likely to occur and to cause problems – electrical cables for instance present a real danger to people. These are the hazards that* should be given a lot of attention. On the other hand, the marquee is unlikely to collapse because it will be put up by professionals and there are large numbers of supporting ropes. There isn't much that the organisers can do – unless it becomes obvious that the marquee is starting to look unstable, for example if a car accidentally dug up several of the guy-ropes. The most careful attention should be given to hazards that are both likely to occur and could cause serious harm. The lake falls into this category, because it's a particular hazard to children and there will be a lot of them about at an event like this. **99**

Aspects of the event

Most hazards can be linked directly to aspects of an event. For example:

- If an event has a main attraction, that can often be the focus of hazards because a lot of people are gathering in one place at one time. Minor or supporting attractions may present fewer organisational headaches – but they still have to be watched.
- One of the main aims of any event is to ensure the safety of customers and anyone else who attends. It's a good idea for health and safety officers to put themselves in the position of customers – it helps them think about how they would experience the event and what hazards they might meet.
- Organisers must consider health and safety implications for staff or helpers. They will experience the event as work – and often physically tiring work. There's often a lot of lifting, carrying and moving heavy articles, as well as setting up electrical equipment.
- Many hazards arise out of timings and movements. For example, people tend to arrive and leave in greater numbers at the start and end of an event – in cars as well as on foot. If there is a main attraction, there could be a large movement of people to see that. There may be a rush for food at particular times causing additional hazards at food outlets.

It is essential to try to think of all these problems in advance. Running through the event in your imagination is one way of trying to spot every hazard that could occur in particular places at particular times.

Risk assessment

Evaluating health and safety hazards is about spotting potential dangers then taking steps to prevent damage or injury. This is desirable in any situation. In many situations, it is a strict legal requirement.

The safety officer explains some of the employers' responsibilities:

66 Where employers are involved in putting on events, they have a legal duty under the Health and Safety at Work Act 1974 to look after the safety of their employees and anybody else affected by their work practices. Since 1993, employers' legal responsibilities include the duty to carry out risk assessments. This was laid down in the Management of Health and Safety at Work Regulations 1992. **99**

A risk assessment should:

- identify the significant risks that might possibly arise because of the work activity
- enable the employer to identify and prioritise measures needed to follow the legislation
- be appropriate to the nature of the work and remain valid for a reasonable period of time.

ACTIVITY

Look back at the list of hazards you drew up in Section 7.2.1 for the Summer Extravaganza. Think about at each one in terms of probability and severity. Decide if they are low, medium or high. Which hazards would you need to pay most attention to?

Produce a summary of your findings, noting:

- which of the hazards present the greatest risk and will need particular attention
- why you think they are the highest priorities.

Measures to ensure health and safety

When the planning team has evaluated the potential and actual hazards, the next job for them is to plan measures that can help reduce or get rid of the risks.

Risk reduction

How can risks be reduced? Read the list of health and safety measures drawn up by the planning team for the Summer Extravaganza to meet the hazards they identified and evaluated earlier.

Examples of emergency actions:

■ drawing up evacuation procedures

■ calling the emergency services

■ having first-aid staff and equipment

■ ensuring access for emergency service vehicles

■ having fire extinguishers

☀ SUMMER EXTRAVAGANZA

- Fence off stallholders' parking area behind the stalls and place restrictions on when cars can be driven in and out of the area – no driving allowed during the hours of the event.
- Keep electric cabling for the PA system, disco tent and other areas covered or hidden and kept off public walkways.
- Site the generators away from areas where the public will be walking and fence them off.
- Put up notices saying the lake is strictly out of bounds and erect some sort of temporary fencing around it.
- Make trolleys available for lifting and transporting heavy equipment – trestle tables, chairs, crates, kegs, etc.
- Arrange adequate waste-disposal facilities.
- Insist that the company supplying toilet facilities should inspect and clean them regularly during the day.
- Arrange for the site to be cleared safely, with supervision.
- Serve drinks in plastic glasses only, and provide additional litter bins in the bar tent area.
- Set acceptable noise levels in the disco before the event takes place.

Emergency actions

As well as putting a lot of thought into reducing or eliminating risks, a planning team also has to think about how they will respond to emergencies if they do arise.

Realistic measures

All the measures suggested by the planning team were realistic in terms of:

- the people available to carry them out
- finance
- time
- materials.

As one of the team commented:

> 66 *It seems like a lot to do, but that's what happens when you choose a site like this for an event. We've got people on the planning team who can deal with most things. One's a skilled electrician, so he'll be in charge of setting up the equipment. Another works for the council parks department and so she'll supervise erecting temporary fencing around the lake. Because it's a charity event the council has agreed to let us have fencing for nothing, and they'll also provide noticeboards. A friend of mine is a solicitor and she has agreed to check the wording of our contracts with the marquee people to make sure we are fully covered. It takes a lot of time, yes, but it will be worth it in the end.* 99

One of the problems of staging a large-scale event is the number of people involved:

- outside companies, such as people running the disco or the bar
- people delivering equipment
- helpers who will only be there on the day.

These people will not be involved in planning of the event. They may not be aware of the potential health and safety hazards, or know about any measures you want to implement.

Outside companies (or contractors) should be consulted about their activities. Only reputable contractors should be used and could be asked to provide evidence of a good health and safety record. Other useful evidence of their competence would be:

- a health and safety policy statement
- membership of a recognised professional body or trade association
- references from other organisations who have used them in the past.

Most health and safety measures depend on people to put them into action. Staffing has to be planned at an early stage. This means asking people to take on particular roles. It also means thinking about training and briefing them about all relevant aspects of health and safety.

ACTIVITY

List any health and safety training staff involved in the Summer Extravaganza might need.

Staff tasks

- stewarding and giving information
- controlling the numbers of people
- evacuation procedures – in case of fire, overcrowding or other emergencies
- first aid
- identifying hazardous chemicals and substances
- lifting heavy materials or equipment
- safe waste disposal
- security procedures

DISCUSSION POINT

Look back at the health and safety measures you suggested for the Summer Extravaganza. Are they realistic in terms of people, finance, time and materials?

Legal and regulatory requirements

What's needed to make health and safety measures effective?

- Common sense – things like siting the children's area well away from the lake and the gate leading to the main road.
- Experience – it's best to include people on the planning team who have put on events before and will have learned from the experience.
- Money – health and safety measures can be expensive, but if they are essential, the money must be found; if they are too expensive, the event should be cancelled, rather than put people at unnecessary risk.
- Laws and regulations – most events are governed by restrictions of one sort or another.

Obligatory regulations

- national (UK) laws – such as the Health and Safety at Work Act
- EU laws – many of the health and safety regulations recently introduced, such as the Provision and Use of Work Equipment Regulations 1992, come from European Union directives
- local laws – bylaws are regulations imposed by local authorities and often place restrictions on use of public land

Voluntary regulations

- agreed rules and regulations of organisations putting on events
- recommended codes of practice – from professional bodies
- advice and guidance from reputable sources – St John's Ambulance for first aid, local authority environmental health officers for noise levels

Legal requirements

Laws and regulations can be obligatory or voluntary.

Laws and regulations that apply to an event may be related to:

- the activities the event involves – music events may need special licences, events involving the preparation and serving of food may be subject to food hygiene regulations
- the facility – guidelines relating to maximum numbers of people in the facility, fire regulations, insurance (both buildings and public liability)
- customers – their health and safety is protected by the Health and Safety at Work Act 1974 (HSWA), and their rights are protected by consumer rights legislation
- staff running the event – employees will be subject to the provisions of the HSWA.

Licences may be needed for some aspects of the event, such as:

- the sale of alcohol
- sale of food and other goods
- provision of entertainment.

Formal permission from the owner of the land or facility may also be needed to put on certain types of event. When a licence or permission is given, it is usually on the basis that the organisers will obey any regulations laid down by the licensing authority or person giving permission. For example:

- time limits imposed on the sale of alcohol
- noise levels
- start and finish times
- using specially trained staff.

DISCUSSION POINT

Here are three other facts about the Summer Extravaganza:

■ the land on which the extravaganza is being held is part of the local hall, which is owned and run by the local authority

■ all health and safety stewards and security officers are employees of the local authority

■ the drinks tent will be serving alcohol.

What implications do these facts have in terms of the laws and regulations that the planning team need to consider?

Section 7.2.5

Implement health and safety proposals

Having drawn up their health and safety proposals, the planning team will have to ensure they are all implemented. This means deciding:

■ who does what
■ when they do it
■ how they do it
■ how they will check that things have been done.

The team leader explains how they've approached this:

66 *We've allocated responsibility for an area of health and safety to individual team members. They all take action for their own area but they also keep each other informed. I coordinate what is done to make sure there aren't any conflicting issues or overlooked areas.* 99

ACTIVITY

Pick one aspect of the health and safety measures planned for by the planning team and devise a checklist they could use to make sure the measures were implemented.

Section 7.2.6

Sources of help, information and guidance

Planning health and safety measures takes experience. It also takes knowledge, particularly about what laws and regulations may affect aspects of the event. No one is likely to have all this information immediately to hand. It's much more likely that people planning health and safety for events will get expert help, information and guidance from other sources.

Sources

- the Health and Safety Executive
- other government agencies or departments
- the local authority
- safety committees
- professional bodies
- employers' codes of practice
- the Fire Service or Police
- company safety officers
- published sources of information

They can provide:

- important information about rules and regulations
- contact names of useful organisations experienced in staging events
- useful hints and tips about aspects of an event.

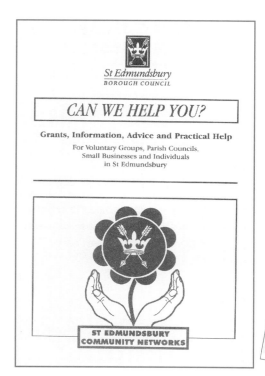

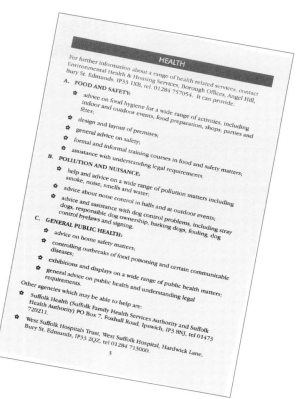

Key questions

1 What is meant by:
   – a current hazard?
   – a potential hazard?
   Give an example of each.
2 What does a risk assessment aim to establish?
3 What steps would you take to reduce or eliminate these risks:
   – accidents and injuries in a visitors' carpark?
   – overcrowding or long queues for the star attraction?
   – children getting separated from their accompanying adults?
4 What areas do licences cover?
5 What are the potential safety hazards of an outdoor event such as a fireworks display?
6 What aspects of an event are covered by health and safety laws and regulations?
7 Where can you get expert help, information and advice on health and safety measures for a leisure and tourism event?

Assignment

You could do this assignment in conjunction with the one in element 7.3 and your work in unit 8.

Plan a set of comprehensive health and safety proposals for the event you are involved in. Your plans should include:

■ measures aimed both at reducing risks and dealing with emergencies
■ details of staffing levels, training and briefing
■ steps to be taken to ensure the health and safety of:
   – customers
   – staff
■ an indication of how you reached your decisions, based on judging what was realistic in the situation
■ the laws and regulations which influenced your planning, and how they affected the measures you agreed
■ notes on which sources of information you used.

When you come to implement your proposals in the event itself, keep detailed notes on:

■ how you identified health and safety hazards and what they were
■ any evaluation you made of them and how it affected your decisions
■ who did what, how and when
■ how successful your measures were.

Your notes could be in the form of:

■ notes and recordings of meetings
■ logs
■ schedules
■ briefing sheets
■ action plans and records
■ checklists
■ written reports.

ELEMENT **7.3**

Security at leisure and tourism events

Safeguarding people's security at an event is just as important as safeguarding their health and safety. Organisers should plan the security of the event carefully and anticipate any problems that might arise – theft, the risk of violence, damage to property and so on. In this element you will be investigating the potential security risks at a leisure and tourism event and describing the measures taken to reduce the risks.

❝ We have to ensure that all the people working with us, even for a very short time, have been checked by the police. We also look for first-aid qualifications when selecting staff. ❞

community play officer in a city council

❝ I get advice from the police about security aspects of the event. There's never been any violence, thank heavens, but there's always a risk of stealing when there are so many people around. The biggest risk is theft from cars so now we hire a security firm to patrol the car enclosure throughout the day. It's not something I want any of our volunteers to do – the presence of a uniformed security guard is a good deterrent. ❞

owner of a riding school which also provides holidays

❝ The main security risk is leaving expensive equipment on site overnight. Fortunately most of it is heavy and bulky and it would be difficult for anyone to take it away without being observed. Smaller items of equipment, such as the lighting control system, are dismantled and stored in a locked room. One year a small amount of damage was done to the stage fittings but it hasn't happened again. But short of putting on an overnight guard, there's not a lot we can do to stop people getting on the stage. ❞

manager of a theatre group

Identifying security hazards

When people attend an event, they expect it to be free from danger or risk, either from health and safety hazards or from breaches in security. They assume that organisers will have taken steps to make sure that the event is safe and secure.

As with health and safety, security poses hazards of many different kinds.

Theft

Anything that has value can be stolen:

- obvious items such as cash, cheque books and credit cards
- valuable stock, equipment and property
- information – if a computer containing the only copy of a customer database is stolen, that can have a big effect on the organisation communicating with its customers in the future (of course, no organisation should have only one copy of a valuable database).

Fraud

Fraud is a kind of theft committed by people working for an organisation. Fraud can be disguised by passing the theft off as a legal transaction or by altering the records. It is sometimes difficult to detect as it is committed by people who have certain powers and are trusted by other members of the organisations to use those powers properly.

Sabotage

There are various reasons why someone might deliberately try to spoil an event:

- a competitor may want to harm a rival's success
- former employees may hold a grudge against the organisation which sacked them
- an individual may have a personal reason for wanting to spoil an event, such as hatred of someone involved in organising it
- a political group may want to stage a protest against some aspect of the event – for example, animal rights activists may try to sabotage a fashion show that includes products made of animal fur.

Sabotage can be committed in various ways:

- intruders destroy vital pieces of equipment or wreck the premises
- animal rights protesters set up a loudspeaker playing the screams of dying animals outside the hall where the fashion show is about to take place
- a competitor tries to disrupt an event by placing advertisements in the paper saying it has been cancelled.

Damage

Damage to equipment or premises can be a major problem affecting the success of an event. It may be accidental, such as a car running over the

Fraud Office to kill off Leeson suit

Number is up for lottery fraudster

Fight promoter on Lloyd's fraud charge

©The Daily Telegraph plc, London, 1995

393

marquee guy-ropes, or it may be deliberate. Organisers of events have to protect against both. Where damage is serious and deliberate, it can lead to prosecution for criminal damage.

Violence

Some events may run a relatively high risk of violence. Many violent incidents in public places are connected with abuse of alcohol. If an event includes the sale of drink, then the organisers will need to look into the risk of trouble from people getting drunk.

Many violent incidents are wholly unpredictable – an argument between two stallholders could get out of hand and result in a fight. The organisers could not predict that, but they can plan measures to deal with it, by making sure there is someone in charge of emergencies.

Evaluating security hazards

Many security problems are relatively minor – a disagreement between two stallholders shouldn't involve anyone else and can be quickly sorted out. But serious security incidents can ruin an event. If vandals destroy essential equipment or damage carefully prepared premises, the event may have to be cancelled.

In planning what measures to take, organisers of events need to look into:
- how likely a security hazard is to occur
- what form any resulting loss or damage may take
- how serious the loss or damage might be.

Some security hazards are more likely than others. Vandalism and theft – including pickpocketing – are more common than sabotage or serious violence. Some people will try to avoid paying the entrance fee to an event. If entrances are left open and unattended, people will feel free to walk in.

Organisers should pay most attention to hazards that are both likely to occur and could cause a high level of serious damage.

Aspects of an event

As with health and safety hazards, many security hazards are connected directly with aspects of the events. For example:
- The main activity of the event is likely to present special security problems. If a famous person is performing at or attending an event, special measures will be needed to look after the celebrity's personal security. That may also be the moment when pickpockets or thieves strike.
- The security of customers or other people attending is most important.
- Organisers must also look after the security of their staff or helpers. They may be in vulnerable positions – a steward at the door may have to deal with people trying to get in without paying, bar staff may be faced with abusive or drunken customers. Careful thought must be given to supporting them.
- Many security hazards result from timings and movements. As with health and safety, the start and end of events present particular problems. It is always harder to maintain security when large numbers of people are moving together in a large crowd.

ACTIVITY

Carry out an evaluation of the security hazards you identified in the last activity. Decide whether they have a low, medium or high probability and whether the severity of the damage is low, medium or high. Then note down what form the loss or damage is likely to take.

Produce a summary of your findings, noting which of the security hazards present the greatest risk and will need particular attention.

DISCUSSION POINT

At the Summer Extravaganza site, the team list some of the security hazards and evaluate their probability and severity:

	Probability	Form of loss or damage	Severity of loss or damage
■ vandals breaking in before the event and damaging stalls, equipment	medium	physical damage	possibly high
■ people trying to sneak into the event without paying the entrance fee	high	financial	medium
■ theft of items during the event	medium	loss of property	medium
■ proceeds being stolen by armed raiders as the event finishes	low	financial loss	high
■ fight breaking out in the beer tent	medium	damage to property, customers and reputation	low

Do you agree with their evaluation ?

Measures to ensure security

When the planning team has identified and evaluated security hazards, they should plan how to cope with them. Many of the measures will aim to reduce the risk from security hazards.

Risk reduction

Read how the planning team for the Summer Extravaganza decided to counter the security risks they identified.

SUMMER EXTRAVAGANZA

- engage security staff overnight to protect equipment set up the day before
- give passes to participants who need to come on to the site the day before to prepare it
- check security fences in the display and children's activity areas, and around the lake
- controlled spectator access via the car park only – put 'No entrance' signs along the perimeter wall
- make sure that enough stewards are on duty along the footpath leading from the car park
- advise all stallholders that they can store cash in the event office
- make sure all helpers know the procedures for lost children.

ACTIVITY

Take another look at the list of hazards you drew up for the event. What measures would you take to improve security? Note down your ideas.

Emergency actions

Planning also needs to focus on dealing with emergencies. It is impossible to predict when an emergency will happen and what form it will take. But it is possible to be prepared for situations such as:

- fire
- a major accident
- bomb threats
- outbreak of violence
- health emergencies such as fainting, heart attacks, sprained or broken limbs.

Any event needs to have someone responsible for planning and carrying out emergency procedures. Plans will need to be drawn up for evacuation of the site (or premises) in the event of a major emergency.

Security and staffing

Many different people are likely to have security roles. For some people it will be their major role – stewards, bouncers or staff employed to patrol events. These services can be bought in from professional security firms and may be essential for activities such as guarding premises overnight. Organisers have to

397

judge whether it is worth paying for this benefit. For some events it is essential, especially where large amounts of money or valuable items are involved.

For other staff, security will be just one part of a wider role – staff serving in a bar or at a stall who need to ensure the security of both stock and takings.

Both categories of staff will need careful training and briefing. All staff need to be clear about what they themselves would do if faced with a security problem. For example:

- How should bar staff tackle customers who start fighting?
- What should staff members do if they see a customer stealing something?
- What should stewards do if they see someone coming into an event illegally?

It is the duty of organisers and employers to make sure that staff and helpers are not put at risk – and don't put themselves at risk by entering into an explosive situation. Staff need to know specific procedures for dealing with such situations. They also need to know what the limits are to their roles.

Securing information

The success of many events depends on good information – financial, marketing or planning information. A database storing details of customers is a good example, as a marketing manager at a facility explains:

66 *We depend on our database to keep customers informed about events and activities. If it got lost or damaged, we wouldn't be able to continue with our normal business. We'd lose touch with customers and lose their confidence. Our database has taken years to develop. It would be a source of highly useful information to competitors. We take strict precautions to keep it safe and secure.* 99

Organisations that store information on computers must comply with the Data Protection Act 1984 (see Section 7.1.5). This places a duty on them to take particular care with information they hold about individuals. This includes not allowing it to be passed on to other organisations.

Realistic measures

Security measures, like health and safety measures, have to be realistic. Factors to consider include:

- people – find out whether staff and helpers have the necessary skills and whether enough people will be available
- finance – balance the cost of security measures against the level of security needed
- time – assess how much time can be devoted to planning and putting security measures into practice, given the demands of planning other aspects of the event and the event schedule
- materials – work out what materials are needed, are available and can be hired or bought, such as fenceposts and rope to create fences, or stationery for distributing information.

Achieving the ideal situation is not always possible. Compromises may be needed to ensure that organisers concentrate on what is essential.

Keeping information secure

- Make sure that at least one back-up copy of information exists.
- Make sure the back-up copy is stored in a completely different place from the original.
- Store copies of important data in fireproof safes.
- Store sensitive information on computers that can only be accessed through passwords.
- Don't leave offices or filing cabinets containing important information unlocked.
- Remember that the storage of computer-based information is governed by legal restrictions.

DISCUSSION POINT

Think about what roles staff at an event might have in ensuring security.

- Who would have important roles in this area.
- Would any additional staff be needed to carry out specific security roles?

Section 7.3.4	# Legal and regulatory requirements

Sections 7.1.5 and 7.2.4 looked in some detail at the different laws and regulations that might apply to different leisure and tourism events. These included both compulsory ones, such as those laid down by the Data Protection Act, and voluntary rules, such as those contained in codes of conduct or an organisation's own guidelines.

Section 7.3.5	# Implement security proposals

See the assignment at the end of the unit.

Section 7.3.6	# Sources of help, information and guidance

Section 7.2.5 listed a number of sources of help, information and guidance relating to health and safety. These same sources can also provide expert help about security matters, as well as useful contacts.

ACTIVITY

Look again at the database you created of people and organisations that can offer help, information and guidance about matters of health, safety and security. Are there any further areas where you may need sources of information, for example about professional security firms?

Update your database to include any new sources of information you can think of. Again, include contact names, addresses and telephone numbers, wherever possible.

Key questions

1 What are the five common security hazards? Give examples of incidents for each at an event such as a fireworks display.

2 What are the security considerations for:
   - event activities?
   - the facility?
   - staff?
   - customers?
   Give brief descriptions for each.

3 How can a leisure and tourism organisation keep its information secure?

4 Some of your friends are in a band and have been booked to play in a few local pubs. What advice would you give them to help them keep their equipment secure when they're travelling to, setting up for and performing at gigs?

5 What factors would you consider when checking that planned security measures were realistic?

6 How would you ensure that all staff involved in security for an event:
   - knew what their responsibilities were?
   - took them seriously?

Assignment

You could do this assignment in conjunction with the one in element 7.2 and your work in unit 8.

Plan a set of comprehensive security proposals for the event you are involved in. Your plans should include:
- measures aimed both at reducing risks and dealing with emergencies
- details of staffing levels, training and briefing
- steps to be taken to ensure the security of premises, property and information
- an indication of how you reached your decisions, based on judging what was realistic in the situation
- the laws and regulations which influenced your planning, and how they affected the measures you agreed
- notes on which sources of information you used.

When you come to implement your proposals in the event itself, keep detailed notes on:
- how you identified security hazards and what they were
- any evaluation you made of them and how it affected your decisions
- who did what, how and when
- how successful your measures were.

Your notes could be in the form of:
- notes and recordings of meetings
- logs
- schedules
- briefing sheets
- action plans and records
- checklists
- written reports.

UNIT **8**

Event management

Element 8.1

Proposing options and selecting an event

Element 8.2

Planning as a team

Element 8.3

Running an event

Element 8.4

Evaluating an event

ELEMENT **8.1**

Proposing options and selecting an event

What is an event? In leisure and tourism, it could be anything from a village fête to a national programme of celebrations, e.g. for the Millennium. In this element you'll be looking at the reasons for running events and the different forms events can take. You'll be investigating the resources needed to plan for and run events, working out the costs and anticipating any problems that might occur. Events normally have a planning team which meets regularly before the event and is responsible for making sure that it runs smoothly and meets the organisation's objectives. You'll be looking closely at how teams like this decide on what events to run.

66 As far as running special events goes, we don't have many. But we run open evenings at Christmas during late-night shopping where we stay open later than usual and give people a glass of mulled wine. It doesn't take much work and everybody feels it's a good way of building up goodwill with the public. 99

manager of a tourist information centre

66 I'm quite wary of running special events – they take so much time and energy to organise. The main one we do is the annual gymkhana, which is a big thing for us both in terms of the amount of organisation it takes and the benefits we get. It's our way of saying to riding people in the area 'Here we are, come and have a look at us.' We always get a lot of enquiries and bookings in the weeks after the show. 99

owner of a riding school which also provides holidays

Characteristics of an event

What do all these have in common?

The answer is that they are all leisure and tourism events, with distinctive characteristics:

- They are seen as something special by the people who organise and attend them.
- They have a starting point.
- They have a finishing point.
- They have fixed deadlines.
- They usually involve extra work for the people who run them.
- They need coordination.
- They need special resources to run smoothly.

An event as something special

Events are seen as something special:

- by the people that organise them – they take place outside the normal run of activities of an organisation, group or individual and need special planning
- by the people who go to them, who usually have to make special arrangements to attend.

An **event** is something that happens, especially something of importance.

DISCUSSION POINT

Look at the promotional material for events above. Are they all seen as something special? Who by? Which appeals most to you?

Starting points and finishing points

Events always have a specific starting time. This is decided at an early planning stage, so it can be included on advertisements and people know when to arrive. Most events also have a finishing time, so that organisers know how long they need to book resources for.

The organiser of a village fête explains why an event needs a starting point and finishing point:

66 *One of the first things we decided when planning the fête was when it should take place, and what time it should start. Once we had a starting time, we booked a celebrity to open it and got posters printed advertising the event. We also decided what time the fête should be winding down, so that we knew how long we needed resources like the bouncy castle and pony rides.* 99

Fixed deadlines

Events always take place within fixed deadlines – a certain period of time decided well in advance. Fixing a date is an important early step in planning and advertising an event. Many leisure and tourism events take place regularly and their deadlines are already decided by people's expectations. For example:

- a village always runs its Easter Fair on the Saturday before Easter
- the Edinburgh Festival takes place every August
- the Olympic Games take place at the end of the summer, every four years.

As an addition to other work

Event organisation is usually an additional part of people's work – they carry it out as an extra responsibility rather than as an everyday part of their job. A catering assistant explains the extra work involved in running a Christmas party for local children:

66 *We were told about the children's party well in advance, and spent a lot of time planning to make sure the event was really special. We held weekly meetings after work, when we decided on entertainment, menus, how many children to invite and who should carry out different tasks. The party itself took place on a Sunday afternoon when the restaurant is usually shut. I'd say in total that I spent an extra 20 hours organising and running the party. But it was worth it, because the event was a special occasion for the children.* 99

Why do pantomimes have fixed deadlines?

What could go wrong if this event hasn't been properly coordinated?

Coordinating

All events need careful coordination if they are to run smoothly. Teams planning events need to coordinate:

- planning before the event to make sure everything is ready in plenty of time
- promotional activities
- timings on the day
- resources for the event (people, equipment, etc.)
- money for the event to make sure it doesn't go over budget.

To do this, the team has to communicate well and have a good overview of planning and running the event. Most teams appoint a team leader or coordinator who takes overall responsibility for making sure the event is well organised.

Allocating resources

Every event is different and requires special allocation of resources to ensure it runs smoothly. These resources include:

- money – a budget which covers the cost of the event
- materials – leaflets, posters, programmes, etc.
- equipment – sound system, catering equipment, etc.
- premises – a venue for the event
- people – staff with the skills and time to plan and run the event.

Often these are specialist resources which are in demand and need to be booked well in advance. For example, many people organise wedding receptions over a year in advance to make sure that they can book the venue, entertainment and photographer they want.

ACTIVITY

Choose a local leisure and tourism organisation that you are interested in or have experience of, perhaps through a work placement or a part-time job. Find out:

- what events it has organised in the past
- what events it is planning for the future.

List the distinctive characteristics of each event. Can you think of other events the organisation runs?

DISCUSSION POINT

Read through the descriptions of these three events organised by leisure and tourism organisations. What distinctive characteristics of an event does each have?

- Your local theatre decides to hold a public launch of its Christmas pantomime in a nearby shopping centre, with several of the stars attending, plus a music roadshow put on by the local radio station.

- A national chain of travel agents holds a promotional evening at every branch to coincide with its merger with another firm of travel agents. The evening includes a free buffet and wine, prize draws and discounts on holidays for people attending.

- A stately home holds a special activities day with attractions such as period dancing in costume, a vintage car rally, children's entertainment and Elizabethan cookery lessons.

Objectives of an event

Common objectives of leisure and tourism events

- to increase profitability
- to increase take-up of products and services
- to heighten interest in products and services
- to promote the organisation, its products or services
- to create a favourable image for the organisation, its products or services
- to help bring the organisation together
- to bring benefits to a community

Putting on an event can be time-consuming and costly in terms of money, resources and staff. Because of this, organisations staging events need to be clear exactly what they are trying to achieve – their objectives.

Increasing profitability

Most leisure and tourism organisations are private-sector companies which have the overall aim of making a profit. Because of this, the main objective of many leisure and tourism events is to increase the profitability of the organisation staging it by:

- bringing in extra money through entrance charges and sales of products or services at the event
- attracting new customers who will spend more money in the future.

The manager of a theatre explains:

66 *As a commercial business, we have to make a profit, and special events can help us do this. For example, we recently ran a gala performance with celebrity acts, good food and drink – and expensive tickets. As well as making a good profit on ticket sales, it attracted a new crowd of people to the theatre. They picked up our programme for the season, and many booked tickets for forthcoming events, helping to increase our profit even more.* 99

Increasing take-up

As the theatre manager explained, increasing profitability is closely linked to customer take-up – the number of people who use a facility.

To increase take-up, organisations need to think of ways to attract new customers. Events can be a good way to do this:

- Gyms and sports clubs often hold open days when people can come and try out facilities. If they are impressed by what they see and do, they will join.
- Hotels organise special weekend events, such as sporting and health breaks, to attract guests who wouldn't usually stay.
- Nightclubs run themed nights, such as 70s and 80s nights, to attract a different range of customers to the club.

DISCUSSION POINT

Suggest events for the following organisations to run:

- a museum that wants to raise interest in its summer workshops for children
- a travel agent that wants to raise interest in its new range of adventure holidays in exotic locations
- a basketball club that wants to raise interest in its family membership scheme for the next season.

DISCUSSION POINT

Have you ever been to a leisure and tourism event that you think was organised with the aim of increasing customer take-up? Did it work? Did you become a regular customer?

Raising interest in products and services

Organisations often run events with the aim of raising interest among the general public – particularly when they have new products and services to offer. For example:

- A sports centre holds an open day for local people, when they can use the new swimming pool free of charge.

- A resort representative organises a cocktail party for newly-arrived holidaymakers to raise interest in the excursions available.
- A pub which is launching a new bar menu organises a 'two for the price of one week' when customers get half-price meals.

Promotion

Events can play an important part in promotion and are often included in an organisation's overall marketing strategy.

The marketing manager of a Victorian living museum explains:

❝ *We carry out regular promotional activities in order to maintain public interest in the museum, including placing advertisements in local and national newspapers, sending direct mailshots to schools, and issuing press releases. But every now and then we decide we need to do something really special, and organise a major event. The aim is to make it as attention-grabbing as possible, and to tie it in with whatever promotional campaign we're currently running. So last year, to tie in with an exhibition, we organised a Victorian Christmas festival in the town. This year we are focusing on the theme of Victorian children, and are organising a performance of Nicholas Nickleby at the theatre, using children from local schools.* ❞

What type of event could an organisation run to help promote this product?

Creating a favourable image

Events can help leisure and tourism organisations to create a good image among the general public if they:

- are well organised
- give people something they want (e.g. free activities, products and services)
- benefit the community (e.g. raising funds or supporting local groups)
- strengthen their overall image (e.g. a sports centre running a health-related event or a children's theatre running a charity event for children).

Organisations are particularly keen to create a favourable image when they:

- are new
- are launching a new product or service
- have received bad publicity.

ACTIVITY

Make a list of different events each of the following organisations could run to help create a favourable image. Make sure that the events you suggest fit in with the organisations' overall aims, image and target audience:

- a Mexican restaurant opening in a large town
- an out-of-town sports centre launching new summer courses for children
- a company running holidays for the under-25s that has been criticised in the media for its 'sun, sex and sangria' approach to advertising.

Unifying the organisation

Most of the objectives of leisure and tourism events are linked to customers – raising the profile of products and services, presenting a good image to the public and promoting sales. But planning and staging an event can also achieve objectives within the organisation itself, giving staff:

■ an opportunity to work together to achieve challenging goals and to develop their teamwork skills

■ a clearer vision of the organisation and what it hopes to achieve

■ the opportunity to enjoy working in a different and stimulating environment.

All of these can combine to improve staff efficiency, motivation and teamwork.

A receptionist at a swimming pool describes her experience when they held a swimming marathon to raise money for a local hospice:

66 *We were all involved in some way in arranging and running the event. I was working closely with people I don't usually work with and I really enjoyed it. I feel I know my colleagues much better now. As part of the event, the three directors agreed to be thrown into the pool if staff pledged £5 each. We all did and in they went! I used to be a bit scared of them but having seen them join in with the fun and the hard work, I feel more at ease with them now.* 99

Providing benefits to a community

The main aim of some leisure and tourism events is to bring benefits to a community, rather than to promote an organisation and its products or services. For example, an organisation might aim to:

■ support community initiatives and activities by running events for youth groups, children, elderly people, and so on

■ stage events which raise funds for charities or organisations in the community.

Profit-making leisure and tourism organisations often stage events to raise funds for charity, with the secondary aim of creating a positive image of the company caring about community issues. In this way, as well as helping people, they attract new customers to the facility. Events like these still benefit the community, but they are also public-relations exercises for the organisation.

CASE STUDY

After a year of building – with all the disruption of dust, dirt, lorries and noise – a new holiday centre was about to open in a seaside town. To thank local residents for their patience during building work, the centre's management decided to stage an event for the community. They set up an event team, and the first thing it did was talk about what they wanted the event to achieve. They listed these as the main objectives:

- To benefit the community – we'll offer them a free event to compensate for the disruption of building.

- To create a favourable image of the organisation – it will be helpful in the long term if local people are on our side.

- To promote our organisation, products and services – local people will be encouraged to use the centre for weddings, parties, etc.

- To increase profitability – if local people know about and use our centre for events, it will increase our profitability.

- To unify our centre team – we'll organise the free event for before our official opening, and it can act as a trial run to make sure our team works well together.

THE SEA

THE BEACH

POOL

BEACH FRONT UNITS

PANORAMA RESTAURANT

PLAY AREA

LEISURE COMPLEX

RESIDENTS' PARKING

RECEPTION AREA

WOODLAND UNITS

ACTIVITY

Most of your work for this unit will involve planning and running an event with the rest of your GNVQ Leisure and Tourism team. Hold an initial planning meeting and talk about what you want to achieve through your event. Look through the different objectives explained in this section, then:

- decide what your aims are going to be

- list your objectives in order of importance (you will probably have more than three)

- keep a record of the objectives so you can refer to them as you plan, run and then evaluate your event.

Proposing options for an event

Once an organisation has decided the objectives of an event, it can start thinking about what event to stage and what sort of products, services and activities it could involve.

The manager of an Italian restaurant was worried by a post-Christmas slump in bookings, and decided that what was needed was an event to renew interest in the restaurant and to cheer everyone up. Here she explains how she came up with different ideas for an event with her team of staff.

66 *It was clear that unless we organised something to snap everyone – including us! – out of our January apathy things weren't going to pick up until Easter. As a team, we decided that our main objectives were:*

1 *to renew interest in our products and services*
2 *create a favourable image of the restaurant in the community*
3 *increase profitability over the next couple of months*
4 *bring our staff together by giving us something to work towards in the quiet times.*

Together, we brainstormed possible ideas for events – I encouraged the team to be as original as possible! The following list is just some of the ideas we came up with. 99

- a Mediterranean-summer-in-February party
- an opera and eating night
- a spaghetti-eating competition
- a series of speciality evenings – food from different regions of Italy, pizza evenings, ice-cream evenings, etc.
- a competition with a holiday to Italy as a prize
- two-for-the-price-of-one evenings for people who come in fancy dress
- a five-a-side football competition: Italy v England

ACTIVITY

What options are there for your GNVQ team event?

In your event planning team, hold a brainstorming session to come up with a list of options for your event. Write down everything that occurs to you, however difficult or outrageous it may seem. Try to think of a range of possibilities which include products, services and activities.

Talk through the different options and start crossing out ideas which you don't think would work. Use the following points as a checklist.

Your event should:

- ☐ meet your objectives (look back at the list you made for the activity on page 409)
- ☐ be big enough to involve the whole team in planning and running it, but not so big that it would take up all your time
- ☐ be aimed at people from outside your school or college; these could include prospective students and their parents but not current parents, governors, staff and students
- ☐ focus on leisure and tourism products, services or activities

- ☐ be attended voluntarily by participants and spectators – you have to make it interesting and appealing so that people want to come
- ☐ take place in three to four months' time
- ☐ need proper planning in advance
- ☐ allow each team member a high level of responsibility – for setting objectives, planning how to meet them, and evaluating how well the event went
- ☐ have a budget (e.g. £300). You may have to find extra money by fundraising or sponsorship.

From your original list, choose three options which meet all of these criteria.

Estimating resources needed

What resources are needed for an event?

- budget (money for staging the event)

- materials (e.g. stationery, posters)

- equipment (e.g. transport, computers)

- premises (a venue for the event)

- staff (with the skills and time to help out)

One of the major steps in planning an event is organising resources. Ideas can be as original and daring as possible. But before putting an idea into practice, an organisation has to estimate the resources needed and make sure it is a realistic option. Without the right resources, the event will fail.

Budget

All events need some money to finance them – a budget. Event budgets vary enormously depending on the size of the event:

- a tea-party for 20 children may have a budget of £75 for buying food, drink, balloons and prizes for games

- the Football World Cup is a multi-million-pound operation, involving sponsorship and television deals as well as different countries investing large amounts of money in participating and staging the event.

Whether the budget for an event is large or small, the planning team needs to work out:

- how much money is needed

- where this money will come from

- where it will be spent.

The manager of a day centre which organises occasional trips for elderly people explains the importance of estimating budget at an early stage.

66 *We don't have a lot of money as an organisation, but we like to arrange special events for the elderly people every now and then. Budget is the most important consideration from the start. We decide what event we'd like to organise – for example a coach trip to Brighton – and then estimate how much it will cost in total. Our budget for the event comes from organising raffles, bingo and bring-and-buy sales. Often we try to get help from other organisations. Last year the coach company we use offered free use of a coach and driver for a day, and a trip to the pantomime was subsidised by our local theatre.* 99

DISCUSSION POINT

What types of financial support might leisure and tourism organisations be able to get for events?

Materials and equipment

Almost all leisure and tourism events need:

- materials – e.g. posters, leaflets, stationery, menus

- equipment – e.g. sports equipment, lighting, seating.

Planning teams should estimate the materials and equipment needed for an event at an early stage so that they can:

- find, borrow and hire equipment

- get materials produced, printed and distributed (this can take several weeks).

411

Estimating resources also enables teams to work out whether an idea for an event is feasible. For example, if a team needs a marquee for 500 people and finds out there are no large marquees available on the date of the event then plans will have to change.

ACTIVITY

Estimate the materials and equipment needed for each of the following events:

■ a Christmas party for 100 infant-school children, to be held in a school hall

■ a sponsored swim for charity

■ a conference for 50 delegates from the hotel industry.

Choose one of the events to look at in more detail. Write a breakdown of what materials and equipment you would need, and where you could get them from. With a large enough budget, do you think it would be feasible for your GNVQ event team to run the event?

ACTIVITY

People are already planning events to celebrate the start of the 21st century – many of the major hotels and party venues in cities such as London, New York and Sydney are already fully booked for New Year celebrations.

If you wanted to hold a large party to celebrate the start of the next century, where would you hold it? The venue should be:

■ an easy drive from where you live

■ have space for 150 people to eat, drink and dance.

Make a list of possible venues – try to be as original as you can. What would be the advantages and disadvantages of each premises?

Premises

Leisure and tourism events all need premises – a venue – of some kind:

■ a football tournament needs football pitches, spectator areas and changing rooms

■ a party needs a room or space large enough to hold the number of people invited

■ a sailing competition needs a clubhouse, cordoned off area of water, and viewing space for spectators.

Is this the right venue for this event?

Often premises are in demand and need to be booked well in advance. When working out the type of premises they need, organisations need to consider:

■ how many people will be attending the event

■ what type of activities will be taking place

■ what facilities are needed (e.g. a bar, food preparation area, dance floor)

■ whether there is disabled access

■ how far people will travel to attend the event

■ how much money it costs to hire different venues.

Staff

People are probably the most important resource for any leisure and tourism event. Teams planning an event need to estimate at an early stage:

■ how many people they need to stage and plan the event

■ how much time people will need to devote to the event

- what skills people need (e.g. first aid, catering, sports coaching, organisational skills, teamwork skills)
- whether enough staff will be available to plan and run the event.

As a GNVQ team organising a children's party found out, you can't cut corners when it comes to staff:

66 *Although we planned the party quite carefully, booking a hall, buying food, sending out invitations and organising games well in advance, we didn't really think about who would do what and what skills we needed. On the day we just divided up the jobs. The result was that the sandwiches were a disaster, the children ran around completely out of control, and no one was on hand with first-aid skills when a little girl cut her knee. And two of the helpers had to leave half-way through the party because we hadn't made it clear how long we needed them for. All in all, we learnt the importance of planning staff resources carefully.* 99

A Women's Institute group wanted to organise a 'Caring at Christmas' event to bring benefits to the local community at Christmas time. One of the options it was considering was a series of outings for people with special needs.

It worked out that it would need the following resources:

Budget:	We estimate that we need £900 for the outings. We've already collected £600 from fund-raising events, so we need to raise an extra £300 through sponsorship and more fundraising.
Equipment:	We need specially adapted transport and access to a computer/printer. We can use the computer/printer at the community centre. We've contacted a local day centre for disabled people, and they've promised to help us out with transport.
Materials:	We need office supplies and stationery for writing to people about the event
Premises:	We need a base room for team meetings, and have been promised open access to an office at the community centre. Outings will include the theatre, cinema, shops and a restaurant. We've contacted all, and found out that there won't be a problem with numbers or disabled access.
Staff:	We have enough volunteers from the Institute for our basic needs. Two members of the team have first-aid training, and three have dealt with people with disabilities before. Outings will mainly take place during evenings and weekends, and we've warned people about putting by time. Helpers from the community centre and local care centres have offered to provide the specialist care skills we need. We've planned a rota, and there seem to be plenty of staff available.

Having estimated resources, we think the outings would be a feasible option.

ACTIVITY

As a team, think about the different resources you would need to run the three possible options for your event. Although at this stage you can only make an estimate, you should be able to judge whether an event would:

- demand far too much in terms of resources, and therefore isn't a feasible option
- demand very little in terms of resources, and probably wouldn't be challenging enough
- place resource demands which are feasible but challenging – the best option.

You may find it helpful to produce a chart for each event, listing:

- budget
- equipment
- materials
- premises
- staff.

It will become clear from your charts whether or not it is sensible to take each idea further.

Estimating costs and benefits

Every event involves costs and benefits for:

■ the customers attending it

■ the organisation running it

■ the facility where it is staged.

Teams organising an event need to weigh these costs against benefits from an early planning stage.

Costs and benefits for external customers

Customers need to feel that the cost of attending or taking part in an event doesn't outweigh the benefits gained or they will feel dissatisfied and won't support future events.

Possible costs to customers include:	Possible benefits to customers include:
■ entrance fees	■ enjoyment
■ time and money spent travelling to the event	■ health and fitness
■ time spent at the event	■ education
■ money spent on products and services at the event	■ special offers on products and services
■ threats to health and safety (e.g. food poisoning, sporting accidents).	■ finding out about products and services which will be useful to them in the future.

Costs and benefits for the facility

Before agreeing to stage an event, a facility needs to weigh up the possible costs and benefits. The manager of a community centre explains:

66 *We have to be quite careful about the events we hire our halls out for. Although we're there for the use of the community, sometimes there's too high a price to pay for helping people out. Recently we hired the main hall out for a youth club disco. They paid the hiring fee of £50 and arrived on time to set everything up. I left them to get on with it, and came in the next day to find the place had been wrecked. There were two broken windows, food and drink all over the floor and walls, a broken trestle table and complaints from local people about noise. I've billed them for the cost of cleaning and repairs, but I won't hire the hall to them again. It cost too much in terms of hassle and bad feeling in the area.* 99

Costs and benefits for the organisation

Organisations and facilities also need to know that costs won't outweigh benefits – whether or not these benefits are financial. Not all leisure and tourism events aim to make a profit, or even cover their costs. Sometimes an organisation is happy to pay large financial costs to stage an event in order to reap the benefits of creating a good community image or attracting new customers.

A sportswear shop is planning an Easter Extravaganza celebrity cricket match at the local leisure centre. The objective of the event is to support local charities and create a positive image for the organisation.

The event planning team worked out the costs and sent a memo to the managing director asking for approval:

MEMORANDUM

To: Wanda Speck, Managing Director
From: the Easter Extravaganza Team
Date: 24th January 1996

Easter Extravaganza – estimated costs

We have estimated the costs of the Easter Extravaganza as follows:

Premises	The event will be held at the leisure centre. As the event is for charity, they're offering the premises for free.	
	Cost for premises	nil
	Site preparation	£300
	Overnight security (4 guards, 12 hours @ £4 per hour)	£192
Staff	Staff will need to take part in planning meetings and may claim overtime.	
	(10 x 1-hour meetings, six staff @£8 per hour)	£560
	Donation to St John's Ambulance for attending	£250
	Staff training (first aid, crowd control)	£200
	Extra staff for marshalling the event (20 staff, 10 hours @ £4 per hour)	£800
	Celebrities are volunteering to play free of charge	
Promotion	Budget for posters, leaflets, press advertising	£600
Admin	Postage, photocopying, etc.	£100
Equipment	Specialist equipment hire (1 tractor and trailer)	£80
Miscellaneous	Transport, refreshments, etc.	£50

Look at the costs estimated by the sportswear company for its Easter Extravaganza.

- Are there any costs which the team has forgotten about?

- Can you think of ways it could save on costs?

- From the figures shown, what will be the total cost to the company of running the event?

It is aiming to make money for charity. If it charges £5 a ticket for watching the match:

- how many people would need to attend for the event to make a profit

- how much money would the company be able to donate to charity if 1000 people watched the event

- how many people would have to attend the event for its benefits to start outweighing its costs to the organisation?

Write a final paragraph to add to the memo to the managing director, explaining whether you think the benefits for the organisation of staging the event outweigh the costs.

ACTIVITY

In your GNVQ event planning team, weigh up the costs and benefits of the different options for your event. You may find it helpful to produce a chart for each option, listing the costs in one column and the benefits in another. Remember to include costs and benefits for:

- your team and school or college

- customers going to the event

- the facility where the event would be held.

The lists of resources you made for the activity at the end of section 8.1.4 will probably be helpful. Keep your cost and benefit charts to help you decide which event to choose.

Constraints which affect events

Constraints are limitations or problems which restrict what can be achieved.

Possible constraints

legal – licensing requirements for alcohol and entertainments, insurance regulations, use of premises for different purposes, trading regulations

health and safety – of staff, of customers, fire regulations, facility capacity, food preparation, hazard and risks, safety standards for equipment

security – people, property, information, money

resources – availability of staff, finances, materials, equipment

customers – how many will attend, who they are, how they will get to the event, how much money they have to spend, special needs (car-parking, disabled access and toilets, baby-changing facilities, etc.)

environmental – potential damage, potential dangers, noise, pollution

disruption to other activities – disturbance for near-by residents, disruption of everyday work activities

Organisations planning a leisure and tourism event have to bear in mind a range of constraints which might affect their success. A nightclub manager explains:

66 *Planning a one-off event, like a big party, can be a minefield. We have to bear in mind legal constraints on opening hours, the number of people allowed on the premises and extended licences for selling alcohol. We have to follow health and safety regulations in food preparation, toilet facilities, fire escapes. We have to make sure we're not going to cause environmental pollution by being too noisy too late at night and that there are enough security staff on duty. A party means that we have to close the normal club for a night, so we have to make sure that this isn't going to cause too much disruption and we can recoup lost costs through the party. And this is all before the practical arrangements for the event, like booking bands and DJs, getting invitations printed, promoting the event, and so on.* 99

When considering different options for an event, organisations need to ask:

■ What constraints are there on the event?
■ How might they affect the event's success?
■ How could they be overcome? If they can be overcome, how much will it cost in time, money and resources?

The box on the left describes some possible constraints on ideas for leisure and tourism events.

A team is organising a conference. The conference is set to start at 8.30 a.m. with breakfast and finish at 7.30 p.m. with an evening meal. The team has this information about the people attending the conference:

■ there will be 80 delegates
■ one uses a wheelchair
■ five are vegetarian
■ several will have to travel over 200 miles to attend the event.

What constraints does this information put on the event? How can the team make sure that the venue they book is suitable?

DISCUSSION POINT

A college is planning to book a band for an end-of-term party for 500 students. Think of:

■ two major legal constraints, that could mean abandoning the event
■ two minor legal constraints, that could be worked around if discovered at an early enough stage.

Useful contacts

- The Citizens Advice Bureau
- Local Office of Fair Trading
- Local authority Environmental Health Officer
- Local fire service Fire Officer
- St John's Ambulance

ACTIVITY

What constraints are there on the different options you are considering for your GNVQ team event?

Fill in a table like this for each option:

Constraints

Legal

_____

_____

Health and safety

_____

_____

Security

_____

_____

Resources

_____

_____

Customers

_____

_____

Environmental

_____

_____

Disruption to other activities

_____

_____

Carry out research to find out more about:

- the constraints on each option
- whether, and how, you could overcome them.

Elements 7.2 and 7.3 contain information that will help you in this activity.

417

Proposing an event

Before making the final decision on what leisure and tourism event to run, each team member may be given an opportunity to propose which event they think would be best. This means that although the final choice of event is a team decision, individuals within the team have a chance to express their opinions.

When putting forward a proposal for an event, a team member must be able to justify it in terms of:

- the team's objectives
- cost and benefit estimates
- the resources available
- constraints.

The Women's Institute group organising a Christmas event considered several different options. One of the event team felt quite strongly that outings for people with special needs would be an excellent way to show caring at Christmas – the aim of the event. Here is a summary of a short talk she gave to the rest of the team. To support what she was saying, she handed round a sheet listing the objectives of the event, resources needed, costs and benefits and constraints.

66 *At our first planning meeting we decided that the team's main objectives were to provide benefits to the community, to work well together as a team and to raise awareness of the Women's Institute. Running outings for people with special needs would achieve all these objectives. It would bring benefits to the community by giving people something to look forward to at Christmas-time. Planning and running a series of outings would be a complicated job, and pose a difficult but manageable and rewarding challenge. And helping people with special needs would make more people realise that the WI is a good organisation.*

We've estimated that the materials and equipment we'd need to run the event would include some things we've got easy access to, like stationery and computers, and some things it will be more challenging (but not impossible) to find, like specially adapted transport. Within the team we've got some first-aid skills and experience in dealing with people with special needs, but we'll have to develop more, which is another positive challenge. Financially, we've got a budget of £600, and have estimated that it will cost £900 to stage the outings. This means finding an extra £300 from sponsorship and fundraising.

Overall, the resources we need will be difficult to get together, but certainly not beyond our capabilities.

We would aim to stay within our budget when running the outings (£900 should be enough), so hopefully there won't be any direct financial costs. We will have to invest quite a lot of time at weekends and evenings, but the team seems happy that the benefits of helping the community would outweigh this cost.

We need to do some more research into constraints on the event. There shouldn't be problems with resources, disruption to other activities or environmental considerations. We do have to think about constraints on the customers – many of the people we take out will have physical disabilities, and we need to make sure they have access to buildings and toilet facilities. We also need to take into account a range of legal, health, safety and security regulations. We've carried out some research into these, which has shown that the outings we're planning are legal. But now we need to go into it in greater detail, to find out exactly what regulations we need to comply with. 99

ACTIVITY

Choose your favourite idea for the GNVQ team event and prepare a proposal to try to persuade the team that yours is the best option. Include in your proposal:

- an explanation of how the event would meet your team's objectives

- a list of resources required and where you could get them from

- an estimate of costs involved

- an explanation of how you think the event will benefit customers, the facility where it is held and your team

- an outline of any constraints you have identified which might affect the success of the event.

Present your proposal to your tutor and other members of the event team.

Selecting an event

Formal meetings:

- have a chairperson
- have a written agenda of what is to be discussed
- have a written record of what happened at the meeting (minutes)
- follow agreed procedures.

Event planning teams often work informally, getting together to talk about progress and to make day-to-day decisions. However, when important decisions need to be taken, teams hold formal meetings.

The chairperson's role

The chairperson:

- runs the meeting (e.g. makes sure that agenda items are followed in order and that the meeting starts on time)
- makes sure people keep to the point
- checks that everyone understands and agrees with what has been decided
- stops arguments or disagreements from dominating the meeting
- encourages everybody to contribute to the meeting, including those who are less confident.

DISCUSSION POINT

Look through the list of responsibilities above and talk about what type of person would make a good chairperson.

The administration role

It's useful to have a team member who takes responsibility for the administration work involved in setting up and having a meeting. This person is usually known as the secretary.

Administrative tasks include:

- letting people know when and where the meeting will be held
- booking and preparing the meeting place
- preparing and distributing the meeting's agenda
- taking minutes on what happens at the meeting
- writing up the minutes and distributing copies to the meeting members
- keeping a file of past agendas, minutes and any other information relevant to the meetings.

An **agenda** is a written list of items to be discussed at a meeting. It usually includes:

- standard items (for example, discussing and agreeing minutes from the last meeting, setting the date for the next meeting)
- special items which team members have asked to be included on the agenda (for example, progress with fundraising, a request for help with a particular task).

Minutes are a written summary of what happened at a meeting, based on notes taken during the meeting.

The agenda lets the team know in advance what will be discussed at the meeting so they have time to prepare any contributions they want to make.

Minutes ensure that the team is up to date on progress and has a record of decisions made at meetings.

A GNVQ team used a wordprocessor to produce this standard way of notifying team members of meetings and agendas. Each time a meeting was arranged, the secretary simply had to fill in the relevant details and change the agenda items.

NOTICE OF MEETING

A meeting of the GNVQ Advanced Leisure and Tourism Event Management Team
will be held on .... at .... in Room ....

Purpose: To consider feasible options for an event which will provide evidence for the
GNVQ Advanced Leisure and Tourism Mandatory Unit 8: Event management

AGENDA

    1 Appoint chairperson and secretary

    2 Agree procedures for meeting

    3 Discuss and agree event objectives

    4 Agree next stage in the planning process

    5 Any other business

    6 Date of next meeting

Note: Additional agenda items for the meeting should be submitted to ....
no later than..

Here are the minutes of their first meeting.

Minutes of the event team's planning meeting on 15 February 1996

1   Appointment of chairperson and secretary

Team members were asked to volunteer for the roles of chairperson and secretary. Kelly volunteered to be chairperson and Stephen volunteered to be secretary. There were no other volunteers and there were no objections to Kelly or Stephen so they were appointed accordingly.

2   Agreed procedures for meeting

We agreed that:

- the secretary would take responsibility for the administration tasks involved in setting up meetings and keeping records
- decisions would be made by voting – in the event of a tie or disagreement, the chairperson would have the final say.

3   Agreed event objectives

We agreed that our event would have the following objectives:

- to raise money for the town's Sue Ryder residential home and day-care centre
- to promote a positive image of the youth of today
- to raise awareness of the college's Leisure and Tourism department
- to raise the profile of the college.

We also discussed the objective of unifying college departments by inviting students and staff of other departments to take part in the event, but we rejected this on the grounds that it would be too complicated. We agreed, however, that we would ask members of staff and students of other departments to act as advisers and helpers if necessary – for example, asking the Arts and Media department for advice on promotional designs.

4   Agree next stage in the planning process

We agreed that the next stage in the planning process was to come up with event ideas that would meet our objectives. All team members will put forward their ideas for discussion and selection at the next meeting.

5   Any other business

There was no other business.

6   Date of next meeting

The next meeting will be held on Thursday 22nd February 1996 at 2.00 p.m.

DISCUSSION POINT

What might happen if there weren't agendas or minutes for meetings?

Formal procedures

Formal meetings need to follow a set of formal procedures, including rules about:

■ not interrupting people who are speaking

■ giving everyone a chance to speak

■ how often meetings should be held and how long they should last.

A chain of fast-food restaurants was planning a major national event with the aims of bringing benefit to the general public, creating a favourable image for the organisation, and heightening interest in the restaurants and their

food. In the long run, it hoped that the event would help to increase customers and profitability.

It formed an event-planning team made up of twelve senior members of staff, and after several meetings had decided on three options, all of which were feasible:

■ a national healthy eating week – providing information for schools, running roadshows in towns across the UK, promoting healthy eating in the restaurants

■ a sponsored toddle – a sponsored walk for young and old, taking place simultaneously in towns and cities throughout the country, and raising money for a national charity

■ opening up restaurants to the homeless over Christmas, offering free food, drink and shelter.

To make the final decision on which idea to go for, the team arranged a formal meeting. They agreed an agenda in advance.

On the day of the meeting, the discussion was led by the team's chairperson, following formal procedures. Each proposal was discussed in turn, and was considered in terms of:

■ how well it met the organisation's objectives

■ whether it was feasible in terms of resources

■ costs and benefits

■ whether there were any constraints which could affect the event.

After an hour and a half's discussion, the team voted on which event to stage. By a majority of five, it decided to run a national healthy eating week. The team's secretary took minutes during the meeting and circulated them afterwards, so that every team member had a record of the decision made and how it had been reached.

ACTIVITY

Arrange a formal meeting of your GNVQ event team to make the final decision on which event to run.

To hold a formal meeting, your team needs:

■ a chairperson

■ a secretary.

As a group, agree an agenda for the meeting so that the note-taker can send information about the meeting to all team members well in advance.

In the meeting itself, talk about the different options for one last time before taking a vote on which event to stage. Make a final check that the options you are voting on are feasible in terms of:

■ meeting your team's objectives

■ resources

■ cost and benefit estimates

■ constraints.

After you have made a decision and the meeting is over, the secretary should circulate the minutes to everyone involved in the event.

Key questions

1   What are the distinctive characteristics of an event?
2   What are the most common objectives of leisure and tourism events?
3   Can you think of five leisure and tourism events which meet the objective
    of providing benefits to a community?
4   What resources need to be considered when planning an event?
5   What do you think would be the costs and benefits of organising a
    children's party?
6   What constraints need to be considered when planning an event?
7   Can you explain why the event your team has decided to run is feasible?
8   What is an agenda?
9   What are minutes and why are they important?

Assignment

Write a brief report explaining the characteristics of a leisure and tourism event
and describing possible objectives an event could have. Choose an event
which you and other students could run yourselves, or one that you will be
involved in, for example in a work experience setting.

Get together in a group with three or four other students. Hold a team meeting
to discuss the events you each chose and select the most feasible one to
implement. At the meeting, each team member should make a presentation
about their chosen event which:

■   describes three options which meet the event objectives
■   gives brief details of the estimated costs, benefits, necessary resources and
    possible constraints of each event option
■   explains which of the three they favour and why.

When everyone has made their presentations, hold a vote to select the best
one.

Write an account explaining:

■   what happened at the meeting
■   the reasons why the selected option was thought to be the best.

ELEMENT **8.2**

Planning as a team

Planning an event is a time-consuming process but it's essential. For big events, planning can start months or even years before the event actually takes place. There are things to do well in advance, such as fix a budget, work out a schedule with the most important dates (sometimes called 'milestones') and allocate resources from within the organisation. After that it may be time to book halls and performers and sort out the publicity. As the event gets closer the pace hots up and there are hundreds of practical things to do. Many event planning teams find it helpful to have a team plan which sets out the responsibilities of each member of the team. In this element you'll have the chance to look closely at the event planning process and construct your own team plan for an event.

66 *When we plan our annual pantomime we start by making sure that it includes stars who will appeal to all the different age groups. We generally have a meeting with the marketing manager, myself and the distribution people at which ideas are shared. We start advertising in early summer and send out customised letters to each particular group – whether it's cubs and scouts or old people. We then start our poster campaign and distribute leaflets throughout the area so that we gradually build up interest. Nearer the date we have a major launch for the pantomime: we invite the press, have a big photocall and give interviews.* **99**

press and publicity officer at an entertainments venue

66 *Last year we ran a small music festival over a weekend. We each took a role in planning the festival – one of us was the business manager, another did the artwork for leaflets and posters, I did most of the administration and the fourth member of the band had the public relations role. We met and planned the programme in advance and agreed which other bands to invite. Then we met several times before the event, each time discussing more and more of the detail as it became available. We built up to a full technical schedule at the same time – who does what and where, what is needed where and when – for rehearsals as well as for performances. We usually had about four drafts of the schedule; the final one was ready about one week before the festival itself.* **99**

leader of a band

66 *I have overall responsibility and I organised everything the first year. Now there is a team of six who became involved in 1987. All have expertise; one is an accountant, one has computer knowledge and skills, the local rowing club provide a couple of their top people to advise and one person from that club organises qualified umpires and marshals. Operational roles are quite clearly defined and documented. We have at least three planning meetings. We have milestones that have to be reached by certain dates.* **99**

organiser of a regatta

Setting targets

As you saw in section 8.1.2, deciding the organisation's objectives in running an event is an important stage in choosing what type of event to run. Once the event has been chosen, these objectives need to be broken down into more specific targets.

There are two main types of targets in event planning:

- individual targets – to be achieved by individual team members
- team targets – to be achieved by the team as a whole.

Planning teams usually hold a special meeting to set the targets for an event.

Individual targets

Individual team members usually have two types of targets when organising an event:

- personal development targets – e.g. 'to develop my leadership skills', 'to play an active part in meetings'
- targets related to their role in the team – e.g. a secretary might set himself the targets 'to circulate information efficiently' and 'to make sure all correspondence is professionally presented'.

Team members usually draw up their own individual targets and then talk them through with the chairperson or the rest of the team to make sure that they fit in with everyone else's goals, timescales and use of resources.

Jess, a box-office assistant at a theatre, was on the team organising a special all-night comedy marathon for charity, and took on the role of publicity coordinator. Here she explains how she set her individual targets:

66 *We all had different roles in the team – mine was publicity officer. The date and time for the comedy marathon were set at an early planning meeting, and the team chairperson asked us all to go away and set our individual targets for the two months we had to plan the event. I set myself the following targets: to produce and distribute publicity within the agreed budget of £2,500; to promote the event in local towns through leaflets, posters, and media advertising; to produce a press release on the event, its objectives and the activities taking place; to ensure media coverage of the event; to cooperate with other team members in ensuring the health, safety and security of participants; to develop my publicity skills, with a view to moving into a publicity job at the theatre in the future.*

At a second planning meeting we all talked through our individual targets with the rest of the team (although I kept my last target quiet in case it seemed too pushy!). They all seemed happy with mine, and I wrote them at the front of my logbook for the event, to remind myself of my goals throughout the planning stage. 99

Team targets

Team targets are the team's specific goals in organising an event. They should be clear and simple, so that the team can evaluate at the end of the event whether it has succeeded in meeting its targets.

The event team for the all-night comedy marathon got together to set its team targets. After spending a lot of time talking about what it wanted to achieve, the team held a brainstorming session and came up with some key words, such as 'cost' and 'fun'. From these, the team put together the following list of targets:

1 to plan an all-night comedy marathon to raise money for Comic Relief

2 to make sure that everyone gives their services free of charge, including performers

3 to keep entrance costs down as much as possible

4 to make sure the venue is suitable for the event and complies with health and safety regulations

5 to make sure the event runs according to plan

6 to list a detailed running order of performers on the night

7 to produce a clear contingency plan

8 to make sure everyone has fun!

9 to make the donations as soon as possible after the event

DISCUSSION POINT

How do you think individual team member's targets would be affected by these team targets? Do you think it is more sensible to set team targets then individual targets or the other way around?

ACTIVITY

Hold a meeting of your GNVQ event planning team and set your team targets for the event. Look back at your original objectives and break these down into clear, detailed goals which you will be able to use at the end of the event to evaluate its success.

Make sure every team member has a copy of these targets so they can monitor progress towards achieving them.

Working on your own, start setting your individual targets for the event. If you already know what role you are going to play in the team (e.g. secretary, promotions manager) you will be able to set detailed targets. If you don't know your role yet, you can set general targets (such as 'to develop my teamwork skills') and then fill in more specific targets at a later stage.

Identifying key factors

Key factors affecting events include:

- anticipated income
- promotion of the event
- resources required and their sources
- providers of services
- health and safety measures
- security measures.

There are always key factors that can affect the eventual success or failure of an event. Teams need to identify these factors and think in advance about how to avoid problems and make sure all goes according to plan.

Key factors vary from event to event:

- Paying for and hiring resources for a conference will be more important if the event is held in a poorly-equipped hotel than a purpose-built centre with its own facilities.
- Health, safety and security will be more important at a disco held at a public venue for a large number of people than at a small private party.
- Promotion and income will be more important if the event aims to make a profit than if it aims to break even.

DISCUSSION POINT

What do you think would be the most important factors at the following events?

- an outing to the theatre for a group with physical disabilities
- a swimming gala to mark the opening of a new pool
- an attempt on the world record for the number of people standing in a row to raise funds for charity
- a charity dinner-dance.

DISCUSSION POINT

A school is organising a sponsored dance for charity. It wants to raise a lot of money, and has identified anticipated income as a key factor in planning. What possible sources of income would it need to take into account in its plans?

Anticipated income

Anticipated income is the amount of money a team hopes to make by running an event. This will vary depending on its targets:

- If a team is aiming to raise money, success depends on income and anticipated income is a key factor.
- If a team has a large enough budget to cover its costs and isn't aiming to make a profit then anticipated income isn't a key factor.

If the success of an event does depend on the money it makes, then the team needs to build anticipated income into plans from an early stage. This means identifying where income is going to come from, estimating how much it will be, and changing plans if it becomes clear the income isn't going to be enough.

Promotion of the event

Teams need to promote events so that people attend. All events need some type of promotion but the amount needed will depend on the event's aims and audience. For example, to attract people to a concert, a venue needs to print posters, leaflets, programmes, advertisements and get media coverage. Whereas a family organising a 21st birthday party will only need to write simple invitations or even tell people about the event by word of mouth.

Whether promotion is a key factor for an event usually depends on:

- whether it is open to the general public. For example, a fête needs more promotion than a wedding reception
- how important it is to attract lots of people from different backgrounds. For example, a nightclub party needs more promotion than an inter-club tennis tournament
- whether it aims to make a profit. For example, promotion is more important for a fundraising ball which needs to attract 200 people to make a profit than for a children's tea party which has a budget to cover its costs.

If promotion is a key factor for an event, teams need to:

- appoint someone to take responsibility for promotion
- decide what types of promotion to use (e.g. posters, leaflets, advertising)
- decide how much money to spend on promotion
- plan writing, designing, printing and distribution of promotional materials.

Resources required and their sources

Resources are a key factor for most events – without them, some events wouldn't be able to take place at all. Imagine a disco without a sound system and lights or a rounders match without bat and balls.

Teams need to identify the resources needed for an event at an early stage and build into their event plan:

- a list of resources needed
- time to find the resources
- money to hire or buy them (and how the money will be raised).

If teams do need to hire or borrow equipment, they need to consider arrangements for payment and loan return.

Providers of services

As well as resources, many leisure and tourism events depend on services in order to succeed. These might include:

- catering
- entertainment
- first-aid.

If a team planning an event identifies services as a key factor, it needs to make sure that it plans where to get them from well in advance and makes sure that the services on offer are of a high enough quality. Here's what can happen if services aren't planned carefully enough:

66 We left everything much too late when planning my daughter's wedding reception and were generally disorganised. The day was a near-disaster – we just hope the guests saw the funny side. We didn't book a photographer early enough, and in the end we just asked everyone to take snaps. I popped into the florists in town the week before the wedding, but by then she was already doin

What providers of services would be needed for an event like this?

three weddings that day. I ended up having to use a florist ten miles away, which was much more expensive. Worst of all, we didn't book catering services early enough and ended up having to use a new firm that nobody knew anything about. The food was cold, bland and badly presented. I've certainly learnt the importance of organising services well in advance! **99**

Health and safety measures

Health and safety is a key factor at almost all events, in particular those involving the general public, sporting activities and food. As many leisure and tourism events combine all three, teams organising leisure and tourism events need to be especially aware of health and safety. If they don't plan health and safety measures at an early enough stage, their event may be illegal and not allowed to go ahead.

Teams need to check:

■ whether their event is affected by any health and safety laws (e.g. number of people allowed to attend, fire regulations, food preparation laws, licences)

■ that they have permission to stage the event (e.g. from the site owner, police, local authorities, school or college)

■ buildings and equipment, to make sure all is in safe working order

■ the layout of the event

■ that they have organised enough first-aid support

■ that everyone involved in running the event understands and follows health and safety routines.

ACTIVITY

A team running a disco for 200 people in a school hall has asked for your advice on health and safety. It wants the disco to go on until 1.00 a.m. and is organising a buffet and the sale of non-alcoholic drinks. Carry out research and write a memo advising them on the health and safety factors it needs to consider.

Security measures

Security is also a key factor in all events. Teams need to make sure:

■ the site for the event is secure, and arrange security staff when necessary

■ equipment is stored safely and can be locked away when the site is empty

■ the public's well-being and personal belongings are safeguarded (this may mean employing security guards or asking for police support).

The theatre team planning the all-night comedy marathon devoted a whole planning meeting to identifying key factors for the success of their event.

After their meeting, the team secretary produced the following chart summarising key factors and how they would affect plans for the event. He gave a copy to each team member and it acted as a useful reminder during the planning stages.

Key factor	Why is it important?	Effect on plans
Anticipated income	The event is for charity, so we need to raise a lot of money	Will definitely need to make an entrance charge Try to think of other ways to raise money during the event Monitor spending carefully during planning stages
Promotion of the event	We need to attract plenty of people so that we can raise a lot of money for charity	Appoint a publicity officer to concentrate on promoting the event, and make sure they have plenty of resources Start promoting in plenty of time
Resources and sources	We can use the theatre's resources for most things, but need to recruit enough comedians willing to offer their services voluntarily	Start contacting comedians NOW, we'll need to book them well in advance People are the most important resource for this event – all the theatre staff have agreed to work for nothing on the night! Hopefully we won't need additional staff
Health and safety	There are going to be a lot of people in the theatre – the event must be safe	Appoint a health and safety coordinator Work closely with the local authority health and safety people
Security	As it's an all-night event, we may get some trouble at pub closing time	Make sure there's enough money in the budget to get good security on the door

ACTIVITY

In your GNVQ event team, identify the key factors which will affect the eventual success or failure of your event. You may find it useful to produce a chart like the all-night comedy marathon team.

Devising a planning flow chart

With targets decided and key factors identified, teams can put together a detailed planning flow chart showing what needs to be done and when it needs to be done by.

Producing a flow chart showing dates and times for everything to do with preparing for an event is a useful planning tool. Teams can refer to it in the run-up to the event, making sure that nothing is forgotten and everything is on schedule.

Planning flow charts usually include:

- dates of key meetings
- the order in which things have to be done (known as the 'critical path')
- dates and deadlines
- targets.

Before you put together a chart, you need to be sure of everything that will go into the plan so you can allocate time to each aspect.

Dated key meetings

During the run-up to an event, there will be all kinds of meetings going on – for example:

- team progress meetings
- single-focus meetings such as finance planning, publicity design, catering planning meetings to discuss particular aspects of an event
- meetings with people outside the team such as managers, health and safety advisers, designers, printers.

All of these meetings have to be given dates. To make sure the whole team knows what's happening, even if they're not involved in all the meetings, these dates should go onto the planning flow chart as well as into the diaries of the people attending the meetings.

Critical path

Critical path analysis involves identifying tasks which are critical to the progress of a project and the order in which they have to be completed. As well as helping to plan the progress of a project, critical path analysis helps teams to make the most of time and resources.

Jess used a computer to produce a critical path analysis of the tasks involved in publicising the comedy marathon. She set out her analysis as a chart known as a Gantt chart.

66 *The Gantt chart was for my own use. It allowed me to see not only the order in which I had to do the tasks my role involved but also where any overlapped.* 99

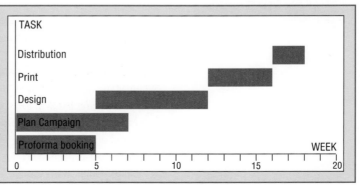

431

Dates and deadlines

Time is always a major factor in planning events – everything has to be ready by the time the event starts. Because of this, teams need to set a range of deadlines for different tasks. Delays can have serious effects on the plan as a whole.

Jess explains how dates and deadlines affected her tasks:

66 *Before I could plan designs for publicity materials, I had to know who was booked to perform. The deadline for bookings was the end of February. That meant my start date for the design stage of publicity materials was the beginning of March. Tickets were to go on sale on 1 May so the publicity materials all had to be distributed by then. So my end date was 26 April, the previous Friday. I scheduled everything from design briefings to delivery of printed material to fit into those deadlines. If the bookings deadline was missed, not only would I have had to reschedule my activities and tasks, but I would also have had my overall time cut by the extra time taken to complete the bookings.* 99

Targets

As you saw in section 8.2.1, team members need to set both individual and team targets for an event. Any targets that are part of the planning – for example, targets for funding, advance sales and so on – should be included on the planning flow chart. Karim Khalil, the finance manager for the comedy marathon, explains which targets they included:

66 *Because we had set a financial target to raise £2,000 for Comic Relief, we needed to achieve a target of ticket and catering sales that would cover our costs and leave us with £2,000 for the donation. We put weekly targets for ticket sales on to the planning chart from 1 May onwards. That way we could monitor our progress towards our overall target. As the catering sales would be made on the night of the event, they didn't go on the chart. But we did include the budget targets for different aspects of the planning process – the publicity budget and so on – as a reminder to those involved to plan their spending carefully.* 99

Putting together a planning flow chart

When all the tasks, dates, deadlines and targets have been established, all the information can be drawn together into one overall plan. The plan can be in any format you like, for example:

■ a hand-drawn flow chart
■ a computer-generated chart
■ a shop-bought wall-planner.

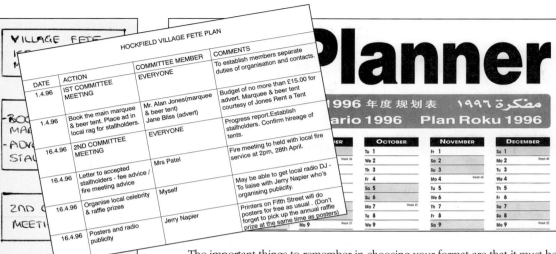

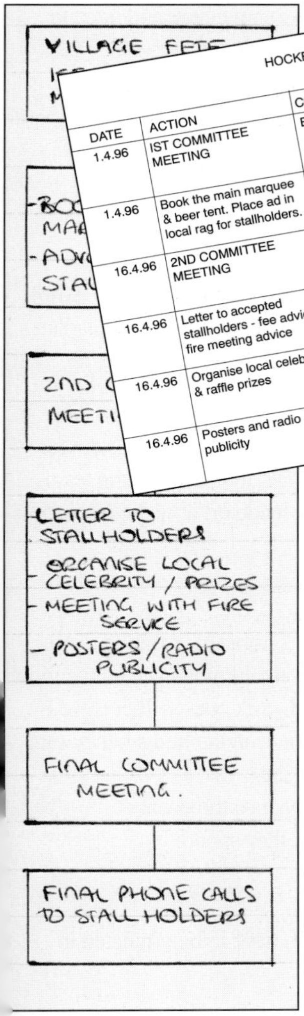

The handwritten notes (flow chart boxes) read:

VILLAGE FETE

- BOOK MA...
- ADV...
  STA...

2ND C...
MEETI...

LETTER TO
STALLHOLDERS

- ORGANISE LOCAL
  CELEBRITY / PRIZES
- MEETING WITH FIRE
  SERVICE
- POSTERS / RADIO
  PUBLICITY

FINAL COMMITTEE
MEETING.

FINAL PHONE CALLS
TO STALL HOLDERS

HOCKFIELD VILLAGE FETE PLAN

DATE	ACTION	COMMITTEE MEMBER	COMMENTS
1.4.96	1ST COMMITTEE MEETING	EVERYONE	To establish members separate duties of organisation and contacts.
1.4.96	Book the main marquee & beer tent. Place ad in local rag for stallholders.	Mr. Alan Jones (marquee & beer tent) Jane Bliss (advert)	Budget of no more than £15.00 for advert. Marquee & beer tent courtesy of Jones Rent a Tent
16.4.96	2ND COMMITTEE MEETING	EVERYONE	Progress report. Establish stallholders. Confirm hireage of tents.
16.4.96	Letter to accepted stallholders - fee advice / fire meeting advice	Mrs Patel	Fire meeting to held with local fire service at 2pm, 28th April.
16.4.96	Organise local celebrity & raffle prizes	Myself	May be able to get local radio DJ - To liaise with Jerry Napier who's organising publicity.
16.4.96	Posters and radio publicity	Jerry Napier	Printers on Fifth Street will do posters for free as usual . (Don't forget to pick up the annual raffle prize at the same time as posters)

Planner

1996 年度规划表   ١٩٩٦ مذكرة

ario 1996   Plan Roku 1996

OCTOBER		NOVEMBER		DECEMBER	
Tu 1		Fr 1		Su 1	
We 2	Week 36	Sa 2		Mo 2	Week 49
Th 3		Su 3		Tu 3	
Fr 4		Mo 4	Week 45	We 4	
Sa 5		Tu 5		Th 5	
Su 6		We 6		Fr 6	
Mo 7	Week 41	Th 7		Sa 7	
Tu 8		Fr 8		Su 8	
We 9		Sa 9		Mo 9	Week 50
Mo 9	Week 37				

The important things to remember in choosing your format are that it must be:

- clear
- accurate
- complete
- easy to update or amend if necessary
- easy to use
- available to all team members
- understood by all team members.

Ellie Pritchard, the event coordinator for the comedy marathon explains how they chose to produce their planning flow chart:

66 *We've got a large whiteboard in the marketing department's office. We hold our event meetings in this office and all the team can come into the office at any time. We chose to draw a planning flow chart on this board. We marked out rectangles side by side, one for each month and divided them into dated days – like giant diary pages. Then we filled in all the information using different coloured pens for different aspects. For example, we'd agreed to hold a half-hour update meeting for the whole team every Thursday at 10.00 a.m. These were all marked on the chart in green. Catering deadlines and details all went on in purple, publicity in blue, finance in brown and so on. For things that were done over a period of time, we drew a vertical line in the relevant colour down through the allocated days. The overall effect was like a huge diary-cum-action-plan. The different colours made it easy to pick out the different aspects and the vertical lines showed any overlaps clearly. It was very motivating to see it all there. It made us feel confident, well-prepared and in control because we could see at a glance what sort of work was involved for us all. We could add to the chart as we went along and if we needed to change the plan, we just rubbed out old details and put in new ones. We also decided to have paper copies of the chart for each team member. Jess produced a template on computer and we were each responsible for keeping our copies up to date. We kept a paper copy of the original plan in the file so we could compare how well we stuck to the plan once the event was over.* 99

Allocating resources efficiently

Almost all planning teams have limited resources for an event, and need to make sure that they make the best possible use of what they've got.

At an early planning stage, teams consider the different resources needed for an event, including:

- budget – how much money there is for the event
- materials – such as stationery, leaflets and posters
- equipment
- premises – the venue for the event
- staff – who is available, whether any extra help is needed, whether people have the skills needed, whether they have time to help.

Once the event is being planned in more detail, these resources have to be shared between different areas, such as publicity, catering and ticket sales. Each team member thinks about the resources they need, getting quotes for hiring equipment, printing and so on. They then talk to the rest of the team about their requirements, and team decisions are made on how the resources should be allocated.

Budget

The team's treasurer or finance coordinator is responsible for working out the overall budget for the event. They look at the amount of money team members want to spend on different areas of the event, and work out whether there is enough money available. If there isn't enough money in the budget, they can:

- check whether all the spending is really necessary
- organise extra fundraising or sponsorship to finance the event
- ask team members to cut back on the amount they spend.

Materials

Any materials like stationery, foodstuffs and so on have to be estimated in advance. This means thinking carefully about:

- what is needed
- what quantities are needed
- what quality is needed
- what the budget can afford.

Here's the experience of the marketing manager at an amusement park:

> 66 As part of a fundraising event, we planned to release a mass of balloons. The idea was that people would 'sponsor' a balloon for 50p and the money would go to charity. As proof of their sponsorship, they would be given a tag with a number on it. We would make a record of their name, address and tag number. A matching tag would be attached to a balloon. At 5.00 p.m. we would release all the sponsored balloons. Anyone finding them could then fill in their name and address on the tag and send it back to us. We would then give free family tickets for a day at the park to the sponsor and the returner. The day before the event, I realised that although I'd ordered the balloons and tags, I'd forgotten to order the gas to fill the balloons. I has to spend two hours ringing round possible suppliers and get my assistant to make an 80-mile round trip to collect it. 99

DISCUSSION POINT

Why is it important that resources are shared out fairly between different areas of an event? What problems do you think might arise if team members all know each other well? How could these problems be avoided?

DISCUSSION POINT

If you were the finance coordinator for an event, which of the following would you say was an efficient use of money?

- spending £100 on printing 300 posters which would be ready a day before the event
- ringing five equipment hire companies to find out about costs and using the one who gives the lowest quote
- going to a wholesalers to buy food and drink rather than the local supermarket
- bulk-buying 500 cans of drink at a cheap rate for an event for 100 people

Equipment

Like materials, equipment has to be thought about carefully. Some equipment may also involve:

■ hire costs
■ health and safety precautions
■ specialist skills for use
■ insurance
■ storage.

Premises

Once the team has decided where to hold an event, it needs to work out how the premises should be used. Often this is straightforward – if a children's party is to be held at a hall with a kitchen area attached, it is obvious that entertainment and games should take place in the hall and catering in the kitchen. Sometimes it is more complicated – if a college open day is being held, different departments need to decide where they will stage exhibitions and demonstrations.

A coach at an athletics club organising its club championship explains why it is important to allocate space sensibly:

66 *In athletics, you have to be very careful that the track and field areas are used in the best way possible. You couldn't have javelin, shot-put and discus all taking place at the same time – it would be chaos and very dangerous. Instead, we spend a lot of time deciding which areas to use for which events and when they should be held. This year we used two separate jump pits – one for long jump and one for triple jump. As long jump tends to be the more popular event, we put this in the pit by the finishing line. We realised that we were going to be tight on time to get the throwing events finished, so we moved the discus to a training ground by the side of the track. It's a case of finding the best compromise to make good use of the space.* 99

Staff

People are the single most important factor in the success of any event. Without the right staff, an event will fail.

All events need staff who:
■ are available to plan and run the event
■ have the skills needed to make sure the event runs smoothly
■ have enough time to plan and run the event.

To make the most of staff, people need to be given jobs which match their skills and the amount of time they have to spare. It would be senseless to put a trained chef behind the bar while a waiter does the cooking. Similarly, there's no point giving someone a responsible, time-consuming job if they don't have enough free time to do it well.

DISCUSSION POINT

Sometimes, leisure and tourism teams don't have enough staff with the right skills for an event, and have to hire extra people. A busy hotel is organising a New Year's Eve party for 100 guests. It needs:

- one chef
- three kitchen assistants
- five waitresses
- a pianist for during the meal
- someone to run the disco afterwards.

The hotel could provide a chef, two kitchen assistants and three waitresses. But no more regular hotel kitchen staff or waitresses were available, and no one at the hotel could play the piano or run the disco.

It would cost the hotel:

- £45 to hire a waitress for the evening
- £40 to hire a kitchen assistant
- £75 to hire a pianist
- £125 to hire someone to run the disco.

The hotel has £280 to spend on extra staff. What do you think it should do?

The team planning the all-night comedy marathon had already made a list of the resources they needed when estimating whether the idea was feasible. At a later meeting, they began deciding how to allocate resources within the team.

The event coordinator, Ellie, describes the decisions they made:

66 *We already had a pretty good idea of the resources we needed to stage the event. We had a budget of £4,000 for the event, most of which (£2,500) we decided to spend on promotion. This was because we realised how important it was that we attracted lots of people to the event in order to make a profit for charity. Luckily we already have all the equipment we need at the theatre, so we don't need to spend money on hire charges. Also everyone's agreeing to give their time voluntarily, including performers and security staff, so we don't have wages to pay. We've allocated £500 to cover food and drinks for performers and staff and accommodation for performers and £500 for extra expenses like additional insurance, telephone calls, stationery and so on. That leaves us £500 for unforeseen expenses.*

We had quite a long discussion about how to organise space on the night of the event. Our auditorium seats 500 people, but we considered clearing out the seating and having standing room only, so we could have more people. But in the end we decided it would be too complicated with fire regulations. We've got two bars and decided to use the upstairs one for food (in particular, breakfast!) and the downstairs one for drinks.

In terms of staffing, everyone at the theatre has offered to work free of charge that night, and there are enough of us to cover tickets, compering, bar work, catering, lighting and sound. We'll all stick to our usual roles, so we know we've got the skills needed. The only people we've got to enlist are security staff, to help out on the door. Jess's brother is a bouncer at a nightclub in town and he's volunteered his services along with a friend in return for free tickets to our next five shows! We've agreed. It will be good to know we've got professionals on hand when the pubs close. 99

ACTIVITY

At a meeting of your GNVQ event team, decide how to allocate resources. Look back to the lists of resources you made at earlier planning stages, and think about:

- how to spend your budget
- who needs equipment, where and when
- who needs materials, where and when
- how to organise space within the premises
- how to organise staff to make sure you make the best use of their skills, time and availability.

Drawing up contingency plans

Fire precautions

All teams planning an event should follow these guidelines:

- practise a fire drill so staff know how to evacuate the building
- restrict the number of people allowed in the venue – never allow more people in than is allowed by law or the fire officer
- make sure fire escapes are clearly signposted and not obstructed
- have people on hand who are trained in fire safety.

Sometimes events are disrupted by circumstances completely beyond the organisers' control. Although teams can't cater for all eventualities, they should try to anticipate possible problems and plan what to do if things do go wrong. This is called a contingency plan.

To draw up a contingency plan, teams need to:
- anticipate what might go wrong
- plan how to prevent these problems
- have back-up measures in case problems do occur.

Teams organising events make contingency plans for two main types of problems:
- emergencies (such as fire or a serious accident)
- foreseeable non-emergency deviations (such as bad weather or equipment breaking down).

Contingency plans for emergencies

An emergency is the most serious type of problem an event might face. Possible emergencies include:
- fire
- a bomb threat
- a major accident
- a health emergency (such as a heart attack).

Teams need to appoint a health and safety officer to take responsibility for:
- organising contingency plans for these types of emergencies
- making sure plans are put into practice efficiently if there is an emergency.

The Fire Precautions Act of 1971 requires some leisure and tourism facilities to get a fire certificate from the local fire authority before they can stage events. To be sure of safety, planning teams should contact the local fire officer for more information on fire regulations and safety.

In case of fire or a bomb threat, health and safety officers need to make sure that plans are in place for evacuating the site. Even quite small events should make sure there are:
- access routes for emergency vehicles
- emergency exits signposted
- meeting points clearly marked
- procedures for calling the emergency services
- stewards who know what to do if there is an emergency and are fully briefed on evacuation procedures.

Procedures should also be in place for calling the emergency services and organising access for vehicles in case of a serious accident or health emergency. All events should have first-aid equipment and a trained first aider on standby who could provide on-the-spot care if necessary.

ACTIVITY

Talk to the manager or a senior member of staff at a local leisure and tourism organisation, and find out whether any of their events have ever been affected by an emergency. Find out what contingency plans they have in place to deal with these situations and whether they worked well. Write a short summary of the organisation's contingency plans and explain whether you think they could be improved in any way.

ACTIVITY

Make a list of the foreseeable non-emergency deviations that could happen if you were organising a tennis tournament. What contingency plans would you make?

ACTIVITY

What contingency plans do you need to draw up for your event? Make two lists, one of plans for emergencies, the other of plans for foreseeable non-emergency deviations.

Contingency plans for foreseeable non-emergency deviations

Foreseeable non-emergency deviations can occur at any time, and although they're not life-threatening, they can severely disrupt an event. Teams need to anticipate all the things that could go wrong, and make contingency plans to minimise the effects of such problems.

A team organising a garden party explains its contingency plans for the event:

We appointed a health and safety officer who made sure that plans were in place in case of emergencies such as fire or accidents. But we also realised there were lots of other, less serious problems which could threaten the success of our event. Knowing the weather in the UK, rain was the most likely problem. We considered transferring the party to an indoor venue if it rained, but decided this would completely destroy the garden party theme. Instead, we managed to borrow a marquee which we had on stand-by in case of pouring rain on the day of the event and erected canopies in case of showers. We did consider taking out an insurance policy against bad weather, but it was going to be too expensive. We also drew up a detailed action plan for alternative procedures on the day if one of the event team was ill, the musicians didn't turn up, catering equipment broke down. We even thought about how we'd be affected by a power cut!

The team organising the all-night comedy marathon made two lists of contingency plans: one for dealing with emergencies, and the other for dealing with foreseeable non-emergency deviations.

Emergencies:

Fire   We've already got a fire certificate from the local authority, carry out regular fire drills, and our fire escapes and emergency exits are clearly signposted. But as this is a special event and we're expecting a full house, we're taking extra care. Ali's our health and safety coordinator for the night, and she's going to get in touch with the local fire officer to re-review our procedures. We'll restrict the number of people allowed in the venue to 500.

Accidents   Ali's trained in first aid and would be able to give on-the-spot care. Dave is responsible for calling the emergency services if Ali's busy. We need to make sure there's access for ambulances round the back of the theatre.

Foreseeable non-emergency deviations:

■ Not enough people turning up: This shouldn't be a problem because we'll know in advance how many tickets we've sold.

■ Comedians not turning up: We're trying to enlist the help of a couple more than we actually need, so that they can cover for each other if necessary.

■ Staff not turning up: We'll organise an emergency rota, giving everyone secondary responsibilities to help out in case of absence or illness.

■ Weather: It's an inside event, so bad weather won't disrupt the actual night's entertainment. It could affect the number of people who come, but as we've organised the event for June it hopefully won't be too much of a problem.

Allocating roles and responsibilities

For people to work well as a team, they need to know what they are responsible for. If everyone tried to do everything, nothing would get done efficiently.

Teams organising an event need to:

- decide the different functions needed (e.g. event coordinator, health and safety coordinator, finance coordinator)
- decide who should be responsible for each of these functions
- establish a structure for the team (e.g. who reports to whom, who is in charge of making final decisions).

DISCUSSION POINT

Think of teams you have been part of. Did team members work well together? Why do you think team members need individual roles and responsibilities?

Functions

The exact functions or roles within an event team will depend on the event being organised. However, most teams organising a leisure and tourism event include some or all of the following:

- event coordinator – responsible for producing an overall plan for the event, coordinating activities and chairing team meetings
- event secretary – responsible for communication within the team, producing minutes for meetings and circulating action lists and planning sheets
- finance coordinator – responsible for working out and allocating budgets and keeping accounts for the event
- resources coordinator – responsible for ensuring that the team has all the materials, equipment and staff it needs to plan and run the event
- promotions coordinator – responsible for public relations and for preparing and producing publicity materials
- health and safety coordinator – responsible for all aspects of health and safety for the event
- security coordinator – responsible for all security aspects of the event.

The event coordinator should also have a deputy coordinator who keeps up to date with progress and would be able to take overall responsibility if the coordinator was absent.

Before allocating roles and responsibilities, teams often carry out a skills audit. Each team member lists:

- their skills (e.g. being able to drive, typing)
- things they are good at (e.g. communication, art)
- things they don't like doing (e.g. maths)
- skills which they would like to improve (e.g. research)
- aspects of the event they are particularly interested in (e.g. promotion).

The team can then use these lists to ensure:

- the event makes the most of team members' skills
- people are given jobs they will enjoy and be good at.

A good coordinator:

- is well-organised
- has good communication skills
- gets on well with people – other team members, people in authority, people from different organisations
- is able to tell people what to do, when necessary
- has time to do the job
- is enthusiastic about the project.

DISCUSSION POINT

A GNVQ Leisure and Tourism team is planning a fundraising barbecue. One of the team members says that she is skilled at word processing, hates using numbers, and quite enjoys public speaking. What role in the team would suit her best?

Interrelationship with others

People in an event planning team need to understand:

■ their role in the team

■ how their responsibilities relate to other people's roles.

For example:

■ a promotional coordinator will need to talk to the treasurer regularly about the budget for producing and printing materials

■ a secretary will need to talk to the chairperson about the agenda for meetings when preparing meeting notes.

Most event planning teams find it useful to produce a chart showing:

■ the structure of the team

■ lines of authority

■ who different people report to.

The more people there are in a team, the more helpful an organisational structure is.

Ten people from the staff of the theatre were involved in planning the all-night comedy marathon. They decided that areas of responsibility should be divided up as follows:

■ event manager (responsible for coordinating the team and event)

■ finance manager (responsible for the budget and ticket sales)

■ secretary (responsible for communications within the team)

■ catering manager (responsible for organising catering for the event with one bar assistant)

■ stage manager (responsible for organising and booking the acts and for coordinating the work of lighting and sound specialists)

■ promotions manager (responsible for publicising the event)

■ health, safety and security manager (responsible for coordinating health, safety and security with the help of extra security staff).

The team's organisational chart looked like this.

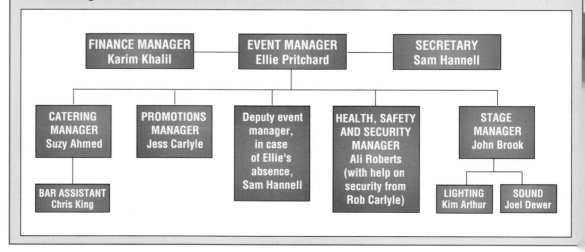

ACTIVITY

In your event planning team:

- agree the different roles needed
- carry out a skills audit and decide who should do what
- prepare an organisational chart for the team.

Preparing briefings for roles

Each team member's role should be explained in a briefing – a written description of their job. Role briefings should include lists of:

- the main tasks the team member has to carry out
- the outcomes they should achieve
- their responsibilities
- contingency arrangements they need to know about
- resources they need and are responsible for.

The planning team for the comedy marathon held a meeting to discuss and agree team roles. As a result they each were given a written job brief. Below is the brief for Jess Carlyle, promotions manager.

Promotions manager: role briefing

Tasks:	Promoting the all-night comedy marathon within a 20-mile radius of the theatre.
	Writing and organising the design, printing and distribution of posters, leaflets and programmes for the event.
	Placing advertisements in local papers (try to get free advertising if possible).
	Organising media coverage and entertaining journalists on the day.
Outcomes:	Good quality promotional materials ready by the middle of May and produced within the budget.
	Coverage in at least two local papers (both before and after the event).
	Attracting at least 400 people to the event.
Responsibilities:	Making sure designers, printers and distributors work efficiently and to budget.
	Making sure promotional materials appear in good time and attract a large number of people to the event.
	Making sure promotional materials and information are up to date and accurate.
Contingency plans:	A list of alternative printers in case there are faults in printing or materials aren't ready in time.
	A plan for a last-minute promotional push, if not enough tickets have been sold.
Resources:	A budget of £2,500 for promotion.
	Secretarial support to help producing press releases, typing copy ready for design, etc.
	Unlimited use of the theatre's photocopiers, telephones and stationery.
	Use of a filing cabinet in the general office to store information on promotional activities.

Jess thought the written brief was a good idea:

66 *Having my role set out like this helped me to remember exactly what I had to do. After the event, I looked back at this role briefing and could see clearly where I had succeeded and failed. It also helped Chris cover for me when I was away on holiday for a fortnight.* 99

ACTIVITY

In an event team meeting, talk about what different roles involve. After the meeting, write a briefing for your own role and show it to the rest of the team.

Section 8.2.7

Cooperating effectively with others

Preparing for an event requires all team members to cooperate – work well together. Without cooperation preparations will be disorganised and the final event is likely to fail.

Team cooperation takes place on many levels:

- in meetings of the whole team
- when team members work together in smaller groups to achieve specific targets
- individually between team members.

Although team members have particular responsibilities, they must always remember that they are contributing to a team effort and focus on the overall team plan as well as their own role and targets.

Checklist for working cooperatively

- Be aware at all times of the team's plan and schedule.
- Don't treat your own area of work as more important than any other. It might seem so to you but it is only one part of the overall plan.
- Be willing to help other team members when you are less busy.
- Follow established procedures for reporting information about progress, problems, tasks achieved, etc.
- Go to meetings and make an active contribution to them wherever possible.
- If problems arise, share them with others. They are generally easier to solve as a team.

Often, good communication is the key to team cooperation. If team members communicate and get on with each other, they will probably work well together.

This is especially true in team meetings, which involve a range of people with different personalities and ideas. Unless people are flexible and willing to listen, meetings can quickly become arguments with no one agreeing on anything. Successful meetings depend on people focusing on the purpose of the meeting and working hard to cooperate with each other.

Meeting skills

- Listen carefully to what people are saying.
- Be brief and concise in what you say.
- Keep focused on the purpose of the meeting.
- Keep your remarks to the point.
- Don't interrupt other people.
- Don't dominate the group.
- Don't let yourself be dominated.
- Use positive body language (e.g. don't yawn or slump in your seat).
- Be objective – don't allow personal feelings to dominate your contribution.

Producing a team plan

Having made decisions about targets, meetings, dates, resources and roles, event teams are ready to produce a team plan for the event. This involves pulling together all of these decisions into a single document.

A team plan includes information on:

- team targets
- planning flow charts
- resources
- key factors which might affect the event
- contingency plans
- roles and responsibilities
- role briefings
- the evaluation process for the event.

The following team plan was produced by the team planning the all-night comedy marathon. Ellie Pritchard, the event coordinator explains its usefulness:

66 *The documented plan, along with our planning flowchart, helped us to keep on track and to make sure all our efforts were concentrated in the same direction. Without them, it would have been easy to forget something or to lose sight of our overall targets.* 99

TEAM PLAN FOR ALL-NIGHT COMEDY MARATHON — 28 JUNE 1996
Our team of ten members of staff has been put together to plan an all-night comedy marathon. Our targets are:
- to raise £2000 for Comic Relief
- to sell all the tickets (500)
- to make sure the venue is suitable for the event and complies with health and safety regulations
- to make sure the event runs according to plan
- to make sure everyone has fun!
- to make the donations as soon as possible after the event
- to operate effectively as a team

Key factors that could affect the comedy marathon
The success of the comedy marathon depends on a number of key factors:
- Making enough money. We want to make sure that we make enough money to give a good donation to charity, so we need to make sure enough people come to the event, we raise extra money, and persuade everyone to give their services free of charge.
- Promoting the event well. The event has to be widely promoted in the local community, or we won't sell enough tickets.
- Resources. We have to get enough comedians to take part in the event.
- Health and safety. If there is any threat to health and safety, the event will fail. We'll work closely with health and safety specialists.
- Security: We need to avoid any trouble on the door, and will use security staff.

Planning flow chart
The planning flowchart summarises our tasks and related targets, critical path, meetings, dates and deadlines. All team members must keep the whiteboard flowchart and their own paper copies up to date and report on progress at weekly team meetings.

Resources
- We have a budget of £4,000 for the event, to cover promotion and any extra expenses. We can use stock from the cafe and bar for refreshments, but will donate profit made to charity. Any money left over from the budget will also be donated to charity.
- We need to arrange for the writing, design and printing of promotional materials.

- The equipment we need is already on hand at the theatre (lighting, sound system, staging, seating etc.).
- The theatre is an ideal venue for the event, with a large stage and seating for 500. The upstairs bar will be good for serving food.
- We have plenty of staff with the skills needed to run the event. Everyone at the theatre has offered to work free of charge that night. The only extra help we need is with security on the door, and this has already been arranged.

Contingency plans

The theatre already has detailed contingency plans in place for emergencies, including fire, bomb threats, medical emergencies and serious accidents. We will make sure that all staff helping out on the night know about these procedures, and re-review health and safety fully before the event

Other problems we might face include:

- not enough people turning up — we can tackle this in advance because we'll know how many tickets have been sold
- comedians not turning up — we'll book a couple more than we actually need, so they can cover for each other if necessary
- staff being off sick — all the key team members will have a deputy, to cover for them if necessary

Role allocations

The team is organised into the following roles:

- event manager — Ellie Pritchard
- finance manager — Karim Khalil
- secretary — Sam Hannell
- catering manager — Suzy Ahmed, (bar assistant — Chris King)
- promotions manager — Jess Carlyle
- health, safety and security manager — Ali Roberts (supported by Rob Carlyle, security specialist)
- stage manager — Jon Brook, (lighting — Kim Arthur, sound — Joel Dewer).

Each team member has a written role brief.

Evaluating the all-night marathon

The success of the comedy marathon will be evaluated against our overall team targets, that is:

- did we raise £2000 for charity?
- did we sell all the tickets?
- did we make sure that everyone gave their services free of charge?
- did we make sure the venue was suitable for the event and complied with health and safety regulations?
- did we make sure the event ran according to plan?
- did everyone have fun?
- did we make the donations as soon as possible after the event?
- did we operate effectively as a team?

We will only be able to carry out this evaluation some time after the all-night marathon, so will hold a final team meeting to evaluate the event on 17 July. In the fortnight after the event we will collect feedback (informally) from people who took part or came to the event.

DISCUSSION POINT

How else might the event team evaluate the success of the all-night comedy marathon?

ACTIVITY

Hold a team meeting to discuss how you will devise a team plan for your event. Make sure everyone in the team makes a contribution to the meeting. Make notes on what you discussed and agreed.

Key questions

1 What is the difference between individual targets and team targets? How do they relate to one another?
2 Can you name five key factors which can affect the success of a leisure and tourism event?
3 What should be included in a planning flow chart?
4 What resources need to be allocated within the team?
5 Why is it important to have a contingency plan? What sort of things should it cover?
6 Why do teams need a team structure?
7 What should be included in a role briefing?
8 How can team members cooperate well with each other?

Assignment

Part 1

For the event you are planning, draw up a team plan which includes:

- targets for the team as a whole and for each person
- key factors to take into account during the planning stages
- a planning flow chart
- resources needed for the event
- contingency plans
- role allocations and briefings
- the evaluation process.

Make notes on how you contributed to the plan.

Part 2

In your team, discuss and agree how you will record your contributions to the event – for example, observation sheets, tape recordings, logs. Prepare any documentation you want to use to record observations.

ELEMENT **8.3**

Running an event

Running a leisure and tourism event can be stressful and exhausting, even if all the planing has been done properly in advance. It can also be tremendously rewarding. The chances of an event going off well are increased if all the people involved are clear about their roles and cooperate with each other. They also need to be on their toes to cope with any unexpected disruptions or emergencies. In this element you'll be looking at what happens in an event and keeping a record of your own contribution.

66 *Communication throughout the day is important, especially when we have separate events going on at different venues. We ensure that leaders of groups can contact us on our mobile phones and in the summer we have a radio link. We also have two people in the van who are out and about in the city and are available to help as backup.* 99

community play officer in a city council

66 *There is so much to do on the day that you don't realise how quickly time is passing. We start with a final meeting in the morning, four hours before the regatta starts. We make sure that the arrangements for teams arriving are all in place – they start to arrive mid-morning. Spectators tend to arrive around one o'clock for a two o' clock start, so the stewards and people in the refreshment tent are all in place by midday.* 99

organiser of a regatta

66 *Things can go wrong unexpectedly. The first year we ran the fête the weather was perfect and all the stallholders were really happy. The next year it started off fine but half way through the afternoon there was a tremendous rainstorm. It turned into a washout, literally. So from then on we organised a marquee in case of rain and encouraged all the stallholders to bring awnings and coverings.* 99

organiser of a summer fête

Following role briefings

ACTIVITY

Imagine that you are Suzy Ahmed, the catering manager for the all-night comedy marathon you read about in section 8.2. Write a role briefing for Suzy, including tasks, outcomes, responsibilities, contingency arrangements and resources. Explain how this role briefing would help you contribute to the event.

Running an event can be a complicated, stressful and nerve-racking job – especially if the event team hasn't prepared well enough.

To make sure everything runs smoothly, team members need to know what they have to do, when and how. This information should be set out clearly in their role briefings, written at the planning stage (see page 441). If role briefings are prepared carefully and everyone follows them, all should go according to plan.

The catering coordinator for a tea party held for 50 children in a local hall explained how her role briefing helped her make sure her part of the event went smoothly:

66 *We wrote role briefings two months before the event at an early planning meeting. My role briefing – for catering – covered all aspects of my job, from preparation through to actually running the event.*

Tasks
Decide the menu for the tea party (food and drink).
Check out food wholesalers to get the best deal.
Work out a budget for food and drink.
Organise five volunteers to help with preparing and serving food.
Buy the food and drink within budget.
Visit the hall and see where food could be prepared and served.
Work out how much crockery and cutlery is needed, and tell the resources coordinator.
Prepare food and drink.
Serve food and drink.
Organise washing up after the event.
Distribute any leftover food and drink among the event team.

Outcomes
A good range of food and drink bought within budget.
Food which is well-presented and appealing to children.

Responsibilities
Making sure food and drink is bought and prepared in time for the event.

Making sure there is enough food and drink for all the children.
Making sure food and drink are bought within budget.
Making sure the kitchen is clean and tidy after use.

Contingency plans
Two reserve helpers in case any of the volunteers can't make it on the day.
20 spare sets of crockery and cutlery.
2 spare bottles of squash, in case fizzy drinks run out.
Mops, cloths and washing up liquid, in case of spillage.

Resources needed
Money for buying food and drink.
Food and drink, trestle tables for food, cutlery, crockery, plastic cups, washing up liquid, cloths, mops.
A kitchen area for preparing food.
An area for laying out food.
A sink and draining board for washing up.
Five volunteers to help with preparing and serving food.

ACTIVITY

Look at the role briefing you prepared for your own role in planning an event (see section 8.2.6). Make sure you read it through again before helping to run the event

I referred to a copy of my role briefing at every stage of planning and running the tea party. I put my tasks into chronological order, ticked them off as I completed them and looked at what I had to do next. I checked my list of responsibilities and the resources I needed regularly, to make sure all was going according to plan. And the contingency plans helped out on the day, when some of the crockery got broken and one of my volunteer helpers phoned in sick. After the event, I looked back at the outcomes given in my briefing, and was pleased to see that I had achieved them. **99**

Section 8.3.2

Health, safety and security

Health and safety in practice

- Wear protective clothing and encourage other team members to do the same.

- Check equipment is in a good condition before using it.

- Don't touch anything which looks like it might be faulty; warn other team members about it.

- Keep the work area tidy and put up signs to warn others of slippery floors, obstacles and other hazards.

- Make sure fire escapes and emergency exits are kept clear.

- Be prepared for possible accidents so you can react quickly and efficiently.

- Report any hazards or accidents that do occur immediately.

DISCUSSION POINT

What action do you think the following people should take, bearing in mind their own and their colleagues' health, safety and security?

- a referee at a football match who sees one of the linesmen being attacked by people from the crowd

- a resource coordinator for a disco who finds that there has been a leak in a storage room and electrical equipment the DJ was due to use that night had got wet

- a first-aider at a rugby match who notices that a colleague is about to treat a badly bleeding wound without wearing gloves

Health, safety and security play an important part in the success of any event. If an event threatens people's health, personal safety or security, then it has failed.

Organisations have a duty of care to both their customers and employees, and event teams need to make sure that this is maintained. Although most teams appoint a team member to coordinate health, safety and security, everyone in the team needs to be aware of risks and take steps to avoid them when running the event. This means considering:

- their own health, safety and security
- the health, safety and security of colleagues
- the health, safety and security of customers
- the security of the facility
- the security of information
- the health, safety and security of the environment.

DISCUSSION POINT

Why are health, safety and security particular concerns for teams organising sporting events? What type of risks would health, safety and security coordinators need to consider at:

- a professional football match

- a school sports day

- a swimming gala?

Health, safety and security of self and colleagues

The Health and Safety at Work Act (1974) gives employees responsibility for their own and their colleagues' health and safety. The Act says that people should:

- take care to avoid injury to themselves and others
- make sure they don't move or misuse anything provided to protect their health and safety
- help to ensure the requirements of the Act are put into practice throughout the event.

In the excitement of running an event, it is easy for team members to concentrate on taking care of customers and neglect their own health, safety and security. A catering assistant who helped out at a Christmas Eve party in a pub found this out the hard way:

66 *It was Christmas Eve, the pub was packed out and the party was in full swing. We'd organised food for 10 o'clock, and because there were a lot more people than we'd expected it was chaos. We were all running round like mad, thinking about getting the job done, not about safety. My friend had already burnt herself quite badly picking up a hot dish without oven gloves, and someone else had cut their hand chopping vegetables. I'd noticed the floor was getting quite slippery but hadn't done anything about it, so really it was my own fault when I went flying a few minutes later. I was taken off to hospital, found out I'd broken my ankle, and spent Christmas in plaster! Not taking enough care had left the party short-staffed and ruined my holiday.* 99

Health, safety and security of customers

Customers should be able to enjoy themselves at leisure and tourism events without having to worry about their health and safety. The event team needs to make sure that they can do this.

The well-being of customers should be one of the main concerns of team members at every stage of an event. All teams should appoint a health, safety and security coordinator, who is responsible for making sure:

- the event complies with health regulations (e.g. for food preparation and hygiene, toilet facilities)
- the event meets safety regulations (e.g. fire regulations, evacuation procedures)
- there are qualified first-aiders available
- the event maintains the security of customers, using security guards or police if necessary.

Once plans are in place, it is up to individual team members to make sure they understand and follow procedures to ensure the health, safety and security of customers on the day of the event. The health and safety coordinator for an indoor football tournament explains.

66 *I spent a lot of time planning health, safety and security arrangements with the leisure centre where we were holding the event. I drew up detailed guidelines for staff who were running the tournament, including procedures for evacuating the building, what to do in the case of fire, calling the emergency services, and getting first-aid help. I gave these to all staff involved, and made sure they understood how to put them into practice. I also gave a special list of regulations to catering volunteers, reminding them of food and hygiene regulations. On the day all I could do was check that they were following my advice – the health and safety of customers was ultimately in the hands of everyone running the event.* 99

Security of the facility

Many leisure and tourism events involve security risks to the facility and the equipment in it. The main security risks are:

- to property
  Security guards patrolling a facility can help to prevent vandalism. Closed-circuit television (CCTV) can also be a useful way to monitor security across a facility
- to possessions and equipment
  Many facilities provide lockers for customers' personal belongings, and lock away any of their own equipment which might be stolen. Security guards and CCTV can deter thieves
- to takings (money from sales)
  Takings should be locked away securely in a till or cash box.

DISCUSSION POINT

- What are the health, safety and security risks to these customers?
- What precautions should the organisers take to avoid accidents and emergencies?

DISCUSSION POINT

Have you been to leisure and tourism events where there have been a lot of security precautions (e.g. police, security staff, closed-circuit TV, video cameras)? As a customer, how does it affect your enjoyment of the event? Could organisations make security arrangements less off-putting for customers?

Security of information

Teams planning leisure and tourism events collect a great deal of information about customers, staff and organisations. In the past, all of this information would have been kept on paper, leaving it at risk from fire and theft, and making it easy to lose. Today, most information is held on a computer. Event teams can make back-up copies quickly and easily and store them on floppy discs.

The administration manager at a company which organises exclusive parties for the rich and famous explains why it is important to keep information secure:

66 *We are paranoid about keeping information about our customers and events secure. As well as potentially losing our company lots of money, there's the issue of confidentiality. We hold information about celebrities that the general public – and journalists – would love to get their hands on. We owe it to our customers to take care. There's a complex password system to get into our computer, and very few people have access to customers' confidential records. Every night we back up the computer's hard disc onto floppy discs and send them to a company nearby which specialises in software security.* **99**

Health, safety and security of the environment

Leisure and tourism events, which bring people together to take part in an activity, can have a serious impact on the environment. Environmental consequences of events can include:

■ noise pollution, particularly from events with music
■ problems caused by traffic as people travel to and from an event
■ litter and waste.

ACTIVITY

Think carefully about how you are going to contribute to health, safety and security at your GNVQ team event. Make notes on what you are going to do to ensure:

■ your own health and safety, and that of your colleagues

■ the health and safety of customers

■ the security of the facility

■ the security of information

■ the security of the environment.

DISCUSSION POINT

If you were organising a large outdoor music event – like the Glastonbury Festival, the Cambridge Folk Festival or Donnington Monsters of Rock – what threats to the environment would you have to consider? How would you try to avoid problems?

Cooperating with others

Section 8.2.7 looked at cooperation between team members planning and preparing for a leisure and tourism event. Just as important is cooperation during the event. The best-laid plans can go astray if team members don't work well – with each other and with their customers – on the day of the event.

The team plan sets out people's roles and responsibilities for the event, and good teamwork is needed to make sure that it is followed. Individual team members are responsible for working together in line with the team plan, their team structure and their roles within it.

How can team members cooperate when running an event?

- by being flexible and helping other team members as needed
- by making sure other team members know what they're doing, so everyone's up to date with progress
- by reporting regularly to their manager
- by being tolerant with each other
- by making constructive criticism, not personal attacks
- by communicating well with each other

Ellie Pritchard, the event coordinator for the all-night comedy marathon, put the success of the event down to good teamwork:

66 *The team worked together well from the earliest planning stages right through to clearing up on the day after the event.*

We all closely followed the team plan. I made sure everyone had their own copy and we referred to it during every planning meeting to check progress.

Cooperation was a major factor in ensuring we met our team targets throughout the planning process and on the day. Everybody kept our overall targets in mind and worked together well to achieve them.

A good indication of the level of cooperation shown by the team was that everybody gave their services free of charge and worked extremely hard. We also worked well with the comedians, and I don't think any of them begrudged giving up time for the cause. Ali, who was responsible for health, safety and security, liaised with local health and safety officers to ensure the venue was safe for the public on the night and there were no accidents or safety problems.

The team really excelled themselves in the way they coped with an unforeseen hitch. Chris, who was running the bar, was taken ill on the day and had to go home. Karim stepped in and the other team members backed him up as necessary. I was really impressed. It could have been a major disruption but they all pulled together to overcome it. The team briefings helped, I think. Because we'd worked so closely together, we knew not only what was expected of ourselves but also of each other.

Overall, we exceeded our team target of raising £2000 for charity, donating £2700 to Comic Relief. I think this excellent achievement is largely due to the quality of teamwork which went into planning and running the event. 99

Recognising and responding to disruptions

Very few leisure and tourism events will take place without any disruptions at all. Disruptions can be annoying, confusing or even dangerous for customers, and event teams need to act quickly to recognise and solve any problems.

To help them do this, they try to anticipate disruptions by preparing contingency plans (see section 8.2.5).

DISCUSSION POINT

The team in charge of a village fête is in a state of complete panic. It's 2.20 p.m. and the official opening was supposed to be at 2.00 p.m. The mayor hasn't arrived, the brass band is awful, a little girl has just been thrown off during a pony ride, the heavens have opened, and people are already wandering home.

Should the team have contingency plans for these disruptions? What should be their priority now?

The most common types of disruptions which affect leisure and tourism events are:

- deviations from the team plan (e.g. changes to timings or to the services on offer)
- emergencies (e.g. fire or serious accidents)
- anticipated disruptions (e.g. bad weather).

Deviations from the team plan

Things in life as a whole – and in leisure and tourism events especially! – rarely go exactly according to plan. However carefully a team has devised the plan for an event, there will almost certainly be some changes on the day. Most often these are changes to:

- the timings of activities
- the roles and responsibilities of individual team members
- the services on offer.

Ellie Pritchard, event coordinator for the all-night comedy marathon, describes some of the disruptions to her team's plan:

66 *We planned very carefully in advance, but of course the best laid plans . . . Unfortunately, Chris King, who runs the bar, went home ill during the day of the event, so Karim, our finance manager, had to cover for him. We made sure that everybody in the team knew and could help Karim out if necessary – I don't think the audience would have known there was a problem. Then a couple of our acts were late arriving. We'd half expected this, so had prepared a very flexible schedule which we put into action. But it threw our programme for the evening, so we had to explain to the audience what had happened.* 99

ACTIVITY

Would you know what to do?

Carry out research into fire safety at events. Talk to your local fire officer about preventing and coping with fires. Interview a manager at a local leisure and tourism organisation about its procedures for fire safety.

From your findings, produce a poster to display at your leisure and tourism event on what to do if there is a fire.

Emergencies

Although emergencies are rare, event teams have to be ready for them and know what to do if one occurs. Health and safety coordinators should make sure systems are in place to deal with emergencies and check that all team members understand procedures, so that the whole team knows what to do if there is:

■ a fire – calling the emergency services, showing people to fire exits, following evacuation procedures, closing doors, going to meeting points

■ an accident – getting help from a first-aider, asking a voluntary medical association for help (e.g. St John's Ambulance), calling the emergency services in the case of a serious accident.

Anticipated disruptions

Event teams can anticipate some disruptions at the planning stage, in particular problems caused by:

■ bad weather

■ change in numbers of participants (either more or fewer people than expected).

Event teams should have contingency plans in place to help them cope with anticipated disruptions so that there is as little inconvenience to customers as possible.

From the customer's point of view, event teams who don't react quickly and efficiently to disruptions they could have anticipated have failed. Here a disgruntled spectator at a charity cricket match complains about an organiser's lack of foresight:

66 *The line-up for the match was quite exciting, so I arrived early to get a good seat. About ten minutes before it was due to start it began to drizzle. The seats weren't under cover, so I put up my brolley and waited. The organisers just carried on playing awful music over the PA system – they didn't tell us anything about what was going on. Eventually, after an hour, they said they'd review the situation after lunch. I decided I might as well go and get something to eat and drink, thinking that at least I'd be able to shelter from the rain for a while. But no! They'd only got a tiny marquee which was jam-packed; the rest of the refreshments were being served in the open air! For people organising an outdoor event in an English summer, I think they showed remarkable lack of planning.* 99

DISCUSSION POINT

What contingency plans would have helped the event team organising this cricket match to cope with the anticipated disruption of bad weather?

ACTIVITY

Are you ready to react promptly to disruptions to your event? Write a list of:

■ how you will react to deviations from the team plan

■ emergencies

■ anticipated disruptions (what are they? what will you do?).

Keeping a log of your contribution

Team members keep a log of their contribution to a team event so that they have a record of the role they played in planning and running the event.

Logs usually contain two main types of information:

Information on process:

The team member's contribution to how an event was planned:

- how the schedule was devised
- how progress was mapped or tracked
- how revisions to the schedule were managed.

Information on content:

The team member's account of their actual experience:

- what they did in planning and staging the event
- their view of the team performance
- whether they stuck to their role and the overall plan
- how they made sure health, safety and security were maintained
- how they cooperated with other members of the team
- how they managed any disruptions or emergencies.

A GNVQ Leisure and Tourism team was asked to help run a canoe competition for a local canoe club. This extract is taken from Andy's logbook, as he explains:

66 *I kept a detailed record of how we planned for the event, and then wrote this personal account of the event itself the day after it had all taken place. I was really busy during the event, but tried to make notes as I went along to remind myself what I was doing when. These were really helpful when it came to writing up my log – I'm sure I'd have forgotten loads of details otherwise! Next time I'm going to borrow my dad's dictaphone so I can record my thoughts and describe things as they happen.* 99

In June I was asked to help out in the planning and running of a canoe competition for the Mid-River Canoe Club. There were 120 canoeists ranging in abilities from beginners to advanced canoeists who had to paddle over a course of 4, 6 or 8 km. The event took place in August and I was one of 20 people involved in the running of the event. My main responsibility was for health and safety with Ravi, Nicki, Jo and Simon in the team.

My schedule for the day was:
0730 Attend briefing meeting
0800 Work on the preparatory tasks in setting up
1000 Help run the event
1400 Prepare for prize-giving
1600 Review and debriefing.
0730 Attended event briefing. As had been discussed in original plans I was to be responsible for setting out tables in the main clubhouse in preparation for caterers. It was reckoned that this would take only a few minutes and I was required to assist where necessary until the event started.
During the race I was to be responsible for the safety boat.
No tasks were allocated to me for the presentation ceremony.
Assist with clearing up at the end.
0800 Set out tables as requested. This took me 15 minutes. No problems at all except that the seating plan had been drawn the wrong way round. I used a bit of common sense to make sure that everything was facing in the right direction.
0815 Helped catering party carry food and drink from transit van in car park upstairs to clubhouse. I had to do this because John had failed to turn up and Jenny

was unable to carry large boxes (sprained wrist).

0920 Went to overflow carpark. Noticed that there was a lot of rubbish that needed to be cleared up and organised party of four with bin bags to assist. The carpark is a council depot opposite the clubhouse. No one had thought that it might be in such a terrible state. There were some areas where parking would have been unsafe because of large oil stains. Cordoned this area off.

Because of the poor state of the carpark I checked with the event organiser. It was agreed that there should be a warden on duty to warn any cars of the hazards (particularly important for those who were carrying canoes).

While I was doing my stint as carpark warden I was asked by a council supervisor to make sure that the council van (on emergency stand-by) had clear access route.

0950 Council van called out for emergency. I had to erect a barrier to ensure that there was parking space available on its return. This was vary annoying since it meant that I was delayed in getting to the safety boat.

1015 Safety boat launched. All pre-launch checks were carried out (checked boat for holes, sufficient fuel, mountings for outboard engine, ropes, rescue equipment, buoyancy aids, etc.)

During the event assistance was required for three canoeists who got into difficulties. The two-way radios which I suggested should be used instead of a flag system were a great improvement. I would suggest that we make sure that they are kept in watertight wrapping (polythene bags or similar) since one was nearly lost in the river. All of the capsizes were near the finishing line and have been captured on video. (Thanks to the publicity team for that, maybe we'll be on television!).

1400 After the event the presentation ceremony took place. The nice thing about this was that the club chairman in his speech thanked all of us for our help. He even commented that we were all on a GNVQ course and how well we had worked as a team! He gave the safety boat a particular mention so obviously the safety team's planning and attention to detail paid off.

1430 Got down to the clearing up!

1530 Before the debriefing the health and safety team met quickly to discuss any ways that things could be improved next year. We agreed that the boat should be the very first thing to be checked since we were very rushed in getting it launched because of the car-parking problem.

1600 At the debriefing we all agreed that the event had been a great success and that all the planning had, generally, gone well. It would certainly have gone much better if John had turned up. I have been asked to submit a written report on the health and safety issues so that the problems of the carpark can be sorted for next year. The club manager agreed that the safety boat should be launched early. He suggested that all the pre-launch checks should, in fact be carried out the day before and double-checked first thing in the morning.

ACTIVITY

Agree with your team members how you are going to log what happened during the event you are planning and running. Are you going to make notes? Or use a dictaphone or mini tape recorder? Is anybody going to video the event?

DISCUSSION POINT

Do you think this gives a clear picture of what the day of the event was like for Andy? He mentions that a video was taken – what would this add to his account of the day? Why do you think it is useful to include both a written account and a video in your portfolio of evidence?

Key questions

1 How can team members make sure they contribute to an event according to their role briefing?
2 How should team members contribute to their own and their colleagues' health and safety at an event?
3 Can you list six ways of putting health and safety into practice at events?
4 How can event teams ensure the security of a facility?
5 Why do event teams have to ensure the security of information?
6 A tennis club is planning a tournament. List five anticipated disruptions. What should the club do so it is ready to cope with them?
7 What should team members include in their log of an event?

Assignment

Keep a log of your own and the team's contributions to the event you are organising and running. Make sure you include details of:

■ how you and the team as a whole met their targets for the event
■ how the outcomes of the event met your expectations
■ how people fulfilled their responsibilities
■ what contingency arrangements were used and why
■ whether the resources were used effectively.

Make sure you include all your contributions, even if they weren't directly part of your team role. Arrange to have your log confirmed, for example, by:

■ your tutor
■ other team members
■ a video recording.

> ❝ We measure the success of our summer play-scheme by the numbers of children being reached, calculating this using half-day sessions. We also ask the children themselves in some of the sessions to say what they thought, by circling cartoon faces looking happy or glum. ❞
>
> *community play officer in a city council*

> ❝ After the festival we discussed how it went and in particular what went wrong. Most of the discussion was on the musical side, but we also discussed the acoustics of the venue, the helpfulness of the staff and other things like the temperature. ❞
>
> *leader of a band*

> ❝ We have a 'wash-up' meeting on the day after the event where we pick up litter, then meet. We count the money, check that all the bills will be paid, and set a meeting for deciding what to do with the profit from the event if there is money left in the pot. Every one of the key people evaluates what they did and decides which bits need to be changed for next year. ❞
>
> *organiser of a regatta*

Evaluating an event

Events can be major activities which take up a lot of time, energy and resources. Leisure and tourism organisations, whether they are in the private, public or voluntary sectors, need to evaluate the events they run to find out if they are worth the time, effort and resources put into them. Normally, criteria for evaluating success are established early on in the planning process. Afterwards, team members usually meet to discuss how it went. There may also be a more formal process of evaluation. The aim is to suggest what can be done next time to improve the event and make it even more successful.

Evaluation criteria for an event

Evaluation criteria

- Did the event meet its objectives?
- Did the team meet its targets?
- Did team members achieve their individual targets?
- How well did you perform in terms of key factors for success (e.g. income, promotional activities, resources, service provision, health, safety and security measures)?
- Did the team stick to the planning flow chart?
- Were contingency plans useful?

DISCUSSION POINT

Why do you think it is important to have evaluation criteria, rather than just having a general chat about whether or not you think an event succeeded?

DISCUSSION POINT

Which of the following objectives do you think would be the best evaluation criteria?

- To attract more primary schools to the museum.
- To double the number of primary schools using the museum over the next term.
- To have 52 visits from primary schools between 4 January and 5 April.

Why is it important for objectives to be clear and specific?

Evaluation criteria are the things against which the event is evaluated. They can be quantitative, such as the number of people attending, or qualitative, such as how much customers enjoyed the event.

Evaluating an event means agreeing what worked and didn't work, and assessing whether the event was a success or a failure. Evaluation can only be completed after an event, when all the facts are available.

To be able to evaluate an event, teams need to decide what to evaluate – their evaluation criteria. It is important that evaluation criteria are clear, specific and easy to measure, as the organiser of a beach party explains:

66 *One of our evaluation criteria was based on our main objective – to provide enjoyable family entertainment. Although the whole team felt that the families who came had enjoyed themselves, we didn't keep any record of customer satisfaction. As it was, we could only report that we thought people had a good time, perhaps because it was a lovely hot day, or the entertainment was good value – we just don't know! If we hadn't wanted to use such vague evaluation criteria, we should have planned how to measure customer satisfaction in advance.* 99

DISCUSSION POINT

How could the beach party organisers have measured whether they 'provided enjoyable family entertainment'?

Did the event meet its objectives?

Although evaluation can only take place after an event, it starts right at the beginning when the team sets objectives and targets. Objectives are often long-term – for example, to increase sales over the next three months – and can't be evaluated until some time after the event.

Objectives are the underlying purpose of running an event and if the event doesn't meet them it cannot be a complete success. A museum's marketing manager explains:

66 *We offer an excellent education service for schools, with teaching packs, workshops, activities and good teaching staff, but at the moment it's under-used by primary schools. So we decided to run an event with the aim of doubling the number of primary schools using the museum over the next term. The day we organised – a fun day for under-eights – was an enormous success. Everyone had a great time, the children learnt a lot and teachers were very enthusiastic. We thought we were onto a winner. But by the end of the next term bookings weren't up at all. We realised, looking back, that most of the schools who took part already used the museum regularly and we hadn't attracted enough new customers.* 99

Were targets met?

Event teams can use two types of targets as evaluation criteria:

- team targets
- individual targets.

Jess Carlyle, the promotions manager for the all-night comedy marathon, explains how she found looking at targets was the most useful way to evaluate an event:

66 *We set objectives at the start of planning, and then broke these down into more detailed targets. I found targets easier to evaluate then objectives, because they were more specific. Before our team evaluation meeting, I wrote a list of my individual targets, and made notes on whether or not I'd met them:*

- *To produce and distribute publicity within the agreed budget of £2,500 – I spent a total of £2,250 on publicity. The remaining £250 was added to the money donated to Comic Relief.*

- *To promote the event in local towns through leaflets, posters and media advertising – I did this.*

- *To produce a press release on the event, its objectives and the activities taking place – I did this and issued it in plenty of time.*

- *To ensure media coverage of the event – ten journalists came to the event. There was one article printed before the event, and five afterwards, in all the main local papers. We also got a short slot on the local evening news.*

- *To cooperate with other team members in ensuring health, safety and security of participants – I helped Ali to make sure everyone understood procedures and organised a fire drill.*

- *To develop my publicity skills, with a view to moving into a publicity job at the theatre in the future – I definitely improved my publicity skills. Time will tell on the second part!*

I showed this list to people at the evaluation meeting and they thought it was a really good way to assess how well things had gone, so we did the same for team targets. 99

DISCUSSION POINT

Why might it be helpful to evaluate whether your team has achieved its targets before deciding whether it has met its overall objectives?

Key factors

Key factors make useful evaluation criteria. For example:

- anticipated income can be used as a criterion for evaluating actual income
- health, safety and security can be used as criteria for evaluating how safe and secure the event was
- resources can be used as criteria for evaluating how accurate you were in estimating resources.

Did the team follow the planning flow chart?

Measuring actual performance against planned performance gives you two forms of evaluation:

- how well you stuck to your plan
- how good your plan was.

459

By comparing what actually happened with what was planned, you can identify the differences and then consider why the differences happened. Sometimes the differences happen because people have ignored the plan. In this case, the people have not performed to standard. Sometimes the differences happen because that part of the plan wasn't possible in practice. In this case, the plan was faulty. In both cases, finding out what caused the differences gives you standards for improving performance and valuable information you can use in the future.

Were contingency plans useful?

Contingency plans – what to do in the case of anticipated disruptions and emergencies – are an important part of the team plan for an event. Evaluating whether contingency plans were needed and how well they worked can help teams plan future events.

Matt, a member of a GNVQ team which planned a local primary school's sports day, carried out the following evaluation of his team's contingency plans:

66 We thought about contingency plans quite carefully, but I suppose we focused on the obvious problems rather than everything that could go wrong. Our health and safety officer was well-organised, and we had good contingency plans in place for emergencies and accidents. And we needed them – unfortunately, one little boy tripped over in the egg-and-spoon race and had to be taken to hospital with concussion. A first-aider helped him and an ambulance was called to the scene quickly and efficiently. The only anticipated disruption we'd planned for was bad weather, and the day of the event was bright and sunny. But we did have other problems which could have been dealt with more easily if contingency plans had been in place – too few competitors in one race, a member of our team was off sick, and the starting gun broke. Overall, I'd say the contingency plans we made were good, but we should have had more of them. 99

ACTIVITY

After your event has taken place, your team should hold an evaluation meeting. To start the discussion, look back at your team plan and make a list of evaluation criteria.

The evaluation process

Once an event team has agreed what to evaluate, it needs to decide how to go about the process of evaluation.

Evaluation can be:

- formal – for example, a written report and review of objectives after the event has taken place
- informal – for example, a team discussion
- based on feedback from a range of sources, including customers, the team, staff, other people
- based on continuous feedback, or ad hoc feedback.

In practice, most event teams agree on an evaluation process which combines several of these different approaches.

Formal evaluation

Formal evaluation is a planned and structured process. It is carried out according to an agreed and established procedure and uses specific, usually measurable, criteria. It can involve:

- measuring actual performance against specified targets
- an interview to discuss and review performance
- a written assessment based on an assessor's observation.

Examples of formal evaluation

- An appraisal interview where a team leader and a team member meet to discuss the team member's performance and plan for future development.
- Team members carrying out set tasks whilst an assessor observes.
- Self-evaluations where team members measure their own performance against their personal targets.
- A customer questionnaire.

Informal evaluation

Informal evaluation is unplanned and unstructured. It is based on personal experience, feelings and general observations. For example:

- chatting to customers to get a feel for whether they are enjoying themselves
- looking around to see how busy the event is
- noticing how well different team members are cooperating.

All of these informal observations can contribute to a useful evaluation of an event. When combined with quantitative data such as attendance figures and takings, they can provide a complete picture of what happened. Ellie Pritchard, the event coordinator for the comedy marathon, explains how formal and informal evaluation gave a more balanced view:

66 *During the event, Chris, who was in charge of the bar, was taken ill and had to go home. Karim stepped in. As it was outside his job role, we couldn't measure his performance against those formal criteria. But we could use informal evaluation based on Karim's and other team members' description of how he coped with the situation and observations of how the customers were affected by the slight disruption. It all indicated that he'd done really well.* 99

Feedback

Feedback is an important part of the evaluation process and event teams need to decide:

- who to collect feedback from
- how to collect feedback.

The leader of a team coordinating a firework display at a theme park explains how she and her team planned gathering feedback:

66 *We realised at an early stage that a thorough evaluation of the event was going to depend on good feedback. As we plan to hold a firework display again next year, we were keen to learn from our mistakes and successes. We decided that our main source of feedback would be the customers themselves, and designed a feedback sheet which we gave to everyone as they left the event. Staff were asked to collect feedback informally, by chatting to customers, and we video'd the event so we had a record of people's reactions. We also decided that it was important to get internal feedback from the staff and the team as they would be involved in the event again next year. Everyone was given a questionnaire to fill in about how things had gone – we said they could remain anonymous if they wanted to, so we really got the truth!* 99

Sources of feedback

- customers
- team members
- staff
- observers
- self-assessment
- evaluation data (attendance rates, sales, profit)

Types of feedback

- continuous – given throughout the planning and running of the event, perhaps formally
- ad hoc – given informally and spontaneously

ACTIVITY

With your team, agree an evaluation process for your event. You should already have included some ideas on this in your team plan (see section 8.2.8). Draw a simple flow chart showing the evaluation process you are going to use.

Gathering evaluation feedback

Gathering evaluation feedback and data from a wide range of sources helps teams to get a well-rounded picture of an event. The event coordinator may think her event has been a major success, but does the catering assistant agree? What about the customers? And do attendance figures back up people's opinions?

To ensure their evaluation of an event isn't biased, team members should consider:

- their own assessment of the event
- feedback from other people, such as colleagues and customers
- evaluation data, such as attendance rates and profit.

Own assessment

Team members are the people who actually experience every aspect of planning and running an event, and their own assessment of what happened can be invaluable. Looking back at a log of an event can act as a useful reminder of what happened when, who achieved what and any problems which arose. Anecdotes about what people said during the event can also be useful for evaluation purposes.

However, it can be easy for team members to allow personal opinions to interfere with the objectivity of their assessment of an event, as this GNVQ student's account of her own and her team leader's performance shows:

66 *I knew from the start that Dominique was the wrong person for the job. She was late for meetings, didn't listen to what I said, and spent all the time giggling with Liz. I was only late a couple of times for meetings, and then I had good reasons. I was ready to work hard and cooperate with Dominique, but she wasn't interested.* 99

This team member has clearly let personal differences (and her own self-opinion) interfere with her evaluation. Her assessment of the event would only be useful if it were honest and fair.

DISCUSSION POINT

From your own experience, why is it difficult to evaluate your own work, and the work of people you know? As a team, talk about how you can try to make sure that your own assessments of the event are as fair as possible.

Assessment by others

As well as collecting their own impressions of the event, team members should gather feedback from other people involved. These might include:

- customers
- colleagues
- staff
- assessors.

Dominique, the GNVQ team leader criticised by one of her colleagues, explains how she gathered feedback from people in preparation for the team's evaluation meeting after the event:

66 *I was determined to get a clear picture of what people thought of the event. I prepared customer questionnaires in advance and handed them out to people as they left. I also gave all the team customer feedback sheets to fill in on the day of the event, and they made notes of comments, criticisms and praise received. Our tutor recorded the event on video, and you get interesting feedback from that. An assessor, as well as the tutor, came to the event, and I've interviewed both of them to find out their views (they're also filling in formal evaluation forms). Finally, I asked all the team members to write a short piece evaluating the performance of the team. Some of these weren't particularly useful as people weren't very objective, so I'd try to do this differently in the future.* 99

Evaluation data

Evaluation data are facts and figures which provide insight into the success or failure of an event. Depending on the type of event, evaluation data might include:

- the amount of money taken and figures for profit (or loss)
- attendance figures
- information about the type of customer who came
- information on how customers travelled to the event
- information on how customers heard about the event.

Different types of evaluation data are useful for judging different criteria. For example, financial data is needed to assess whether an event has made its target profit, whereas information on customers is needed to find out how many over-50s came to an event.

DISCUSSION POINT

What data would be needed to evaluate the following criteria? How do you think the organisations could gather it?

- Evaluation criterion: Have we made £500 from our bring and buy sale?

- Evaluation criterion: Did we attract over 100 under-21s to the movie preview?

- Evaluation criterion: Since the event, have more people who live outside of town come to the leisure centre?

ACTIVITY

Summarise the evaluation feedback you gathered during your GNVQ team event. You should include:

- your own assessment of the event
- feedback from other people
- evaluation data.

Providing evaluation feedback to other team members

Once the team has gathered feedback from a range of sources, it should hold an evaluation meeting to share thoughts and opinions.

It is only useful to comment on other team members' performance if the feedback is constructive. Constructive feedback is both negative and positive – it picks up on problems and weaknesses, but suggests ways to improve in the future.

UNIT

8

ELEMENT **8.4**

DISCUSSION POINT

Which of these are examples of constructive feedback?

- 'I enjoyed your presentation.'
- 'I thought the way you presented your report was really interesting. It would be good if you could include some of the visuals used in the presentation in the report itself.'
- 'Your enthusiasm at meetings always kept things moving, but I sometimes thought that because of that other people didn't get to say their bit.'
- 'You never let anyone else get a word in edgeways!'

How could you phrase the following comments more constructively?

- 'You were too slow circulating the agendas – it was useless only getting them to the team half an hour before the meeting!'
- 'The posters you designed looked like my little sister had scribbled on them.'

Points to remember when giving feedback

- Take time to think about whether you would like to hear what you are going to say. For example, would you like to be told that your ideas were boring? Would it improve your performance in the future?
- Try not to accuse people. What's the point of saying 'You're always aggressive', or 'You never think about other people'?
- Include yourself in the feedback statement when possible. For example, 'I sometimes thought you dominated the team and even though I realised we'd got stuck that made me feel like I didn't have anything to offer.'
- Be clear and honest about what you think. For example, don't say to someone that they're multi-talented in all aspects of teamwork if you have felt throughout the project that they have interfered and caused disruption. Try to find a constructive way to say what you think and feel.

ACTIVITY

Before your team's evaluation meeting, think carefully about the feedback you want to give to other team members. Make notes in each case, taking particular care when you want to make a constructive criticism. It's worth taking time in advance to make sure that you voice your feedback in a constructive way.

465

Responding to evaluation feedback

Receiving feedback can be difficult. People are sensitive about being criticised, even if, like this financial coordinator on an event team, they realise they need an evaluation of their performance:

66 *I wasn't absolutely sure about my ability as financial coordinator on this project, and was very worried about whether people would think I was useless and criticise me during our evaluation meeting. But at the same time, I knew that I needed someone to look at what I had done and say 'This aspect of what you did was good, but you could have tried this here . . . ' – constructive criticism, I suppose. In the end, I quite enjoyed the evaluation meeting and found it incredibly useful. Even when people pointed out ways I could improve my performance, at least I knew where I stood.* 99

DISCUSSION POINT

Think of two occasions when you were given positive and negative feedback. How did you respond? Did you think the feedback was accurate, or unfair?

To get the most out of a feedback session, team members need to:
- be open to criticism
- ask questions about areas of their performance where they lacked confidence
- react honestly
- listen carefully and make sure they understand what is being said
- remain calm and take time to reflect on what has been said.

Feedback from team colleagues

Feedback from colleagues can be particularly difficult for team members to accept. Before responding, they should ask themselves:
- Are the criticisms fair?
- Do I deserve the praise?
- What can I learn from this feedback?

As one event coordinator found out, if you can accept criticism from your colleagues, it can be extremely useful:

66 *It never occurred to me that the team thought I was trying to take over. I really did think they were grateful that I offered to take responsibility – at least seemed to get things moving. It was only during a feedback session at a late planning meeting that I was made aware of how my behaviour was affecting other members of the team. I was cross to start off with, you know – if only so and so had done this or that then I wouldn't have had to run everything. But after I'd calmed down I realised that actually they were right, that I always wanted to do things my way. It was awful to realise that even though I went on and on about democracy, I wasn't being very democratic!* 99

Feedback from customers

Customers are on the receiving end of products, services and activities, so can give some of the best feedback.

Team members often receive feedback informally from customers during an event. For example, customers might:

- compliment a catering assistant on the range of food on sale
- complain about the long wait to get in
- comment on the programme design.

Team members need to keep records of this feedback, so they can respond to it constructively and share it with other team members.

Feedback from teachers and tutors

Teachers and tutors are in a good position to give GNVQ team members evaluation on their performance. They:

- have monitored the event from its earliest stages, so they have a good overview
- understand the constraints the team was working under
- aren't directly involved, so they can give balanced feedback on the event.

DISCUSSION POINT

How should team members handle complaints? How can you respond constructively to customers' complaints, both during and after an event?

ACTIVITY

Ask your teacher or tutor to come to your team evaluation meeting. They will be able to give you valuable feedback on your team and individual performances

Factors affecting performance

When evaluating performance, it's important to think about the whole picture. Certain factors will have contributed to the success of the event and the affects they had need to be taken into consideration. For example:

- the team may have performed well because they had previous experience of running similar events
- the team may have had to alter their plan at the last minute because of an unforeseen occurrence
- attendance may have been below what was expected because of an external factor like a flu virus.

Some factors may affect individuals – for example, inexperienced team members may have been nervous and let it show in the way they dealt with customers. Some factors may affect teams – for example, the team may all be good friends and therefore good at cooperating with each other. Some factors may affect the event – for example, an unexpected thunderstorm causing a power failure.

You can identify the factors affecting performance by asking three questions:

- What happened?
- Why did it happen?
- Was the outcome good or bad?

Answering these questions will help you identify these things about yourself, the team and the event:

- strengths – things you're good at
- weaknesses – things you need to improve
- constraints – things that set limits such as legal restrictions, health, safety and security requirements, availability of resources, environmental considerations.

Ellie Pritchard, the event coordinator for the comedy marathon, explains how they examined the factors that affected the event:

> 66 *I asked all the team members to think about how they felt the event had gone, how well they thought they'd worked as a team and how satisfied they were with their own performances. We then agreed a date for a meeting when we could share our views and discuss what we'd learnt from organising and running the event. At the meeting, I gave the team feedback on our performance against our objectives. We'd exceeded our donation target of £2000 by £700 and I congratulated everyone on that. Customer feedback showed a high level of customer enjoyment, and we'd got a good write-up in the local press. Overall, we'd done very well and everyone had enjoyed the work involved. The general view was that we'd worked well as a team. We felt this was due to the fact that we know each other well and we trusted each other to carry out our allocated roles. This is a definite strength and we'd like to build on it in future. Jess, who'd handled the promotions, felt that she'd been a bit overstretched. She suggested having two people on the promotional side for future events. Suzy, who'd handled the catering, felt she could have got a better deal from some of the drink suppliers and said she'd like to develop her negotiation skills.* 99

ACTIVITY

Working on your own, draw up a list of the strengths, weaknesses and constraints that affected:

- your individual performance
- the team's performance
- the event.

Discuss and compare your views with those of your team colleagues.

Presenting evaluation findings and suggesting improvements

An evaluation sets out to establish what went well and what could be improved. It provides evidence which can be used to highlight achievements and identify areas for improvement and records what was done, why it was done and how well it worked – all valuable information for future occasions.

In making an evaluation, you will have analysed all aspects of the event and assessed how each aspect contributed to the overall success. As a result, you may come up with improvements in one or more of these areas:

- the event as a whole
- setting objectives and targets
- the planning process
- the resources required
- contingency plans
- the feedback and evaluation processes
- your own performance
- your performance as a team.

Presenting evaluation findings and suggestions for improvements is a useful skill. The marketing manager at an amusement park explains some benefits:

> 66 We are in a very competitive business and we're always looking for improvements. We're all encouraged to make suggestions and to try new ways of doing things. But for us to learn from what we and others do, we need to evaluate and then share our evaluation with colleagues. It's all done very informally but it takes confidence to speak to others – especially when you're describing how and why something didn't work. We're given training in both evaluation and presentation skills. Evaluation techniques help us to be more objective in our judgement of ourselves and of others. Presentation skills help us to communicate more confidently and improve our abilities to put together and present ideas in a structured and logical way. 99

DISCUSSION POINT

There is some advice on presentation skills on page 355 in unit 6. Read it through and discuss with your team what other things you need to consider when giving a team presentation.

ACTIVITY

Hold a team meeting to plan and prepare a presentation of your evaluation of the event you organised and ran and your suggestions for improvements you would make if you were to run a similar event in the future.

UNIT

8

ELEMENT **8.4**

The team who organised and ran the comedy marathon were asked to present their evaluation of the event and suggestions for improvements to the theatre's managing director. Ellie Pritchard, the event coordinator, explains what they did:

> 66 We held a team meeting to discuss the presentation. There was so much we wanted to put into it that it could have taken a whole day. But we only had an hour and a half so we needed to structure it very carefully. We decided we'd give a brief account of the event – explaining the objectives and what it involved. We would then briefly explain how we'd organised the event and the roles we all played. Then we would give our evaluation of the event's success and then our evaluation of our performances – as a team and as individuals. We would need to include a clear definition of our evaluation criteria in this bit. Finally, we would make our suggestions for improvements. We felt it was important to justify any recommendation we made with a statement of the benefits.
>
> Once we'd decided on the content of our presentation, we thought about ways of making it interesting. There was a lot of visual possibilities – graphs showing actual sales against predicted sales, the promotional materials, press reviews and pictures and so on. Kim, who'd done the lighting for the show, came up with an idea of making a mock-up of a huge cheque to show our donation. The whole event had also been video'd and we decided to pick some extracts to show.
>
> Then we decided who would do what. We all wanted to contribute to the presentation and we thought it would be a good opportunity to show the managing director how we worked as a team.
>
> Once we'd got all the materials we needed and drafted our scripts, we practised until we were all confident. In a way, it was just like the event – everybody had a role, everybody had their responsibilities, we were working to a deadline and the presentation had to take place between fixed start and finish times. And our success would depend on good teamwork. 99

Key questions

1 Why is it important to have evaluation criteria?
2 Why is it important to establish an evaluation process for all the team to follow?
3 How many sources of evaluation feedback can you think of?
4 What benefits are there in getting feedback from other people?
5 What should you bear in mind when giving feedback on someone else's performance?
6 Why should you identify the factors which affect performance?
7 How can an evaluation help you to make improvements?

Assignment

Working as a team, decide how you are going to evaluate the event you organised and ran. Your evaluation process should include:

■ agreed criteria
■ feedback from appropriate sources
■ feedback from team members
■ self-evaluation.

Identify which factors affected the performance of the event and explain their effect. Then identify improvements to team and individual performance that you would implement if you staged a similar event in the future.

Prepare and give a team presentation on the findings of your team and the improvements you identified through the evaluation process.

Keep notes and other documentation on how you carried out the evaluation and prepared for the presentation.

Arrange to have your tutor present as an observer at any meetings you have:

■ as part of the evaluation process
■ in preparation for the presentation.

Index